Iran

From encounters with Western powers in the nineteenth century through to a Constitutional Revolution at the beginning of the twentieth century, and from the overthrow of the democratically elected Prime Minister Mosaddeq in the 1950s to the current Islamic Republic, Iran's history has rarely been anything other than tumultuous and dramatic. The ways in which Iranian society has participated in and reacted to these events have been equally fascinating and revolutionary.

Here for the first time in English, Yann Richard offers his take on the social and political history of Iran since 1800. Richard's account traces the common threads of national ideology and violent conflict that have characterized a number of episodes in Iranian history. By also concerning himself with the reactions and feelings of Iranian society and by referring frequently to Persian sources and commentaries, Richard gives us a unique insight into the challenges encountered by Iranians in modern times.

Yann Richard is Professor Emeritus at the Sorbonne Nouvelle – Paris. A specialist of the history of contemporary Iran, Persian literature, and the sociology of modern Shiism, he is the author of a number of books on modern Iran and is also the coeditor of the "Iran Studies" book series.

Iran

A Social and Political History since the Qajars

Yann Richard
Sorbonne Nouvelle – Paris
With the assistance of Willem Floor

CAMBRIDGE
UNIVERSITY PRESS

University Printing House, Cambridge CB2 8BS, United Kingdom

One Liberty Plaza, 20th Floor, New York, NY 10006, USA

477 Williamstown Road, Port Melbourne, VIC 3207, Australia

314–321, 3rd Floor, Plot 3, Splendor Forum, Jasola District Centre,
New Delhi – 110025, India

79 Anson Road, #06–04/06, Singapore 079906

Cambridge University Press is part of the University of Cambridge.

It furthers the University's mission by disseminating knowledge in the pursuit of
education, learning, and research at the highest international levels of excellence.

www.cambridge.org
Information on this title: www.cambridge.org/9781108476836
DOI: 10.1017/9781108569071

© Yann Richard 2019

This publication is in copyright. Subject to statutory exception
and to the provisions of relevant collective licensing agreements
no reproduction of any part may take place without the written
permission of Cambridge University Press.

This edition is a revised, expanded and updated translation of *L'Iran de 1800 à nos jours*,
published by Flammarion, 2009 and 2016, and previously published as *L'Iran:
Naissance d'une république islamique* by La Martinière, 2006.

Printed in the United Kingdom by TJ International Ltd. Padstow Cornwall

A catalogue record for this publication is available from the British Library.

Library of Congress Cataloging-in-Publication Data
NAMES: Richard, Yann, author. | Floor, Willem M., translator.
TITLE: Iran : a social and political history since the Qajars / Yann Richard.
OTHER TITLES: Iran de 1800 à nos jours. English
DESCRIPTION: Cambridge, United Kingdom ; New York, NY : Cambridge University
Press, [2019] | "This edition is a revised, expanded and updated translation of L'Iran de
1800 à nos jours, published by Flammarion, 2009 and 2016, and previously published as
L'Iran: naissance d'une république islamique by La Martinière, 2006." | Includes
bibliographical references and index.
IDENTIFIERS: LCCN 2018056862| ISBN 9781108476836 (hardback : alk. paper) |
ISBN 9781108701624 (paperback : alk. paper)
SUBJECTS: LCSH: Iran – History.
CLASSIFICATION: LCC DS298 .R52513 2019 | DDC 955–dc23
LC record available at https://lccn.loc.gov/2018056862

ISBN 978-1-108-47683-6 Hardback
ISBN 978-1-108-70162-4 Paperback

Cambridge University Press has no responsibility for the persistence or accuracy of
URLs for external or third-party internet websites referred to in this publication
and does not guarantee that any content on such websites is, or will remain,
accurate or appropriate.

NOTE ON THE TRANSLATION

The original French version of this book has been translated, adapted, and expanded through the friendly help of Willem Floor.

CONTENTS

MAPS

PREFACE

With the eruption of violent conflict and the opposition between the Americans and their allies on the one hand and the national and religious power structures in the Middle East on the other, the media have often spoken about Iran and the Iranians. But what do they know about them?

Why do Iranians seem to be the main beneficiaries of American interventions in Afghanistan (2001) and Iraq (2003)? Does the signing of the nuclear agreement with the Americans, Europeans, Russians, and Chinese in Vienna in 2015 provide Iran with a new opportunity for regional hegemony? Or is Iran a real danger to the security of Israel? Is the American withdrawal from the nuclear deal in 2018 a path towards peace or a challenge to the stability of the Middle East?

To answer the many questions that have been raised about the violent anti-western reaction of the "Islamic Republic," one needs to appreciate the history of the country since its first encounter with European nations and to take into account the way this history is understood by Iranians: history as told and imagined is often a very different narrative from documented history.

This book offers fresh insights into the history of modern Iranians. In the West, we hardly know them any better than our Enlightenment forebears who saw Persia as paradigm of strangeness. The book aims to show how Iran, after a period of systematic secularization, has become an Islamic republic, and, at the same time, a foil for western intellectuals. Since ayatollah Khomeyni founded a state that can scarcely be said to resemble a paradise of liberties, as western intellectuals had dreamt when fulminating against the Shah, the country has fallen into collective disgrace for reasons that are not only due to its religious orientation. Those who denounce the chadors, veils, stoning, and other questionable practices in Iran have long remained silent about the situation in Saudi Arabia, a much less liberal country, but one linked to the western economic system; there women are veiled in such a way that one cannot even see their eyes, and their rights are much more limited than their Iranian sisters'.

To complicate the situation, Iranians themselves are tormented by their collective superego. Regardless of their political leanings, they are crushed by the image of their past, less by nostalgia than by a paranoid anguish about external conspiracy and fear for their future. Periodically rediscovering the grandeur of their history, they compare it with the tribulations of the present and think that the cause of all their problems rests with others. "*Az mā-st ke bar mā-st,*" ("what happens to us comes from ourselves,") answers a Persian saying. But Iranians' concern for their future is fueled by painful memories.

The weight of its rich heritage creates an identity strain in Iran. Like the French, who for many years thought that, unless you spoke their language, you could never appreciate their genius, Iranians are not far from believing that only they have the right to talk about themselves. That a foreigner speaks and reads their language seems to them an intrusion, as they like to hide behind their identity. While contemplating themselves, they see only what should be seen. Indeed, far from homogeneity, Persia has been governed by Turkic-speaking dynasties for many of the last ten centuries.

In 1987, an Iranian academic journal launched a debate on the status of the Turkic Azeri language, which is spoken by about 40 percent of the population, and which a recent book proposed as the country's second official language.[1] In response to the editor's highly nationalistic speech, a defender of Turkish referred him to his own genealogy: after the Mongol invasion that saw his ancient forefather killed, the latter's widow taught Persian to her child, but a child that was the result of rape – the memory of the wounds of the past always haunts a country that, since the time of Genghis Khan and Tamerlane, has suffered invasions, pillaging, and occupations. Iranians often think that their identity has been stolen from them, that it has been violated,

---

[1] N. Purjavādi, "Irān-e mazlum."

perverted by foreigners. Some nationalists, looking for truth in the ancient past, point the finger at Islam and the Arab invasion in the seventh century. Others point to Turkic, Seljuq, and Mongol invasions. For the last two centuries the culprits have been the Europeans and, most recently, the Americans, whose interference the Iranians rail against. Thus, they readily overlook or excuse their own weaknesses.

History and Ideology

How can one have a dispassionate and objective discussion in such a highly charged environment? Can the historian of Iran ignore the emotional weight of certain facts? Is the neutrality of the researcher not akin to treason? The ideological discourse, either nationalist, communist, monarchist, or Islamic, incessantly uses historical data to give it a moral or political slant. With the exception of some rare heroic figures, such as Karim Khān Zand or Amir Kabir, no other actors in that history are embraced by everyone. Prominent personalities such as Hasan Taqizāde, an important politician since 1906 until his death in 1970, are still the subject of laudatory or resentful biographies: a neutral presentation would be suspected of hidden intentions. The founding heroes for one side are the black sheep for the other. Fazlollāh Nuri, the highly regarded theologian who was sentenced by a revolutionary court and hanged in the public square in 1909, is at the same time the champion of an Islam that resists reforms imposed by Europeanization and the traitor who allied himself with the plotting monarch. For one group, Rezā Shāh revived Iran; for others, he is the most corrupt despot who sold out to foreigners. Mosaddeq, adored by nationalists, has been dragged through the mud by Islamists since the 1979 Revolution.

In this context is it possible for a westerner to write a history of Iran that will be read by an Iranian? Although at every moment I risk acting like the proverbial bull in a china shop, such is the challenge I am trying to respond to here, in order to explicate the paths taken by Iran before it became an Islamic republic.

The challenges are multiple: how can one understand Iran today if one ignores the history of the failed encounters between Iran and the West? The historical discourse on a rapidly changing society needs distance from emotions and journalism. Documentary evidence can be unearthed at any time, in contradiction to previous statements. The historian of contemporary societies and the journalist inevitably meet, and, in the face of unpredictable social behavior, both feel help-less. The "journalist" is under pressure to give his readers immediate information and understanding, while the "historian" can go back as far as is necessary. More so than the journalist, he has to be free of the two contrary and complementary rationalities of history: that of the long view where each event is the result of a long maturation process, where the only pertinent facts are beyond individual control, where statistics and numerical data form a barrier to speculation; and that of individual destinies, human will, and the force of circumstance. Each individual is subject to different influences and sometimes acts according to contradictory and changing motivations. Thus, the historian has to identify multiple strategies to shed light on their convergence. Generalizations are always wrong, because they depersonalize events as if they resulted from occult forces or from abstract laws, while in fact each person acts in the name of an ideal or from personal interest.

The Creation of a Modern Nation

Since the time of Darius over two millennia ago, Iran has been fortunate to lay claim to elements of an identity that has changed very little. These include its language (which has evolved from Old Persian in much the same way as other Indo-European languages have developed), the very name of the country (*Irān*, the country of the Aryans), and the borders of its imperial heartland (bounded by two seas, two mountain chains, plains, and deserts). The changes that have taken place in relation to the dynasties and regimes ruling the region have not impacted the continuity of a nation. But what is a nation? The Europeans, who invented the concept in the nineteenth century, can be said to be in the process of destroying it by introducing new concepts, the supranational (the European Union) and the subnational (Corsica, the Basque Country, Scotland, regionalism). What is the value of these concepts at a time of globalization?

Since the beginning of the nineteenth century, Iran has known difficult times, although the country has never been colonized. In many of the new nations of the Third World born in the twentieth century during the breakdown of the big empires, colonization has often led to the replication of imperial power structures by the national elites. In Iran, too, the imitation of foreign political structures played an important role. Were the "imitators" progressives or, on the contrary, did they betray their homeland by selling it to a faraway power that dominated them? This debate has torn Iranian intellectuals for decades. The leaders have identified themselves with "civilized" countries and, of course, tried to reproduce their institutions and rules. But the real change happened in social behavior and policies, even when there was a regular return to authoritarianism, or even absolutism. The weakening of Iran was regularly blamed on conspiracies. In reality, the visible progress hid an undertow that the reformists were unable to suppress. Since 1906 the Iranians had a Constitution, but they had difficulty in respecting the constraints of a parliamentary system.

How can one define modernity in this society that is so different from our own? The Iranian reformers dreaming of "progress," of "civilization," wanted to identify with a European model. Beyond the exterior forms of democracy and the parliamentary system, they had to integrate types of action that were incompatible with the traditional communal system and with the sanctification of authority. It was not yet modernity, because this concept also implies active participation, never foreign imports or imitation. Politically, modernity excludes authoritarianism and absolutism, two grooves into which Iran seems to fall back periodically.

According to "developmental" sociology, which analyzes the modernization of traditional societies, a return to political absolutism is impossible in a society where citizens can read the newspapers, listen to radio stations, and watch television stations, navigate the Internet – in a word, use the instruments of participation and education in the diversity of modern culture.[2] Does Iran constitute a counter-example where modernity has not prevented political violence and where the media have fostered an idea that was rejected by the industrial societies of the West, that of a unique collective will and of greater interference of religion in politics?

This book aims to show "the creation of the nation" of Iran, and begins with the rise of the Qajar dynasty and the first national wounds suffered by Iran following the interference of its Russian and British neighbors. Despite the efforts of reformers and self-proclaimed nationalists, we have to wait until the end of the twentieth century to see the true emergence of patriotic, popular feeling in confrontations and

[2] See D. LERNER, *The Passing of Traditional Society. Modernizing the Middle East*, New York: The Free Press, 1958.

conflicts, first against Great Britain (1951–53), then Iraq (1980–88). The confrontation with the West – which, in another form, is an echo of the crises of the more distant past with the Ottoman Empire, Russia, and Great Britain – and the current regional ambitions of Iran, cannot be fully understood without recourse to the country's history.

Basic Definitions

Irān is the name that Iranians have always given to their country; however, Westerners have preferred, until modern times, to use *Persia* and *Persians,* originally the name of the tribe that founded the Achaemenid Empire. In accordance with the usage of diplomats and travelers until 1935, one can still speak of Persia and the Persians for the country and its people. In 1935, Rezā Shāh ordered western embassies to abandon this name, which had connotations of tales, legends, and ancient culture, since he wanted to present his country, Iran, as a modern power oriented toward progress. In 1989, saddened to have to conclude that the Iran from which he had been exiled only reminded westerners of violence and fanaticism, an Iranian academic asked them to return to the ancient usage, which had a positive cultural image (such as Persian literature, painting, architecture).[3] I use both terms here without making a distinction between them.

At present, most Iranians (about 85 percent) are Shiites. Shiite Islam, imposed as the official religion in Iran at the beginning of the sixteenth century, is, with Sunni Islam, one of the two main constituent branches of Islam. In Shiism, piety is surrounded by intermediaries and intercessors, the twelve Imams and numerous saints. Religious authority is represented by theologians who are traditionally independent from the ruler and who constitute what may be called a "clergy" (*ruhāniat*). Despite certain discordant voices, most Shiites accept the Koran as established by Caliph Osman.[4] In Persia there are also, since Antiquity, Zoroastrians, Jews, and Christians and, since the end of the nineteenth century, a Bahai community (300–500,000 in 1979). Today, after the massive departure of Baha'is, Jews, and Christians, non-Muslim minorities represent less than 2 percent of the population,

---

[3] E. YARSHATER, "Communication."
[4] On the distortions of the Koran, see Md. A. AMIR-MOEZZI and Ch. JAMBET, *Qu'est-ce que le shî'isme ?*, pp. 89f.

perhaps only 1 percent. However, a spectacular surge in apostasy and conversion to Zoroastrianism and Buddhism, and above all to Christianity, might reverse that trend.

Within its borders, Iran has relatively well-integrated ethnic minorities: Azeris, Kurds, Turkmen, Arabs, Lurs, Baluchis, to name but a few. Regional languages are allowed, but Persian is the only official language recognized by the Constitution. The teaching of Persian is compulsory in schools, even in provinces where a local tongue may be taught in addition. Persian (called *fārsi* in Iranian Persian, *dari* in Afghanistan, *tājik* in Tajikistan) is an Iranian language, as are Kurdish and Pashto, the official language of Afghanistan.

The Qajars ruled over Iran from 1779 to 1925. The Pahlavis then ruled the country until the revolution of 1979, which is often called, to follow official usage, the "Islamic Revolution," although, as we will see, it has no intrinsic relation to Islam.

Persian onomastics are complex, as befits an imperial society where matters of hierarchy, social ranking, and protocol have a long tradition. *Mirzā* means prince when it follows the name, but a man of letters when it precedes it. *Seyyed* indicates a descendant of the Prophet, a title often usurped, but it is used as a noble title. *Khān* serves as a title, without rigorous distinction, and is sometimes simply a respectful manner in which to address men. In the Qajar period, the actual titles of nobility (*laqab*, pl. *alqāb*) in principle indicate a function in court or in the administration and are liable to sudden changes of holder, such that over the course of his life, the same person may have three or four successive titles, those that he gives up, during his lifetime, passing to another person, sometimes his son (but not necessarily so). Titles that end in *od-Din, ol-Eslām, ol-Olamā* in general are given to religious persons. Those ending in *os-Saltane* are in principle higher ranking than those ending in *os-Soltān, od-Dowle, ol-Molk* or *ol-Mamālek* (servants of the monarchy more highly honored than servants of the monarch, state, or country).

Dates are given according to the Gregorian calender, with the inevitable margin of uncertainty when converting dates of the lunar Hegira calender. For the last 100 years in Iran, a solar calender of 365 days has been used, which has the Hegira as its beginning. In bibliographical references where I give the date of publication according to the calender of origin as well as the calculated date of the Christian calender, one will sometimes find, between 1976 and 1978, dates of the Iranian Imperial calender that the Shah tried to substitute for the Hegira calender (2535 for 1355, corresponding to 1976–77). Many references in the notes refer to Persian works in order to take account of Iranians' own perceptions of their past, even when, to me, they may seem to be erroneous: it is important to understand Iranian historiography from the inside and to articulate our view alongside that of the Iranians themselves, even when they vary considerably.[5]

The first French edition of this book was published in 2006 by La Martinière under the title of *Iran. Naissance d'une république islamique* (Iran: The Birth of an Islamic Republic) and then with some improvements by Flammarion (2009 and 2016) as *L'Iran de 1800 à nos jours* (Iran from 1800 to the Present Day). It owes much to a large number of colleagues and friends who have been with me for many years in the discovery of Persian culture and Iranian history. It pleases me to mention a few masters to whom I owe much in particular in this field: Nikkie Keddie (Los Angeles), Maxime Rodinson (d. 2004), and Jamshid Behnam, among others. The students who participated in my seminar at the Sorbonne Nouvelle, notably Oliver Bast and Nader Nasiri, now colleagues at Paris and Strasbourg respectively, my colleagues at the CNRS, as well as many others deserve my acknowledgment. But I have thought much, while writing, about all the Iranian researchers who look at the works of Orientalists with some distrust and to those among them who generously helped me in my choice of reading material and sources, whose works constituted the main foundation of my knowledge, notably Fereydun Ādamiat (d. 2008), Iraj Afshār (d. 2011), Kāveh Bayāt, Mansoureh Ettehadiyeh, Homa Nategh (d. 2016), Mohammad Torkamān and many others.

The difficulty in creating a reliable translation into English led my friend and colleague Willem Floor to write a first English draft and take the opportunity of suggesting a number of corrections. His readings brought many improvements for which I am very grateful, even when our standpoints don't always match. This English version differs in many details from the original French. I owe the elegant English rendering to Elizabeth Stone (at Bourchier) and my editor Kilmeny MacBride. My thanks to all.

---

[5] On modern Persian Historiography, see T. ATABAKI, ed., *Iran in the 20th Century: Historiography and Political Culture*, and particularly H. CHEHABI's. contribution.

I dedicate this book to the Iranian officials who, by denying me access to their country since 2002, have increased my desire to understand the Islamic Republic. Without dissuading me from returning there, they have given me, in the meantime, greater freedom of speech. This book is also dedicated to the Iranians who are thirsty for justice having suffered torture, repression and censorship, before and after the 1979 Revolution.

1 IRAN UNDER THE QAJARS

During its long history, Persia has witnessed numerous invasions. But each time, it took revenge on its assailants, who were generally from Central Asia, by turning them into Iranians through a culture of assimilation. In 1722, the army of the ruler of Qandahār, once again from the East, took Isfahan and brought an end to the ruling Safavid dynasty. Persia thus became a battlefield between dynasties that were unable to permanently establish themselves. This continued until the end of the eighteenth century, when the Qajars were finally able to take power. It is to this period that we now turn in order to understand the difficult relationship between Shiism and politics and how a conventional monarchy was able to give birth to an Islamic republic. It was also at this time that the European empires began to take an interest in Iran and to drag it into the modern world. Iranian historians today see the Qajar period as a time of confrontation between their country and Europe, with the concomitant humiliations and wounds that resulted from it.

The Qājār dynasty, descended from a tribe whose early traces in Iran date to the eleventh century, held the reins of power until 1925. Much like the Safavids, they were Turkmen and spoke Turkish: their ethnic group of about 10,000 people led a nomadic life in northern Iran when it conquered the principalities that had fought over the Iranian plateau after the death of Nāder Shāh (1747). The founder of the dynasty, Āqā Mohammad Khān (1742–97) had been kept prisoner during his youth in Shiraz by the Zands, rulers of southern Persia from 1750 to 1794. Following his castration, he dreamt of revenge and of reconstituting the Safavid kingdom. Once freed, he gathered the members of his clan and took power in 1786, establishing his capital in Tehran. From there he could easily move northwards through the passes open for much of the year, through which the caravans linking Tabriz to Mashhad passed. It took him another ten years or so to unite Persian territory. It was only after having conquered Georgia and having ravaged Tiflis that he accepted the title of Shāh ("king"). Shortly thereafter, in 1797, he was assassinated by a servant, whom he had condemned to death and whom he had imprudently released.

Āqā Mohammad Khān, although without offspring, had decreed the law of succession, according to which the crown prince had to be the son of a princess of Qajar blood. This law was respected, but the nomination of a successor was often a merciless battle, with the two main clans within the tribe fighting for supremacy: the Qavānlu, who were in authority, and the Davalu. Despite marriages between the two clans that in theory neutralized internecine fights, each succession weakened the dynasty by giving rise to rivalries and plots within the royal family. From 1828, it was the support of a foreign power – Russia – that determined the legitimacy of a succession. Moreover, the Qajars preferred to choose members of their own tribe as governors or important ministers. This blood relationship allowed them to control Iran for more than a century by assuring the political cohesion of the kingdom but had the effect of impeding the renewal of the elite.

A Vast Territory

Toward 1800, the Persian kingdom extended over the Safavid territory, without Herāt to the east and the holy cities of Mesopotamia to the west. To the north, the founder of the Qajar kingdom had achieved the conquest of the Caucasus, with its rich arable land, where Iran delegated its sovereignty to Muslim and Christian vassals. The Caucasian provinces were not only a reservoir of slaves, soldiers, and concubines, they also formed a buffer zone against the threat of neighboring Ottomans and Russians.

In the south, in the Persian Gulf, the Safavids had evicted the Portuguese from Hormuz in 1622, with English help. Thereafter, thanks to the prosperity of the port of Bandar Abbās, Iranians dominated maritime trade. They also benefited from the port of Bushehr, which Nāder Shāh had developed to become the base of his fleet. Closer to

Shiraz than Bandar Abbās, despite a mountainous barrier, it soon became the most important Iranian port. The British established themselves there in the mid-nineteenth century to put an end to piracy and ensure transport between Bombay and Mesopotamia. Iran claimed the Bahrain archipelago, home to an Arabic-speaking population but one which since Antiquity had also exhibited a strong Iranian influence; since early Islamic times most of the population was Shiite.

In Iran, a territory three times the size of France, it took weeks to travel from the capital to the cities in the periphery. In 1800, it had five or six million inhabitants. The population was scattered. Because of the desert climate of the Iranian plateau, villages were found at the bottom of the valleys, the only place – apart from the Caspian plain, which had abundant rains – where rural settlements could be established, as irrigation was ensured either on the surface or by draining and canalizing underground waters from the foothills. The model par excellence of this settlement was the garden, irrigated by cleverly arranged canals and protected against the dry wind by high mud walls.

The geographical and climatic environment had resulted in another peculiar form of land usage – nomadism. Benefiting in summer from pastures at higher altitudes freed from the snow, and in winter from the moderate temperature of the plains, the nomads of Iran did not have to make long seasonal migrations (on average 300 km or 190 miles). Their social structure was very hierarchized and tribal in nature, because the group had to defend its territory at any time against encroachment by rivals. At the beginning of the nineteenth century, it is estimated that Persia had half a million nomads, about 10 percent of the population. The nomadic population proportionally decreases with demographic growth, but numerically it remains almost constant and symbolically central. At present, it only represents a small proportion of the population.

Three centuries after the Safavids, it was a tribe of the same Turkmen group that held power: the Qajars themselves knew how to deal with the other tribes. The central Qajar government levied taxes on each head of livestock and allocated territories to the tribal groups, sometimes by moving entire tribes in accordance with the needs of land occupation and border surveillance. Nomadism and sedentary agriculture had gone hand in hand in Iran for centuries. In this semi-desert territory, the inevitable conflicts between settled populations and nomads were infrequent, especially since the two produced complementary goods that they could barter (meat, dairy produce, skins, and wool for wheat, fruit, and artisanal products).

The attraction of seasonal migration, like the attachment to gardens, remained essential elements of Iranian psychology until the end of the twentieth century. Yet with widespread urbanization, cohabitation in large settlements and worker migration, sometimes abroad, the ancient dreams of liberty and of solidarity that involved these two ways of life were shattered. The frustrations that modern Iranians have felt as a result of this uprooting undoubtedly explain in part the success of contemporary political preachers, who have brought back the utopia of solidarity and paradisiacal freedom to a society where one could see only walls and grievous displacement.

Between Heaven and Earth

Shiite Islam

Persia became Shiite in 1501. The first Safavid ruler imposed this form of Islam on his subjects, most of whom, although initially unfamiliar with its traditions, gradually adopted the new faith. The Safavids – falsely – claimed to be descended from the Imams and the Prophet and thus embodied religious legitimacy. According to Imamite Shiism, the legitimate authority belongs to the twelve Imams, descendants of the Prophet Mohammad via his daughter Fatima. Only the first Imam, Ali, was caliph; the others were set aside and, according to the Shiites, were martyred by the majority Sunnis. The twelfth Imam, also called the 'hidden Imam,' is believed to be still alive, although in occultation from the eyes of man. He rules the world in an invisible manner and will only reappear at the end of time to install a reign of justice and truth. His authority is "usurped" by all human government. Shiites have sought the most diverse theological and political solutions to overcome this obstacle. Commonly, the Safavids held the secular power in the name of the Imam and as delegates of theologians who were installed as official interpreters of religious legitimacy.

From the sixteenth century, Iranian culture was impregnated with the devotion of the Imams, either by pilgrimages to Mashhad, Qom, and the holy cities in Mesopotamia or by mourning ceremonies for the Imams. On the day of Āshurā, the tenth of the month of Moharram, Shiites commemorate the martyrdom of Hoseyn, the grandson of the prophet, the third Imam, at the battle of Karbalā in 680, during which he was killed by the army of the Ummayad caliph. During this month, and above all during the first ten days, the clergy commemorate the sufferings of the Imam by special sermons; the faithful weep and cry to show their sharing in the savior's sacrifice. In addition to these sermons, there are performances of religious theater, played by lay actors.

During the Qajar period, these mourning representations (*ta'ziye*) became increasingly grandiose. They were patronized by the Shah or a magnate and sometimes performed with splendor in a public enclosure.[1] Even now, they are accompanied by processions of flagellants, grouped by guild or by quarter, who go through the streets whipping themselves with metal-tipped whips, while reciting and chanting lamentations that are taken over by the flagellants and the public. The most impassioned participants strike themselves with a sword so that their bloody heads add a touch of realism to the martyrdom of the savior. By associating themselves with the suffering of Hoseyn and his army, who were massacred at Karbala by the political authorities, the flagellants symbolically damn the despot and participate in a venture of salvation. Some Shiite reformers at the end of the twentieth century (Shariati) criticized this expression of grief and its promotion of suffering as it deadened the revolutionary spirit. In the 1960s, a radical interpretation came into being which sought to give the commemoration of the martyrdom of the Imams a revolutionary spirit, that of sacrifice for the sake of justice. The Shiite clerics, who fear outbursts, rarely encourage these ostentatious manifestations.

Since the time of the Safavids, the ulama have been divided into two camps, *Akhbāri* and *Osuli*, each having opposing conceptions of the interpretation of tradition (*sunna*) and of the role to play in relation to civil power. The *Akhbāri*-s adhere to the traditions established by the Imams during the first centuries of Islam. For them, each believer must find the Imam who will guide him to salvation, and this is achieved by learning Arabic and studying the teachings of the Imams. In the meantime, the believer continues to practice his religion in accordance with the teachings of tradition and avoids any practice that results in acknowledging a master other than the hidden Imam. In particular, he

---

[1] See J. CALMARD, "L'Iran sous Nāser od-Din Chāh"; P. CHELKOWSKI, ed., *Ta'ziyeh: Ritual and Drama in Iran.*

has to refuse participating in the Friday prayer or in a holy war, deeds that only may be undertaken under the direction of an Imam. Contrariwise, the *Osuli*s maintain that their most learned ulama, the *mojtahed*-s, have full legitimacy to teach and discuss the principles of faith (*osul*), and, consequently, to reinterpret tradition, because they engage in scholarship in the name of the hidden Imam. They maintain that non-*mojtahed* Muslims have to "imitate" the *mojtahed*-s by applying the religious precepts as defined by them. This idea of "imitation" had to result, in the mid-nineteenth century, in the definition of a "source to imitate" (*marja-e taqlid*), who in some way is the interpreter of the will of the hidden Imam to the believers.

Religion and Political Legitimacy

At the end of the seventeenth century, several great ulama of Qom, in particular Mohsen Feyz, had developed *Akhbāri* tendencies in reaction to the excessive power the official *Osuli* ulama had assumed under the Safavids. The influence of the *Akhbāri*s increased in Najaf, which had become a center of their school in the eighteenth century. But a dogmatic theologian, Mohammad Bāqer Behbahāni (1705–93) soon cursed them and chased them from the holy places in Mesopotamia.

The religious question acquired new impetus under the Qajars. Unlike the Safavids, the Qajars claimed neither descent from the Imams nor part of their heritage. Although protectors of Shiism, they had to negotiate with the ulama to have their legitimacy acknowledged. The Shiite clergy had suffered ordeals during the collapse of the Safavid kingdom: humiliation and persecution by the Sunni Afghan rulers and, subsequently, confiscation of their numerous endowments by Nāder Shāh and an attempt to drown their doctrinal idiosyncrasies in a syncretism which this monarch saw above all as a means to subdue the Shiite clergy. On several occasions, Nāder Shāh brought the ulama together and demanded that they redefine Shiism as a fifth religious school of jurisprudence (*mazhab*), at the same level as the four religious schools recognized by the Sunnis. Most Shiite theologians refused this compromise, which was imposed on them by force and which meant that they would have to stop cursing the Sunnis.

In 1848, a theoretical work aimed at the political education of Nāser od-Din Mirzā, who was to become Shah, gives this definition of the relations between the political power and authority of the ulama:[2]

> Royalty and Prophethood are two gems that are found mounted in the same setting. The Imamate and the government are two twins that are born from the same belly . . . One owes obedience to the just sovereign, because he is the *Shadow of God* on earth. Likewise, the conduct of political affairs is the younger brother of the *Velāyat* [a term that generally refers to the Imams in a Shiite context, both spiritual love and temporal authority] and the latter is the highest degree of humanity.

Thus, the Qajar monarch, like the *mojtahed*, has the right to interpret faith, based on reason, and to distinguish good from bad in the different political domains, whether it concerns military, economic, or social affairs. "Therefore, the monarch has the right to intervene [in the affairs of this world] and to interpret [the religious traditions], while the *mojtahed* does not have the right to govern." This right, which fully belongs to the Imams, was not devolved to the ulama.

Nevertheless, after 1813, the doctrine of clerical power was affirmed by Mollā Ahmad Narāqi (1771–1829). This theologian for the first time defined a concept that Khomeyni borrowed one and a half centuries later, turning it into the lynchpin of his theory of "the authority of the theologian" (*velāyat-e faqih*). But Narāqi did not give this principle the importance which it acquired in the Islamic Republic. For Narāqi, authority was not only the prerogative of the Prophet and the Imams, it also belonged to those whom God appoints by their intermediary. While trying to define as closely as possible the power of the jurisprudents of religious law (*foqahā*), he distinguished several types of authority: political, judicial, administrative, but also the authority or mandate relating to orphans and the insane. While awaiting the return of the hidden Imam, in his view, the ulama are the real rulers, the only ones capable of legitimizing political action.

Some modern commentators point out that Narāqi wrote his tract during the first war between Persia and Russia (1804–13), at the moment when the ulama were calling for a holy war and needed to legitimize their political authority, but that he himself did not include

---

[2] Treatise by Mohammad Hoseyn Damāvandi, in F. Ādamiat and H. Nāteq, *Afkār-e ejtemā'i va siāsi*, pp. 13f.

the government in the tasks devolved to the jurisprudents, even though he had given a hint of being a possible intractable rival of public power; for example, on several occasions he sent back from Kāshān a governor appointed by Fath-Ali Shāh because he had acted unjustly. His most famous student, Mortazā Ansāri (1799–1864) played a major role in strengthening clerical authority, while adopting a clear position in favor of the withdrawal of the competence of the ulama in the judicial sphere.

After having been chased out of Karbalā, the *Akhbāri* ulama resurfaced in the Qajar period, but under the name *Sheykhi* and with a more speculative doctrine. Being less preoccupied with the legal status of the ulama while waiting for the return of the hidden Imam than with the presence of the Imam in this world and his way of revelation, the Sheykhis tried to restore the esoteric dimension of Shiism that the political victory of the Safavids had stifled. The founder of this school, Sheykh Ahmad Ahsā'i (1753–1826), was born in Bahrain and during his youth had experienced visionary states. Encouraged to attend the court of Fath-Ali Shāh he introduced a more ambiguous doctrine, one that was able to accommodate the mystical fervor of this monarch. He developed the already ancient idea of an intermediary region, situated somewhere between the spiritual and the material world, which he named Hurqalyā, where the Imam resided in occultation and where the resurrection would take place. Rejecting the teachings of the *Osuli* school, the *Sheykhi*-s moved closer to the very individualized practice of the *Akhbāri* school. But the majority of Shiites rejected several of their beliefs; for example, they refused the idea that in each era there is a single Imam, who speaks on behalf of God and the Prophet, or that the "perfect Shiites" are, in each era, secretly, the representatives or "the Gate" of the twelfth Imam. But Sheykhis themselves would reply that he who claims to be invested with this esoteric dignity violates the very principle of the eschatological expectation of the return of the Imam.

Bābism and Sufism

The Sheykhi school might have been able to survive discreetly if, in Karbalā, had not developed a teaching intensifying the eschatological expectation of the Imam and had not an enthusiastic disciple emerged, Ali-Mohammad Shirāzi (1819–50). The latter, believing himself to be the "Gate" (*Bāb*) leading to the Imam, soon claimed, by posing as the

Imam himself, the abolition of the Koranic revelation to the benefit of his new message.

One cannot understand the emergence and the success of this religious movement, Bābism, without referring to the millenarian beliefs that flourished in Iran during the 1840s.[3] The major political catastrophes that had preceded the establishment of the Qajar dynasty had not been forgotten. The defeat that the Persian army suffered in the Caucasus against the Christian Russians presaged imminent cataclysm. Those who sought to benefit by announcing these misfortunes reminded the public that the occultation of the twelfth Imam had begun in 260 of the Hegira (874) and that his return would be one thousand lunar years later, in 1260 of the Hegira (1844). The buoyant return of Sufism in Iran only increased that feverous anxiety. Other causes, social and political, contributed to the success of the Bābis, which triggered a very violent reaction from the ulama and which was severely suppressed by the monarchy. This trauma weighed on Iranian politics for more than half a century.

Sufism, the mystical tradition of Islam that acquired institutional form beyond the mosques, has profoundly influenced Persian literature, notably lyrical and narrative poetry. The Safavids, who themselves emerged from a Sunni mystical order that became Shiite, had different attitudes toward Sufism. To establish their power in the name of Shiite Islam they had to rely on Shiite jurisprudents and theologians who already were clandestinely in Iran or came from present-day Syria or Bahrain to serve them. Thus, official Shiism was very much closed against Sufism, even more than were the Sunnis. By its peculiar religious practice, often critical of official doctrine, and by its devotion to a succession of mystical witnesses eventually leading to a "Pole" (*qotb*) – that is a living spiritual leader – Sufism sometimes appears to be a carbon copy of Shiism. It claims to be a spiritual derivation that goes back to the Imams.

The introduction of Sufism within Shiite Islam took multiple forms: concrete forms through the intermediary of mystical orders that developed above all after the eighteenth century, but also philosophical forms with mystical speculation, in which the Shiite philosophers – whom Henry Corbin called 'theosophers' – of the Safavid period excelled. The Sufis claimed to be the representatives of *erfān* (mysticism,

---

[3] As shown by A. AMANAT, *Resurrection and Renewal*, ch. 2.

gnosis), an ambiguous term that classical theologians readily accepted, unlike the term *tasavvof* (Sufism), which implied allegiance to a spiritual leader and to a brotherhood. The discourse of Shiite philosophers consisted in saying that knowledge of God is generally accessible through prophetic revelation, but that some have access to it in a more direct way via mysticism. Eventually, Koranic revelation and mystical knowledge merged, the latter able to annul the obligatory rituals to which orthodoxy clings. Moreover, the references to the great classics of Sunni Sufism, notably to the mystical martyr al-Hallāj and the thoughts of Ibn al-Arabi are identical in Shiite Sufism, even if they are interpreted differently.

The Shiite Sufis did not belong to the great Sunni mystical orders that had flourished before the Safavids, in the Persian language and on Iranian soil, such as the Naqshbandiye or the Qāderiye. But three major Shiite orders have flourished since then, the Zahabi, the Ne'matollāhi, and the Khāksār. The most important in terms of number of followers and branches, the Ne'matollāhi order, bears the name of the Sunni saint Shāh Ne'matollāh Vali, who died in 1431 and is buried in Māhān, near Kermān. At first, the order developed in India, in the Deccan, and it was only in the eighteenth century that one of its missionaries, Ma'sum-Ali Shāh Dekkani, began preaching in central Iran, in Shiraz, Isfahan, Hamadan, and Kerman. He was executed in Kermanshah on the orders of the *mojtahed* Mohammad-Ali Behbahāni, surnamed the "killer of Sufis" (*sufi-kosh*). The immediate disciple of this Sufi martyr, Nur-Ali Shāh Esfahāni, a prolific poet, was also poisoned by order of the "killer of Sufis." After the latter's death, the Sufis of this order avoided provocative statements and attitudes and enjoyed some respite. They even gained a disciple and soon protector, the third Qajar monarch, Mohammad Shāh (r. 1834–48), who choose as chancellor his Sufi master, Mirzā Āqāsi. This swing of Sufism toward power must have deeply irritated the ulama.

Neighbors and the Avidity of Foreign Powers

Far from the Mediterranean, cut off from other Muslim Mediterranean and Asian powers by its religion, Persia could have lived in peace, tormented only by the internal conflicts of dervishes and the expectation of the twelfth Imam. However, even at the beginning of the nineteenth century, this ancient land was already caught up in the conflicts of the colonial era. In fact, the Iranians represented an increasing challenge; they threatened Ottoman rule in Mesopotamia and hindered Russian advances in the Caucasus. They were also on the land route that led from Europe to India, but the colonial designs of France and Great Britain set Iran apart, as too distant and too large, turning instead toward north Africa and the Near East.

The Ottomans

The historical rivalry between the Persian and Turkish kingdoms had a religious justification. The Ottomans were the traditional defenders of orthodox Sunnism, the Persians, after 1501, of Shiism. Since the sixteenth century, the two sides had worn themselves out in a series of wars, until in 1639 a border compromise was found, roughly the actual western border of Iran, even though the claim to Mesopotamia continued on both sides. After having ruled, under the Safavids, for a few years (1622–38), over the Shiite holy places – a historical return to the sites where pre-Islamic Iran had its capital – in the eighteenth century, Iran twice tried in vain to conquer all or part of Mesopotamia, first under Nāder Shāh in the 1730s and later under Karim Khān Zand in 1775–79. These attempts to conquer Mesopotamia were not driven by hostility toward the Arab Bedouins, but by the desire to control that rich region, the site of the tombs of several Imams through which passed one of the pilgrim routes to Mecca. The Shiites went on pilgrimage to the holy cities of Najaf, Karbalā, and Samarrā. The greatest Shiite ulama, often of Iranian origin, had established themselves there since the strengthening of the *Osuli* school, attracting young theologians who had just finished their studies. Under the paradoxical protection of the Ottomans, they were sheltered from political interference by Tehran during the entire nineteenth century and until the creation of Iraq by the British in 1920.

Under the Qajars, despite a relative peace between the two states, the holy places of Mesopotamia remained a sensitive point. The relations between the subjects of the Sultan and those of the Shah were far from cordial. Sometimes persecutions of Shiites in the Baghdad region resulted in Iranian mobilization, more ostentatious than threatening, while sometimes governors in the south mounted razzias in Turkish territory, west of the Shatt ol-Arab; at other times, Ottoman Kurds descended on Iranian valleys where they took advantage of the women and the harvest. The British, who usually took sides with the

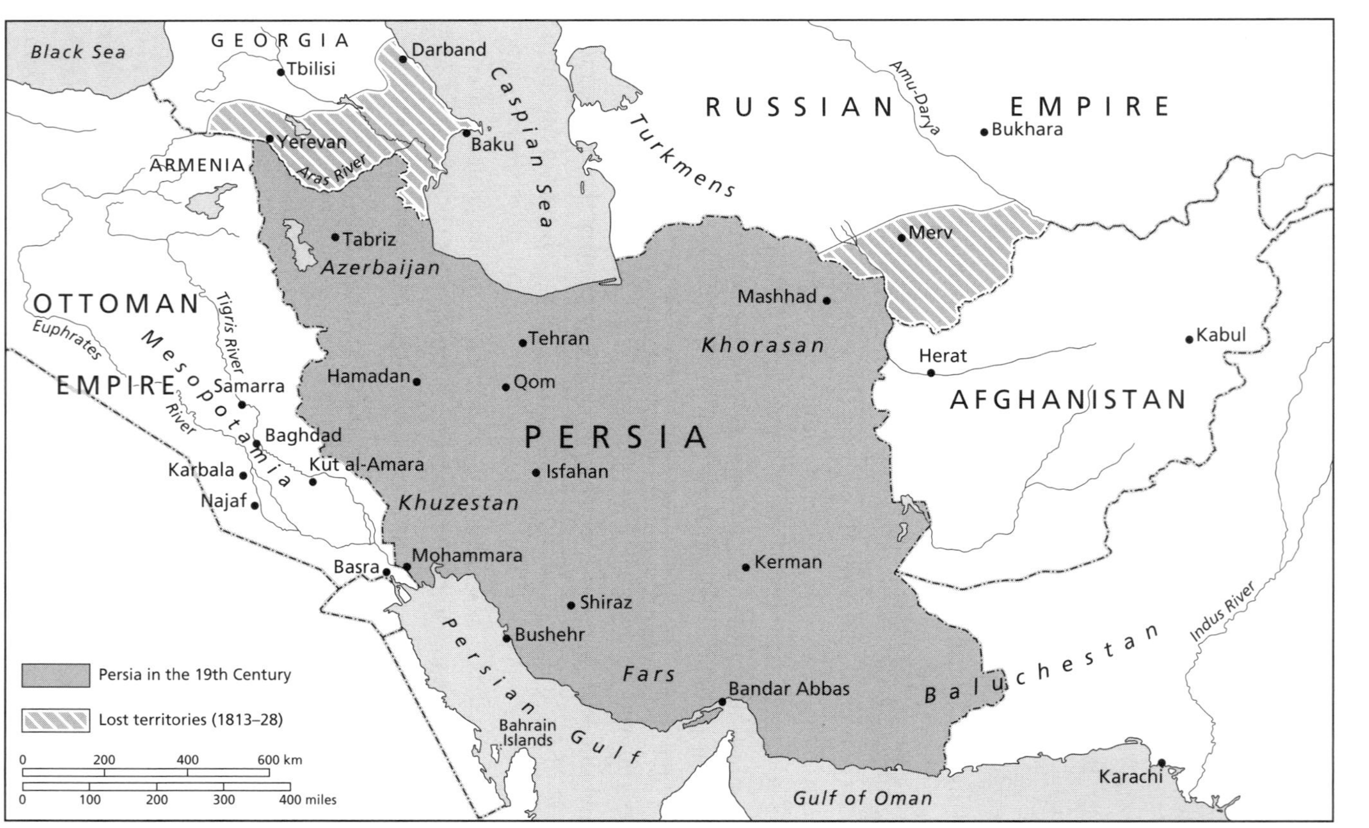

M1 Persia in the nineteenth century

Ottomans, meanwhile forced the Iranians to show reserve. During the Crimean War (1853–56), Persia sided with Russia, more because of what it hoped to gain (in relation to its dispute over Herāt) than out of enmity for the Sublime Porte, which it did not attack.

The river border that allowed commercial vessels to go to Basra was itself a sufficient challenge to give rise to skirmishes. Access to the Persian Gulf via the Shatt ol-Arab had always been of greater strategic importance for Arab Iraq, then under Ottoman rule, than for the Iranians, who benefited from a long coastline and important ports.

In 1838, the Ottomans took advantage of the long siege of Herāt, which kept the Persian troops busy, to attack the port of Mohammara (now Khorramshahr), which took away too much trade from Basra. Following the joint intervention of Russia and Great Britain, the Ottomans and Persians were forced to negotiate. The treaty, signed in Erzurum in 1847, contained the seed of a border conflict which remained unresolved until the beginning of the twenty-first century. It fixed the river border along the Shatt ol-Arab not in the middle of the river bed, or *talweg*, in accordance with the general rule of border rivers, but on the eastern bank, and consequently the right to navigation for Iranians was but a concession. The treaty recognized Iranian sovereignty over the Arab tribes on their side of the river, but that sovereignty was totally theoretical. In fact, the allegiance of the Banu Ka'b tribe, whose territory extended on both sides of the river, was fluctuating, being more an allegiance to their chief than to any state.[4] The southern Iranian province was then officially called Arabestān, "the land of the Arabs." Under Rezā Shāh it became known once again by its ancient name, Khuzestān.

The Russians

The Russian empire, Persia's big non-Muslim neighbor, was separated from Iran by the Caucasus, the Caspian Sea, and Central Asia. Since the reforms of Peter the Great and, above all, of Catherine II, Russia had become a threatening power. It was through this Russian window that Iranians imaged Europe: violent, dominating but oriented toward progress and reforms. For a long time, they were haunted by

---

[4] W. FLOOR, "The Rise and Fall of the Banu Ka'b. A Borderer State in Southern Khuzestan."

a document forged under Catherine II that was presented as Peter the Great's testament. It stated:

> We must progress as much as possible in the direction of Constantinople and India. He who can once get the possession of these points is the real ruler of the world. With this in view we must provoke constant quarrels at the one time with Turkey, at another with Persia. We must establish wharves and docks in the Euxine and by degrees make ourselves master of that sea, as well as the Baltic, which is a doubly important element in the success of our plan. We must hasten the downfall of Persia, push on to the Persian Gulf, if possible re-establish the ancient commercial ties with the Levant through Syria, and force our way into the Indies, which are the storehouses of the world. Once there, we can dispense with English gold.[5]

The Russian advance to the south during the nineteenth century seems to concretize a strategic plan that threatened Persia. The Caucasus had been conquered in the eighteenth century by Peter the Great, whose troops even had pushed as far south as Gilan and Mazandaran. But Nāder Shāh, having established his rule over Persian territory, then put an end to the Czar's control over Baku and Darband. The Iranian vassals of the Caucasus, such as Georgia and Armenia, two Christian nations, hesitated between putting themselves under Russian protection, whose Christian culture was more familiar to them, and Persian protection, which fiscally and politically was less threatening. Iran laid claim to these lands until 1921. In the Qajar period, the Russians moved people – willingly or unwillingly – to rechristianize the Caucasus. Around Erevan in particular they established villages of Armenians from Iranian Azerbaijan who were incited to leave their homes and their church with their livestock and their priest. The policy resulted in weakening Armenian Christians and Assyro-Chaldean communities who remained in Persia. It also shrank the space of Armenian culture; historically Greater Armenia had encompassed part of Anatolia and also Azerbaijan.

Moreover, the Russians used all means available to them to export their goods to Iran: textiles, metals, and sugar. At the beginning

---

[5] D. V. Lehovich, "The Testament of Peter the Great." *The American Slavic and East European Review*, vol. 7, No. 2 (Apr., 1948), pp. 111–24.

of the nineteenth century, when coffee was still the most popular beverage, Iranians gradually adopted the Russian way of preparing tea with samovars using charcoal and drank from small glasses placed on a deep saucer, which the Iranians continue to practice to this day.[6]

The French and English

Russian designs clashed with other conflicts that arose in Persia itself between the French and the English. Fath-Ali Shāh, who succeeded the founder of the Qajar dynasty in 1797, sought an alliance to retake Georgia, which Czar Paul I had just annexed. At that time, the French Emperor Napoléon wanted to ally himself with Persia to weaken the Russians but, above all, to be able to get land access to India. This dream, born during his legendary Egyptian adventure, would allow him to take revenge on the British, who were already established in Bengal and Bombay.

From their side, the British hoped to make Persia the shield of their Indian empire. In 1800, to impress Fath-Ali Shāh and to offer him military and financial assistance, the East India Company sent captain John Malcolm on an embassy with valuable presents. It had no great effect, because the Iranian monarch understood them to be a tribute brought to him as a sign of submission. But the British changed their position when the possibility of action by the Persian army in the Caucasus became a real prospect, Russia being their ally against France. Malcolm had not yet left Persia when his trusted interlocutor, grand vizier Ebrāhim Kalāntar Shirāzi, a survivor of the Zand regime, was accused of treason, had his eyes pulled out, his tongue cut out and was executed some months later. Kalāntar had seen an alliance with the British as a possible support for his dream of a federation of cities and tribes of the south, and a counter-weight to the unification of Persia of which he had been an efficacious agent.

Napoléon had a message taken to the Shah by Commander Romieu and Amédée Jaubert, who were sent as envoys in May 1805. The Shah replied that he himself had already considered an alliance with France and that he proposed to start hostilities with Russia as soon as possible. France and Russia's alliance had not yet down, which happened in September 1805. Two years later France signed a treaty with

---

[6] W. FLOOR, "Tea Consumption and Importation in Qajar Iran."

Iran at Finkenstein in which it committed itself to place its forces at the service of its ally to regain Georgia; in return, Persia had to evict the British instructors from its army and replace them with Frenchmen. The new envoy of the emperor, his aide-de-camp general Gardane, had also prepared the passage of a French army of 20,000 men, to which about 12,000 Persian soldiers were to be added, trained by French officers and armed with French rifles and cannons founded in Isfahan.

However, shortly thereafter, on 7 July, Napoléon signed the treaty of Tilsit with Russia. In this new and fragile alliance, he was more concerned to widen the anti-British coalition than to help Persia. One may assume that the Czar, if his French ally had put pressure on him, would have withdrawn from Georgia without a fight. In Tehran, the French ambassador desperately tried to convince the Shah that France was doing its best. As one might expect, the Russo-Persian negotiations in Tehran about Georgia led to nothing. The Russians, seeing Napoléon's difficulties in Spain, were somewhat skeptical about the help the French were going to extend to Persia. They took advantage of the situation by trying to retake Erevan, the Armenian capital, but were met by Persian resistance (October 1808). Despite the Shah's request, the French refused to intervene against their Russian ally.

Gardane was still in Tehran when John Malcolm, who again had been sent by the East India Company, arrived with great pomp via the Persian Gulf, but he was stopped at Shiraz in May 1808, because the Shah refused to receive him at Tehran in the hope that the French alliance would be reactivated. Piqued, Malcolm returned to Calcutta, disavowed by London. Finally, Fath Ali-Shāh decided to dismiss the French and to receive a British delegation. The British were starting to feel the backlash of their colonial grandeur, and the Indian administrators clashed with the policy agreed in London. The new British envoy was Sir Harford Jones, a man who knew Persia very well and who was at that time based in Baghdad. In 1809, Jones concluded the first alliance between Great Britain and Iran. In retaliation, the governor of Bombay refused to meet the costs of this mission.

Jones' success signaled the end of French hopes in Persia, apart from military assistance, because the governor of Tabriz, Crown Prince Abbās Mirzā, employed former officers of the Napoleonic army – soldiers of fortune – to modernize the Persian army. The latter benefited from the assistance of the two enemy powers, whose relations with the Russian enemy were constantly changing.

Napoléon rode roughshod over the Finkenstein commitments only a few months after the treaty was signed, and without even warning the Persian side, thus demonstrating the impotency of the Qajar dynasty in the face of external conflicts. But part of the Qajars' reservations in respect of France derived from the French Revolution. The echoes of the republic that had begun with the beheading of a king did not inspire them with great confidence, and the English found it easy to exaggerate the horrors of the Revolution. In contrast, Napoléon's military exploits inspired real sympathy, above all his coronation in 1804 and his campaigns against the Russians, whose threat was directly felt as far as Tehran. Subsequently, when the British themselves turned into cumbersome and arrogant allies, the symbol of that populist emperor, who for such a long time had kept them in suspense, represented an even more attractive model, and the biographies of the emperor were translated into Persian.

The confrontation of Persia with the European nations was also challenging for the Persian envoys. Noting the indisputable superiority of the western powers and fascinated by an open society aiming at progress, some of them turned to Masonic lodges. From the beginning of the nineteenth century, Persia was involved in imperial conflicts without mastering the military and political instruments that would have allowed it to defend its integrity. To overcome this heavy handicap the Qajar monarchs started to fight in a different manner.

2 THREE SHAHS, THREE WARS, THREE REFORMERS (1797–1896)

The three Qajar monarchs who ruled between 1797 and 1896 each had their own ideas about the obligations of royal office. Yet all considered themselves to be defenders of common assets and felt a sense of pride in their achievement of having essentially maintained the status quo while at the same time introducing reforms concomitant with modern conceptions of institutional structures and governance. Over the course of a century, the Qajar dynasty contemplated its own image as a reflection of Safavid heritage, aspiring to conquests and the proliferation of its prestigious cultural heritage. It did not merely imitate Safavid culture but basked in its own cultural production, creating a cult of personality around the dynasty's – increasingly precarious – grandeur. Although several initiatives were undertaken to reform the state, weaknesses in Persia's military and economic situation allowed foreign influence to obtain exorbitant privileges. This was not the era of a flourishing or a renaissance of Persian culture. Rather, when assessing the conditions of Persia in the nineteenth century, one has the impression of the gradual emptying of the state's coffers.

Fath-Ali Shāh (1797–1834) and His Court

Fath-Ali Shāh was born in 1769. During his youth, to rein in the ambitions of his tempestuous father, the Zands took him hostage, detaining him in Shiraz, where they already held his uncle Āqā Mohammad Khān, the future founder of the dynasty. Despite his emasculation, after having launched the conquest of the Iranian kingdom, the latter married Fath-Ali Shāh's mother, who was now widowed. Thus he became the adoptive father of the prince, whom he made his heir when he himself acceded to the throne in 1786.

Fath-Ali Shāh's succession in 1797 gave rise to violent jealousies within the Qajar tribe. To confirm his right to the succession, the young king practiced every cruelty that he had witnessed his uncle and predecessor mete out, not hesitating to pluck out eyes, cut out tongues, and wall up alive those who contested his supremacy. Nor did he spare his brother Hoseyn-Qoli, governor of Fārs, who rebelled on two occasions in his pursuit to share in royal power, from such punishment; and he reserved the same treatment for his first grand vizier, Ebrāhim Khān. This policy of intimidation allowed him to consolidate the gains of his uncle's conquest, despite the rebellions that threatened his throne. Concerning his own sons, who might have been able to conspire if they had been left to their own devices in the capital, he kept them busy with political and military missions. Gradually he entrusted them with the governance of the provinces, assigning to them a tutor when they were too young to govern alone. The crown prince, Abbās Mirzā (1789–1833), the scion of two rival branches of the Qajar tribe (Qavānlu on his father's side, Davalu on his mother's), was appointed governor of Tabriz, capital of Azerbaijan, according to a practice that remained until the end of the dynasty. There he kept a real court, with a vizier, and had an army. His father quickly tasked him to retake the Caucasian lands from the Russians.

The second Qajar Shah was obsessed with amassing a fortune. His lavish lifestyle and continuous military campaigns critically drained his treasury and reduced the Crown's reserves of gold and precious jewels. He did not hesitate to sell religious endowments that Nāder Shāh had confiscated for the benefit of the Crown.

From Tehran, which was but a small township, Fath-Ali Shāh kept himself informed about the political and social customs of the Europeans, but he thought that it would have been disastrous to inculcate them in Persia, particularly the parliamentary model, which would have weakened the government at a time when the Russian threat was ever present. To elevate the status of the capital he designated it the "abode of the caliphate" (*Dār al-Khelāfe*), an expression – surprising for a Shiite – adopted to state its supremacy over Tabriz, which was but an "abode of royalty" (*Dār os-Saltane*), and over Isfahan, the prestigious capital of the Safavids. In similar decorum, he restored the honor of the ancient titles of the Persian empire, in particular *Shāhanshāh*, "king of kings," or *Khāqān*, the Turkish word to denote the Chinese emperor, which he adopted himself as a surname to proclaim his superiority over his Ottoman counterpart, who was but a sultan. He commissioned several full-length portraits of himself, showcasing his long, pointed beard and his ceremonial dress – portraits that he sent to foreign rulers as a present. He even went so far as to have his deeds sculpted over a Sasanian bas-relief at Ray and in Fars, near prestigious sites of pre-Islamic Iran.

Fath-Ali Shāh was not only concerned about strengthening the prestige of his dynasty or of his own glory; he also reinforced the religious character of his monarchy. He had many mosques built and decorated the cupolas of the tombs of the Imams and Shiite saints at Qom and Mashhad, but also in Mesopotamia. He invited well-known theologians to court such as Sheykh Ahmad Ahsā'i, who declined, and Mollā Ahmad Narāqi, a theologian who was most outspoken about clerical prerogatives. Moreover, Tehran attracted poets and writers who received pensions. It was the age of "literary renewal" (*bāzgasht-e adabi*) – though many of the authors of the day are now largely forgotten – in which the Shah himself did not hesitate to publish rather banal poems under the pseudonym of Khāqān.

Other than for his difficulties with Napoléon, Fath-Ali Shāh is above all known for his sexual prowess and his numerous wives and concubines. He kept a thousand women, if one includes the servants and young girls awaiting marriage, to which one must add a large number of eunuchs. He begot no fewer than 260 children; sixty boys and fifty girls survived him, for whom he had constantly to enlarge the harem. Some fifteen years after the death of this prolific Shah, it is estimated that he had more than 10,000 relatives and descendants. Even if many of his associations were above all political in nature, he had a certain number of favorites. Some were women who attained recognition for their financial competence and were used to manage the harem or the accounting of the royal treasury. It was for a favorite from Isfahan, Tāvus Khānom Tāj od-Dowle, that the famous Peacock throne (*Takht-e Tāvus*) was commissioned (which was later transferred from Golestān Palace to the Museum of the National Treasury at Tehran, where it is housed today).

From the Loss of the Caucasus to the Capitulations

The first Irano-Russian war (1804–13), led by Crown Prince Abbās Mirzā, allowed Persia, initially, to reinforce its position in the region. After the Peace of Tilsit, which France signed despite its commitment to Persia, the Czar offered Abbās Mirzā a peace agreement in which he promised his neutrality toward Persia in his border conflicts with the Ottomans, but refused point-blank to return Georgia. The Shah rejected the terms, counting on British aid. The Persian campaigns continued, encouraged by the call of the ulama for a holy war. In June 1812, Napoléon attacked Russia, but a few months later he faltered in the Muscovite snow. The Russian victory encouraged the Czar to undertake a new campaign in the Caucasus.

In 1813, the Iranians were forced to sign a humiliating peace at Golestān, a village in Qarabāgh. A British representative was allowed to participate in the negotiations, the first in a long series in which the two rival empires would preside over the destiny of Persia. The territorial clauses were a bitter pill for the Iranians. They permanently lost the entire region of the Caucasus north of the river Kur, that is, Darband, Bāku, and Shirvān. Moreover, the Russians obtained the exclusive right to maintain a naval presence in the Caspian Sea. Until the Peace Conference of Versailles and the Irano-Soviet Treaty of 1921, and perhaps even to the present day, the Persians longed to regain these territories, where many of the Shah's subjects remained throughout the nineteenth century. It was in Baku, the center of the oil industry, that they became aware of the revolutionary socialist movement.

Under the Treaty of Golestān, the Czar acquired the right "to acknowledge the Persian prince designated to inherit the throne and to render him assistance in case of need to eliminate his rivals" (art. 14). This prerogative constituted a precedent that hampered the designation of a crown prince for almost a century. Its official objective was to consolidate the territorial gains in case the crown prince was ousted by pretenders who would wage war. But according to another interpretation, often seen in nationalistic polemics hostile to the Qajars, the initiative was up to the crown prince who strengthened his position, at the cost of seventeen cities of the Caucasus that he sold to the Russians.

It was not long until a second Irano-Russian war broke out. Exploiting the ambiguities of the Treaty of Golestān, which defined the new border as the ceasefire line, thus leaving in contention two important zones, the Russians occupied the region situated between Erevan and Lake Sevan (also called Gokcha) in 1825. Immediately, declarations of a holy war could be heard in Tehran and in Tabriz. Abbās Mirzā decided to resume hostilities in 1826 and achieved some successes in Armenia, but the Russians soon gained the upper hand and took Tabriz in October 1827.

The treaty that followed in 1828 was negotiated in Torkamanchāy, east of Tabriz. It was even more disadvantageous for Iran, which lost all its territory north of the Aras. Even more serious for the vanquished, it established a regime of "capitulations."[1] This stipulation was in response to the demands of Russian merchants and of Europeans in general, who would thus benefit from extra-territorial judiciary rights over Iranian soil. By virtue of their nationality and their religion, foreigners before 1828 hardly had any means to claim any rights in the event of a dispute with an Iranian Muslim. The Ottoman Empire had signed capitulations with the French in 1569, and later progressively with other nations. These guaranteed safe passage to persons as well as to merchandise, which was subject to a fixed-rate tax (5 percent) of their value. Moreover, foreign nations were free to organize their own mail routes, which were not under the control of the Ottoman Empire (this freedom was not questioned until the empire joined the Universal Postal Union in 1875).

The Treaty of Torkamanchāy, which included a lengthy clause on commercial arrangements, granted similar rights to the Russians (excluding the mail), notably with the fixed-rate 5 percent tax as a customs duty. It defined a legal framework for foreign merchants. Gradually these capitulations were applied and soon extended to other nations, by virtue of the clause of the most-favored nation, and foreign merchants found themselves in a situation that was diametrically opposed to the legal inferiority from which they had suffered before. Apart from the fact that their merchandise was henceforth subject to a single tax, and thus exempt from internal tolls, they had the guarantee that all contestations of their rights, and all events justifying judicial arbitrage, could only be settled in the presence of their consul, or his representative, in the presence of a representative of the Iranian Ministry of Foreign Affairs (*kārgozār*) and above all in accordance with the law of their country of origin.

---

[1] See Md Mosaddeq, *Kāpitulāsyon va Irān.*

This situation created more resentment among Persian merchants. Yet, despite the negative reaction to the Treaty of Torkamanchāy, its impact on Russo-Persian trade was negligible. In Entner's words, "The great expectations did not materialize." Owing to various conditions, Russian trade in Iran did not increase; at some stage, Persian merchants, benefiting from the same 5 percent tax rate in Russia, would use this means to re-export from Tabriz to Russia European goods competing with Russian industrial production.[2]

To claim for themselves some of the advantages granted to foreigners, some merchants went so far as to ask the foreign legations for legal recognition as a "protected subject." In 1850, when the right of sanctuary (*bast*) in religious places was abolished, numerous Iranians asked the British to give them shelter. This practice did not cease when the right of sanctuary was re-established, and its use was such that Nāser od-Din Shāh, then on the throne, warned his vizier: "If we are not careful, the entire nation progressively becomes British."[3] In the Treaty of Paris of 1857 the Persians demanded from London "henceforth to give up diplomatic protection to all Persian subjects who were not actually in the service of the British mission." In reality, the abuse continued sporadically, driven by the attraction of the privileges of the capitulations.

Later, the Ottomans strove to abolish the capitulations on the basis that the law, in a secularized society, in principle granted equality to Christians and guaranteed an equitable status to foreigners. In parallel, notably after the revolution of 1906, Iranian nationalists denounced the continuation of this humiliating system. These extra-territorial privileges finally were abolished by Rezā Shāh a hundred years after their formal introduction, much later than by Turkey, and despite protests from Europeans. Iran then promulgated a modern and secularized civil code where the equality of citizens and the rights of foreigners were defined without prejudice toward non-Muslims.

Following the Treaty of Torkamanchāy, an incident further complicated the relations between Persia and Russia. One of the Russian negotiators, Alexander Griboyedov, a well-known author as well as a diplomat who had married a Georgian woman, was appointed minister plenipotentiary in Tehran. His mission was to supervise the

---

[2] M. L. ENTNER, *Russo-Persian Commercial Relations, 1928–1914*, p. 7, 13.
[3] A. AMANAT, *Pivot of the Universe*, pp. 237f; F. ĀDAMIAT, *Amir Kabir*, p. 432.

proper execution of the treaty, notably the payments of war reparations and the repatriation of prisoners of war. He understood that this included captive Georgian or Armenian women, who were kept in the princely harems of Tehran.[4] The affair resulted in a mob attack, fed by popular resentment against the Russian victory and by the arrogant attitude of this diplomat, who offered asylum to women of Christian origin who had converted to Islam and were the mothers of Muslim children – numerous women had in fact been taken from the Caucasus by the Persians. The mob sacked the Russian legation and killed Griboyedov as well as several members of his embassy (1829). In response to the crisis, Fath-Ali Shāh and Abbās Mirzā sent one of the royal princes to St. Petersburg bearing lavish gifts as a reparation.

How can we explain this excess, which cost Persia more in terms of the loss of international credibility than the monetary cost of the gifts? A religious outrage fomented by the ulama? Some think that Griboyedov was victim of a complot aimed at preventing the Abbās Mirzā's succession to the throne, of which the diplomat had been an ardent defender at Torkamanchāy. The violation of the guarantees granted to embassies is curiously similar to the storming of the American embassy in 1979. The irruption of Islamic law into the controversy ran counter to international conventions and placed Persia in a position which the country would find itself in once again, in 1989, after the fatwa against Salman Rushdie.

The Army and the Need for Reforms: Abbās Mirzā

After the disastrous result of the second Russian war, Crown Prince Abbās Mirzā was called to re-establish order in the country at Yazd, Kerman, and Deh Kord, near Isfahan. Fath-Ali Shāh even conferred on him the governorship of Khorāsān in addition to that of Azerbaijan where Abbās Mirzā had delegated his functions to one of his sons. He launched two military campaigns around Mashhad (1832 and 1833) to retake control over former Iranian territories. These operations were only the prelude to a more serious conflict aimed at taking control of northern Afghanistan. This campaign, most likely considered to be easier than the one in the Caucasus, would have

---

[4] See A. SHAMIM, *Irān dar dowre-ye saltanat-e Qājār*, p. 76; H. ALGAR, *Religion and State*, pp. 94f.

allowed the future king to restore his image and to impose himself as the best candidate to inherit the throne. But, in 1833, having suffered from ill-health owing to liver problems, he died, one year before his father, despite the efforts of his two British physicians. He was buried in Mashhad in the shrine of Imam Reza.

Of the many westerners who met Abbās Mirzā, most gave a complimentary account of him. One may speculate about the changes that this "reformist prince" could have brought if he had reigned. An admirer of Sultan Selim III, who reformed the Ottoman empire, he transformed Tabriz, which was located on the caravan route that came from Europe, into a center of westernization. Staying abreast of the social and political reforms sweeping across many European countries, he hesitated between French and British influence, notably on the question of military reform. Having early on realized his army's weakness when faced with the Russian threat, he put to use the literature available on Ottoman military reforms and, in 1819, enlisted Russian deserters to train a regiment of 800 men in modern military discipline. He also recruited British, Sicilian, and Polish officers and founded a military academy – managed by a Frenchman – where Ottoman, French, and Russian officers provided training. Cannons and gunpowder were produced at an arsenal. By 1831, he had trained 12,000 foot soldiers and 2,000 gunners in addition to a cavalry regiment. The fortifications of Tabriz, Khoy, and Ardabil were modernized. It was the first large-scale reform after the defeat by the Russians. Abbās Mirzā also attempted to improve the network of caravanserais and the efficacy of the administration. His ambitions were not to be realized, however, owing to a lack of competent staff, but his plans did offer fresh impetus to modernization.

Two people of the time stand out. Both were functionaries of the court of Tabriz, both bore the title of Qā'em-Maqām (lieutenant, deputy), and both were to hold the role of provincial vizier: Mirzā Isā Farāhāni (d. 1822) and his son Abo'l-Qāsem Farāhāni. The latter, a well-known man of letters, helped to create a new style of Persian prose of an uncluttered elegance. After Abbās Mirzā's death it was he who arranged for the son of the princely master to take power in an environment of fierce rivalries. The prince ascended to the throne under the name of Mohammad Shāh, but, far from being grateful, had Abo'l-Qāsem Farāhāni strangled in 1835. Qā'em-Maqām II had tried to curb political encroachment by both Russian and British imperialism, and the British minister in Tehran, who hated him, would have encouraged his execution.[5]

Influencing a King: Mohammad Shāh (1834–48)

Prior to his accession to the throne, Abbās Mirzā's son had spent several months on the front line at Herāt. He struggled to be accepted as heir apparent; his father's army was exhausted by the Afghanistan campaign and the treasury was empty. He needed the joint support of the Russians and the British, as well as the skill of his father's vizier, Qā'em-Maqām to avoid Persia descending into anarchy.

Born in 1808 Mohammad Shāh was educated by a French governess at Tabriz who taught him French.[6] Toward the end of his life, he also had two French physicians. In his youth, he was particularly influenced by his teacher Hājj Mirzā Āqāsi (1783–1848), a protégé of Qā'em-Maqām. Abbās Āqāsi was a Sufi from the Caucasus. Before becoming a tutor at the court of Tabriz, he studied in the holy cities of Iraq and then led the life of a peripatetic dervish before entering the service of the Armenian patriarch of Erevan, his native city, where he stood out because of his intelligence.

Opinions on this atypical mystic diverge widely. In her book on Iran and its cultural development under Mohammad Shāh, recently published in Europe, the historian Homa Nategh, though little inclined to praise Sufism, presents a collection of the slanderous stereotypes, gossip, lies, and misinformation that circulated about Mirzā Āqāsi, demonstrating the jealousies and subterfuge at work among the pretenders to the throne and other conspirators, who were pushed aside when he was appointed by his royal pupil.[7]

Āqāsi occupied this post for thirteen years. One of his first acts was to approve the execution of his predecessor. Subsequently he established in Persia a regime that was systematically hostile to any kind of political violence and provided the model of a simple, corruption-free life. This was peculiar behavior in a climate where politicians were often the very worst offenders, using public goods to enhance their personal standing, which political positions alone could not provide. The accusations of

---

[5] F. Ādamiat, "Sarnevesht-e Qā'em-Maqām," pp. 5f, based on Sir John Campbell's diaries.

[6] On Louise de la Marnierre see J. Calmard, "Une dame française à la cour de Perse"; H. Nāteq, *Irān dar rāhyābi-e farhangi*, p. 105.

[7] H. Nāteq, *Irān dar rāhyābi-e farhangi*, p. 12.

pederasty, greed, and prevarication with which his enemies blackened Āqāsi's reputation were matched by those of imbecility and villainous dishonesty. He was also slanderously imputed to have been surrounded by Caucasian crooks and to have amassed landed estates. His Sufi beliefs led him in fact to an overtly ascetic life and inspired him to impose restrictions on the import of ideas and goods coming from Europe, such as British textiles – a measure that was not sufficiently efficacious to prevent the progressive disappearance of the traditional textile industry.[8]

Under the influence of Mirzā Āqāsi, Sufis acquired influential social positions, much to the annoyance of the representatives of official Islam, who, until recently, had them killed indiscriminately. As one Muslim historian says: "That the country was governed by a king of heterodox belief was a scandal in itself."[9] The tombs of great Sufi thinkers were restored, mostly of Sunnis such as Attār at Nishapur and Shabestari in Azerbaijan. Soon it became the norm, even fashionable, to call oneself a Sufi, which was also a way to call oneself a Muslim without attending the mosque. The result was a more liberal space and free-thinking that had not previously existed, and which was favored by more frequent contact with Europeans. A Qajar prince, who had participated in the peace-making mission to Russia after the killing of Griboyedov, returned an admirer of social progress and freedom of thought, blaming the yoke of Islam for the backwardness of Iranian society.

The ulama could not intervene in politics without the risk of banishment to faraway places, for they were exiled to Najaf or Mashhad, away from their devoted flocks. To negotiate their return, they were forced to promise that they would no longer criticize the government. The confrontations had the makings of a military resistance, since some ulama maintained armed men to intervene when the central government was incapable of doing so. In Isfahan, a *mojtahed* who, from poverty, rose to enormous wealth, had dominated the city under the preceding Shah: Seyyed Mohammad Bāqer Shafti (1766–1844) had an army of henchmen (*luti*) and made life difficult for Khosrow Khān, the governor of the city. To force the religious leader into giving up his temporal power, Mohammad Shāh himself led an

---

[8] H. Nāteq, *Irān dar rāhyābi-e farhangi*, pp. 15f, 214f.
[9] H. Algar, *Religion and State*, p. 107. Opposite statement in H. Nāteq, *Irān dar rāhyābi-e farhangi*, who stresses the tolerance and freedom which were then prevalent.

army that bombarded Isfahan's fortifications with cannon (1839) and had him reduced to submission and abandon the support of ruffians.[10]

The Western Missionaries

The few Christian missionaries who had traveled to Persia up to the beginning of the nineteenth century had limited themselves to making contact with the elite, to translate the gospel, and to engage in polemics against Islam. Henry Martin (1781–1821), a British missionary and Cambridge graduate, who had lived in Calcutta, stayed in Persia for a year and completed a fresh translation of the New Testament into Persian – slightly improved, this version is still used today. Local Christians were reluctant to read the gospel in a 'Muslim' language, preferring Armenian or Syriac; thus this task was a novel one to foreign missionaries.

The traditional Christians of Azerbaijan, who since the Mongol era lived in mostly rural and insular communal quarters, attracted Protestant and Roman Catholic missionaries.[11] After their victories in the Caucasus in 1813 and in 1828, the Russians had induced the Christians of Iran – Armenian and Assyro-Chaldean[12] – to place themselves under the Czar's protection, offering them tax exemptions for two years. Almost 45,000 Armenians chose exile, which very much weakened the presence of Christians in Azerbaijan. At the beginning of Mohammad Shāh's reign, American Presbyterians established themselves at Urmia, in Iranian Kurdistan, where the Assyro-Chaldeans lived. Here they opened a mission, with a church, a school, a printing press, and a hospital. Five years later, in 1839, they were followed by a French Catholic, Eugène Boré (1809–78), a linguist and epigraphist, who established a school in Tabriz and soon attracted a missionary congregation, the Lazarists, to come to Persia. The Lazarist schools in Azerbaijan, and later in Tehran and Isfahan, provided bilingual

---

[10] H. ALGAR, *Religion and State*, p. 112, quoting *Nāsekh ot-tavârikh* and *Qesas ol-olamā*.

[11] The Church of Persia brought the gospel to Central Asia and China, at the end of the Sassanian era and until the time of the Abbasid caliphate. The decline of the Church of the East followed the conversion of the Mongols to Islam.

[12] The Armenian Church (Gregorian) is part of the national identity of Armenians; Christianity was introduced in Armenia in the third century. The name "Assyrian" was given to the Church of the East (also improperly called "Nestorian") in the nineteenth century; the "Chaldeans" (also a false denomination) are those who joined the Roman Church at the beginning of the sixteenth century.

education and became bastions of westernization; gradually, Muslim students were admitted. In Tehran, the École Saint-Louis was founded and provided modern schooling to a wealthy elite; it continued to operate until the revolution of 1979. At the end of the nineteenth century, other schools were created in major towns, in particular through the Alliance Israélite Universelle, an international network with the aim of educating Jews.

At first, the missionaries were not allowed to accept Muslim pupils – apostasy was punished by death in Islam, and, as a result, the evangelization of Muslims generally did not have much success. Nevertheless, they enjoyed relative freedom because of the existence of the Christian and Jewish minorities. The leaders of the Eastern Churches, above all the Armenians, for their part, looked very much askance at these rival churches, which benefited from considerable material support and had a poor opinion of local traditional Christianity. They obtained restrictive measures from the authorities, but these remained provisory. Thus, in 1841, Catholic missionaries were forbidden to preach among the Armenians.[13]

The flourishing of missionary activities benefited from the favorable conditions created by the capitulations (consular privileges granted to "Christian" nations), a status that the missionaries had already claimed in the Ottoman empire. The European colonial, commercial, and religious expansion was such that the legitimacy of such a step was never questioned by the missionaries. In their eyes, they were bringing progress to people who until then had lived in the dark. They believed they could regenerate the fossilized Christianity of the traditional churches.

The Catholic and Protestant schools favored urbanization. Many Christians, most of whom lived in villages, went to live in Tabriz or Tehran; later, they migrated to the USA or Australia. The traditional Christians, above all those who had received a modern education, were relatively well integrated within society where their training as technicians, physicians, industrialists, and merchants was valued. One of their specialties, and likewise for the Jews, had always been the production of wine, which Muslims drank, but which they

---

[13] H. Nāteq, *Irān dar rāhyābi-e farhangi*, p. 260; M. Golnazarian-Nichanian, *Les Arméniens d'Azerbaïdjan, histoire locale et enjeux régionaux, 1828–1918*. Further, Th. Flynn. *The Western Christian Presence in the Russias and Qajar Persia c. 1760–c.1870*.

seldom made themselves because of religious prohibition. The same was true for music and dance, which Muslims appreciated, but which were performed by the "minorities." The Armenians, by far the most numerous of the Persian Christians, obtained important diplomatic, military, and financial functions prior to the 1906–07 Constitution, which made Islam a condition for higher public functions.

The cultural identification with a foreign church contributed to the marginalization of the *minorities* and, to mark this point of difference, Persians got into the habit of addressing them as "Monsieur" or "Madame" rather than the typical titles used among Iranians (*Āqā, Khānom*). The theoretical civic equality which they enjoyed was exaggerated by Iranian historians, who were concerned with showing Iran in a favorable light and as following the example of the Ottoman empire. In 1840, Mohammad Shāh accorded the autonomy of personal status (marriage, inheritance, and so on) to the Catholics, as well as the ownership of the churches, which they had the right to build and restore, but not religious liberty, which would have implied preaching to and the baptism of subjects who were born Muslims. In short, he had merely formally given what traditional Islamic law had always tolerated.

An Old Version of Shiite Islam: Ismailism

As noted above, there were two major schools of Shiite Islam: the majority *Osuli* school that wanted to expand clerical authority; and the *Sheykhi* school that flourished at Karbalā in Iraq, and which, in 1841, after the death of its spiritual leader, was mainly established in Kermān and formed alliances within the Qajar family.

Much less numerous, the Ismailis, who were also Shiites, but dissident ones, had been persecuted since the Seljuq period and, to survive, had merged with the Sufis with whom one finds them at Kermān and Mahallāt (Central Iran) at the beginning of the nineteenth century. The forty-sixth Ismaili Imam, known under the Sufi name of Hasan-Ali Shāh (1804–81) received the title of Āqā Khān (commonly "Agha Khan") from Fath-Ali Shāh, a title that the leader of the Ismailis continues to hold to this day (together with his Iranian citizenship). In 1835, Mohammad Shāh appointed him governor of Kerman, where he soon established order and expelled rebellious elements who opposed paying taxes. As thanks, he was removed from his office for the benefit of a Qajar family member, and in reaction he rebelled. He resisted the

Shah's troops for fourteen months until, in 1841, he decided to permanently go into exile in India. This semi-political, semi-religious rebellion was tied to different Sufi affiliations of the vizier Mirzā Āqāsi and Agha Khan. It was in some respects a prelude to the rebellion of the adherents of the Bāb.

Bābism: A New Religion

One may recall that, after the death of the spiritual leader of the *Sheykhi*s, a number of his disciples, among whom was Seyyed Ali-Mohammad Shirāzi, were convinced that the Twelfth Imam would return to earth to install his reign 'of justice and truth' in 1844, a thousand lunar years after his Occultation. To add to this eschatological expectation various social upheavals appeared to announce the end of time: for the peasantry, it was their torment in the aftermath of the Russian wars and the resulting fiscal pressure; for the ulama, it was the rottenness of the government of the 'impious' vizier – which is how they saw Mirzā Āqāsi; and for the faithful, it was the news of the sack of Karbalā, first by the Wahhabis in 1801 and then by the Ottomans in 1843 to evict bandits who ransomed pilgrims.

It is at that time that Ali-Mohammad Shirāzi, a young merchant, convinced he was the "Gate" (*bāb*) leading to the Imam, announced this divine identity to some of his friends among the *Sheykhi*s. Inspiring admiration and sympathy, the Bāb recruited his first disciples among the mollas from low-income backgrounds, coming from all across Iran. At first, he refrained from announcing his identity in public. During an interrogation in the Vakil mosque in Shiraz, he denied the claim to avoid being lynched. He finally found refuge at Isfahan thanks to the governor of the city, Manuchehr Khān Mo'tamed od-Dowle. This Armenian convert to Islam, attracted by the trail-blazing discourse of the Bāb and eager to stimulate inter-religious debates, asked the Imam-Jom'e to provide shelter to the prophet of Shiraz. Yet a large number of the theologians of the city, supported by those of Isfahan who resisted the charms of the young prophet, alerted the vizier. Mirzā Āqāsi had the Bāb arrested and refused to grant him an audience with the Shah, fearing the latter's weak judgment and that the Bāb might convert him to his cause, and thus impose his new religion on all of Iran.

The resistance to the new religion by the main *Sheykhi* leader, Hājj Mohammad Karim Khān Kermāni (1809–70), contributed to the isolation of the relatively numerous Babis. An exceptional woman joined them, however: Fāteme Zarrintāj Baraqāni (1814–52). The daughter of a theologian of Qazvin, she had received an advanced education and wrote poetry. She was nicknamed Qorrat ol-Eyn (Consolation of the Eyes) and the Bāb called her Tāhere, the "Pure One." She was the first Iranian woman who dared to go out in public without a veil; feminist scholars have often cited this example. She was arrested in 1847 and refused to repent. A wave of repression brought sporadic revolts, with the Bābis capitalizing on the rural discontent to bolster their resistance.

Despite their suppression, the Bābis resisted for some years. Arthur Gobineau, a French diplomat who lived in Iran shortly after these events and who spoke with numerous witnesses, reported that, apart from the mollas, another social group traditionally linked to the clergy, namely merchants and artisans, joined the Bābis.[14]

According to a historian of Bābism, the success of the movement was owed in part to the merchants' predicament, consequences of the western commercial offensive that stifled the Iranian market at a time when it had begun to benefit from relative political stability.[15] Moreover, the Ottomans had tried to blockade the port of Mohammara (Khorramshahr) and impose discriminatory measures on Iranian merchants at Baghdad, in response to which the Iranian authorities did little. In 1841, as a result of the signing of the new Anglo-Persian trade treaty, the British and their protégés benefited from the right to import their textiles into Iran, in direct competition with the traditional textiles industry in Isfahan and Kāshān. These believers from a low-income background, who saw their hope for prosperity disappear with the European encroachment, believed they had found an answer to their worries in the Messianic aspirations of Bābism. In fact, the foreign importers were less damaging than the local merchants profiting from new imports.

After having been protected at Isfahan, in 1847 the Bāb was imprisoned in Sunni Kurdistan where he continued to spread his predictions of catastrophe via his disciples. The Russians, fearing the effect

---

[14] A. DE GOBINEAU, *Les Religions et les philosophies dans l'Asie centrale*, ch. 6, pp. 504f.
[15] A. AMANAT, *Resurrection and Renewal*, pp. 332f.

of Bābi propaganda near their border – they already had faced two Messianic preachers in the Caucasus – demanded that the prisoner be moved away from their territories. The Bāb was thus taken to the Ottoman border to the Chehriq fortress, but still numerous visitors came to see him. As the agitation continued, Mirzā Āqāsi decided to have him judged at Tabriz to humiliate him in front of his followers when he continued to claim to be the Twelfth Imam. Despite the determination of the ulama who interrogated him and judged him to be guilty of apostasy, he was declared insane and got away with a bastinado. At the same time, the Bābis rose up in the north of the country, notably around the stronghold of Sheykh-Tabarsi in Māzandarān. After a ten-month siege they surrendered; the survivors were disemboweled and had their throats slit. But the Bāb, although better supervised in the fort where he had been taken after his trial in Tabriz, continued to make himself heard by visitors to whom he spoke via his prison's window. He was still there when the Shah died.

The new king, Nāser od-Din Shāh, aged seventeen, was dominated by Amir Kabir, a vizier who did not have the restraint or scruples of Mirzā Āqāsi when raison d'état required it. He had the Bāb brought to Tabriz for execution, considering this good timing as the uprisings had been subdued. On 9 July 1850 the prophet was led through the city with bare head and feet to be shot.

The Bābi agitation continued, and, two years after the execution of the founder, an attempt to kill Nāser od-Din Shāh failed. Throughout his life, the Shah was haunted by a possible Bābi revenge attack. The crushing of the rebellion, including the execution of Qorrat ol-Eyn, did not result in the total suppression of the sect, which survived under two very different forms.

The Bāb had appointed Mirzā Yahyā Nuri (1830–1912), despite his youth, as his successor. Known by the name of *Sobh-e Azal* (Dawn of Eternity) he fled to the island of Cyprus in the Ottoman empire. His adherents, the *Azalis*, were among the most radical political activists until the beginning of the twentieth century. Their final revenge on the Qajar dynasty was to put an end to absolute monarchy through their role in the constitutional revolution.

In 1866, Mirzā Hoseyn-Ali Nuri (1817–92), a half-brother of Sobh-e Azal, older than him and also a convert to Bābism since his youth, claimed to be "he whom God will manifest" (*man yozheroh Allāh*), a messianic figure announced by the Bāb. Known by the name of Bahā'ollāh (God's Splendor) he quickly acquired more adherents than his brother while preaching a syncretistic doctrine that nowadays is known by the name Bahāism. His message of openness and modernity attracted not only many middle-class Iranians, but also many dwellers from rural areas and even among the tribes, notably in Azerbaijan and to the east of Tehran. His faithful were recruited among Shiites who had followed the Bāb, although Bahā'ollāh rejected all violence and all ambition to politically dominate the world. They were joined by many Jews, notably from the Hamadān region, and soon the movement spread its wings abroad, in particular in the USA. The renouncement of violence did not eliminate the loathing toward Bahāism in which many Iranians continue to see a heresy aimed at leading Muslims astray from their faith. Considered as apostates (even when they are children of Bābis or Bahāis, or former Jews and Christians) the Bahāis have never obtained the right of citizenship in Iran where even now they form the largest non-Muslim community (today numbering 350,000 compared to 500,000 before the 1979 revolution).

Another reproach that Iranians have made against the Bābis and Bahāis concerned their links abroad. It is certain that the repression of this new religion, which questioned the legitimacy of the Shiite ulama, stressed their needs to become known abroad. Conversely, apart from pressure by a Russian diplomat to remove the Bāb from the borders of the Caucasus, some Europeans saw in the new religion a means to breach the monolithic position of the Muslim community that seemed to be an obstacle to freedom and progress and was slowing down their political and economic penetration. Moojan Momen, a Bahāi historian, praises Gobineau as being the first to make Bābism and Bahāism known to the outside world, and he is astonished that this was achieved by a theorist of racism who put white Aryan peoples well above Semitic ethnic groups.[16] This overlooks the fact that Gobineau, followed by a long line of Orientalists, saw heterodox beliefs of Iranians as the faithful remnant of an Aryan source of inspiration, opposed to the Semitic religion, Islam, for which, when all is said and done, they had no great esteem. Later, driven by other motivations, among other things their involvement in the struggle for liberties in Iran, the Frenchman A.-L.-M. Nicolas (1864–1939) and the

[16] M. MOMEN, ed., *The Bábí and Bahá'í Religions, 1844–1944. Some Contemporary Western Accounts*, p. 17.

Englishman E. G. Browne (1862–1925), two great experts on Iran, spoke sympathetically about the new religion from which they saw the rise of progressive militants. Western experts have been generally more interested in dissent than in conformity and in suppressed causes than in repressive forces. Because of their hostility toward absolutism, the *Azali*s were met with sympathy from liberals and free-thinkers, and indeed from rationalists and humanists affiliated with Masonic lodges. As for the Bahāis, preaching a religion that claimed to be non-violent, pacifist, cosmopolitan, internationalist, and ecumenical, they appealed most to those social groups who were open to external influence and notably the West, rejecting the rigidity of traditional Islam. This cosmopolitism looked like treason to many nationalists.

The Bābi uprising resulted in the strengthening of relations between the traditional Shiite clergy and Qajar power, which henceforth shared a common enemy. The physical suppression and the theological denunciation of the sect that defied them by arrogating some of the main creeds of Shiism (like the return of the Imam), stirred the Shiite ulama to unite as a religious community around a kind of theological magisterium or clerical authority (*marja'iyat*), an ideal launched during the Safavid period, but whose realization was prevented by personal rivalry and religious sensitivity among the *mojtahed*s. The construction of telegraph lines after 1865 facilitated this centralizing tendency. Now one could very quickly ask for the opinion of a faraway theologian and receive an immediate reply, thus nothing impeded the selection, as "a guide to imitate" (*marja-e taqlid*), of a *mojtahed* who lived hundreds of miles away.

A Modernizing King: Nāser od-Din Shāh (1848–96)

Nāser od-Din (born in 1831) acceded to the throne at the age of seventeen; having barely known his father, he did not share his mystical tendencies. He was instead torn between the authority of his mother, Mahd Olyā, and that of his military chief, Amir Kabir, whom he made his vizier.

At the age of three he became crown prince, which princes of the Davalu Qajar blood did not fail to contest until his enthronement. If one had questioned his right to succession, due to his right of primogeniture, one also questioned Mohammad Shāh's right to the throne – the very reason the latter had insisted on the appointment. The Russians pushed another candidate, Qahramān Mirzā. In truth, Mohammad Shāh had suspicions as to whether he was the father of his first son, which explains a certain hesitancy to appoint him heir and, above all, the distance at which he kept him during his education. Mahd Olyā, of the same Qavanlu clan as himself, in fact had a bad reputation. She lost her status as permanent wife but was kept on in a "provisional" marriage (*mot'a*), which put her at a distance without dishonoring her. But she was strong-willed and held on to the right of succession for her son, an objective that she shared with the vizier Mirzā Āqāsi. A few months before his death, in January 1848, Mohammad Shāh secretly appointed Nāser od-Din governor of Azerbaijan and sent him to Tabriz so as to prevent any plotting at court to impede this; the move definitely signaled that he was his chosen successor.

Though finding himself rather suddenly elevated to power and lacking paternal affection, Prince Nāser od-Din received an excellent education, even having, like his father before him, a French governess. Attracted to history and literature and showing skill in drawing, his good humor was evident in the caricatures he produced of his close friends. The young king showed much interest in the latest technological advances, notably photography, which he practiced himself. But above all, he was a Qajar who liked to move, preferring the tent and the hunt to the palace and the intrigues of the harem. Despite Mirzā Āqāsi's efforts to make him an adherent of Sufism, he maintained a more conventional religiosity. He had not inherited the non-violent principles of his father. Though certainly impressed by the trial of the Bāb in Tabriz, over which he presided in person, he did not have particular sympathy for the prophet, who had even failed to situate well-known places on a world map, a test the monarch had invented himself to test his prophetic gift.

Amir Kabir's Reforms

The young king was launched into his career by Mirzā Taqi Khān "Amir-Nezām," often called Amir Kabir (1807–52). This son of a cook in the service of the princely court of Tabriz had been noticed because of his intelligence by the second Qā'em-Maqām who had him educated with his own son. In 1829–30, Amir Kabir was a member of the mission sent to St. Petersburg to present the Iranian apology after the killing of Griboyedov. Over a period of ten months, he visited schools, various modern institutions, an arsenal, a mint, factories making coaches and glass, an observatory, banks, chambers of commerce, theaters, and modern offices in the many ministries. In 1837, he deepened his knowledge of Russia when he accompanied Crown Prince Nāser od-Din Mirzā for a short official visit to the Czar, who was passing through the Caucasus.

But it was in the Ottoman Empire that Amir Kabir discovered modern political culture. It was here that he had served as the principal Iranian interlocutor when the British pushed the Persians and Ottomans to negotiate, after the latter's attack on Mohammara (Khorramshahr), a port which competed with Basra, and after several border conflicts in Kurdistan. The negotiations took place in Erzurum, in Anatolia, and lasted four years (1843–47). There, Mirzā Taqi Khān witnessed the implementation of the Ottoman judiciary, financial, administrative, and military reforms (*tanzimāt*) granted by Sultan Abdulmejid in his Edict of Gulkhaneh in 1839. He was initiated into the diplomatic circles and the power struggle between the European nations and the Muslim states. The British feared that any outbreak of war between the Persians and the Ottomans would provide impetus for a Russian advance and thus participated in the conference as mediators.

On his return, Mirzā Taqi Khān was appointed army administrator (*vazir-e nezām*) and later chief tutor for the crown prince. He was indispensable in ensuring the enthronement of Nāser od-Din Shāh in 1848, and it was a natural move to appoint him vizier (or "First Person," *shakhs-e avval*, according to the contrived system of titles adopted by his predecessor Mirzā Āqāsi). He went on to receive a new title, Amir Kabir. It was he who taught the young monarch his craft, telling him how to behave and who to trust. Courtiers and pretenders to the throne were turned away and neutralized by Amir Kabir.

The vizier first focused on strengthening the Treasury. He reduced pensions, granting them only based on the criterion of service to the state, and he reorganized the tax burden according to the principle of the collective distribution per village, a system called *boniche*. The levying of troops followed the same system (*boniche-ye sarbāz*), and recruits were paid for by the village for the entire period of their service. In 1851, Amir Kabir opened a modern school, the *Dār ol-fonun* ("polytechnic college") where, with the help of interpreters, Europeans taught. To avoid any backlash, the educators were recruited from European countries other than Great Britain, Russia, and France, and an ambitious program was launched promoting modern science, medicine and the military arts. The government also took direct control of the management of customs duties, which had been farmed out, as well as of the Caspian fisheries, which had been left in the hands of a Russian monopoly.

Amir Kabir also took steps to strengthen the agriculture sector and encourage better management of Crown lands. These activities were boosted by a policy of construction; a new covered bazaar was built at Tehran (*bāzār-e Amir*) and work began on the digging of an irrigation canal, linking the capital with Karaj – a distance of about 40 km (25 miles). Other irrigation works and the construction of a dyke and bridges were undertaken in the west of the country, and, in Khuzestan, Amir Kabir instructed the planting of sugar cane. He also had American cotton planted near Urmia and Tehran.

To distribute government decrees and make the reforms known, an official newspaper was founded, *Vaqāye'-e Ettefāqiye* ("the Events") to which all high officials had to subscribe. Finally, the judiciary was thoroughly reformed, with the creation of a judicial customary system (*orfi*) parallel to that of the religious court system (*shar'i*), from which Amir Kabir had corrupt judges removed. The traditional right to sanctuary (*bast*) granted to all criminals or suspects who used to flee to the residences of the ulama and the shrines was abolished – a temporary measure, as discussed above.

To limit the influence of the ulama, Amir Kabir also tried to ban the theatrical mourning manifestations for the Imams (*ta'ziye*) and the processions of flagellants, with the help of a *mojtahed* who opposed these activities. Yet these bans gave rise to strong resistance, and he was forced to give in. He protected Christian minorities, granting priests tax exemptions and encouraged the construction of schools. He prohibited the vexatious pressure aimed at Sabeans and Zoroastrians to convert to Islam. Finally, in response to the high-handed presence of the Russians in the north and the complacent solidarity of the British, the vizier strived to limit the commercial penetration of both powers.[17] Moreover, he organized a counter-intelligence organization to monitor the activities of the diplomats of these two powers, applying for the first time, in a systematic manner, a policy of "negative equilibrium," a concept that one encounters again one century later at the time of Mosaddeq.

---

[17] F. ĀDAMIAT, *Amir Kabir va Irān*, pp. 461f.

Amir Kabir had upset and upended too many feudal lords, traditional powers, tribal privileges, and advantages. The Qajar notables, led by the queen mother, Mahd Olyā, tried several times to have this son of a servant who had started these reforms removed. The Shah, too, began to fear the vizier's arrogance and became convinced that Amir Kabir wanted to have himself crowned. In reality, Amir Kabir tried to promote Abbās Mirzā III, a half-brother of the Shah, as crown prince, whose mother was of the Davalu clan and who enjoyed British protection. To rid himself of this pretender, the Shah appointed him governor of Qom. The vizier's insistence worried the Shah; throughout his reign he maintained an acute mistrust of pretenders to the throne protected by foreign states.

On 17 November 1851, Amir Kabir was dismissed from all his functions. He considered demanding British protection, which would have been willingly granted to him to prevent the Ottomans from doing so. And it would have been possible to find a solution similar to the one adopted in the case of Mirzā Āqāsi, who was able to reach Ottoman Iraq when he was dismissed at Mohammad Shāh's death. The Russians also offered their protection, as they had done for Bahman Mirzā, the succession candidate. Yet Amir Kabir was afraid that if he left the capital he would become vulnerable and be assassinated. Finally, he had to accept the honorary governorship of Kāshān, where he was relegated to the Fin royal garden, away from the city. Foreign officials didn't hesitate to offer him their help, on humanitarian grounds as well as for reason of political gain, hoping for a possible return of the dismissed man. After forty days, on the personal orders of the Shah, his four limbs were bled by incision in his veins in the baths of his residence until he died; a towel was pushed into his mouth to silence him. The violence of the solution in some ways was a response to the foreign legations' insolent interference. Despite the short duration of his government, Amir Kabir remains a hero in the memory of Iranians. Coming from the people, he had tried to profoundly reform the state and had faced royal arbitrariness until martyred.

Nāser od-Din Shāh only truly acceded to the throne after this infamy. He appointed Mirzā Āqā Khan Nuri (1807–65) as vizier, who in turn abolished some of the reforms that interfered with the interests of the Qajar tribal leaders, and permanently intrigued with the British legation. However, many of Amir Kabir's measures were maintained, notably the establishment of the *Dār ol-fonun* school.

Mirzā Āqā Khān Nuri and the Treaty of Paris (1857)

The willingness of the Shah to reform the political system and to sanitize the public finances remained unchanged. But he was paralyzed by the demands of fighting corruption and nepotism, while the Anglo-Russian rivalry continued to threaten Persia's independence. Only an upstanding minister, conscious of such danger, might have been able to counter the corruption effectively.

Nuri remained in power for seven years and was incessantly sought out by the diplomats with whom he corresponded, sometimes in secret. He ruthlessly led the suppression of the Bābis. And, after the failed attempt on the life of the Shah in 1852, he showed himself even more implacable with the suppression of the pretender to the throne, Abbās Mirzā III, whom Amir Kabir had wanted to protect. The prince was accused of having Bābi sympathies and being complicit in the assassination attempt. Mahd Olyā wanted to have him killed, but Great Britain intervened, and the prince was exiled to Baghdad with a British passport. Later, he returned to Iran where he died in 1898.

In a reversal of alliances, a move at which Nuri was adept, the vizier availed himself of the mobilization of British troops in the Crimea (1843–56) and turned toward Russia to organize a long and costly campaign to take Herāt, an attempt that two previous Shahs had undertaken in vain. The Iranian government considered that Herāt was part of its territory, because it was a prestigious Persian-speaking city that had belonged to the Safavids. The Russians, placed in a difficult position by French-British forces at Sebastopol, considered this operation an easy way to redress their humiliation. But the British wanted to keep a buffer state in Afghanistan as far as Herāt to protect their Indian empire. Seeing the Shah reneging on an agreement he had given in January 1853 not to send troops to Herāt,[18] the British reacted decisively, disembarking an Anglo-Indian army at the port of Bushehr and threatening to conquer the country's coastal area. The move forced the Shah to make an inglorious withdrawal, and the affair was concluded with the Treaty of Paris, which ended the Crimean War. The agreement signed in 1857 between Great Britain and Persia restored diplomatic and commercial privileges to the British, strengthening their

---

[18] A. AMANAT, *Pivot of the Universe*, pp. 233f.

influence in Iran with the establishing of new consulates. Persia permanently abandoned its claim to Herāt.[19]

Persia "shrank" to the east, but at the same time also to the north, in the Khanates of Bokhārā and Khiva. The Russian advance into Central Asia forced Nāser od-Din Shāh to enter into further treaties with the Czar, in which he abandoned these Persian or Turkic-speaking territories that Iran had laid claim to – though never actually possessed – since the Safavid period.

The agreement signed within the context of the Treaty of Paris also ended a crisis that had erupted as a result of the arrogance of the British minister plenipotentiary, Sir Charles Murray. Feigning that he had the right to protect a Persian subject and to grant him impunity, the diplomat provided sanctuary to a certain Hāshem Khān Esfandiyāri, one of Nāser od-Din Shāh's companions during his youth, who had married the sister of the Shah's second wife. This woman of loose reputation lived in the British embassy, and it was said that she had an affair with Murray. The rumor reached the Shah. Outraged, he expelled all the diplomatic personnel of the British legation, who were forced into exile in Iraq for several months. The same Murray triumphantly returned to Tehran, mounted on a horse with gilt tack from the royal stables and surrounded by an impressive mounted guard. According to Gobineau, who was present at the time, there was a lack of popular enthusiasm during this imperial return, and he noted that the infantry battalion of the honorary guard was under-strength. In a subtle act of revenge, Nuri and the Shah humiliated the British diplomat by imposing on him unexpected protocol in formal visits where he had to sit in a less prestigious place, beneath his status.

In 1858, Nāser od-Din Shāh dismissed his vizier and decided to govern the country directly, with the support of a council of ministers, whose powers were severely limited to prevent any individual from gaining any significant political weight. The financier Mirzā Yusof Mostowfi ol-Mamālek (1812–86) led the conservative wing, while Farrokh Khān Amin od-Dowle (1812–71), the Iranian negotiator of the Treaty of Paris, led the more reform-minded camp. In reality, there were several major provinces that were not under the Shah's direct control, in particular the region of Isfahan where the Shah's eldest son, the governor Zell os-Soltān (1850–1918) held immense power,

---

[19] A. AMANAT, *Pivot of the Universe*, p. 308.

with his own army, court, and administration. He did not accept being passed over for succession because of the low rank of his mother.

For some time, the Shah was under the influence of Mirzā Malkom Khān, a Christian Armenian who had converted to Islam. He had participated in the negotiations in Paris and tried to promote his Masonic ideas in Iran. Nāser od-Din Shāh sincerely wanted to modernize his kingdom, however he was unsure of the direction this should take. Moreover, his autocratic conception of power prevented him from working with those politicians who may have been capable of the task at hand, since his disposition discouraged any genuine freedom of speech and dialogue. Arbitrary decisions, personal fantasies, and harem intrigues often took over. Many documents, testimonies, and letters of the period – written by Europeans who had stayed in Tehran or by educated Iranians who were beginning to emerge as a keen intelligentsia – attest that this arbitrary display of power weakened his government. A telling example is the voluminous diaries of a courtier, E'temād os-Saltane (1834–96), a curious and well-read man, who was one of the first students of the *Dār ol-fonun*. For some forty years he enjoyed a career as a servant of the state, and for many years was the Shah's confidant.

In his private journal, which he wrote in secret, he records with humor and wisdom, but also with some trepidation, daily observations about the court and the monarch between 1875 and 1896.[20] In one entry he recounts events of July 1888 when the Shah, in typical fashion, had established a royal camp in the mountains north of Tehran, with an army of servants, part of the harem, ministers, and even diplomats (the minister of France, de Balloy, came there to fish for trout). E'temād os-Saltane, who gave the Shah French and history lessons, translated the foreign newspapers for him and regularly had to attend the royal tent despite a nagging toothache. He recalls:

> One hour after nightfall I was led to the royal tent. The Shah was very happy, for two reasons: first because Aziz os-Soltān[21] was free of fever, next because a telegram had arrived from Astarabad [now Gorgan, south-east of the Caspian Sea] saying that 5,000 cavalry of the regular army had attacked some

---

[20] I. AFSHĀR, ed., *Ruzname-ye khāterat-e E'temād os-Saltane*, pp. 579f.
[21] Son of Malijak, a personal servant of the Shah and of the sister of Amin-e Aqdas, his favorite wife; at that time he was nine years old, and the Shah loved him beyond measure, getting up at night to see if he had a temperature, freeing prisoners when he recovered.

families of Vāz and had killed nine of them, had taken prisoner 30 of them and had made a booty of several thousand sheep and camels. The rest of the tribe, fearing the victorious army, had fled. Twenty men of the force of law and order, which was commanded by Seyf ol-Molk [a corrupt prince], had died. The comments made by the courtiers who were present were so exaggerated that they would not have been more laudatory if India and Bokhara or all of China had been conquered. A robe of honor of white brocade was given to Amin os-Soltān [the vizier] to celebrate the victory. After dinner, I went to Amin os-Soltān to congratulate him with this robe of honor.

[One week later] His Majesty tells me that the officers of Astarābād instead of beating and pillaging the rebellious tribes had attacked groups that are loyal to the government, had taken their wives and killed their men. He tells me that he has written to Rokn od-Dowle [the governor] to indemnify the tribes and to return their property. This royal decree has been issued, but how to implement it? Let's assume that they are given part of what has been taken from them, that the raped women are returned to their husband, can one return life to the victims? Our valiant officers have sown such a rebellion at Astarabad that the Turkmen tribes will all leave and place themselves under Russian rule.

[Nine days later, after lunch] I read the newspapers for His Majesty. He tells me that Amin os-Soltān will give me a text to be printed in the newspaper *Irān*. I have guessed that it concerned Astarābād. It became clear that the British consul who is in that city has made a precise report on what has happened for the British legation, and the British minister has sent it to His Majesty by courier. The royal temper was awful. He received Amin os-Soltān in private after lunch.

Some months earlier, the Shah had wanted to tease E'temād os-Saltane by telling him that, because he had refused to attend the palace the previous evening to translate the words of foreign visitors, he had asked a physician to act as interpreter in his place.[22] "At the time of Fath-Ali Shāh, I replied, Napoléon I had written a letter to the Shah

----

[22] I. Afshār, ed., *Ruznāme-ye khāterat*, pp. 524f.

containing matters of the utmost importance and there was nobody to translate. The letter was returned as such. Now, four or five thousand people in Tehran know French." His August Majesty smoothed his moustache. "It was better in those days, he replied, the eyes and ears of people were not as open as they are nowadays!"

The Discovery of Europe: Sepahsālār

In 1870, the Shah undertook a pilgrimage to the holy places of Mesopotamia, accompanied by his ambassador to the Sublime Porte, Mirzā Hoseyn Khān Moshir od-Dowle. On this occasion, he witnessed the tangible results of Ottoman reforms implemented some thirty years earlier. Impressed with their scope, he immediately appointed the ambassador as minister of justice and then vizier, or more precisely, chancellor (*sadr-e a'zam*), establishing a function whose necessity was again required.

Mirzā Hoseyn Khān (1828–81), better known under the title of *Sepahsālār* (Marshal), had spent most of his life abroad. After studying in France, he was made consul in Bombay and Tiflis, before being appointed ambassador at the Sublime Porte in 1858. In Istanbul, he befriended Mirzā Malkom Khān, who had been expelled from Iran. Unlike Amir Kabir, who had tried to distance Persia from the two great neighboring powers, Russia and Great Britain, to ensure the country's independence, Sepahsālār hoped to attract British interest in development projects that would be profitable for both sides. On his appointment in Iran he would begin to negotiate various concessions to the British, a subject we will return to in the next chapter.

Encouraged by his vizier, the Shah made three trips to Europe (1873, 1878, 1889). The first one, carefully prepared, broke with an ancient taboo; traveling in a non-Muslim country implied, above all for a Shiite, all kinds of compromises with the rule of ritual purity and religious prohibitions, such as eating food prepared by an infidel or shaking hands with women and so on. Nāser od-Din Shāh was accompanied by about sixty persons, each one traveling with his servants, and took with him an impressive quantity of gifts – in particular he gave horses as a display of his royal largesse – without counting the very voluminous private luggage. He had barely arrived at the Russian border when Sepahsālār convinced Nāser od-Din Shāh, contrary to royal lifestyles, to leave his women behind and to take only his favorite,

Anis od-Dowle, to Moscow, because the various wives and concubines of the Shah were constantly fighting out of jealousy. Once he arrived at the Russian capital, she caused a sensation with her veil and her eunuchs, and the vizier decided to also send her back, which only added a decisive voice to the camp of his enemies. In a show of submission to the vizier's rivals the Shah dismissed him on his return to Persia, allowing him to continue the reforms but only under the title of minister of war.

In addition to Russia, the Shah traveled to Poland, Prussia, France, Switzerland, Italy, and Austria – where he visited the World Exhibition – and finally on to Istanbul, the Caucasus, and the Caspian Sea. The impact of this journey was reciprocal. As the Shah took pleasure in discovering technical and industrial inventions, the European public looked on with curiosity at these men with moustaches who came from so far away. The interest in Iran was increased due to the presence of this monarch who hired physicians, administrators and professors, and who granted concessions to European firms.

The Shah kept a journal during his trip in which he conscientiously noted his meetings and impressions. Thus, upon his arrival in Paris (July 1873), he offers a rather faithful description of the city which still showed the scars of the Commune and the war of 1870. Lodged at the Palais Bourbon – the Parliament was then at Versailles – and in what had been the bed of Napoléon I, he wrote:

> From another, I heard that during the night he cried "Long live the monarchy and its unwavering rules." Thus, it seems that there are numerous factions in France. Most are monarchists, but they are divided in three parties, one that wants the descendants of Napoléon, another the descendants of Louis-Philippe, and a third the descendants of Henry [probably the Duke of Orléans] who is of the Bourbon family and related to the heirs of Louis-Philippe, but is separated from them. The Republicans also have much power, but they are neither in agreement: some want a red republic that is the radical republic, others want a moderate republic that comprises some rules of the monarchy without a monarch; others again want another form of a republic. It is very difficult to govern in an independent manner amid all these parties and this leads again to bloodbaths and destruction, unless all agree on either an independent

monarchy, or an independent republic, in which case the French state will be the strongest of all and everybody has to take heed of it. But one will not be able to do anything with these differences of opinion, and the situation grows worse day by day; what a shame![23]

Taking into account the lavish expenses, the Shah's journeys only brought some minor political benefit. To replenish the state's coffers, given the inefficiency of the fiscal system, any means was seen as licit, including the selling off of large sectors of the economy to foreign companies or, later on, by contracting foreign loans; and the Iranian economy plunged further into dependence. The reforms of Sepahsālār finally resulted in the concentration of more power in the hands of the Shah.

However, on the eve of the twentieth century, the absolutism of the Qajars started to be contested openly. After the violent crisis of religious sectarianism that spread across Iran between 1844 and 1850, and the pitiless suppression of the movement, the Bābis remained, in secret, fierce opponents of the dynasty and vivid exemplars of the surprising inventiveness among the pre-modern Iranian elite. The two big modernization projects, started by successive viziers, Abbās Mirzā, Amir Kabir, and Sepahsālār were halted before having been able to prove themselves. Increasingly frequent direct contact between Iranian leaders and Europeans, as well as the military disasters first in the Caucasus and then in Afghanistan, all resulted in increasing interference by Europeans in the Persian economy. At the time of the first Qajars, under Fath-Ali Shāh and Mohammad Shāh, the desire to emulate the Safavids, to reconstitute their kingdom, and to protect religion dominated the royal imagination. Now, the elite looked at themselves through the eyes of Europe, considering European institutions to be more efficacious, more rational than in fact they were; many despaired whether Iran would ever become an equal. Yet this tendency toward self-denigration intensified the wave of protests against European interference and led to Nāser od-Din Shāh's assassination, the first act of a major revolutionary movement.

Religious convictions had given the Iranians, at least since the Safavids, the feeling of an uneasy relationship with other Muslims in the

---

[23] F. Qāzihā, ed., *Ruznāme-ye khāterāt-e Nāser od-Din Shāh dar safar-e avval-e Farangestān,* pp. 210f.

region. Behind the fortifications of their Persian identity, they felt under siege, a feeling which European intrusion only fostered. The birth of a nationalist ideology fueled Iranians with a sense of forgotten pride, inspired by the myth of ancient empires, expectations of a renewal at the price of casting aside central values such as Islam or Qajar royal absolutism. The Iranian reformist elite molded itself as an image of a collective superego, that of an eternal Persia that had once brought Greece and Rome to its knees. The devotion to the homeland was transformed by the Bābi revolt that stressed the forces of repression and antagonism between the state (*dowlat*) and the nation (*mellat*). These two concepts would truly take shape in the Constitutional Revolution of 1906.

3 FROM REVOLTS TO THE REVOLUTION (1880–1906)

Was the Constitutional Revolution of 1906 provoked by Anglo-Russian rivalry and supported by the British to put an end to the arrogance of the Russians, the protectors of Qajar absolute monarchy? Many Iranian observers, notably those who wish to understand the failure of liberal democracy, have put forward foreign intervention, above all by the British, for the unfolding of the revolution. Detractors, particularly those trying to justify the Islamic Revolution, raise many arguments against the reformist movement of those early years: manipulated elites (by Freemasons among others); religious symbols raised by mollas with ties to British diplomats; the belated manifestation of political demands, in particular those for a "constitution" (*mashrute*); and the still more visible intervention by British diplomats in the final formulation of demands during the occupation of the British embassy garden in August 1906. Foreign intervention likely distorted the reforms from the very beginning and would explain why the transfer of power failed to produce a strong viable regime.

On the other hand, the success of the movement rather appears to be the result of a convergence of social, economic, and cultural tensions and developments that made the continuation of the old order more and more improbable. It was the product of the maturation of internal resistance and politicization that, while rejecting the Russian model, likewise resulted in defining a national will against any foreign interference, including that of the British. It was a powerful movement and deeply revolutionary, even if, as is often the case with social crises, what it wanted to bring down – absolutism, corruption, and dependence – was more clearly defined than what one wanted to put in its place. To structural causes – low agricultural productivity (despite rising exports) and strong competition of European industrial products – were added ideological causes: the penetration of the same ideas that had inspired the French Revolution, albeit with a delay of more than hundred years. Although convinced of a deep injustice of history because of the many cases of interference by Europeans in their country, the Iranians did not sink into fatalism. The memory of their past grandeur, their injured pride, and the insolent lack of concern of their leaders persuaded them, on the contrary, that fate was reversible.

Nevertheless, the mobilization of the Iranian people was particularly difficult because of the country's lack of urbanization. At the beginning of the twentieth century, Persia barely had a hundred urban centers of more than 5,000 inhabitants. Neither Tehran nor Tabriz (200,000 inhabitants each) nor Isfahan (with 100,000–120,000 inhabitants) resembled a modern city. The streets were not asphalted, there was no public lighting nor any drainage system or mains water supply. As for the villages, they were too scattered and isolated to allow peasant uprisings in the manner of "jacqueries." Many constituted a type of semi-desert habitat that made use of every valley floor, of each humid foothill, and of any irrigation possible. In short, the configuration of most Persian villages was unconducive for mobilizing and uniting the masses. Conversely, on the Caspian plain – where precipitation is high, there was intensive agriculture, and the pattern of rural settlement was more closely knit – social movements were a frequent occurrence.

Low Agricultural Productivity

The agrarian economy, in which almost 80 percent of the population were employed in 1900, had been profoundly transformed and weakened since the 1860s.[1] The huge sale of Crown lands to private individuals accelerated the growth in mercantilism. The new landowners, often bazaar merchants, were more focused on making a profit than the traditional estate caretakers, and orientated agriculture toward cash crops such as opium, cotton, tobacco, and the mulberry

---

[1] J. BHARIER, *Economic Development in Iran, 1900–1970*, p. 5, says that around 90 percent of the Iranian population was directly or indirectly involved in agricultural production.

trees needed to raise silk worms. Production for local consumption largely diminished and the peasantry became subject to market forces.

However, in places where wheat and animal husbandry remained, conditions had been improving since the middle of the nineteenth century due to the relative political stability (at least up to the beginning of the twentieth century). In the Caspian provinces, an increase in arable land was made possible with deforestation, as soon as the crops could be exported to the Russian market. Russian merchants, using a better network of transportation, could re-export Mazandaran rice to Mashhad. However, drought remained a serious concern for the peasantry, as Curzon states in his famous description:[2]

> He [the peasant] is poor, illiterate, and stolid; but in appearance he is robust, in strength he is like an ox, he usually has clothes to his back, and he is seldom a beggar. With the grossest ignorance he combines a rude skill in turning to account the scanty resources of nature, and though he neither expects nor aspires to prosper, he is patient and persevering. His times of misery occur when there is a break-down of the water supply, or when, after a long drought, there is a famine in the land. Unfed and uncared for, the Persian peasantry then die off like flies.

Aside from weather conditions and the threat of pests and locusts, bad landlords and deficient infrastructure prevented Iranian peasants from reaping the benefits of their efforts. Cash was often scarce, resulting in a barter exchange economy, and roads, other than the main roads used by government officials, were insecure and poorly maintained.

The example of opium is indicative of the growing importance of the world economy to Persians. The opening of China to foreign trade (with their exports of tea and silk) injected fresh capital into the market. The treaties that had ended the Opium Wars (1842 and 1860) granted the British the right to export Indian opium to China. Soon demand increased when India turned to the production of cotton in response to the market demand created by the deficits resulting from the American Civil War (1860–65). Iranian opium exports increased by 750 percent

---

[2] G. N. CURZON, *Persia and the Persian Question*, p. 490. Note the nuance of scorn: described as noble savages, their deaths generate little empathy; they are not even caused by human factors, simply nature.

between 1858 and 1870. However, trade fell sharply soon after owing to poor harvests and, by the beginning of the twentieth century, because of the troubles in China following the Boxer uprising and the emergence of strong competition from Japanese commodity exports.

Today, some researchers tend to minimize the impact of commercial factors, given the relatively modest position of opium cultivation in the Iranian economy, and the continuation of wheat production for local consumption.[3] For opium, as with cotton, tobacco and also silk, dependence on the foreign markets became increasingly dominant, and Iranian autarky no longer had any meaning. Public opinion swayed sharply toward hostility at the direct interference by foreigners in their economic life, as we will see in the case of the Tobacco Regie. The Iranian producers, badly protected and subject to arbitrary tax collection – and to an unjust system of army conscription – were the first victims of the commercial fluctuations.

With the resumption of American exports, the slump in sales of Iranian cotton ruined those who had benefited during the temporary cessation of the US cotton trade (though exports to Russia partially compensated for this lost market). However, the case of the silk trade even better illustrates the economic decline in the northern provinces.[4] With its rapid expansion at the beginning of the nineteenth century due to foreign demand, silk production led to widespread deforestation to clear areas for the mulberry plantations. Production quintupled in fifty years; by mid-century it represented about 40 percent of the value of total Iranian exports. However, silk worm disease (*Pébrine*), having ravaged the silkworm farms in Europe in 1845, appeared in Iran around 1860, reducing production to one-tenth of normal output. In the interim years, before the peasants could transition to the production of rice and tobacco for the Russian market, the resultant distress prompted the population to riot. Moderate production was re-established toward 1890, due to the import of *bombyx mori* (silkworms) from the Ottoman Empire and Japan, but it was still dependent on foreign markets and continued to decline. Moreover, foreign investors dominated the entire production chain, from the supply of worms to the

---

[3] W. Floor, *Agriculture in Qajar Iran*, pp. 25f, criticizing Gad G. Gilbar's views.
[4] See Ch. Bromberger, "Changements techniques et transformation des rapports sociaux." Data on silk production in W. Floor, *Agriculture in Qajar Iran*, pp. 357–401.

export of silk; in 1908 there were not more than sixteen Iranians among the owners of cocoon-processing plants in Gilan.

Apart from changing forces on the world market, natural factors impacted agriculture, particularly as people lacked the means to cushion themselves from the effects. During two successive winters in 1870 and 1871, rainfall was so rare an occurrence that most of the crops wilted before the harvest. Even the river of Isfahan, the Zāyanderud, ran dry. A devastating famine followed, with many cases of cannibalism reported (the same drama was repeated in 1918, heightened by the war). In both cases, the number of deaths might have been reduced had food reserves been better distributed. The merchants, and sometimes aristocrats or even religious leaders, stockpiled large reserves to sell on the black market in times of scarcity. The bad state of the roads made the situation worse because they did not allow the transportation of wheat, which was generally abundant in Sistan and Azerbaijan, to the most badly affected cities and provinces, and more banditry resulted in greater insecurity. Owing to the lack of usable roads, the transportation of merchandise continued to be carried out by caravan until 1900, but the pack animals, dromedaries and mules, were insufficient in number, which added further to the cost of food. It is estimated that 40 percent of the price of goods and foodstuffs sold in Tehran was attributable to transport costs.

Finances and Concessions

Under the Qajar tribal system of governance, the monarch was considered the father of the nation. The country belonged to him personally, and the privy purse was not separate from the public treasury. The two defeats at the hands of Russia in 1813 and 1828, the assassination of Griboyedov and its fallout, and the military campaign of Herāt had seriously weakened the country's finances. After Fath-Ali Shāh, who was survived by more than one hundred children, a large number of pensions and honorific functions were added to the state's financial burden that weighed heavily on the public finances.

From the beginning of the nineteenth century, Iran was dependent on foreign financial aid to pay its debts, thus hampering its independence. Often it switched from one dependency to another. After the two conflicts with Russia, Great Britain lent significant sums of money that made it possible for Iran to pay its war damages and to demand the evacuation of Russian troops from Persian territory. (These sums were never repaid; they became subsidies.) In 1854, the Russians wrote off the last payment so as to ensure Persia's neutrality in the Crimean War.

However, other than these two exceptions, government revenue generally showed a surplus and allowed the acquisition of jewelry and gold (pieces or ingots) for the royal treasury. This situation was reversed by the Shah's trips to Europe after 1873.

The means to restore royal wealth were not lacking. Crown lands had increased in size in the eighteenth century under Nāder Shāh through the confiscation of religious endowments. These lands, called *khālese*, were leased as temporary fiefs as a method to pay for services rendered, notably to the army, and in exchange for yearly 'presents' extracted from property revenues, exerting further pressure on the peasants. The sale of *khālese* made it possible for the monarch to immediately access large sums of money. Sales were not always recorded and could be arbitrarily annulled, with the same estates being sold for a second time. Large properties were progressively transferred to new and increasingly powerful landowners (*arbāb*), often bazaar merchants who wanted to extend their activities to the export of agricultural goods. Landed property gave them the status of local masters and was expected to generate domestic revenue with fewer fluctuations than was previously the case with the reliance on foreign trade, at which only a few could successfully compete with Europeans. In the twentieth century, Iranian political life would be dominated by these landed proprietors who held the majority in Parliament until the "White Revolution" in the early 1960s.[5]

Another cause of impoverishment concerned not only the merchants, but all Iranians: the slow devaluation of silver relative to the gold price on the world market. Iranian money, the kran (*qerān*), which was indexed to silver, lost 80 percent of its value between 1800 and 1914 (and half of its value between 1875 and 1900 alone).[6] The devaluation stimulated exports but raised prices for essential goods such as bread, affecting the urban poor. Lacking local industry, the Iranian economy could not counter inflation and the competition of European-made products (textiles, metals, luxury products) resulted in the ruination of

---

5 Z. SHAJI'I, *Nokhbegān-e siāsi-e Irān* [Political elite in twentieth-century Iran].
6 Ch. ISSAWI, ed., *The Economic History of Iran 1800–1914*, p. 335; R. MATTHEE, W. FLOOR, & P. CLAWSON. *The Monetary History of Iran from the Safavids to the Qajars,* pp. 243f.

local craftsmen and artisans. Only Persian carpets saw an increase in exports to Europe and the United States after 1873, growing to 12 percent of total visible exports in 1914.[7]

Thus European investors created more favorable conditions to satisfy their appetite by monopolizing entire portions of the economy. In exchange for a considerable sum and a share in the profits, the Shah sold the rights to concessions often with lengthy terms, if not for perpetuity. Entire sectors of economic activities were thus ceded to foreign companies during the last three decades of the nineteenth century. However, apart from the oil concession sold to Knox d'Arcy in 1901, these deals had little in the way of economic consequences for Persians owing to the already low industrial output.

In 1872, after the great famine and in anticipation of his first journey to Europe, Nāser od-Din Shāh sold the concessions for the construction of railways and trams, coal and metal mines (except for those already being exploited), irrigation works (dams and bridges), a national bank, the farming out of the customs administration and various other sectors to Baron Reuter, a British citizen, effectively creating a seventy-year monopoly.[8] The British minister, who raised concerns about the sale, decided not to support it. For the Iranian monarch, who finalized the concession agreement during his trip to Great Britain, it meant no less than establishing the most efficient new European industries. But the protests that arose against the sale by members of the Qajar family, as well as, finally, cold feet by the Shah himself, led to the cancellation of the concession in 1873, a few weeks after his return from Europe. The first works to establish a railway from Tehran to Ābādān were already underway, in conformity with Reuter's commitment, who demanded full indemnity. The British embassy was relieved by this reversal, because the north–south line would have favored access by the Russians to the "warm seas."

The British were also keen to prevent the realization of a railway linking the Caucasus to Tabriz; over a period of fifty years, proposals to expand the railway network in Persia were put on ice as a result of Anglo-Russian rivalry, each power fearing that the other's interests would be given priority. In 1887, the Shah signed a secret agreement

---

[7] W. FLOOR, *The Persian Textile Industry in Historical Perspective, 1500–1925; Agriculture in Qajar Iran*, p. 25.
[8] The German-born Julius Reuter (1816–99), the son of a rabbi, started out as a journalist and publisher and founded the still-extant Reuter news agency.

with the Russians under the terms of which he committed himself to refuse any railway construction without their agreement.

The Shah granted other concessions, mostly sectoral. After 1862 he sold the concession for a telegraph line linking London with Bombay, followed by secondary lines which linked the principal Iranian cities to the main network; for roads and railway in the west and the south of the country; for navigation and port installation in the Caspian; and, in 1893, the construction of the road from Anzali to Qazvin was likewise granted to a Russian company. Nāser od-Din Shāh's successors continued this policy, in 1902 ceding, again to Russian companies, the construction of a new road, and then the railway from Jolfa to Tabriz and in 1911 the oil pipeline from Anzali to Rasht.

The creation in 1889 of the Imperial Bank (Bānk-e Shāhi) by the son of Julius Reuter in some ways was the epilogue to the Reuter concession, for which the complete balance still had not been reimbursed. Shortly thereafter, the Russians reacted to this acquisition by the entirely British firm by obtaining the seventy-five-year concession for the Russian Loan Bank (*Bānk-e esteqrāzi-e Rus*, or Banque d'escompte de Perse) with a smaller initial capital outlay. The Russian bank was linked to an insurance company and a transport company, but it did not have the right to issue paper money, which was a British monopoly, and it rapidly fell into decline before it was purchased by the Russian state; it became a branch of the Russian Bank under the name of Bank of Loans.

Faced by these two powerful and well-organized companies, the traditional Iranian bankers (*sarrāf*) were unable to compete. In their own country, Iranians paid with money issued by a foreign bank and could not execute most banking operations unless via the intermediary of foreigners. In 1889, an attempt to create a "public" (*omumi*) bank, established with the support of a few leading mercantile families such as the Tumāniān Brothers and Malek ot-Tojjār, was forced into bankruptcy by the Imperial Bank, which also did its best to bankrupt the Tumāniān Brothers. The project by the constitutionalists to establish a "national bank" had no success at all. Iranians had to wait till 1928 before a real national state-controlled banking system that issued money and attracted savings was established; this replaced the Imperial Bank within a few years.[9]

---

[9] On the cumbersome traditional banking activity in Iran, see W. FLOOR, "The Bankers (*sarrāf*) in Qājār Iran"; on the encounter with foreign trade, see W. FLOOR, "The Merchants (*tujjār*) in Qājār Iran."

The Military Situation: Cossacks and the Army of "Levies"

Prior to 1921 a formal national Iranian army did not exist. By the close of the nineteenth century, the coveted kingdom had lost its Caucasian provinces and was defended by heterogeneous military forces. This was reinforced after 1879 by the creation of the Persian Cossack Brigade, placed under the command of Russian officers and intended primarily to protect the Shah.

At the beginning of Nāser od-Din Shāh's reign, Iran's military strength was estimated at about 30,000 men. The army's loyalty to the Shah was not at all guaranteed, and their inefficacy was demonstrated each time Iran had to face foreign forces, Russian or British. Moreover, as during the suppression of the Bābi revolt, which resulted in several campaigns, the army only had the role of maintaining order. In August 1853, under a fierce sun, Nāser od-Din Shāh organized, despite British warnings, a major and costly military review at Soltāniye, which turned into a demonstration of weakness. The soldiers, seeing that some of them had cholera, tried to flee. The Shah ordered the cancellation of the review at the last moment and, for his "triumphal" return to the capital was accompanied solely by the British chargé d'affaires who did his best to show his disapproval.

By the mid-century, Abbās Mirzā – and after him Amir Kabir – had implemented military reforms, mainly imitating those of the Ottoman Empire, and invited European, and particularly French, instructors to further assist in the modernization of the armed forces. Troops were recruited in the villages according to a system developed for the collection of taxes, the *boniche*. The number of soldiers was fixed by region, district and village, with the population required to fund their equipment and wages. The arrival of army recruiters in the villages was the occasion where the most hale and hearty peasants, those most needed for the necessary work in the fields, were able to avoid enlistment. The recruits lacked the conviction, the strength, and the discipline to become good soldiers. During campaigns they lived off the peasants' toil; in wintertime they returned to their villages, and in summer they tried to escape to engage in seasonal work, since their wages were not paid. In the tribal zones, where warlike traditions were preserved because of the need to maintain safety in the camps, the supply of military force was a fiscal duty subject to allegiances negotiated between the tribal chiefs and the government.[10]

In addition to the official army, there were numerous militias and semi-private or tribal armies. Occasionally, these militias were the source of internal conflict when they defied the authority and legitimacy of the central government. Until his disgrace in 1888, Zell os-Soltān controlled the entire south of the country owing to the strength of his personal army, of which one regiment was trained in the Prussian discipline. His half-brother, Kāmrān Mirzā Nāyeb os-Saltane, minister of war, who maintained an army of 90,000 men, at the same time, in the 1880s, was accused of selling arms to Kurdish and Lor tribes.

In 1878, Nāser od-Din Shāh had been impressed with the Cossacks' discipline when he passed through Moscow on his second trip to Europe. He persuaded the Russians to agree to the creation of a Persian Cossack Brigade that would be commanded by Russian officers appointed by the Czar and placed at the service of the Iranian monarchy. The Russians were, of course, very pleased with the open door to a permanent and efficacious way to fight British influence. Colonel Domantovitch, the first commander of that small army, in the beginning had a regiment of 400 horsemen, later 600, under his command. A second regiment was created the following year; by 1899 its strength reached 1,500 men consisting of cavalry (666 men), mounted artillery, and infantry. There were ten Russian officers commanding thirteen Iranian subaltern officers. Only 10 percent of this force, mostly volunteers, were from Persian-speaking areas; the others were from Turkic and Kurdish tribes. The creation of a unified national army would be one of the demands of the constitutionalists of 1906.

Birth of a National Ideology

After the wars with Russia and Great Britain, and with the increasing economic penetration by Europeans, bitterness grew among the Iranian elite. Diplomats who had lived abroad, notably in Russia and the Ottoman Empire, had witnessed the benefits of reforms and the functioning of a modern political institution that strengthened national cohesion in the face of foreign covetousness. Some among these "reformers" tried to use their influence as ministers or advisers to promote

[10] J. CALMARD, "Les réformes militaires sous les Qâjâr (1794–1925)."

change from within the government. Others, rapidly discouraged, took a more overtly oppositionary stance. Still others placed religious issues at the heart of their discourse.

Mirzā Malkom Khān

A controversial figure, Mirzā Malkom Khān (1833–1908) played the role of an awakener to modernization and adviser to the monarch, but he is also described as corrupt and trying to make a profit from his role as intermediary. Born to an Armenian family and a convert to Islam – or rather to a kind of Masonic humanism with hints of Islam – he studied in France for seven years under the tutelage of the Mekhitarist Fathers. Later, undertaking translations for the new Dār ol-fonun school, which employed European tutors, he wrote lampoons and political tracts advocating Europeanization. After having accompanied Farrokh Khān Ghaffāri's mission to France, where they negotiated for the Treaty of Paris with the British (1857), he founded a secret quasi-Masonic club in Tehran, the House of Forgetfulness (*Farāmush-khāne*), to which he was able to attract some notable people, including some members of the Shiite clergy. Nāser od-Din Shāh, who believed the club was a republican revolutionary society, had it dissolved, and Malkom Khan was exiled to the Ottoman Empire.

In Istanbul, Malkom befriended Mirzā Hoseyn Khān, the future Sepahsālār, then Persian ambassador at the Sublime Porte (see Chapter 2). Once he had become prime minister (1871), the latter invited Malkom back to Tehran to serve as an adviser. Malkom was involved with several negotiations to grant concessions to Europeans; besides the official discussions with foreign companies, he – like anyone else in those days – negotiated directly for a personal share in the deal. In 1873, he was sent to London as a resident minister plenipotentiary, partly to resolve the problems of the revocation of the Reuter concession, and only returned to Persia for short visits. However, an embezzlement scandal resulted in him losing his diplomatic post: he managed to interest European investors in a concession to establish a national lottery and casinos in Iran, while already well aware that the concession had been cancelled.

Banished and disgraced, he soon launched an ideological campaign to exact revenge on Iranian leaders, whom he accused of corruption, and to promote the idea of a constitution. In 1891, he began a newspaper, *Qānun* ("the Law") which ran for forty-one issues until it was discontinued in 1898. Printed in London and then sent to Istanbul and on to Iran, it was distributed by friends of the House of Forgetfulness, henceforth gathered in a League for Humanity (*Majma'-e Ādamiat*). *Qānun* had an enormous influence among the reformers, despite Malkom's own ideological inconsistencies. To appease religious resistance to reforms that aimed at adopting European democratic institutions, Malkom asserted that all these reforms were already contained in the Koran. The tone of *Qānun* became milder after Nāser od-Din Shāh's assassination (1896), and the publication was stopped two years later when Malkom was reinstated into Iran's diplomatic circle and appointed Iran's representative in Rome.

The influence of the *Qānun* publication is one example of the growing importance of the modern media in spreading political, social, and cultural ideas. Amir Kabir had already understood this power by creating, a short while before his dismissal, the government newspaper *Vaqāye'-e Ettefāqiye* ("Events"). But each time the Persian State used the press to influence public opinion, the exiles reacted by creating their own journals. Since the arrival of the printing press, Iran had only known short intervals of freedom of speech, during which an opposition press was able to operate freely in the country. At that time, the aspiration to a free press of this sort was maintained by newspapers published in India (Calcutta), in the Ottoman Empire (Istanbul, Cairo), and in Europe.

As Malkom's newspaper, published in England, enjoyed great freedom, it systematically exposed, sometimes with more virulence than others, ideas that were also disseminated from Istanbul by *Akhtar* ("Star"). This newspaper, published from 1876 to 1896 by secular and nationalist opponents, was quite well read by the Persian diaspora and in Iran itself (almost half of the letters from readers came from Tehran or Tabriz). Though the paper had to contend with Ottoman censorship, the intellectuals who contributed to it were able to agitate for three main demands. First, they praised Western civilization, explaining that it was based on sound principles of science and technology, and that its essential, quasi-magical, engine was social progress and the advancement of universal education, the true enemies of the morbid indolence that paralyzed Iran. Secondly, they posited themselves as defenders of the Iranian patrimony, which they wanted to develop through the teaching of ancient history and Persian literature and language. One of the important themes among Iranian intellectuals of that time, which was echoed by *Akhtar*, was the need for the reform of the alphabet to allow a more rapid spread of education and modern science, but not at the expense of the integrity of the language itself, for which *Akhtar* wanted to adopt the model of the Académie française which presides over the preservation of the national language. Finally, the publication supported Pan-Islamism, a theme that pleased the Ottoman authorities, to whom these Iranian Shiite reformers advocated giving the task of uniting the Muslim world around a new caliphate. *Akhtar* thus placed itself between two opposing figures, Mirzā Āqā Khān Kermāni and Jamāl od-Din Asadābādi.[11]

Āqā Khān Kermāni

Mirzā Āqā Khān Kermāni was born in Kermān in 1854 and arrived in 1886 in Istanbul, having fled Iran where he had been accused of embezzlement and, above all, where his "new and progressive" ideas had put him in danger. Having converted to *Azali* Bābism, the spiritual leader of the sect, who was exiled in Cyprus, gave him the hand of one of his daughters in marriage. A sworn opponent of Islam, which he accused of having corrupted the Iranian nation with a culture of "lizard eaters,"[12] Mirzā Āqā Khān criticized the absolutism and obscurantism of Nāser od-Din Shāh. Entirely in agreement with Mirzā Malkom Khān, he distributed the newspaper *Qānun* in Istanbul and also established there a branch of the League for Humanity. In 1892, strangely enough, still secular, but otherwise a less fierce defender of Bābism, he also collaborated directly on the cause of Pan-Islamism with Jamāl od-Din, a man, as we will see, who believed as much in progress as in the Koranic revelation, but who wanted to use the mobilizing force of Islam against imperialist undertakings. Arrested in Istanbul by the Ottomans in 1895, Mirzā Āqā Khān, together with two other Iranian opponents, was handed over to the Shah's agents who executed them, holding them accountable for the killing of Nāser od-Din Shāh.[13]

---

[11] A. Pistor-Hatam. "The Persian Newspaper *Akhtar* as a transmitter of Ottoman Political Ideas," in Th. Zarcone & F. Zarinebaf-Shahr, *Les Iraniens d'Istanbul*.

[12] This racial and insulting stereotype toward Arabs, rather common among Iranians, can be found as far back as the early eleventh century in Nāser-e Khosrow's travelogue.

[13] F. Ādamiat, *Andishe-hā-ye Mirzā Āqā Khān Kermāni*, pp. 42f; H. Nāteq, Introduction to Mirzā Āqā Khān Kermāni's exile correspondence, *Name-hā-ye tab'id*, pp. 37f: before the

Jamāl od-Din Asadābādi – "al-Afghani"

Seyyed Jamāl od-Din Asadābādi (1838–97) is an even more ambivalent figure. It took the research of two historians to uncover not so much who he was but rather that he was not who he claimed to be.[14] Born to a modest family in Asadābād, near Hamadān, he generally claimed to be an Afghan, born in a village called As'adābād, near Kabul. In Afghanistan, he claimed to be an Ottoman citizen, but when he talked with Westerners, he passed himself off as an Arab. Despite his religious education, he did not want to present himself as Iranian at any price, fearing he would become a prisoner to his Shiite identity that would have lost him the audience in Sunnite countries.

Until the age of twelve, Jamāl od-Din studied in Qazvin where he witnessed the ferocious suppression of Bābism, a movement whose force of attraction undoubtedly left a mark on him. He went on to study for four years in Najaf in the Ottoman Empire, and from there traveled to India. Remaining for many years in Bombay and Calcutta, he moved in Muslim circles at the time of the Sepoy rebellion in 1857, a mutiny driven by religious sentiments and by the rejection of colonialism; in northern India he witnessed the temporary setback of British colonial ambitions. Later, he visited Mecca and the Mesopotamian regions. These journeys, which may be considered a normal itinerary for a young traditional scholar, turned this Seyyed into a true child of the *Umma* (the "community" of Muslims), open to the problems of the time, and into a multilingual person. In 1866 he went to Afghanistan, undoubtedly after a stay in Istanbul. British sources describe him as an adviser to the Emir of Kabul and considered him to be a Russian agent, having called himself Seyyed Rumi (originating from Anatolia). Haunted by the idea that the Russians were destabilizing their empire, the British were perturbed by the Seyyed's anti-colonial rhetoric. Having fallen into disgrace, Jamāl od-Din left Afghanistan at the end of 1868 and went to Istanbul via India and Egypt.

He spent two years in the Ottoman capital where he began to call himself "Afghāni," the name by which he is generally known. Above all, he was notable for his audacious ideas, which placed prophet and philosopher in opposition; he maintained his belief in the pre-eminence, at all

Shah's assassination, the three Iranian opponents were arrested, and possible extradition was considered in exchange for Armenian insurgents who had taken refuge in Persia.

[14] Homa PAKDAMAN (Nāteq); Nikki KEDDIE (see bibliography).

times, of a guide who leads humanity out of obscurantism – a formulation close to that of the Sheykhis.[15] Moreover, he drafted a project for the union of the Muslim peoples of Central Asia and northern India against the Russians; in reality he was also aiming it at the British. Exiled to Egypt, he taught there for eight years and formed lasting friendships, in particular with one of the great Salafist reformers of Islam, Sheykh Mohammad Abduh. His denunciation of the de facto collusion between the Khedive and the British saw him exiled once again to India, this time for three years.

In 1883, Jamāl od-Din Asadābādi went to Paris where he quickly enjoyed considerable fame. Invited to respond in the *Journal des débats* to Renan's lecture on Islam at the Sorbonne, "Afghani" essentially agreed with Renan: historically, Islam had been an obstacle to science.[16] This surprising assertion conveys the ambivalence of Jamal od-Din's message. With his Egyptian friend Abduh, who joined him in Paris, he published a newspaper in Arabic, *al-Urwat al-Wuthqa* ("the Indissoluble Link"), which, disseminated Pan-Islamic ideas across the Muslim world. The Seyyed was constantly in political talks with the British over India, Egypt, and particularly Sudan, and also stayed in London where he participated in political negotiations, even trying to rouse the British against Russia in Central Asia in the hope of awakening hostile sentiments that would, ultimately, stir the Muslim world into an anti-colonial jihad.

While in correspondence with the Ottoman Sultan, Afghāni arrived in Iran in May 1886, at Bushehr in the Persian Gulf. Soon invited by the Shah to Tehran, Jamāl od-Din had now to present himself as an Iranian, born in Asadābād. He lodged with an important merchant, Amin oz-Zarb, who assigned Mirzā Rezā Kermāni to him as servant. The latter, ten years later, would earn notoriety as the Shah's assassin. Afghani's burdensome attractiveness resulted in tension among the Shah's advisers, who forced the Seyyed to leave for Russia. Here, he took on the role of commercial agent in the service of Amin oz-Zarb, helping him in what proved a stillborn project of establishing a railway; he continued to participate in various industrial endeavors, all the while

---

[15] See N. Keddie, *Sayyid Jamāl ad-Din "al-Afghāni,"* p. 69.

[16] Even though, says Afghani, such statement could also apply to Christianity. See *Journal des débats*, 18 May 1883.

fostering tensions between the European powers, playing one off against another.

Jamāl od-Din had not abandoned all hope of playing a role in his country's future. In 1889, during Nāser od-Din Shāh's third trip to Europe, he contacted the Shah's entourage, saying that he was charged with a mission by the Russian government; shortly thereafter he returned to Tehran, where, despite an audience with the Shah, he failed to find an ear sympathetic to his claims, hindering his wish to secure for himself a role in the many negotiations the government was engaged with, specifically on identifying viable economic sectors for modernization, with the development of navigation in the Karun river and the construction of railways, as well as on more sensitive concessions (lotteries, wines, and spirits), which encroached on religious and cultural spheres of influence. In parallel, Jamāl od-Din held semi-secret meetings in which some fifty people participated, who from that time played leading roles in the reforms and soon in the revolution. Among them were intellectuals (Zokā ol-Molk Foruqi and E'temād os-Saltane), ulama (Mohammad Tabātabā'i and Hādi Najmābādi), and politicians (Amin od-Dowle, minister of posts and Moshir od-Dowle, minister of justice, who was dismissed at the behest of the British). Under the guise of promoting Pan-Islamism, Jamāl od-Din criticized despotism and agitated for constitutional reform, and even for the establishment of a republic.

In July 1890, when the decision was taken to banish him to Qom (120 km or 75 miles south of Tehran), the Seyyed claimed the right to asylum (*bast*) at the sanctuary of Abd ol-Azim, near Tehran. From there, where in principle he was beyond the reach of the authorities, he defied the government over a period of seven months:

> This time, when people want to see me, it was no longer to hear me talk about science, arts and morality. Finally, they came to ask me to help tear the veil of darkness and break the chains of despotism. They claim a liberal regime, laws and equitability for a country that in the exercise of justice remains even more backward than the most savage tribes and that, because of the faulty character of Nāser od-Din staggers on the edge of the precipice.[17]

---

[17] L. Asadābādi, *Sharh-e hāl va āsār-e Seyyed Jamāl ol-Din Asadābādi*, p. 149.

Finally, in mid-winter, in a humiliating move and in terrible physical conditions, he was expelled to Ottoman Iraq, first to Baghdad, and later, at Tehran's intervention, to Basra.

Boycott of the Tobacco Regie

Iran entered a period of volatility and widespread revolt against the monarchy, which first took shape with the rejection of the Tobacco Regie, a company created by a Briton, Major G. F. Talbot. The entire country was affected. Jamāl od-Din's expulsion from Iran was linked to the protest movement.

In March 1890 Talbot had obtained the concession to cultivate and trade tobacco, securing a monopoly all over Iran. Popular reaction against the Regie concession was widespread. Tracts circulated accusing the Shah of cupidity and threatening him with death. Though the spread of agitation certainly did not have a direct link to Afghāni's declarations nor with his letters, which he continued to send from Ottoman Iraq to his adherents, inciting opposition to the Tobacco Regie, his protestations remained under the state's radar. Malkom Khān, in London, was also involved in the campaign, and any Iranian found to be in correspondence with these two dissidents was promptly prosecuted and imprisoned, with many being tortured; this was notably the case with Mirzā Rezā Kermāni, the future assassin of the Shah, and with a prominent merchant from Isfahan, Hājj Sayyāh.

In April 1891, when the uprising against the Talbot monopoly had spread to Shiraz, a Seyyed from that city who had played an active role was expelled to Karbalā, from where he contacted Jamāl od-Din, still under house arrest in Basra. Shortly after, Jamāl od-Din sent a long letter to one of the leading Shiite theologians of that time, Mirzā Hasan Shirāzi, who lived at Samarrā, in northern Iraq. In his letter he denounced European economic interference and accused the prime minister, Amin os-Soltān, of being a Bābi. Shortly thereafter, faced with the intensity of popular revolt, the monopoly of the Tobacco Regie was suspended at Tabriz, a partial victory that encouraged opponents in other provinces.

The ulama, seeing that popular resistance was widespread, abandoned their neutrality and condemned the Regie. At Isfahan, the powerful theologian Āqā Najafi (whose local business interests were at stake) led the denouncement against Prince Zell os-Soltān, who had placed his interests in the British company. Jamāl od-Din's letters only further enflamed the opposition. In September 1891, from Samarrā, Mirzā Shirāzi wrote to Nāser od-Din Shāh to beg him to oust the Europeans from the central sectors of the economy. This political intervention by a leading Shiite theologian, who was free from the reach of the Iranian government because he lived in the Ottoman Empire, opened the gates to a century of exchanges between the sanctuaries of Iraq and the Iranian nation.

The boycott of the tobacco concession began at Isfahan in the fall of 1891, and progressively spread across the country. A fatwa attributed to Mirzā Shirāzi was released: "In the name of Allah the Merciful and Clement. Now the consumption of *tambāku* and tobacco in all its forms is considered to be a war against the Imam of the Age (may Allah hasten his glorious advent)."[18] This terse message was heard even within the royal harem where the princesses and concubines refused to prepare the water pipe for their royal husband. As of then, the concession was doomed. The Shah began the process of annulling it, first, removing the monopoly on domestic trade, but he was soon forced to rescind and buy back the entire concern to appease the crisis. Mirzā Shirāzi awaited the written confirmation of the annulment before, in turn, withdrawing his fatwa. On 26 January 1892 the public crier finally announced that one was allowed to smoke again in peace. The prestige and the finances of the Crown were irretrievably damaged by the reversal. As N. Keddie points out, the repeal of the concession led to a situation of greater dependence, as the royal treasury was compelled to rely on foreign loans, with fierce competition between the Russians and the British to maintain financial pressure.[19]

Meanwhile, having escaped the reach of the Ottoman police in Basra, Jamāl od-Din traveled to London, where he joined Malkom Khān. The two men offered a much more liberal account of the struggle against the Tobacco Regie, that of a fight for social justice, with Islam in no way presenting an obstacle to democratic liberties. They denounced the autocracy of the Shah and begged the British to help them fight tyranny. Deceived by the promise of liberty that Sultan Abdul Hamid II offered him, Jamāl od-Din decided to end his days in an environment

---

[18] F. Ādamiat, *Shuresh bar emtiāznāme-ye Rezhi*, p. 84, says that nobody had ever seen the original fatwa; whatever its authenticity, it worked efficiently.

[19] N. Keddie, *Religion and Rebellion in Iran*, p. 131.

where his commitment to Islam would not be tarnished by the obligation to speak the liberal and nationalistic language of Europe. The Sultan, from that time on, behaved in just as reactionary a way as the Shah, but he remained the symbol of the union of all Muslims against colonialism. In that fight, the Iranian Seyyed succeeded in attracting the free-thinkers, the Bābis, who all wanted to defeat despotism and to free the oppressed nations. In his last correspondence with Shiite ulama of Mesopotamia he militated for the unification of Muslims behind the Sultan and called on them to depose the Shah. Pressure from Iran became increasingly insistent, and, finally, in 1895, the Porte accepted to arrest three of the most virulent opponents, Mirzā Āqā Khān Kermāni, Hasan Khabir ol-Molk (consul-general of Iran), and Sheykh Ahmad Ruhi. Jamal od-Din, who was ill, enjoyed special protection. He died two years later in Istanbul.

The Assassination of Nāser od-Din Shāh

On Friday 1 May 1896, as he was about to leave the tomb of Abd ol-Azim, south of Tehran, where he had just offered a prayer of thanks for his reign of fifty lunar years, Nāser od-Din was approached by a man who had taken refuge in the sanctuary to escape police pursuit.

This man, Mirzā Rezā Kermāni, had been in Jamāl od-Din's service during his sojourn in Tehran. After the expulsion of his master from the same sanctuary, Mirzā Rezā was imprisoned and tortured over a period of four years; when he was freed, he joined the Seyyed in Istanbul. He had returned with the sole intention of exacting revenge on the governor of Tehran, Nāyeb os-Saltane, who had been the instigator of his imprisonment. Yet, thinking it was better to cut down the tree than prune the branches, he acquired a revolver. The opportunity that presented itself on that day, in the very mausoleum where his mentor had been mistreated a few years earlier, was too auspicious to miss. Approaching the monarch as though to submit a petition, he drew his revolver and shot the Shah several times in the heart, killing him instantly.

There is no doubt about the motivation of Mirzā Rezā, who was executed only after enduring a lengthy interrogation. The killer had sought revenge as he had promised Jamāl od-Din in Istanbul he would. Yet his insistence, during the interrogation, on the suffering that he had experienced and his protestations of the misery and injustice that reigned in Iran, revealed well-thought-out political motives. The assassination was a reaction to social distress. For Mirzā Rezā, it was an act of solidarity with disaffected elements across Persian society.

> Are not these poor folk, says the assassin to his court interrogators "without pressure of torture," and this handful of Persian people a trust from God? Step forth for a moment from this land of Persia, and you will see in Mesopotamia, the Caucasus, Ashgabat, and the border-lands of Russia, thousands of poor Persian subjects who have fled from their own dear country from the hands of oppression and tyranny, and have perforce adopted the most miserable means of earning a livelihood. The porters, sweepers, donkey-men and labourers whom you see in those regions are all Persians. After all, these flocks of your sheep need a pasture in which they may graze, so that their milk may increase, and they may be able both to suckle their young and to support your milking; not that you should constantly milk them as long as they have milk to give, and, when they have none, should devour the flesh from their bodies. Your sheep are all gone and scattered: this is the result of tyranny which you see. What and wherefore is this boundless tyranny and oppression, and what can exceed this? They strip the very flesh from the bodies to devour it, and to feed therewith their hawks and birds of venery. Under the burden of their oppressions they do so constrain the poor, captive, helpless people that men are compelled to divorce their own wives so that these their lords may take to wife a hundred. Every year they spend on the *Aziz os-Soltān* [young boy, 'favorite' of the Shah] who is of no use to the state or the nation, nor serves for the personal gratification of any one, half a million tumān wrung from the people by this bloodthirsty and merciless tyranny. These are matters known to all the people of this city, though they do not dare to utter them aloud.[20]

Mirzā Rezā perceived that he was acting with the support of many, although he acted without an accomplice in fear that his intention would be disclosed without him seeing the deed through. "Those who

---

[20] Persian text published in 1907 by *Sur-e Esrāfil*; reproduced by H. Nāteq, *Kārnāme va zamāne*, pp. 182f, translation by E. G. Browne *Persian Revolution*, pp. 63f (quote pp. 71f).

share my view in this city and in this country are many, alike amongst the ulama, the Ministers, the nobles, the merchants, the trades-people, and all other classes ... Now everyone holds the same views that I do." Acknowledging those who wept for the Shah, as if he were one of their own, he replied: "But go and look at the miserable condition of the people outside."[21]

The assassination toppled the quiet decadence of the Iranian political system, instigating a spiraling into chaos. The new king, Mozaffar od-Din Shāh, was already forty-three years old and not the preferred candidate for the throne. Nāser od-Din had wanted to designate Kāmrān Mirzā, although much younger. Another older pretender, the powerful governor of Isfahan, Zell os-Soltān, was excluded from succession because he was the son of a low-born mother, despite his efforts to have his rights recognized with the help of the Freemasons. Both the British and Russians, who influenced each succession, entered into a compromise with the sickly prince, whom contemporary diplomats sometimes called "*Mauvaise-affaire* od-Din Shah."

This difficulty in designating an heir had been felt during Nāser od-Din Shāh's reign. Two princes, whom he loved, had died young. The Shah showed little affection to Mozaffar od-Din, who in his eyes was a second-best choice, and whom he soon relegated to Tabriz. Since about 1860, the Shah had been afflicted by a kind of sterility, undoubtedly linked to the congenital weakness of the children who survived him. In a country where sexual prowess was measured by the number offspring, the fact of not having more children certainly frustrated Nāser od-Din and increased his anguish of failing to consolidate more firmly dynastic perpetuity, despite having held the reins of the country for half a century.

Foreign Loans and the Reorganization of the Customs Administration

The timorous and sickly Mozaffar od-Din Shāh (1853–1907) immediately faced volatile political conditions. The pressure from reformers steadily increased, and though the new Shah was not averse to certain reforms, he loathed public violence. Notably he authorized the establishment of the Roshdiye schools, whose system, based on the

---

[21] Translated in Browne, *Persian Revolution*, pp. 72, 80.

European pedagogical system, had already been adopted in the Ottoman Empire. The move was violently decried by the ulama, because they saw the spread of modern pedagogy as the end to their monopoly on education.

After the buyback of the Reuter concession, and even more so of the Talbot concession, the Treasury was empty. The Persian state had little choice but to borrow £500,000 from the Imperial Bank – that is, Great Britain – to be repaid over forty years. In 1900 and 1902 the Russians granted Mozaffar od-Din Shāh two new loans to fund his trips to Europe; these totaled an amount almost seven times higher than the British loan, at a rate of 5 percent for a duration of sixty-five years. It placed an unprecedented pressure on the Iranian government throughout the period.

The level of indebtedness was an entirely new financial situation for Iran; however, it was not catastrophic. Nevertheless, the dependence on foreign powers, who manipulated financial pressure to obtain political advantages, revealed an inherent weakness in the state. The real decisions, from that point, were made abroad. The loans and concessions of monopolies gave the impression that the country had been sold off to foreigners; and more than ever these foreigners demanded that customs duties were pledged as a guarantee for the loans. The spectacle of a monarch who confiscated his subjects' property, imprisoned them, wasted the royal treasury, and amused himself at the expense of the population, with little restraint and to the detriment of the clear interests of the nation, became increasingly unpalatable. Here one finds comparisons with the climate of France in 1789; the nation demanded a control on public expenditure, on the collection of taxes and their use, and that royal arbitrariness be subject to the approval of a Parliament.

Yet at the end of the nineteenth century, the customs administration, which was both arbitrary and ineffective, remained in place. Other than an import or export tax, goods were subject to fees at the city gates to cover road maintenance. The discriminatory regime established by the Treaty of Torkamanchāy (1828), which in theory placed Iranian merchants at a disadvantage compared with their Russian counterparts,[22] was progressively extended to other European nations,

[22] M. L. ENTNER shows that in fact, it was Iran not Russia that benefited most from this treaty: see *Russo-Persian Commercial Relations*, pp. 6f. But the setback to Iranian trade at the end of the nineteenth century was attributed to the derogatory terms of the capitulations.

whose goods were taxed at a flat fee of 5 percent of their value and exempt from any internal fees.[23] To rationalize the management of these revenues, which no public administration had been able to take charge of, the Shah's government decided to farm out the management of the customs duties. In 1898, when negotiations for the first Russian loan began, the administration of the customs administration in Azerbaijan was entrusted to Belgian officials, and within a year this was the case throughout Iran, a state of affairs which would last until the 1930s.[24]

The first chief of customs, was Joseph Naus, who soon became a scapegoat for the merchants and liberals, because customs, now under state control, introduced new rules, forms to fill out, and other controls that humiliated Persians and put them at a disadvantage. The chief administrator of customs became a central figure in the political administration, with the Shah appointing him "minister of higher rank" to allow him the necessary powers when the prime minister accompanied the sovereign to France in 1902. The 10 million rubles issued under the Russian loan had been absorbed by the costly trip of His Majesty. Naus negotiated a new customs agreement with the Russians and, later, with other powers. The treaty (1903) augmented the hatred toward the Belgians, who were now clearly supported by Russia.[25] After having taken control of the Directorate of the Posts, he began to reform the taxes. This was to prove a too ambitious venture for the Belgian.

The first official questioning of the appointment of the Belgian customs administration began with the British, who were dissatisfied that the Russians through their loans had taken hold of that coveted territory. The Belgian officials posted along the Indian border, which was vaguely delineated, and where trade was pretty-much non-existent, were considered representatives of Russia. At best, they only conformed to Persian sovereignty to the detriment of British efforts to improve transport links between India and Persia through the modernizing of highways and to establish local agreements with semi-autonomous tribal chiefs. Until 1905, the head of the powerful British consulate of Kermān was the flamboyant Major Sykes, a spy, colonial officer and romantic and megalomaniac consul, who for a certain time had as his

---

[23] See preceding chapter. Cf. Ch. ISSAWI, ed., *Economic History*, pp. 70f.
[24] A. DESTRÉE, *Les Fonctionnaires belges au service de la Perse*; W. FLOOR, "The Customs in Qajar Iran"; "Custom duties," *Encyclopædia Iranica, s.v.; A Fiscal History of Iran in the Safavid and Qajar Period*, pp. 376f.
[25] M. L. ENTNER, *Russo-Persian Commercial Relations*, pp. 53f.

interlocutor the eminent anglophile Prince Farmānfarmā (1857–1939).[26] In other words, the Belgian customs officials did not have an easy task.

More serious, the customs tariff reform of 1903 led to a temporary slowdown in imports, as merchants preferring to get rid of their stock before ordering goods that were taxed at a higher rate. The customs revenues decreased considerably compared with the forecast, and Naus was forced to borrow money to pay administrators' salaries. In Tabriz, the Shiite clergy supported a revolt against the customs administration, and the new provincial director, Jérôme Priem, was forced to leave the city for a few weeks. This state of affairs appears to have been encouraged by Mohammad-Ali Mirzā, the crown prince, who detested the prime minister, Eyn od-Dowle. Thereafter, the new customs system was applied without major problem and increased government revenues.

Here one sees how many socio-economic problems were amplified by political conflicts and rivalries. The intervention of the ulama, at the request of the crown prince, who wanted to undermine the prime minister, lent the revolt a quasi-insurrectional character. This use of clergy influence, in the face of what was perceived as foreign interests (even though Naus had negotiated rather a good deal for Iran), created a particularly complex dynamic to Iranian popular mobilization. The theologian referents (*marja-e taqlid*) lived in the holy places of Mesopotamia where they could be consulted by telegram, letters being very slow. From their faraway *madrasa*, these ulama did not fully grasp the real stakes; their replies essentially reaffirmed the function of those who posed the questions rather than addressing the questions themselves. Above all, they did not want to alienate the faithful, from whom they received subsidies by way of Islamic taxes that were voluntarily paid to the mosques by Shiites. In any case, they could not accept that Christians levied taxes on Muslims in their own country.

An Elite Increasingly Loosing Self-Confidence

Was the Constitutional Revolution kick-started by the grassroots rejection of the political order or by the manipulation of the British – whose demands sought to undermine the increasingly strong

[26] A. Wynn, *Persia in the Great Game. Sir Percy Sykes, Explorer, Consul, Soldier, Spy.*

Russian hold on the Persian monarchy? With the Persian elites weakened, there is little question that they were more susceptible to foreign
exploitation. The slow and inexorable erosion of Iran's sovereign interests and wealth by determined foreign interference left the population in
a state of resignation. Many Iranians were convinced that the fate of
their country was decided far away, in London – later Washington – and
Moscow.[27] As Russia underwent structural upheaval after 1917, it was
above all Great Britain, whose power was blown out of all proportion
by public opinion, that remained a powerful influencer in Iranian affairs
and the target of conspiracy denunciations. After World War II,
American policy gradually took its place.

By the beginning of the twentieth century, in one way or
another, the Iranian elite had come to resent the erosion of traditional
certainties. They were no longer capable, or even desirous, of perpetu-
ating the social and cultural norms in which they no longer believed.
This theme of self-denigration is a recurrent theme in the Persian literature of the time. In the *Travel Account of Ebrahim Beg*, Marāqe'i mocks
the drunk and corrupt Iranian authorities who led the country to
ruination.[28] He adopted the scathing style of the *Adventures of Hajji
Baba of Isfahan* by James Morier, a satirical novel of 1824, the 1886
Persian translation of which set peoples' teeth on edge. For Iranians it
was a bitter pill to swallow, and they had difficulty in accepting that so
accurate a portrait was written by a European.

It is often said that the Russian defeat at Port Arthur against the
Japanese in 1905 triggered an immense wave that provoked a political
fever in the peoples south of Russia and of the Muslim world.[29]
In Persia, there was a fascination for Japan, a country which had already
been the subject of laudatory articles and which some Iranian travelers
began to visit. In 1891, Malkom Khān noted a difference that the
Iranian nationalists would not forget: "It is true that the Japanese
have copied Europe. There is no obstacle there, as there is for us, because
religion does not play such a strong role there."

Through the Japanese paradigm, Iranians saw the emergence of
a new goal which could not be attained without great skill: they called it

---

[27] See Ahmad Ashraf, "Conspiracy Theories," *Encyclopædia Iranica, s.v.*
[28] Zeyn ol-Ābedin Marāqe'ī, *Siyāhat-nāme-ye Ebrāhim Beyk*.
[29] Kl. Kreiser, "Der japanische Sieg über Rußland (1905) und sein Echo unter den Muslimen";
A. Pistor-Hatam, "Progress and Civilization in Nineteenth-Century Japan: The Far Eastern
State as a Model for Modernization."

"*sivilisāsyon*" (civilization). Some Persian words, *tamaddon, farhang, tarbiat*, refer to similar concepts, but the French term was imported into Persian with distorted and more rousing connotations suggesting that it was the key to technical progress and to a successful political system. No more pride, no longer any reluctance to call on "the unwashed bums"! From then on, Iranians would dress like Europeans, speak like them, and even read the same things. The people wanted to abolish their differences with them, because the Europeans provided the model for a unique civilization. And what about the means to conquer progress and mythical modernity? The answer was clear to many: the first priority was universal education, access to European science, and the rejection of fanaticism and superstition. The overarching aim was the adoption, by whatever means, of modern institutions where power was no longer arbitrary, and thus, of a parliamentary constitution. This new humanism, whose basis was fragile and barely assimilated, could not be achieved through normal progress along the lines of what had gone before; it was rather to be the focal point of the Constitutional Revolution of 1906–09.

4 THE CONSTITUTIONAL REVOLUTION: FROM ILLUSION TO REALITY (1905–08)

The 1896 attack on Nāser od-Din Shāh was not, as we have seen, a random or isolated act. It was symptomatic of the intensifying tensions between arbitrary rule and the deep social aspirations for justice and political leverage. It was not a change of monarch that could put an end to this, nor even action by certain leaders who were more concerned about the social malaise. What was needed was structural reform. To trigger the process, external events came to the aid of the reformers. The Russian Revolution of 1905, shortly thereafter followed by the surrender of the Czar's troops to the Japanese at Port Arthur (Lushun) had a profound impact on Iran, where the obsession with the Russian threat seemed to deflate overnight like a balloon. As the Iranian public began to find its voice, newspapers and lampoons proliferated. The British were only too happy to encourage Iranian opinion along a path that might curtail the influence of their Russian rivals.

The Prolegomena of the Revolution

Having ascended to the Persian throne in 1896, Mozaffar od-Din Shāh would remain in power until 1907. Ill-prepared to face the demands of his subjects, he was preoccupied by only two things: to calm the mutinies of the army, often paid with a delay of two years, and to finance his journeys to "take the waters" in Europe, where he went three times (in 1900, 1902, and 1905).

To cover the considerable expense that these cures entailed, on the recommendation of his physicians, he asked his prime minister,

Amin os-Soltān, to secretly negotiate two loans which he obtained from the Russians. Having been appointed prime minister under the preceding Shah from 1885 to 1896, Amin os-Soltan had left a bad memory of having encouraged the Tobacco concession. Mozaffar od-Din Shāh had only called him back to the government in 1898 to rescue the state's coffers. Upon his return from his first visit to Europe, he bestowed on him the title of Atābak-e A'zam, "supreme father," to offer him some clout against the cabals of his opponents.

The Russian loans were unpopular, because the customs revenues from northern Iran were collateral for their repayment – the south was considered untouchable, because of the British. For the latter, the indebtedness to Russia put Iran under the domination of their rivals for decades, and thus they were fiercely opposed to these loans. Also, they encouraged in secret the ulama, sometimes by giving them money, to denounce Amin os-Soltān as a heretic, under the pretext that he sold the country to infidels.

In September 1903, when the government had already spent the successive loans and when the Russians and British continued to exercise pressure on Iran to be its financier, a fatwa cursing Amin os-Soltān circulated in Tehran. This document, which seemed to have originated from the grand mojtaheds of Najaf and Karbalā, was most likely a fake, but its effect was immediate. Amin os-Soltān was quickly replaced by his rival Eyn od-Dowle (1845–1927). This arrogant and brutal prince was known for his hostility toward European influence. It did not take long before he was even more detested than his predecessor.

In the eyes of the public, and particularly the merchants, everything had gone wrong. The administration of customs duties was under the complete control of Belgian officials. At their head, Joseph Naus, who had pledged to modernize the fiscal system, became minister of finance and posts, playing a major role in the government. Iranian merchants believed that the new customs tariffs were too favorable to the Russians. The dissatisfaction grew at the beginning of 1905. Repercussions from the defeat of the Czar's armies by the Japanese, and the troubles that followed in its wake were felt as far away as Tehran, where prices rose sharply; in certain cities, the cost of sugar increased by more than 30 percent and wheat by 90 percent. Moreover, popular fervor increased because of the conjunction in 1905 of the lunar month of Moharram – when religious sentiments reached their zenith in the mourning of Imam Hoseyn and in celebration of the Iranian

New Year (21 March). To this climate was added the uproar sparked by the rumor of a proposed third trip by the Shah to Europe. In reaction, Mozaffar od-Din Shāh left Iran, claiming he was going on pilgrimage to Mashhad.

Shortly after his departure, the protest focused on Naus. It all began with a calculated provocation by the religious camp, which found a picture of the Belgian two years before, in which he was dressed like a molla at a masked ball in Tehran. In order to incite public anger, the photo was reproduced and distributed as proof of the government and its administration's mockery of Islam. The demonstrators cried sacrilege and took asylum in the Abd ol-Azim mausoleum, south of Tehran. The Shah promised that on his return to Tehran he would dismiss Naus and replace him with a council of merchants.

Revolt rumbled all the more since the Czarist power that protected the Shah was itself in a weakened position. The "positive equilibrium" between Russia and Great Britain which Iranian politics had been able to establish since the 1880s by granting concessions first to one and then to the other, so that each of the powers felt that it was in a dominant position, was upset. The British profited from the situation by turning the course of events to their advantage, pressing the religious camp and then the liberals and the reformers to demand reforms to strengthen their growing influence and thus to break with the absolutism that the population identified with the Russian model.

As the months passed, mobilization took varied forms. Initially it was popular and religious, because the ulama, supported by the mojtaheds from the holy places in Iraq, played a growing role. However, it soon became covert and elitist in nature, with secret clubs and associations, the *anjoman*-s which distributed clandestine tracts, *shabnāme*, a neologism that could be translated as "nightly" by analogy of *ruznāme*, "daily." The reformers were driven by heterogeneous motivations. For some, the sentiment that Islam was in danger directed their animosity against all non-Muslims, above all, Christians and Bābis. Conversely, the Freemasons and secular reformers finally saw the impending prospect of the defeat of absolutism and the implementation of radical reforms without any link to religious law. More radical elements, notably *Azali* Bābis, some of them acting under the garb of Shiite clerics to avoid being cursed as heretics, challenged not only the corrupt civil powers, but also the conniving clerical powers. More significantly the radical revolutionaries, who themselves were influenced by the Social Democrat movement of the Caucasus – which in the suppression of the Russian Revolution was pushed to Tabriz – sought in the name of social justice to stir up dissatisfaction against the monarchy and against the corruption of the elite.

At Tabriz, the agitation began in 1903 against the local director of customs, the Belgian Jérôme Priem. At Mashhad, the religious discourse initially took on Pan-Islamic overtones, for similar reasons; in April 1905, a riot broke out against wheat hoarders; peasants from the province of Sistan had been forced to abandon their villages because of famine and were living in temporary shelters at the city's gates. At Isfahan, Kermān, and Yazd, riots with a sectarian character erupted, notably aimed at Christians and foreign missionaries, and elsewhere at the Bābis. At Rasht, the population which was joined by Armenian Christians with their own religious rituals, organized a prayer for the victory of the Japanese against the Russians. At Shiraz, in September–October, an uprising occurred against its brutal and greedy governor, Sho'ā os-Saltane (1880–1920), son of the Shah, because he had unjustly punished merchants whom he blamed for the price increases; a mob of 500 people occupied the Shāh-e Cherāgh sanctuary and secured the governor's removal.

These events are less notorious and sometimes less spectacular than the large demonstrations that started in Tehran at the end of 1905 and which European diplomats witnessed directly. They call into question the belief that the constitutional movement began in the capital and only then spread to the rest of the country, even though some unrest was a common reaction to social discontent and did not necessarily lead to, or in fact demand, political change. Moreover, the claim that agitation in Tabriz was the result of a personal campaign by the crown prince, who lived in the city, against Prime Minister Eyn od-Dowle should be rejected. There is no question that there was an accumulation of tension in most Iranian provinces. If the events in Tehran were met with a quasi-unanimous echo across the rest of the country, it was because they finally allowed the general discontent to find an outlet.

Nevertheless, it is undeniable that the religious dimension often dominated the hostilities, and those aimed at foreigners took the form of the defense of Islam more than the defense of the country. Traditionally, the ulama's role was to obtain justice against the rapacity of hoarders and the brutality of governors, if they themselves were not directly implicated. Accusations of heresy, such as that of Amin ol-Soltān, amounted to the accusation of betraying the community and playing the game of the "Christians," that is, the Belgian customs officials, or the Russian and British bankers, groups of Europeans whose main motivation had little, if anything, to do with Christianity.

A Tinderbox

The demands of the revolutionaries, which at first were very imprecise, focused on Naus but also on the prime minister. Eyn od-Dowle accompanied the Shah to Europe in the summer of 1905, but the demonstrations started again after his return. In December, clumsy punitive measures taken by the governor of Tehran – in reality on the orders of the prime minister – against two merchants who were accused of selling sugar at too high a price resulted in the closure of the bazaar. The two men were condemned to the bastinado; one of them was an old Seyyed, who had made the pilgrimage to Mecca several times and enjoyed a sound reputation.

To alleviate the tension, a meeting was organized the next day by the Emām-jom'e (the official mosque leader), a son-in-law of the Shah. Two famous clerical personalities, who soon were called "the Two Seyyeds," presided over the meeting. The first, Seyyed Abdollāh Behbahāni (1846–1910), was an ambitious and venal clergyman who had defied the famous fatwa against the consumption of tobacco in 1891 and dared to smoke in public, to please, it was said, the British legation. Fiercely hostile to the prime minister, it was he who had distributed the photo of Naus dressed as a molla. As for the other Seyyed, Mohammad Tabātabā'i (1841–1918), he was a liberal theologian, close to Masonic circles and strongly politicized. He had made Malkom's ideas about the need for a Constitution his own and had visited Jamāl od-Din during his stay in Tehran. He would relate, in an autobiographical narration, that he had awaited the coming of Mozaffar od-Din Shāh, who was more moderate than his father, before becoming involved in politics.[1] The alliance of the two very different men appeared to have been the work of one of the secret societies that plotted in favor of the revolution and that may have convinced Behbahāni to fight for a more radical goal than the simple dismissal of the prime minister.

[1] E. Kāzemiya, ed., "Yād-dāsht-hā-ye Seyyed Mohammad Tabātabā'i."

A third "cleric" intervened during that meeting at the mosque, Seyyed Jamāl od-Din Isfahāni (1863–1908). This *Azali* Bābi, dressed in clerical habit, was known for his fierce oratory. After having preached on the need for justice, the main concern of the ulama, he explained that if the Shah were a Muslim he could not but support the people's demands – a way of turning religious issues into political protest. The Emām-jom'e ordered the meeting to disperse. By defending the prime minister, he believed that the crowd, dissatisfied about the rise in prices, would expel seditious ulama. However, he achieved the opposite. The ulama, accompanied by about 2,000 people, sought sanctuary in the Abd ol-Azim mausoleum south of Tehran, where they remained for several weeks (December 1905–January 1906). The *bast*, the non-violent occupation of a place holding the right of asylum, became a privileged form of protest during the revolution.

The demonstrations at Abd ol-Azim rapidly received the support of the bazaar merchants who hoped for the fulfilment of their own demands, that is, the dismissal of Naus and the prime minister. But less patent supporters joined the protest, in particular followers of the former prime minister, Amin os-Soltān, then in exile; or the patronage of Mohammad-Ali Mirzā, the crown prince (a reactionary who thought only of getting rid of Eyn od-Dowle, his personal enemy) and finally the support of different reformers among the political elite. After some weeks, the role of the bazaar notables diminished when they saw that the men whose departure they demanded maintained their positions.

Negotiations took place through the intermediation of the Ottoman ambassador. As a condition for his interventions, the latter demanded that the demonstrators formulate their claims in a general manner and that these should not be limited to persons or corporatist interests, such as fiscal exemptions, which the ulama wanted to preserve. From their side the demonstrators not only demanded amnesty for the ulama who were banned from their mosques, but also: (1) the establishment of a "house of justice" in each province so that the Shah's subjects could make their complaints heard and have them followed up appropriately; (2) the application of Islamic law in each case and for each person, without individual distinction; (3) the dismissal of Naus; and (4) the dismissal of the governor of Tehran (they did not mention the prime minister).

A royal rescript of 10 January 1906 partially gave in to the demonstrators who returned in triumph to Tehran. According to this, a new system of tribunals was to be established to respect and apply "the law of Islam." Everyone seemed to be appeased. But the promise remained dormant for months, during which time the government tried to divide the opposition, while the secret societies continued to campaign for political change. In the spring of 1906, one of the Two Seyyeds, Mohammad Tabātabā'i, wrote to the Shah and to the government to remind them of their promise. The government did not bother to reply.

In June 1906, violence broke out and the army intervened. A certain Mahdi Gāvkosh, a man close to Behbahāni, the other leader of the movement, on suspicion of plotting against the government, was brutally arrested in his home where the police molested his pregnant wife. This was too much for Tabātabā'i. The Seyyed mounted the pulpit and preached a sermon to denounce tyranny and the arbitrary use of power. The people of Fārs (a southern province) complained about the abuses to which they had been subjected for a year. At Quchān (a northeastern province), he added, people had no wheat to pay their taxes and the governor took their daughters by force to sell them to the Turkmen, who took them to the slave market. Such oppression was no longer acceptable. People were ready to sacrifice their lives and property for a monarch who defended and protected them, but not for one who was blind and deaf to their suffering.

> We don't want a Presidency, declared Tabātabā'i in his sermon, we are not in favor of a republic, we don't want a constitutional regime that rapidly, because the people of Iran are not educated enough and are not ready for either a constitution or for a republic. Because republics are for educated nations. What we say is, why do you authorities apply all that oppression, why that violence for your subjects? If these subjects were not there, then you [the Shah] you would have nothing ... What we want is justice and a house of justice, we want the application of the law of Islam, we want an assembly (*majles*) in which the king and the beggar will be treated in the same manner, in accordance with the law. We neither want a constitution nor a republic, we want an assembly of religious justice (*majles-e mashru'a-ye adālat-khāne*).[2]

---

[2] Nāzem ol-Eslām KERMĀNI, *Tārikh-e bidāri*, vol. 1, p. 450, 453. The sermon of July 5, 1906, has probably been edited by the historian of the reports, pretending to have eye-witnesses who had taken notes as sources.

The various examples of violence that the sermon cited showed Tabataba'i's denunciation was not so much cultural or religious but clearly social and political in nature. Iranians demanded that the rule of law and their rights be respected, and account be taken of the economic misery into which the government's mismanagement had plunged them. The preacher wanted it to be understood that the desire for justice was deep but almost always defined in religious terms. His denials about being in favor of a republic implied that the demand for such a regime was current at that time and most likely subject to strict censorship by the government and that the leaders of the movement rejected all provocations. Finally, behind the demand for equal justice, the most virulent opponents did not worry over much about Islam, even when they used it as a mobilizing force. Those among them who were excluded in the name of Islam, the Babis and the Freemasons would become the first beneficiaries of a law that would treat all of the kingdom's subjects as equals. In a word, the sermon seemed to attest that there was no well-defined program in place at the beginning of the summer, not even a project for a constitution.

Victory for the Constitutionalists

On 11 July, a few days after Tabataba'i's sermon, a preacher named Mohammad Esfahani was arrested. The demonstrations that followed were suppressed by force, resulting in the death of a theology student, a Seyyed, whose corpse was carried in procession to the mosque. Immediately, the most important ulama were alerted, including the most eminent of the theologians of Tehran, Sheykh Fazlollah Nuri (1843–1909), already suspected of being hostile to the demanded reforms, thus obliging him to show his solidarity with the other mollas.

The Shah, afraid of the public reaction the incident might unleash, promised compensation to the victim's family, but he still refused to dismiss his prime minister, Eyn od-Dowle. In reaction, the ulama demanded that they should be allowed to go on pilgrimage to Najaf; however, they went to Qom instead, 120 km (75 miles) south of the capital, where they remained from 15 July until 14 August. This form of demonstration was of a particular nature, which in Iranian historiography is known as the "Great emigration" (*Mohajerat-e kobra*) – to distinguish it from the first "emigration" to the Abd ol-Azim sanctuary eight months earlier. The exodus apparently removed from the capital a powerful organ of contestation and virulent criticism.

Within a month, Tehran was deprived of its religious class, that is, its notaries, its judges, and its preachers. A woman demonstrated by lifting her veil at the end of a stick while crying: "As of now it is Mr. Naus the Belgian who will marry your girls, because we have ulama no longer!"[3] As a "protector of Islam," as the monarch would have liked to have been known, he lost all credibility. Whatever may have been the political nature of this activity, the initiative now belonged to the ulama. They remained in contact with Tehran by telegraph – the line was later cut – or by road, and remained the interlocutors when negotiations began. The merchants and craftsmen mobilized their forces to increase the pressure, which was easier in the already disorganized economic life of the capital since the departure of the ulama. The bazaaris were linked to the ulama by marriage ties as well as by institutional ties; no important transaction, no notarized contract, no legitimization of a profit could be made without their agreement, tacitly or in writing. The symbol of this link, the mosque, the place of spiritual healing, but also of meetings and discussions, was inserted within the bazaar itself. It is significant that the opposition movement of the Tehran sit-in came from "lesser merchants," and the Shah, at the same time, was able to speak to "major merchants" whom he tried to dissociate from the former.[4]

From the start of the bazaaris' demonstrations, Behbahāni used the good relations that he had maintained with the British to demand financial aid from their diplomats. Perhaps to force their hand, he gave his followers orders to seek asylum (*bast*) in the, then unoccupied, garden of the British embassy, since the British, like most of the wealthy Tehranis, moved to the higher slopes of the city in summertime, when the heat was most fierce. Grant-Duff (1863–1926), the chargé d'affaires, who had been posted in Tehran since 1893, was informed of the right of asylum. He refused to give financial aid and said no to the bazaaris who wanted to use the embassy grounds as a refuge against repression. Yet his "no" lacked conviction; it was a diplomatic "no" of convenience that to the demonstrators sounded like "yes."

---

[3] A. KASRAVI, *Tārikh-e Mashrute-ye Iran*, p. 107.
[4] V. MARTIN, *Islam and Modernism*, p. 91.

The occupation of the British embassy's garden began on 19 July 1906 and lasted until mid-August. Merchants and craftsmen of different guilds, theology students, and soon many of Tehran's most dynamic thinkers joined the first *bastis* and pitched tents on the British lawns, where soup kitchens were improvised. The common people en masse joined this political fest where food was free of charge. There were said to have been up to 16,000 demonstrators,[5] men only, since women did not attend – the mixing of the two sexes would have posed insoluble problems in such a limited space. During the day, political discussions were organized, newspapers from abroad (such as *Habl ol-Matin* printed in Calcutta) were read, and people freely discussed liberty, equality, and the notion of a constitution, concepts which most Iranians had never heard about. During the evening, under the light of the lamps, preachers made the participants weep by relating the martyrdom of the Imams while other groups played music.

Imagine, writes a British diplomat, the garden with tents in every available place and crammed with thousands from all classes, merchants, ulema, members of all the guilds etc., sitting there day after day with stubborn patience, determined not to leave the shelter of the British flag until their demands were satisfied.[6]

The demonstrators only wanted to negotiate via the intermediary of Grant-Duff. Wise to the many promises that were not kept, they demanded that the proposals made by the court or the government were guaranteed by the British diplomat, but he was in contact only with the minister of foreign affairs, Moshir od-Dowle. After some days, Grant-Duff finally visited his "guests." He surprised them by taking off his hat, because in Islamic countries a man always had his head covered. "The British monarch is your dear and benevolent father, he told them. We too are your friends and we have come to show this to you. Be welcome and know that you are safe here."[7] The chargé d'affaires found it difficult to get explanations about the demands that he was expected to transmit to the government. The Persian language had not yet adapted to the vocabulary of the new political institutions; in particular the word designating a constitutional regime, *mashruta*, was not

---

[5] Yahyā DOWLATĀBĀDI speaks of 20,000, Sharif KĀSHĀNI 24,000, whereas 16,000 would be a large crowd in the precinct of the Legation. Many went home to sleep.

[6] Walter Smart in a letter to E. G. Browne, in D. WRIGHT, *The Persians amongst the English*, p. 201.

[7] Vakil od-Dowle's (secretary of the Shah) letter, quoted in E. SAFĀ'I, ed., *Asnād-e Mashrute*, p. 59.

yet well established. Nevertheless, some insinuated that Grant-Duff must have suggested it to the demonstrators.

– What are the demands that you want me to convey to the Shah? asked the diplomat. It seems that you asked the ulama may return safely [from Qom] . . .
– No, they replied, not only that!
– Do you also want the dismissal of Eyn od-Dowle?
– These two demands will not change anything in the dramatic situation in which we find ourselves. We want the *mashrute*.
– What is that, the *mashrute*? asked Grant-Duff. Some replied without being able to explain it. Grant-Duff gave them a definition and an explanation and the people replied:
– That is exactly what we want.[8]

During this time, Prime Minister Eyn od-Dowle tried in vain to divide the movement by targeting less radical clergy, such as Fazlollāh Nuri, who had remained in Tehran. Openly mocking the ulama and the demands that were brought to him, all demanding his dismissal, he gave bonuses and promotions to soldiers who fired on the crowd in June. The sick Shah had not been informed about the occupation of the embassy garden and his physicians prohibited his wives from saying anything whatsoever that might cause another stroke. When he finally learned of the situation, he suggested several measures, which the demonstrators rejected. Eventually, under pressure from the British, he dismissed Eyn od-Dowle. It was said that he wept while showering the prince with presents to soften the blow of dismissal. The minister of foreign affairs, Moshir od-Dowle then became prime minister.

Shortly thereafter, on 5 August 1906 the Shah signed an edict convening the nation's elected representatives to form a deliberative national parliament. This text triggered fresh fighting. The demonstrators demanded that the British guarantee its implementation, but they were refused. Moreover, the new prime minister demanded that this parliament be called "the deliberative Islamic assembly" (*Majles-e shurā-ye eslāmi*),

---

[8] Hājj SAYYĀH, *Khāterāt*, p. 560; Y. DOWLATABADI, *Hayāt-e Yahyā* (Memoirs), vol. 2, p. 73. British sources are also used by V. MARTIN, *Islam and Modernism*, and D. WRIGHT, *The Persians amongst the English*.

while the demonstrators only wanted to hear about the deliberative national Parliament (*melli*) in name of the power of the people.[9]

This was not only a verbal fight. Many militants had abandoned Islam, overtly or not, and some among them were originally Zoroastrians, Christians, Jews, or Bābis. To accept the adjective "Islamic" would have given too much power to the ulama, whose reticence about liberty and citizens' equality outside of the Muslim confessional framework they were well aware of. Despite the tensions created by the restriction, the ulama, who wished to return to Tehran in triumph, feigned ignorance of the secular tendencies of their allies in the capital. After all, when the assembly met nobody would contest the right of the first-rank mojtaheds to take a seat at the table, such as the "Two Seyyeds" and the eminent theologian Fazlollāh Nuri. None of them had stood for election.

The *melli/eslāmi* struggle would raise its head several times in the history of contemporary Iran. It rests on a double misunderstanding. Until August 1906, Iranians used the Arabic term *mellat* to designate a religious community, but this word was also used to translate the European concept of "nation." Among the Ottomans, the term *mellat* traditionally designated the non-Muslim minorities of the empire. The Iranian constitutionalist demonstrators, rather than use *eslāmi*, kept the adjective *melli*, to which they gave the exact opposite meaning, because in their eyes it designated the entire nation, the people, without religious distinction. During the days of the "Islamic" Revolution of 1979, following clashes of "nationalists" (who were liberals and more secular) and "Islamists," *eslāmi* tended to replace *melli* in the sense of "popular."

Another important distinction to play a role in later history appeared, between *mellat*, "the nation, the people" and *dowlat*, "the government, the state." According to this distinction, the assets of the "nation" did not belong to the public domain, but to the private domain. The Constitution of 1907 distinguishes thus between "private" (*mellati*) schools and "public" (*dowlati*) schools. The term *mellat* was also often used to designate "the people," such that *melli* had to be translated as "popular" or even "democratic."[10] The term *eslāmi* does not have another meaning in the revolutionary phraseology of 1979. These contradictions in the terminology, whose interpretation has

---

[9] BROWNE, *Persian Revolution*, p. 123 does not mention the different stages of the negotiation. The firman is dated 14 jomādā, II, 1324/5 August. See N. KERMĀNI, *Tārikh-e Bidāri*, I, p. 561, 567; E. SAFĀ'I, ed., *Asnād-e Mashrute*, p. 120; A. KASRAVI, *Tārikh-e Mashruta-ye Irān*, p. 120.

[10] H. KATOUZIAN, *Political Economy*, p. 171.

greatly evolved within a century, resulted in an ideological tautology, but after much abuse and many sectarian rifts.

The First Parliament

Following the royal edict, an electoral law, drafted in haste, organized the elections based on social class and guilds, a more realistic system than universal suffrage, because of the absence of civil records. It was decreed that Tehran would have sixty deputies and the provinces eighty-four altogether and that the Parliament could start deliberating immediately after the elections upon the confirmation of the deputies from the capital. The representation of Qajar princes (4), the ulama (4), landlords (10), and powerful merchants (10) was determined before-hand, but their combined number did not exceed that of the guilds (36).

This assembly had as its first task to draft a constitution and to have it adopted by royal edict before Mozaffar od-Din Shāh's death, which seemed imminent. Deliberations began on 7 October, with a conservative majority, but they included few lawyers with competence to write such a delicate text as a constitution. Finally, it approved a "Fundamental Law" (*nezāmnāme-ye asāsi*), which was amended, and then presented to the Shah for his signature on 30 December 1906. They also had his son, the crown prince, sign the law – it was the condition to accede to the throne; the new deputies thus thought they had the assurance that from then on they would exercise popular sovereignty. In fact, they mistrusted the future Mohammad-Ali Shāh, because his behavior in Tabriz and his education – under the influence of Shapsal, a Russian tutor of Karaime origin[11] – led them to believe that he was little prepared to modernize the political system, even if his support of the revolutionaries had gained him some sympathy. Above all, he had wanted the fall of Prince Eyn od-Dowle, who challenged his right to succeed.

This text in reality was but the first part of the Constitution; it had to be completed by a supplement that the deputies began to compile after the coronation of the new Shah in January 1907. In this first part, several regulations could be found that were also in force in western constitutional monarchies: six articles (of a total of fifty-one) were copied from the Belgian Constitution and five from the Bulgarian

---

[11] On him, and on the use of "Karaime" instead of "Karaite," see N. Nasiri-Moghaddam, *La Révolution constitutionnelle à Tabriz*, pp. 529f.

Constitution of 1879, two models of constitutional monarchies in countries with statute law; other articles were inspired by the new Russian Constitution of 1906. The Constitution created two chambers. The assembly (*majles*) had the right to make laws and had to approve the state's budget as well as international treaties, loans, and concessions; it did not have the right to censure the government, but it could question a minister and demand his dismissal. The Senate, half composed of members appointed by the Shah, with the other half elected members, had to ratify laws. Democratic liberties were proclaimed, notably freedom of speech, of the press, of correspondence; the right to be judged based on fair predefined judicial criteria; and so on. Only the rights of religious minorities were glossed over, as were those of women, to whom, as in other democracies of the time, no political rights were granted.

Mohammad-Ali Shāh: Islam and the New Institutions

Mohammad-Ali Shāh (1872–1925) began his short reign in January 1907 with, at the very least, a hostile gesture. He did not invite the parliamentary deputies to his coronation, other than the Qajar princes who were members. Very quickly, strong tensions arose within Parliament. The committee charged with the task of writing the Supplement to the Constitution came up against the delicate problem of the very definition of the parliamentary monarchy and the primordial question of the legitimacy of popular suffrage in an Islamic society. The question was even more thorny in this Shiite country, where the Hidden Imam was, by definition, the only legitimate sovereign.

The members of the clergy immediately understood that they had been outwitted by the secular allies. Nothing in the Constitution guaranteed to maintain the integrity of Shiite Islam as the official religion. The text spoke only of democratic freedoms: the rights of the nation, the equality of citizens before the law, and freedom of opinion and speech. The press, dominated by secular intellectuals, put their full weight behind the Constitution, which put the clergy on the alert as soon as the authors of the constitutional text got involved with the formulation of the principles that governed the relations between the state and religion.

On the back of clerical pressure and hard negotiations, the Supplement stated from the very beginning that the official religion was "Twelver Shiism of the Ja'fari rite." Other articles confirmed this. The monarch and the ministers had to state their loyalty to Islam (art. 1), Islam that ruled the "religious" (*shar'i*) courts, but not the "secular courts for civil cases" (*mahākem-e adliye dar orfiāt*, art. 27). The famous theologian Sheykh Fazlollāh Nuri objected in principle to the laws that would be approved by the deputies of the people, arguing that they might be contrary to Islamic laws desired by God. Thus he wrote article 2 of the Supplement to the Constitution in which each word was weighed up:

> Art. 2. At no time must any legal enactment of the Sacred National Consultative Assembly, established by the favour and assistance of His Holiness the Imam of the Age (may God Hasten his glad Advent!), the favour of His Majesty the Shahinshah, of Islam (. . .), and the whole people of the Persian Nation, be at variance with the sacred rules of Islam or the laws established by His Holiness the Best of Mankind (i.e. the Prophet).
>
> It is hereby declared that, it is for the learned doctors of theology (the ulama) – may God prolong the blessing of their existence! – to determine whether such laws as may be proposed are or are not in conformity with the rules of Islam; and it is therefore officially enacted that there shall at all times exist a committee composed of not less than five mojtaheds or other devout theologians, cognizant also of the requirements of the age, [which committee shall be elected] in this manner. The ulama and Proofs of Islam shall present to the National Consultative Assembly the names of twenty of the ulama possessing the attributes mentioned above; and the Members of the National Consultative Assembly shall, either by unanimous acclamation, or by vote, designate five or more of these, according to the circumstances, and recognize these as Members, so that they may carefully discuss and consider all matters proposed in the Assembly, and reject and repudiate, wholly or in part, any such proposal which is at variance with the Sacred Laws of Islam, so that it shall not obtain the title of legality. In such matters the decision of this clerical committee shall be followed and obeyed, and this article shall

continue unchanged until the appearance of His Holiness the Proof of the Age (may God hasten his glad Advent!).[12]

First Threats to the Constitution

The concession that the secular oriented members had made with this Supplement was not sufficient for Fazlollāh Nuri and his followers. Returning from their support of the new institutions, they became involved in a campaign to denounce the anti-Islamic propaganda of the constitutionalists, which made them the object of physical attacks. In protest they left to take refuge again in the famous sanctuary of Abd ol-Azim in Rey, in the south of Tehran. Thus, paradoxically, they showed the intolerance and the limitations of "the freedom of opinion" of their enemies.

As of May of that year, Nuri had found a new ally to resist the free-thinkers of the Majles in the person of Amin os-Soltān, who became prime minister for the third time. Denounced – in fact or fictitiously – as a heretic in 1903, Amin os-Soltān had gone into exile and embarked on a journey around the world that took him to Russia, Siberia, China, Japan, and the USA. At the request of Mohammad-Ali Shāh he hurried back from Europe. Revolutionaries opposed his disembarkation at Anzali, on the Caspian Sea, but on the good faith of his protestations of new parliamentarian convictions, which he said he had acquired on his journey, and appeased by his oath of loyalty to the Constitution, the deputies finally allowed him to reach Tehran.

Upon his return to power, Amin os-Soltān not only found a country on the brink of bankruptcy, but insecurity reigned in the border areas: the Ottomans had made incursions in the west, and the Turkmen in the north. Moreover, the Russians, who had begun to recover from the revolution a year earlier, attempted to regain influence with the new monarch to counterbalance the ascendancy that the British had gained during the demonstrations of the summer of 1906. Despite his new constitutional persuasion, the prime minister was not unhappy to find in Fazlolllāh Nuri a man he could count on to defeat the pretensions of the revolutionaries.

---

[12] As translated by E. G. BROWNE, *The Persian Revolution of 1905–1909*, p. 373.

Parliament flexed its political muscle by limiting the civil list of the monarch and by obtaining the repeatedly demanded dismissal of Naus. The Shah, who tried to withdraw from his constitutional oath, counted on his new government to fight the Majles. The prime minister, for his part, looked for the support of moderate elements such as Seyyed Abdollāh Behbahāni and tried to prevent the Shah from making any errors in judgment. For example, he forced him to arrest a tribal chief, Rahim Khān, who had attacked the constitutionalists of Tabriz, while the Shah himself had encouraged him. In that city, where the revolutionary movement was particularly active, the local assembly (called *Anjoman-e Melli*) acted as the provincial parliament – as defined by article 90 of the Supplement to the Constitution.

As for Sheykh Fazlollāh Nuri's followers, financed in secret by Amin os-Soltan, from the safety of the Abd ol-Azim sanctuary, they accused the constitutionalists of having surrendered to western materialism. They were helped by the excess verbiage of the revolutionaries; some among them did not hesitate to mention the end to all privileges (of Qajar princes) and even the perspective of a republic, which made many afraid. The tracts, telegrams, and newspapers printed and diffused from Rey by Fazlollāh Nuri made a deep impression on religious circles who until then had supported the revolution. The new institutions still remained steadfast thanks in part to some of the clergy who remained loyal, but Nuri opposed a constitutional regime (*mashrute*) and proposed to replace it with a regime that submitted to religious authority (*mashru'e*).

> It is not possible, he wrote, that an Islamic country be submitted to a constitutional regime other than by eliminating Islam. Thus, if a Muslim makes an effort to impose on us, Muslims, a Constitution, this will be in fact the destruction of religion, and such a man, whatever his level of education and his social status, is a renegade, who deserves the punishment reserved for apostasy [i.e. death].[13]

The already catastrophic situation became even worse because of two events, apparently unrelated, that happened on the same day

[13] Md Torkamān, ed., *Rasā'el, e'lāmiye-hā, maktubāt ... va ruznāme-ye Sheykh-e Shahid Fazlollāh Nuri*, p. 114.

(31 August 1907): the assassination of the prime minister and the Anglo-Russian Convention.

Even now, the precise details of Amin os-Soltān's assassination remain unclear, despite the confidence of the Iranian historian Ādamiat who discloses the participation of Taqizāde in the plot, and who exonerates the Shah from any responsibility.[14] On 31 August, Amin os-Soltān obtained a new declaration from the Shah in favor of the government and the Parliament, which gave reason to hope for the normalization of political life. At nightfall, while leaving the Majles, where he had presented two new ministers, the prime minister was killed by a militant, who shot him several times and who was himself immediately killed; however, it is unknown whether he committed suicide or was killed by an accomplice. The man, who called himself Abbās Āqā, was a member of a secret society. For many years, radical revolutionaries were accused of having organized the killing, but, contrariwise, some have submitted that the killer was in fact the Shah's man. The killer's tomb was spontaneously showered with flowers, as if the death of an unpopular politician was a reason for celebration.

The Anglo-Russian Agreement, signed at St. Petersburg, was in fact a victory of French diplomacy, in the international relations that preceded World War I.[15] It was the first step toward the Triple Entente destined to become the military alliance against the Axis states. France feared that in the case of war with Germany, the Russians and British would not be in the same camp, because of their territorial disputes in Asia. Since the beginning of the twentieth century, each side had attempted to outmaneuver the other in order to consolidate influence in Persia. The Treaty of 1828 had opened up Iran to Russian merchants even if the level of trade, as said before, never met expectations. In 1907, oil was not yet on the British radar (since the reserves were only discovered in 1908), but in terms of the strategic defense of the northern borders of their Indian empire, Persia remained of critical importance. The British dominated trade in the south of the country, mainly via the Persian Gulf, while Russia dominated trade in the rest of the country. In fact, by 1916, 65 percent of Iran's foreign trade was with Russia.

---

[14] F. Ādamiat, *Ideolozhi-e nahzat-e Mashrutiyat-e Irān*, II, *Majles-e avval*, p. 169. See further J. Calmard, "Atābak-e A'zam, Amin-os-Soltān"; M. Shamshiri, *Asrār-e qatl-e Mirzā Ali-Asqar Khān Atābak*.

[15] D. McLean, *Britain and Her Buffer State*, pp. 74, 80 only refers to the French role in passing. See M. Habibi, *L'Interface France-Iran, 1907–1938*, pp. 23f.

M2 Anglo-Russian Agreement 1907

Ceasing to aggressively compete with each other and agreeing on respective "zones of influence" allowed the two powers sufficient reassurances and security for each to continue their policy in Persia.

The agreement foresaw a neutral buffer zone separating the zones, from the Pamir to the Caucasus, which the two empires mutually recognized as their own. In Persia, the Russian zone was much larger and covered the entire northern region as far as Isfahan; the British zone covered the south-east, from Bandar Abbas to Zabol, so as to protect the land border with India, leaving the entire south-west in the neutral zone, including Khuzestan where soon oil would flow.

For Iranian nationalists, the publication of this agreement, negotiated without any consultation with them, was an unacceptable slap in the face. How could they accept that the two powers had not only carved up Iranian territory from St. Petersburg but that the Persian politicians had also lost their trump card of being able to take advantage of the two powers' rivalry? The constitutionalists, moreover, were well aware that the British would no longer support them as they had done in 1906. From that moment on, they were vulnerable to intimidation by Mohammad-Ali Shāh, who himself was supported by his Czarist friends.

The Two Coups d'État

The Anglo-Russian Agreement might have indirectly strengthened the Shah, but the desperate state of the public finances continued to cripple the Persian state. In January 1907, to liberate the country "from the claw of the lion and the talon of the eagle," that is, from foreign debts, a National Bank (*Bānk-e melli*) was created at the initiative of the Majles. Popular enthusiasm was not sufficient to ensure success of the operation, which required the active participation of the wealthy, but in this they failed. Eugène Bizot, a French financial adviser was hired, whose contract did not mention the bank so as not to scare the Russians and the British (the very idea of a bank had vanished, as nobody wanted to finance it). Bizot arrived in 1908. The Iranians remember "a member of the French elite whose intelligence, honesty and distinction were without reproach," if one may believe Seyyed Ziā. Shuster, an American expert who succeeded him in 1911, gave a less flattering portrait: "During the two years which he remained in Teheran he accomplished no actual reforms and conditions went from bad to worse."[16] The National Bank, barely born, died. The British, eager to retain the Imperial Bank's monopoly on issuing bank notes, undoubtedly administered the *coup de grâce*.

The financial collapse of the state forced the various political actors to face the gravity of the situation. After Amin ol-Soltān's assassination, the followers of Sheykh Fazlollāh Nuri returned to Tehran and reached a compromise with their political enemies. As of then, the Supplement to the Constitution, with its article 2, was accepted unanimously. The Shah presented himself in person to Parliament to sign the text on 9 November 1907 and formally renewed his loyalty oath.

However, a few days later, while claiming to adhere to the very principles of the Constitution, Mohammad-Ali Shāh wanted to regain

---

[16] M. SHUSTER, *The Strangling*, p. L, 28.

control. He reproached the Majles of exceeding its authority by interfering in the executive power. He accused some political factions of fomenting intolerable trouble, in particular deploring the demonstrations organized by members of the *anjoman*s from within Parliament. The Shah's protests were met with jeers.[17] In response, the deputies announced that they intended to create a law-enforcement force, composed of volunteers and modeled on the French national guard pre-1871, and to include military training in schools. They also wanted to place the Cossack Brigade – which was still under the Shah's command and obeying Russian officers – under the control of the minister of war. The deputies insisted on the principle of freedom of assembly which prevented them from prohibiting the *anjoman*-s as the government demanded.

From this point, the Shah sought the opportunity to dissolve this seditious Parliament, which, to isolate the sovereign, tried to alienate the government of Nāser ol-Molk (1856–1927). The latter, a Qajar prince, had studied in Oxford; he resigned after six weeks, not wishing to be implicated in the putsch that was being prepared.

On 15 December, militias and hired hands attacked the Majles. The deputies barricaded themselves within the building and stood strong, despite their lack of preparation and ammunition. The attackers withdrew to Canon Square (*Tupkhāne*), where they were reinforced by the royal guard. A crowd of poor people and muleteers were given alcohol and encouraged to yell slogans against the Constitution. Sheykh Fazlollāh Nuri, whose support was indispensable to the Shah to legitimize his coup, was also literally taken to the square so that he might take a public position against Parliament. He balked at remaining among the crowd of drunks. At the same time, the monarch arrested and put in chains his prime minister who had resigned – he was later freed and sent to Europe after the intervention of the British minister – and gave orders to the Cossacks, commanded by Colonel Liakhoff, to attack Parliament. For two days, one might have believed that the *coup d'état* had been a success.

Telegrams of solidarity arrived from across the provinces, proclaiming support for the deputies at the Majles. Parliament had no difficulty mobilizing militias among members of the *anjoman*-s, some of whom were already armed. The next day, when the deputies

---

[17] F. Ādamiat, *Ideolozhi-e nahzat-e Mashrutiyat-e Irān*, II, *Majles-e avval*, pp. 205f.

demanded the Shah's deposition, they received reinforcements of 7,000 men, who positioned themselves around the Bahārestān Palace, where the deputies were seated, and in the neighboring Sepahsālār school-mosque, which was summarily fortified to defend the deputies. Faced with the militias, the 1,500 men of the Shah did not count for much. The Shah had to decide to accept a compromise, which, from their side, the Russians and British pushed the constitutionalists to accept, making them understand that it was preferable to have the monarch remain on the throne to avoid disorder.

Thus Mohammad-Ali Shāh gave in to the demands of the deputies. He accepted that the Majles would be protected by a guard commanded by the deputies themselves and sent a handwritten letter to Parliament to reaffirm his oath of loyalty to the new institutions. For their part, the deputies renewed their allegiance to him. The Shah promised to abstain from intervening in political and legislative decisions. To show that he renounced confrontation, he dismissed his most intransigent adviser, Amir Bahādor, who fled to the Russian legation.

The deputies, no longer having any external enemy, fought among themselves, and split into the Freedom Party (*Āzādikhāhān*) and the Moderates (*Mo'tadelin*). The former, mainly Azerbaijanis, were uncontrollable hotheads. Their leader Seyyed Hasan Taqizāde espoused all social causes but scared the religious elements. Among the moderates, notably, were the ulama and some powerful merchants.

The disagreements became public in March 1908, after the election of the new president of the Majles, Momtāz od-Dowle, who rather favored the Freedom Party. The Shah suspected him of complicity in an attack that had almost cost him his life a few days earlier, when a bomb exploded as the royal car was passing, killing two bystanders. The attack was planned by a group of revolutionaries from the Social Democrat movement, led by an activist and electrical engineer from the Caucasus named Heydar Khān (1880–1921), a classmate of Stalin – and most likely the same man who was behind the assassination of Amin ol-Soltān on 31 August the previous year. Radical elements in the Majles – in particular, *Azali*s such as Seyyed Jamāl Esfahāni and Yahyā Dowlatābādi – were aware of the planned attack. The deputies avoided the worst by advising Mohammad-Ali Shāh to exercise restraint – which he did, with regard to both the police investigation and the punishment of those guilty of causing the death of the victims. The radicals were furious to see that the attack had failed to even damage relations between the Shah and Parliament. Invoking the Constitution, they argued that Heydar Khān and his two conspirators were illegally detained at the royal palace and interrogated without a judicial mandate; the men were released.

Thereafter, the Shah was determined to rid himself of the Constitution and Parliament. On 4 June he left Tehran to take up residence in Bāq-e Shāh under the protection of the Cossacks. A few days later, he had three constitutionalist princes arrested, who were suspected of conspiring to put Zell os-Soltān, his uncle, on the throne, and sent them into exile. He recalled his adviser Amir Bahādor to help him organize a military operation against Parliament. This time, he took care to cut the telegraph line with Tehran. With the excesses of the *anjoman*s turned against them, the situation had become less favorable for the constitutionalists. The Azerbaijani deputies openly demanding the deposition of the monarch worried proponents of the Constitution. While the deputies took up position in the Sepahsālār school-mosque, the Shah demanded the dispersal and departure into exile of eight of the most radical, among whom was the preacher Seyyed Jamāl Esfahāni. The deputies refused.

The attack against the Bahārestān Palace where Parliament resided took place on 23 June 1908, under the command of Colonel Liakhoff. The building was seriously damaged by cannon fire, and, according to British estimates, about 250 constitutionalists lost their lives. Seyyed Jamāl Esfahāni, who had attempted to flee, was captured at Borujerd – about 300 km (190 miles) west of the capital – and executed. Some liberal and radical deputies found refuge in the British embassy and obtained a laissez-passer to leave for Europe. Many among them continued in their support for the constitutionalists. The satirical poet Ali-Akbar Dehkhodā (1879–1956) launched a newspaper in Persian, circulated from Yverdon in Switzerland. The radical Taqizāde mobilized British newspapers and intellectuals but showed himself to be much more moderate and democratic with his friend Edward G. Browne; the professor of Persian literature at Cambridge tried to convince the British liberals to support – politically and financially – the revolutionaries of Tabriz, a city in rebellion, to which Taqizāde returned in December 1908.

In Tehran, Mohammad-Ali Shāh now governed without a constitution and without a parliament, but his power was limited and he was faced with a growing rebellion in the provinces. Martial law was decreed, the anjomans were dissolved, and opponents systematically pursued – some hundred militants were imprisoned. The Russian legation supported the Shah, while the British, afraid of the immoderate behavior of the radicals in the Majles and having to respect the new alliance with the Russians, did little to check the violence or to help the liberals, apart from making some of the opposition leaders leave for Europe. Some ulama obtained safe passage to the holy sites in Ottoman Iraq. The center of resistance was Tabriz, a cosmopolitan city where revolutionary agitation was encouraged from Najaf and Karbala by the grand mojtaheds who condemned the return to absolutism.

5 THE NATIONALISTS' BITTER VICTORY (1908–12)

The first Parliament had not come to the end of its legislative period before internal divisions led to an impasse. Elected hastily, the deputies agreed on very few matters. Some did not hesitate to defy royal authority, while others refused any interference by the clergy in political life. Foreign powers pushed for appeasement; though unanimity was not in their interests, under the premise that a divided Iran would be easier to manipulate, dissolution of the assembly did not serve their interests either.

What did the Iranian people want? The convening of the first Majles had been achieved through the alliance, in Tehran, between the clergy and the reformers in order to limit royal absolutism and to bring political and legal rights to the nation. In the absence of a clearly formulated constitutionalist ideology, and given the immoderation of some radicals, Mohammad-Ali Shāh presented the abolition of the Constitution as a return to order, a move tacitly approved by the Russians and the British. His victory involuntarily gave the Iranian people a political objective and allowed the various classes of society to form a united front. The movement, this time stemming from the provinces, was outspoken in its determination to take over the capital. A new-found solidarity with Europe, the Caucasus, and above all with the provinces (Rasht to the north and Isfahan in the center), as well as with the nomadic tribes, gave the protest movement far greater power.

Following the coup d'état of June 1908 there was little to offer any real hope to the revolutionaries, other than the conviction that the evolution of all societies would lead inexorably to the nation's increased participation in political power. The survivors of the coup fled to Europe or to legations where they were protected by diplomatic law from the threat of the Iranian police. Depending on their place of refuge, or combat, from this time on they presented themselves as revolutionaries, strongly influenced by the Social Democrats of the Caucasus, as nationalists desiring to rid their country of foreign interference, as reformers concerned about social progress and democratic freedoms, or merely as constitutionalists who wanted to ensure, by way of the return of a parliamentary regime, the permanence of the reforms already obtained. The same Hasan Taqizāde who had given revolutionary speeches in progressive circles in Iran presented himself, in his exile in Great Britain, as a democrat concerned with reforms and national sovereignty, values that were more easily communicable in liberal British circles, which supported the constitutionalists against Mohammad-Ali Shāh.

Resistance from the Constitutionalists of Tabriz

It was in Tabriz, situated not far from the Russian border, that the first revolutionary activities had broken out as early as 1903. In 1906, the constitutionalists formed a provincial assembly there and called it *Anjoman-e melli*. This assembly had the status of a political club, like the *anjoman*-s that were covertly or overtly formed in Tehran, as well as that of a "provincial council" as defined in the Supplement to the Constitution.[1] When the first Majles was in session, the Tabriz *anjoman* constantly demanded, by telegram, explanations from the deputies of Azerbaijan about the situation in the capital, while giving them instructions of a generally radical nature – a radicalism that was not shared by other political groups. After the bombardment of the Parliament in Tehran it was the progressives of Tabriz who led resistance against the Shah.

Until then, Tabriz had been the only modern city in Persia. It was populous (with 200,000 inhabitants) and somewhat multi-ethnic; the capital of Azerbaijan was home to an established Armenian Christian community that had been strengthened, at the end of the nineteenth century, by the arrival of Armenian refugees from Anatolia during the first Ottoman persecutions. The schools founded in Tabriz

---

[1] Articles 90 and 91, which were never implemented.

and Urmia by Protestant and Catholic missionaries contributed to maintaining a high level of education, all the more so as they were discreetly open to Muslims. It was in Tabriz that the first caravans from Europe arrived until the opening of the Suez Canal in 1869. From then on, trade increasingly used the route of the Persian Gulf or, after the construction of the railway linking Moscow to Tsaritsyn (now Volgograd) and then to Baku, the route to Russia, via the Caspian Sea. Economic activity progressively moved to Tehran, the destination of new road networks; less off-center in relation to the rest of the country, the capital also increasingly attracted intellectuals.

Despite its historic decline, Tabriz remained the seat of the governorate of the crown prince, who had his own court there, as at the time of the early Qajars. It was here that groups of modern activists gathered, influenced by social democracy and the revolutionaries of the Caucasus. Since the mid-nineteenth century, oil had been exploited in the Baku region, and numerous Iranians from Azerbaijan went to work on the other side of the border, often as seasonal labor. Moreover, although Azari Turkish was the language of the court and the mother tongue of about half the population in Iran, many Azerbaijani intellectuals suffered a kind of ethnic minority complex which induced them to redouble their Persian nationalist fervor. They did not identify with the Sunni Ottomans, even though newspaper reports from Istanbul reached them, and the example of the Ottoman reforms inspired their desire for change. Pan-Turkish propaganda placed Azerbaijan within the boundaries of "Greater Turkey" but had no effect on the Iranian side where allegiance to the Shah and Shiite beliefs were strong. On the other hand, Pan-Islamism, which advocated the coming together of believers to combat European imperialism, found a certain resonance in its resentment toward the Russians and the British.

Thus, Tabriz took the lead in political radicalism. As of 1906, alongside the *Anjoman-e Melli*, semi-secret groups formed militias with the help of armed and experienced men who came to help from the Caucasus. A "Social Democratic Party" (*Ferqe-ye Ejtemāʿiyun-Āmiyun-e Irān, Mojāhed*), sometimes mistaken for a secret society or "Secret Center" (*Markaz-e qeybi*), established links with political groups in Baku, but also with the Second International. The Russian Social Democrats encouraged them, while believing that Iran had to continue its bourgeois revolution and obtain its economic independence before freeing itself from foreign influence.

After the Shah's coup, the *Anjoman* of Tabriz sent a group of 300 volunteers to Tehran to support the Majles, but they returned when they learnt that Mohammad-Ali Shāh had sent troops to besiege their city. The insurgents, relieved by solidarity campaigns in the Caucasus, received support from Armenians, Tatars, and Georgians and plundered the arsenal. At the head of the revolt were two popular and colorful heroes, Bāqer Khān and Sattār Khān. The former was a mason, who had become the strong man of the Sheykhi Khiābān quarter; the latter was a horse-dealer. Their revolutionary convictions and the example of their courage were decisive in maintaining the insurgents' morale. Confronted by government forces, Bāqer Khān was forced to abandon the fight, but Sattār Khān convinced him to take up arms again.

The siege of Tabriz was led by Eyn od-Dowle, the former prime minister, whom the Shah had recalled and appointed governor of Azerbaijan. Unable to break the resistance of the revolutionaries, he declared an end to hostilities and returned to Tehran in October 1908. Other troops were sent to relieve them. We are quite well informed about the political and military evolution of the resistance thanks to the records of various European consuls who remained in the vicinity alongside the colonies of merchants and missionaries. The French consul Alphonse Nicolas, who was born in Iran, left impassioned reports from that period; sympathizing with the liberals, he was informed of even the most trivial pieces of news and rumors.[2] Finally, it was the Russians who imposed the lifting of the siege in April 1909. Profiting from the catastrophic financial situation in which Mohammad-Ali Shāh found himself, they used the pretext of the need to resupply their subjects to relieve the insurgents, but instead established a permanent occupation force.

When the revolutionaries of Tabriz were besieged, many towns in Gilan, a neighboring province, joined their struggle. In Rasht, Sepahdār Tonekāboni, a powerful landed proprietor, was initially sent by Eyn od-Dowle to subdue the rebellion in Tabriz, but he changed sides and placed his men and his large fortune in the service of the constitutionalists. He received support from Armenian *mojāhedin* from the Caucasus, who were headed by an exceptional leader, Yefrem Khān (1868–1912). Yefrem, or Eprem, was born in the Caucasus and during his youth participated in campaigns for the liberation of Armenia, then

---

[2] N. NASIRI-MOGHADDAM, ed., *La Révolution constitutionnelle à Tabriz …*

part of the Ottoman Empire, with the Dashnak Party. Arrested by the Russians and sent to Siberia, he managed to escape and reached Tabriz in 1896. He became an Armenian teacher and finally took up residence in Rasht. In the summer of 1908, this intrepid militant had been able to travel to Baku, where he obtained arms and joined a group of volunteers. Thus, in Rasht he formed a "Sattār committee" – named after the Tabriz activist – which was composed of Armenians and Persians, and another one in Anzali, the more revolutionary *Komite-ye Barq* (Lighting Committee). In May 1909, in Tehran, the Shah tried in vain to take control of the situation, but Yefrem liberated Rasht and Anzali and had Sepahdār Tonekāboni appointed governor of the province, before taking control of Qazvin with an Armenian and Georgian force.

After the siege of Tabriz was lifted, the Azerbaijani revolutionaries were divided on the movement's future. Some, among them Taqizāde, aware of their lack of preparation, were reluctant to march on Tehran. They doubted that they would ever be able to take control of the state and feared that the conquest of the capital by the "rebels," among whom were subjects of the Czar, might give the Russians a pretext to intervene militarily.[3]

During the winter of 1908/9 the liberation movement had also taken over Isfahan, but under very different circumstances. The leaders of the Bakhtyāri nomadic tribes had become masters of the city thanks to their horsemen. They decided to control the government, an agenda notably pushed by Ali Qoli Khān Sardār As'ad (1858–1917), a Bakhtyāri khān who undoubtedly hoped to secure for his tribe a substantial share in the future management of the country. Sardār As'ad had made several journeys to India, the Middle East, and France, where he had been initiated into Freemasonry. He was an anglophile, and the British held him in high esteem. "The people adored him," writes an Iranian historian, usually critical of Qajar elite, "he was a just man, insusceptible to bribery at a time when corruption was the norm."[4]

Within a year, despite the heterogeneous nature of the revolutionary troops, the military situation had shifted rapidly in favor of the partisans of the Constitution.

---

[3] See I. Afshār, ed., *Owrāq-e tāze-yāb-e Mashrutiyat va naqsh-e Taqizāde*, pp. 25f.

[4] M. Bāmdād, *Tārikh-e rejāl-e Irān*, II, p. 451. See A. Sa'idi-Sirjāni, "Baktiari / Haj 'Ali-Qoli Kan Sardar As'ad."

The Return of the Constitutionalists

In May 1909, under the pressure of events, and even more of British and Russian influence, the Shah attempted to restore the Constitution. But the battle was lost before it began. After many months, the troubles in the provinces had isolated the capital, and slowly Mohammad-Ali Shāh had lost the credibility he had initially enjoyed as guarantor of the return of order because he had not been able to use his advantage to stimulate trade. The *bāzāri*-s were divided between two concerns. On the one hand, there was a need for security so that goods might circulate and be sold in safety. On the other, was the need for social stability: transactions often relied on mutual trust and sometimes needed to be legitimized by clerical endorsement. In the absence of a strong state, religious authority and popular consensus were indispensable to them. The Constitution seemed to them to be a rational framework to counter the effects of despotism, and they favorably received the revolutionaries despite their political inexperience.

In mid-July 1909 the constitutionalists took Tehran. The monarch fled to the Russian legation and accepted abdication in favor of his 11-year-old son, Ahmad, who was installed with a regent. A pension was given to the deposed king who went into exile in Odessa.

Ahead of new elections, the revolutionaries put in place a "supreme assembly" led by the Bakhtyāri chief, Sardār As'ad. The assembly, which numbered 300 persons, replaced Parliament in urgent decision-making, while the government was entrusted to Sepahdār-e A'zam Tonekāboni, the powerful landowner of Gilan, who was protected by the Russians. A Russophile landlord and an anglophile tribal chief: such were the leaders chosen by the victorious constitutionalists. After the death of the first regent in 1910, his successor, Nāser ol-Molk, was a prince who had studied in England. In other words, the revolution had more a liberal flavor than a popular one, a flavor that was soon to become more nationalist, despite its paradoxical links with imperial powers, than it was religious.

Those who had been compromised by their support of Mohammad-Ali were in danger. First and foremost this included Sheykh Fazlollāh Nuri, who was recognized as the greatest of the Tehran ulama at that time. He consulted the mojtaheds of Najaf by telegram to ascertain whether he could count on their support. "We cannot give you a guarantee," they replied, "only the nation may ensure your safety." The Russians offered their protection, but, outraged, he refused to raise their flag over his house, a condition of their support. Those clergymen close to Nuri left for the provinces, others "went on pilgrimage," and still others went to the Russian or Ottoman embassies.

The theologian himself was only arrested two weeks after the Shah's abdication, as though he had been granted time to flee. Brought before a revolutionary tribunal presided over by Sheykh Ebrāhim Zanjāni (1857–1934), a very progressive theologian with connections to Masonic circles, Nuri was found guilty of having legitimated Mohammad-Ali Shāh's demands in the name of Islam and was condemned to death. Yefrem Khān, the Armenian who meanwhile had become chief of police, had, according to some witnesses, intervened in the trial, an act of infamy for traditional Muslims who considered non-Muslim minorities as "protected" and excluded Christians from any judicial function. The Shiite religious authorities of Ottoman Iraq were consulted and approved the sentence. Nuri was hanged on 31 July 1909 in Tupkhāne Square in front of a large crowd, on the anniversary of the birth of the first Shiite Imam.

The Split between the Clergy and the Constitutionalists

Nuri's execution caused the moderate ulama to withdraw their support for the revolution. Even though they disapproved of Fazlollāh Nuri, they recognized that partisans of the contemporary Western order would not hesitate in getting rid of too scrupulous Muslims.

Iranian historiography echoed the hostility of the constitutionalists toward Sheykh Fazlollāh, an example of a deeply conservative theologian. It was only in the 1960s that the brilliant essayist, Jalāl Āl-e Ahmad (1923–69), a former communist militant, recalling the clerical origins of his own family and desiring to promote the historical image of a besieged country, changed history's interpretation of Nuri, by referencing a flattering biography that had just been published by a grandson of the anti-constitutionalist theologian. Since then the reactionary theologian has become an Iranian martyr, a victim of Westernization, and a lone figure in voicing his opposition among Europeanized intellectuals who had renounced their heritage in the face of the seduction of modern imperialism.[5] The Islamic Revolution in its turn presented him as a forebear of their cause, despite Nuri's support for absolute monarchy and his categorical rejection of popular suffrage, two points on which modern reformist politicians could not make concessions in the face of clerical objections.

The elimination of this theologian established the split between the Shiite clergy and progressive intellectuals. It also simultaneously doomed the Constitutional Revolution to failure because it violently marked the rift between secular reformers and Islam. Several events illustrate how the clergy distanced themselves from constitutional institutions after 1909. An Iranian theologian who lived in Ottoman Iraq, Mirzā Mohammad-Hoseyn Nā'ini (1860–1936) had earlier written a theological treatise in Persian to bolster constitutionalism with Islamic arguments. Taking the theme of Muslim apologetics as his focus, he maintained that the principles of popular representation, the delegation of authority, parliamentary deliberation, and other causes such as social justice and equality could be found in the Koran or in the traditions of the Prophet and the Imams – in short, that these institutions conformed to Islamic principles. Stricken with remorse after 1909, he gathered copies of his own book to destroy them.[6]

To understand the mood in relations between the different wings of the constitutionalists in November 1909 when the second Parliament met, the words of one of the secular deputies who welcomed Seyyed Abdollāh Behbahāni when he presented himself to the Majles on his return from exile, without having stood for election, are particularly informative:[7]

> You deceive yourself if you think that you may continue as in the past to interfere in political matters; things have really changed. Just as nobody envies Azod ol-Molk's post of regent [because the royal authority faded out], nobody envies your role as religious leader. It is preferable that you occupy yourself with religious law without henceforth interfering in any manner

[5] J. Āl-e Ahmad, *Dar khedmat va khiānat-e rowshanfekrān*, II, p. 232. Āl-e Ahmad's source is T. Kiā, *Nahib-e jombesh-e adabi. Shāhin.*
[6] See A. Hairi, *Si'ism and Constitutionalism*, p. 158. Nā'ini's book, *Tanbih ol-omma*, was republished by ayatollah Mahmud Tāleqāni in 1955.
[7] Y. Dowlatābādi, *Hayāt-e Yahyā*, [Memoirs], III, p. 128.

whatsoever in politics, and that you would do well to make a distinction between religious and civil law.

The other Seyyed, the liberal Mohammad Tabātabā'i, who also had played an important role at the beginning of popular mobilization, confirmed, prior to his death, this impression of failure. He recalled that after having been banished to Mashhad, when he came back to participate in politics at the return of constitutionalism, he indeed found a Parliament, but "not the one that I had wanted."[8]

In 1909, some ulama remained to exercise the function stipulated in article 2 of the Supplement to the Constitution and to become members of the council of religious scholars who had the power to censure parliamentary decisions. But the legislators who met in 1914, and after 1921, were forced to abandon the application of this article, which had been so difficult to write and proven impossible to gain majority approval on, as no one could be found who was willing to enact this religious censorship in an institution that appeared to have turned its back on the clergy and Islam.[9] The clerics who sat in the Majles later stood for election – or the simulacrum that took its place.

The Second Parliament

The elections for the second Parliament were organized shortly after the writing of a new electoral law. Henceforth, suffrage was no longer determined by guild or social category, but only by region. A notable novelty was the enfranchisement of non-Muslim minorities (with the exception of the Bahāis and Bābis), who could now each elect a representative. This rule would remain in force until the Islamic Revolution and was inserted into the Constitution of 1979. In reality, under the guise of granting electoral rights to "minorities," this system separated them from the nation, because a Jew, a Zoroastrian, or a Christian could not vote for a Muslim nor put himself forward for the vote of Muslims. Finally, the number of deputies from Tehran (15) was considerably reduced as compared with the provinces (101), which comprised a more conservative majority.

---

[8] "*Majles dorost shod, vali na āntowr ke man mi-khāstam,*" in E. KĀZEMIYE, "Yād-dāsht-hā-ye," p. 473.
[9] See Md TORKAMĀN, "Nezārat-e hey'at-e mojtahedin."

The second Majles met after November 1909, with two major parties: the Democratic Party (*Hezb-e Demokrāt*), dominated by Taqizāde; and the Moderates (*E'tedāliun*), still dominated by the two Seyyeds, Behbahāni, and Tabātabā'i. To deflect attention from their link with social democracy (*Ejtemā'iun-āmmiun*), which had caused widespread public anxiety in 1908, the Democrats dropped the word "social" (*ejtemā'iun*). But their foreign-sounding name ensured a question continued to hang over them in the public's mind: some of the most well-known militant democrats, such as Heydar Khān (the culprit behind the bomb attempt on the Shah of February 1908 and, most likely, of Atabak's assassination the year before) and the Azari journalist Rasulzāda, both had Russian citizenship. In Tabriz, the Democrats were known as "*Melli*," meaning either "national" or "popular."[10]

Neither of the two parties held a majority, which placed the Majles in a position of weakness, precisely at a time when there was no real king and the state finances had not improved. The unity of the country was not directly in danger, but Russian troops continued to occupy part of the north after the "liberation" of Tabriz. This situation played into the hands of the Bakhtyāri tribal chiefs, who dominated the government thanks to their wealth, military efficacy, and prestige. Despite the immobility of political power, two important decisions were taken: the hiring, firstly, of an American financial mission and, secondly, of Swedish officers to organize a gendarmerie in order to establish security on the trade routes and, by the same token, counterbalance the military might of the Cossack Brigade.[11] In these two cases, the constitutionalists appealed to citizens of countries that were considered to be neutral owing to their remoteness and weak international ambitions.

The opinion had always been sensitive as to the Muslim character of the new institutions. In 1910, two Ismaili Muslims (Āqā Khān's community) upon returning from a pilgrimage to Mashhad, were put on trial by a local theologian because they refused to renounce Ismailism and convert to Twelver Shiism. The theologian with the connivance of the ulama of the holy city condemned them to death, a sentence which

---

[10] See M. ETTEHĀDIYE, *Peydāyesh va tahavvol-e ahzāb-e siāsi*, pp. 199f.
[11] The counterbalance is a later justification. The gendarmerie was created to avoid the British creating a British-officered force to protect the roads in the south. The British also paid for the gendarmerie until 1915.

was carried out. Addressing the assembly, Taqizāde demanded that the police chief, the Armenian Yefrem Khān, arrest the judge responsible for this double murder. But Seyyed Abdollāh Behbahāni, who wanted to defend the clergy, appealed to the Najaf ulama to condemn Taqizāde, asserting that he dishonored Shiite clerics. The Iraqi ulama gave in and issued a fatwa declaring Taqizāde guilty of "ideological corruption" (*fesād-e maslak*). Without waiting for the anathema to be pronounced, Taqizāde requested leave from Parliament and left for Tabriz, from where he fled to Europe and then the USA.[12]

Shortly thereafter, on 16 July 1910, a radical militant killed Behbahāni as he was preparing to read Taqizāde's sentence to the Majles. In merely a few days, Parliament had lost two of its most diametrically opposed figures, whose cooperation had undoubtedly contributed more than anything else to the success of the constitutional movement.

The Shuster Mission and the Russian Ultimatum

The American Morgan Shuster (1877–1960) arrived in Persia in May 1911, heading a delegation of five financial advisers, about six months after he was first officially contacted about this mission. He remained in Tehran for between seven and eight months. The constitutionalists, in hiring this esteemed foreigner, finally wanted to put an end to financial excesses, corruption, privileges, and foreign interference – in short all the ills encountered by young democracies when social revolution has not changed attitudes and the balance of power, as Shuster's memoirs suggest.[13] But it also evidenced the cultural distance between the American advisers, convinced of the benefits of a modern and effective administration, and the reality of a traditional, rigidly hierarchical society, where the complex relations of loyalty and family guaranteed individuals rights which no rational law could offer them.

Despite the contempt that he showed for his Belgian and French predecessors, Shuster adopted their projects, notably when he tried to establish a proper fiscal administration and an income tax. The

---

[12] See I. AFSHĀR, ed., *Owrāq-e tāze-yāb-e Mashrutiyat*, pp. 207f, especially pp. 230–31; H. TAQIZĀDA, *Zendagi-e tufāni*, pp. 152f.
[13] M. SHUSTER, *The Strangling of Persia*.

implementation of this tax, which more than a century later has still not been entirely achieved, assumed that quite a large number of Iranians had salaries and that these salaries were actually paid. As one Iranian historian rightly remarked, the naiveté of Shuster, who had been educated in a politically free country, was comprehensible, but less so was that of the Persians who entrusted him with enormous powers without waiting for him to have grasped the particularities of the country's financial system. Instead, at this time, Iranians and, in particular, the Democrats, would lose their ability to think critically and give any European (unless perhaps he was Russian or British) or American advisor carte blanche.[14]

Shuster felt real sympathy for the constitutionalists. His efforts to formulate a financial law to protect against foreign interference and which could be enforced demonstrate the challenges Iran now faced because no real administrative modernization had ever been undertaken before. Shuster's main adversaries, from whom he could not disentangle his constitutionalist friends, were the Russian and British legations. The Russian troops which had liberated Tabriz in April 1909 had not left, despite their promises to do so. Meanwhile, the British were trying to curtail the powers of the Treasurer-General by luring the Persian government with the promise of a new loan of £1.25 million, whose repayment would be managed by the Belgian Joseph Mornard, thereby undermining Shuster's efforts. Moreover, on 16 October 1910, the government was given an ultimatum – which appeared to be unrelated to Shuster's operations – demanding that British-Indian guards be posted along the roads, which, although paid for by the Iranian government, would be under British control.

Two cases would intensify British and Russian hostility toward Shuster and result in his untimely dismissal. Shuster had planned to form a special force tasked with the collection of the various taxes in the Persian kingdom, because neither the army nor the newly created gendarmerie was able to accomplish that task. This force of armed agents, in the service of the Treasury, at first numbered 1,000 men, and it was planned to increase that number to 10,000 or even 12,000 men. To head up the taskforce Shuster wanted to hire a British officer, Major Stokes (1875–1948) who knew Persia very well. He had served with the Indian army and had just ended a four-year mission as military attaché in Tehran;

---

[14] A. Kasravi, *Tārikh-e hejdah sāle-ye Āzarbāyjān ...*, p. 229.

he spoke, read, and wrote Persian fluently. But the British legation placed a condition on his appointment, one that was dictated by the Russian minister: Stokes could be recruited for the Treasury but without any jurisdiction in the northern region. Acceptance of this condition would have meant recognizing Russian sovereignty in the northern territory, and Shuster refused to do this. Such an application of the Anglo-Russian Accord of 1907, despite its recognition in the preamble of the inalienable sovereignty of the country, clearly undermined the basic rights of the Persian people.

The second case is linked to this, because it involves the Russian and British legations. The ex-Shah's brother, Prince Sho'ā os-Saltane, had tried to arrange the return of Mohammad-Ali Mirzā to the throne with the help of the Russians in September 1911, an attempt that failed thanks to the talent and military courage of Yefrem Khān – the latter was promoted on that occasion to the rank of commander of the army in the north. Soon after, on 4 October, the government decided to seize the rebellious prince's property for the benefit of the Treasury, notifying the legations concerned about these actions because of the protected status of the prince. The Treasury gendarmes took the main residence of Sho'ā os-Saltane situated in a garden close to Shuster's Treasury headquarter, in which some of the prince's wives and children still lived. The men were busy doing an inventory of the furniture when they were removed by Cossacks. The Russian legation had intervened, alleging the capitulary privileges, on the pretext that the proprietor of the palace was a Russian subject. Furthermore, to legitimize his actions to the British legation, the Russian plenipotentiary minister produced evidence of a debt the prince owed to the Imperial Bank, against which the palace was listed as security.

The affair took an unexpected turn when correspondents for Reuters and *The Times* of London interviewed Shuster. At the instigation of the Foreign Office, *The Times* published an unfavorable commentary about the American stating that his judgment was "inequitable" and "without foundation." On 21 October 1911, Shuster published in *The Times* a very detailed open letter about the affair and appealed to the generous and democratic sentiments of the British readers, defending the sovereign rights of Persia against the unjustifiable interference of the imperial powers.

To settle the matter, when the government of the Czar was certain that Washington would not support Shuster, the Russian legation sent an ultimatum to the Persian government, ordering it to dismiss the American, not to employ foreign advisers without the agreement of the Russian and British legations, and to meet the cost of moving the Russian troops to the north of Persia (the first elements were already stationed in Rasht). The ultimatum expired after one month, on 24 December. The deputies rejected the ultimatum, preferring to dissolve the Majiles without calling for new elections, despite the acceptance of Russia's demands by the government.[15] Shuster was dismissed de facto.

End of the Majles, End of the Revolution?

In the days that followed, Russian troops invaded the north of Iran, where they engaged in a merciless political purge, notably in Tabriz and Mashhad, which were disarmed. The leaders of the constitutionalists, including the venerated theologian Seqat ol-Eslām (1861–1911) were hanged in Tabriz on 31 December, which, in that year, fell on the day of mourning for the passing of Imam Hoseyn. The reverberations of this takeover prompted numerous meetings and declarations of solidarity in Europe within socialist circles. The British minister spoke of a "reign of terror" in Tabriz, where the reactionary Samad Khān Shojā od-Dowle had become de facto governor with the support of the occupying troops.[16]

The Russians went on to provide further evidence of their extreme brutality in Mashhad on 30 March 1912, when they shelled the sanctuary of Imam Reza, one of the most important Shiite shrines, and used machine-guns to disperse the crowd, killing more than 500.[17] This attack, which severely damaged the sanctuary's dome, was carried out under the pretext of restoring order. In reality, it was an agent on the Czar's payroll who had provoked the troubles by concocting propaganda for the restoration of Mohammad-Ali Shāh. The European press, soon occupied with the sinking of the *Titanic*, did not mention the event, but the

---

[15] See W. M. SHUSTER, *The Strangling of Persia*, pp. 206f; A. KASRAVI, *Tārikh-e hejdah sāla-ye Āzarbāyjān*, pp. 234f.

[16] Details about this "reign of terror" can be found in E. G. BROWNE, *Letters from Tabriz: The Russian Suppression of the Iranian Constitutional Movement*.

[17] Detailed report in Md-Hasan ADIB HARAVI, *Hadiqat ol-razaviye*, pp. 210f; H. L. RABINO, *Mashrute-ye Gilān az yād-dāsht-hā-ye Rābino*, pp. 113–46.

Iranians felt it was an unpardonable insult. The situation was less dramatic in the south, where the population stood up to the British occupation by boycotting foreign goods and demanding the Imperial Bank change the paper money in circulation for hard cash.

Six years after the first demonstrations, the Constitutional Revolution collapsed into chaos. Political conscience, the diffusion of ideas, and the desire for reform had made considerable progress. Some achievements were touted as historic conquests, and the monarchy did not regain the freedom of action that it had enjoyed under the early Qajars. But society at large was stymied by the increasingly visible and brutal interference of foreigners, and the British, in whom Iranian liberals had at first placed their hope of support in their struggles against absolutism, henceforth showed solidarity with the Russians.

The most serious failure of the Constitution was the disaffection of the Shiite clergy. The latter had been one of the first actors to plead for the people's right to justice, but it had refused to go all the way toward extending full democratic rights, held back by the limitations of traditional theological discourse. The ulama were not ready to accept that political life could be independent of the hegemony of Islam. Demands for equality before the law, for freedom of the individual, and for national representation could only result, in their view, in the negation of the central role that Islam had until then played in structuring social relations.

The great diversity of opinions, the participation of non-Muslims in events, and the profusion of written documents attesting to the ideological explosion of the time all serve to show that the desire for reform had ripened. Aspirations for freedom and justice remained. The spirit of hope that had swept across Persia between 1906 and 1911 had left a lasting impression. The reformers had learnt that political conquests should no longer rely on foreign assistance. Iran had to its cost entered the international game of strategy that would soon see Europe and the entire world set ablaze.

Despite overthrowing a reactionary monarch, the new regime did not have the strength to resist foreign pressures effectively. The dissolution of Parliament in December 1911, without immediate plans for new elections, showed the weakness of public support for the reformers and created a precedent for the political class, which from then on considered the authority of the nation's deputies as secondary. The manipulation of the constitutional regime that continued until 1979 would probably not have happened if from the very beginning national representation had been able to withstand the Russian ultimatum.

6 IRAN IN THE GREAT WAR

In 1912, the Persian state had never been so weak. The suspension, for the second time, of the Constitution and the occupation of northern Iran by Russian troops plunged the country into a situation that was diametrically opposed to what it had known in 1906, when the Shah, in his famous edict, had convened the first Parliament and responded to the desires of the demonstrators. The state was deprived of an efficient government, devoid of financial means, without an army, and being drained off by politicians who passively admired the progress of Europe, many of whom were idle and wealthy aristocrats behaving as parasites. The great revolutionary ideals, timorous stirrings of national or patriotic sentiment, and social democratic activism seemed only to have served to destroy the arrogance of royal power and to hand the benefits of that destruction over to foreigners. The Anglo-Russian Accord of 1907 had divided Iranian territory into zones where the Persians themselves did not know who ruled them. The financial reorganization, the objective of which was to guarantee the state's resources, had been paralyzed before it had even started to take place .

Even more seriously, the dissidence of the mollas would henceforth deprive the political establishment of popular support and of the trust of those elements of the population less open to Westernization. In 1891–92, during the boycott of the Tobacco Regie, the ulama had rallied behind a protest movement that, thanks to them, was of a considerable size. But since the ulama's split with the constitutionalist reformers, politicians were moving ever further from their fellow citizens who for the most part retained their traditional loyalty to the clergy. What reforms could prove sustainable, given the numerous ambiguities of a modern ideology drawing sometimes on religious traditions, sometimes on humanist democracy, and sometimes on the commitment and determination of the Bābis and the Freemasons?

In the early 1910s, the Persians nevertheless felt there were reasons to be hopeful. First, the political and administrative institutions of their country had undergone modernization, even if they were not yet fully in place. The Constitution was no longer applied, but it remained as a reference. Better adapted institutions transmitted modern knowledge that would create a more exacting elite more conscientious of their civic duty; among other modern schools, were the Dār ol-fonun school, the Roshdiye schools, the School of Political Science of Tehran (established in 1899 by Hasan Khān Moshir od-Dowle Pirniā, who hired French teachers for it), not to mention the numerous schools run by Christian missions and the Alliance israélite universelle. French remained the common language and the medium to diffuse international culture, scientific curiosity, and political ideology to this elite, elements that would limit the effects of Anglo-Russian domination. Rooted in history and the wounds inflicted by foreign interference, national or patriotic consciousness appealed ever more insistently for revival.

Finally, since the assassination of Nāser od-Din Shāh in 1896, the Persian question had continued to preoccupy political circles and receive coverage in the Western press. Numerous scholarly books and articles published in Great Britain (Lord Curzon, E. G. Browne), in France (V. Bérard; G. Demorgny; A. Nicolas), and in the USA (M. Shuster) soon after the Constitutional Revolution show how closely the events in Persia were followed abroad. The revolution, the fall of the Shah, and the military intervention by the Russians were a clear concern to the British who kept a close eye on events unfolding in Persia. As we have seen, Shuster brought his dispute with the Russians to the readers of *The Times*. The India question and the looming prospect of competition between colonial empires and a shift in global strategy in Europe kept Western diplomats on tenterhooks long before concerns were raised about the security of oil production. Persia was a major theater of international affairs, even if it did not actively play a leading role.

Although the principle of Persia's independence was confirmed in the preamble of the Anglo-Russian Accord in 1907, this did not mean that the two neighboring empires respected its sovereignty, but rather that each party would not encroach on the domain of the competitor and would maintain their alliance in the case of conflict with Germany. In reality, Persian independence was trampled upon, despite the immediate and courageous protests of the Minister of Foreign Affairs Hasan Khān Moshir od-Dowle (1871–1935). In the absence of British resistance, in 1911, the Russians were even ready to exploit the dissolution of the Majles and march as far as Tehran – their troops were already occupying Qazvin – to restore Mohammad-Ali Shāh to the throne. Both sides tried to grant a new loan to the Persian government to allow it to re-establish order while at the same time pushing it further into dependence.

From 1912, the British Admiralty's transition from coal to oil to propel its ships gave Persia new strategic importance. Henceforth, oil became a leading concern in London's direct interests. The oil reserves brought Iran considerable revenue, leading increasingly to greed and resentment when Iranian nationalists realized that their subterranean resources were making foreigners richer than they were making the Iranians themselves and that they had little control over any stage of the exploitation of their mineral interest. Meanwhile the British attempted to bypass Iranian sovereignty over Khuzestan to safeguard access to the strategically important oil supply.

Decadence of a Dynasty

At the head of the state was Ahmad Shāh (1898–1930). Aged eleven when his father was deposed, he now represented the only guarantee of political continuation. He would have to wait until his sixteenth birthday, on 21 July 1914 to formally sit on the throne that his father contested after having made several unsuccessful attempts to reclaim it.

Now a constitutional monarch, Ahmad Shāh only reigned during the war. Subject to many foreign pressures, he remained the symbol of Iran's decadence. This timid, young monarch, hung up about his puffy and potbellied physical appearance, libidinous, and avaricious to the point of obsession, amassed wealth as though his father's dismissal had convinced him that he in turn would suffer the same fall from grace and that he should cushion himself against such an inevitablity.

The British did not fail to exploit his weakness, knowing that essentially their interests could be bought from the Shah.

Ahmad Shāh was proficient in Russian and French, and was the first Iranian monarch to converse directly with Europeans and read Western literature and newspapers. Yet despite the efforts of the constitutionalists to provide him with an education appropriate to his function, he never showed any real interest in politics nor any concern for the happiness of the Persians whose welfare preoccupied him much less than his own. In 1919, he made his first journey to Europe and invested his fortune in the Paris Exchange, only taking an interest in the prosperity of French capitalism and in bourgeois pleasures. He despaired of his country, while the people loved him all the more because he had not presented a threat to them. In 1925, when the prospect of returning to his country to defend his throne was open to him, he preferred the casinos of Monte Carlo and Deauville to the uncertain pleasures of political intrigue, and favored whining political declarations to European ears over the starchy palaces of his own country, where he found the festivities provincial and the women insufficiently easy .

On the eve of the outbreak of war in Europe, the Persian state found itself in a precarious situation. The former Shah continued to plot to retake the throne, and the Russians had not given up on such a restoration, doing so only after implausible negotiations – with the British. The weakening of the constitutionalist camp in Tehran and Tabriz, with the elimination or exile of most of the political leaders, was such that many Iranians seemed resigned to a return to the previous order. With the acceptance of the Russian ultimatum of December 1911, the government of Samsām os-Saltane could not hire foreign officials without first consulting the British and Russians. From that point, Tehran de facto adhered to the stipulations of the Anglo-Russian Agreement of 1907.

The Constitution remained in force, but new elections were postponed indefinitely. The new Majles would not meet until 1 November 1914, when the international storm had already reached Persia. The British wanted the restoration of Parliament, which seemed to them a guaranteed way of to staving off excessive Russian influence. The Russians, for their part, feared the excesses of Social Democracy and preferred the pragmatism that had been imposed following acceptance of their ultimatum.

The rivalry between the two powers was played out in other arenas, in particular in Azerbaijan where they were opposed as to the choice of governor. During the invasion of the Russian troops in December 1911–January 1912, a feudal landowner, Samad Khān Shojā' od-Dowle (1855–1917), took advantage of the opportunity to take revenge on the constitutionalists of Tabriz who loathed him. He starved the city by plundering the caravans that supplied it and as a final insult the Russians installed him at the head of the province. The official governor, a prince and officer of the Persian Cossack Brigade was forced to seek refuge in the British consulate but committed suicide at the very moment that the Russians agreed to give him a laissez-passer. Everyone expected that the new governor would proclaim the return of Mohammad-Ali Mirzā to the throne.

In a countermove, the British had Sepahdār-e A'zam ("supreme commander of the armies") Tonekāboni appointed governor by the Tehran government. This powerful landowner from Gilan was known to have enjoyed Russian protection before siding with the revolutionaries and leading the first government after the conquest of Tehran in 1909. The Russians objected that they could not accept a governor who was an ally of Armenian *fedā'i*s, who were reputed to have been infiltrated by revolutionaries and Social Democrats. Finally, they gave in and Shojā' od-Dowle, leaving the position in Tabriz, would remain governor of his fiefdom of Marāqa, but on the condition of not spreading propaganda in favor of Mohammad-Ali Mirzā. Moreover, to consolidate their influence over the province, the Russians demanded an increase in the number of Cossacks stationed in Azerbaijan.

In an apparent reversal – though not unusual in his case – the *Sepahdār*, who went to Tabriz in September 1912, did not waste time in finding common ground with Shojā' od-Dowle. The two men agreed on the return of the former Shah and thus, on the overthrow of the constitutional government, which, at the time, was dominated by the chiefs of the Bakhtyāri tribe. With the help of the Russians, Sepahdār and Shojā' od-Dowle sought to confer the government of Tehran on Sa'd od-Dowle (1841–1929), a constitutionalist who had rallied behind Mohammad-Ali Shāh after the coup d'état of June 1908. This scheming soon came to an end. Sepahdār-e A'zam left for Europe, after writing a bitter letter to the Regent about the demise of the kingdom; Sa'd od-Dowle disappeared from the scene; and Shojā' od-Dowle remained de facto governor of Tabriz. Confusion was endemic.

In 1913, the British, aware that the Bakhtyāris had become unpopular, succeeded in securing the appointment of a government led by Alā' os-Saltane (1838–1918), "a man with hardly any competence, an old naive man in whom the British had confidence."[1] In the government sat moderate constitutionalists belonging to the political establishment such as the former presidents of the Majles, Mostashār od-Dowle, Momtāz od-Dowle; the former detested prime minister of 1906, Eyn od-Dowle; the two brothers Mirzā Hasan Khān Vosuq od-Dowle (1872–1951) and Ahmad Khān Qavām os-Saltane (1873–1955); and nationalist intellectuals such as Mirzā Hasan Khān Moshir od-Dowle. These liberal and nationalist ministers would reappear in the raft of governments that were formed and dissolved over the years to come.

Iran's "Neutrality"

The aftershocks of the outbreak of war in Europe in August 1914 were felt in even the most remote Iranian provinces. On 1 November, in Tehran, the Allies put pressure on Iran to obtain a commitment that it would side with them. A royal edict proclaimed the neutrality of the country:

> Given that the blaze of war has unfortunately set fire to Europe and that it is possible that the conflict will extend to our borders, as we have friendly relations with the different belligerents, so as to inform the population of our intention to preserve our good relations with the belligerents, we declare and command . . . that our government will choose a position of neutrality vis-à-vis the belligerents and will maintain its friendly relations with them. [The state's agents] will have to avoid, in all circumstances, on land and at sea, any act in favor or to the detriment of one or the other of the warring parties or to supply or transport arms destined for one of them.[2]

It was an expedient declaration which Persia hoped would disentangle it from its Russian and British neighbors. In reality, until the end of the conflict both the Persian public and political personnel

---

[1] J. ZARQĀM-BORUJENI, *Dowlat-hā-ye asr-e Mashrutiyat*, p. 83.
[2] A.-A. SEPEHR MOVARREKH OD-DOWLE, *Irān dar Jang-e bozorg-e 1914–1918*, p. 89.

sympathized with the Ottoman and German camp, both out of hostility to the powers that had violated its sovereignty and out of a sense of Pan-Islamic solidarity.

The question of neutrality was not merely theoretical and ideological, at least for the British who were the only ones to verbally agree to the government's neutrality. They were aware that the great majority of Iranians detested them and that most Persians would prefer to side with Istanbul and Berlin rather than with London and St Petersburg. But the British, with their fleet dependent on oil, had a major strategic reason to keep Iran out of the conflict. For this reason, in 1914, the British state took a majority share (53%) in the company which exploited oil in the South – since 1909 Knox d'Arcy had sold the rights of this concession to a company called the Anglo-Persian Oil Company (APOC). Thus London ensured the delivery of technical and material supplies to the installations involved in oil production and refining during the war, without depending on American reserves.

The Iranian Nationalists: The Committee of National Defense

In October 1915, the war in Europe seemed to shift in the favor of the Axis powers, who succeeded in linking up with the Ottomans across Serbia and Bulgaria, while the Franco-British operation in the Dardanelles proved a fiasco.

Despite their declaration of neutrality, the Persians began secret discussions with the Germans about an alliance. But they demanded guarantees of sovereignty and integrity which the Germans were reluctant to provide, because they themselves did not want to thwart Ottoman ambitions for the annexation of the Turkic-speaking Persian provinces. Persia also demanded a significant financial commitment, so that, notably, it might pay off the Russian and British debt.

On their part, the Russians, to prevent Persia from joining with the Ottoman and German empires, decided to send an army corps to Qazvin. Commanded by General Baratov, it consisted of 8,000 cavalry and 6,000 infantry. In Tehran, there was little doubt that the Russians would march on the capital. The diplomats of the allied countries supported this advance, arguing that a pro-German coup d'état would put the legations in danger. On 15 November, Ahmad Shāh caused a political storm by making preparations to move to Isfahan escorted by the gendarmerie

under the orders of Colonel Edwall a Swedish officer. In the end, he decided
not to leave. Following negotiations conducted in great confusion, pro-
British ministers were appointed to the government, giving the Allies
a guarantee of the state's neutrality, while *nationalist* deputies, accompanied by the German plenipotentiary minister left Tehran. The nationalists
(*melli*) stood for the rejection of the increasingly overt Russian and British
supervision and demanded actual respect for Iranian sovereignty, in which
they trusted Germany more; the term *melli* could here equally well be
translated as "patriots." They gathered in Qom where they founded
a Committee of National Defense (*Komite-ye defā'-e melli*) under the
leadership of a deputy of the Democratic Party, Prince Soleymān Mirzā.[3]
The committee claimed to represent central authority and relied on the
support of the gendarmerie, reinforced by Ottoman elements. But General
Baratov had little difficulty in defeating them. His troops marched as far as
Isfahan, from where, on 16 March 1916, they ejected the Democrats who
had, with German help, taken over the local government. Persia was by
now in an even more precarious situation than in 1911. The third Majles
had ceased to exist. The deputies who remained in Tehran were insufficient
in number to allow the assembly to meet and the two-year term of the
legislature had ended before new elections could be organized. The central
government was no more than the puppet of the Allies and had only
telegraphic contact with the provinces, with little direct control.

The Committee of National Defense established itself in
Kermānshāh, near the Ottoman border (Iraq) where it formed
a "national government" in exile. Regrouping members of the
Democratic Party, under German protection, it was led by the governor
of the region of neighboring Lorestān, Nezām os-Saltane, whose role
was incongruous in view of the fact that he was an anglophile.[4] Of the
gendarmes who had remained loyal to him he tried to maintain 8,000
badly equipped men, who formed a "national" army. It was both
a heterogeneous and divided force, because its officers – Swedes,
Ottomans, and tribal chiefs – all wanted to be in command.

---

[3] Also known as Mohsen Eskandari (1862–1944). This outstanding personality was later
portrayed as a British spy by Khālesi, because Rezā Khān drew him skillfully into his
government in 1923 (see Md-M. al-KHALISI, *La vie de l'ayatollah Mahdi al-Khâlisi*,
p. 314f; 350); however, in 1925 he refused to vote for a change of dynasty. Later, he
participated in the creation of the Toudeh (Communist) Party in 1942.

[4] P. AVERY, *Modern Iran*, p. 195. Rezā-Qoli Khān Nezām os-Saltane Māfi (1867–1924) at the
end of the war lived in exile in Istanbul; after a sojourn in Paris he became governor of
Khorasan under the government of Rezā Khān in 1923.

The foremost Persian officers were arrested and sent to Mosul, and Nezām os-Saltane dismissed the Swedes, whom he did not trust. The Russian advance, in May 1916, forced this government to flee to Baghdad. The following summer, when the city was retaken by the Ottomans, Nezām os-Saltane returned to Kermānshāh and for eight months maintained the fiction of a nationalist government. After the British conquest of Baghdad in May 1917, the nationalists withdrew to Mosul, and the Germans ceased to support them.

German Propaganda and Operations

From the start of the war, the Germans held secret discussions with the government in Tehran so as to enlist Persia against the Russians and British. To finance their propaganda, notably among the Swedish officers of the Persian gendarmerie, many of whom had joined the "nationalist" cause, they sent a large sum of money to the capital. Thus, they had a network of spies and numerous contacts among the population. From Berlin, they encouraged all expressions of nationalism that could be used against their enemies, even going so far as to give Muslims the impression that Kaiser Wilhelm II had converted to Islam, and renamed himself Hājj Wilhelm – though there is a grain of truth in this in that German Kaiser had long held a fascination – more strategic than religious – with Islam.[5]

The Germans were quick to recruit Taqizāde, who at the time was in the USA working as a library cataloger. In Berlin, the former deputy of the Majles had to collaborate with a committee of nationalist Indians, who were occupied with liberation from British imperialism. But Taqizāde demanded to have a separate committee for Persia and got his way. Thus he founded the *Persisches Komitee*, initially with an almost unlimited budget, but which decreased during the war years. It was his task to establish contacts with nationalists inside Iran and in particular with the National Committee of Defense. With a small group of carefully selected collaborators he was also tasked with informing the

---

5 On the Germans in Iran during the war, see O. Bast, *Les Allemands en Perse pendant la Première Guerre mondiale*. The pro-Muslim engagement of Wilhelm II was less important for Iranian intellectuals than his leading role against the Russians and the British; see, for example, the way Taqizāde presents him in the second issue of *Kāve* or the *Qeysar-nāme* of Adib Pishāvari (see A. Mir-Ansari's contribution in O. Bast, ed., *La Perse et la Grande Guerre*).

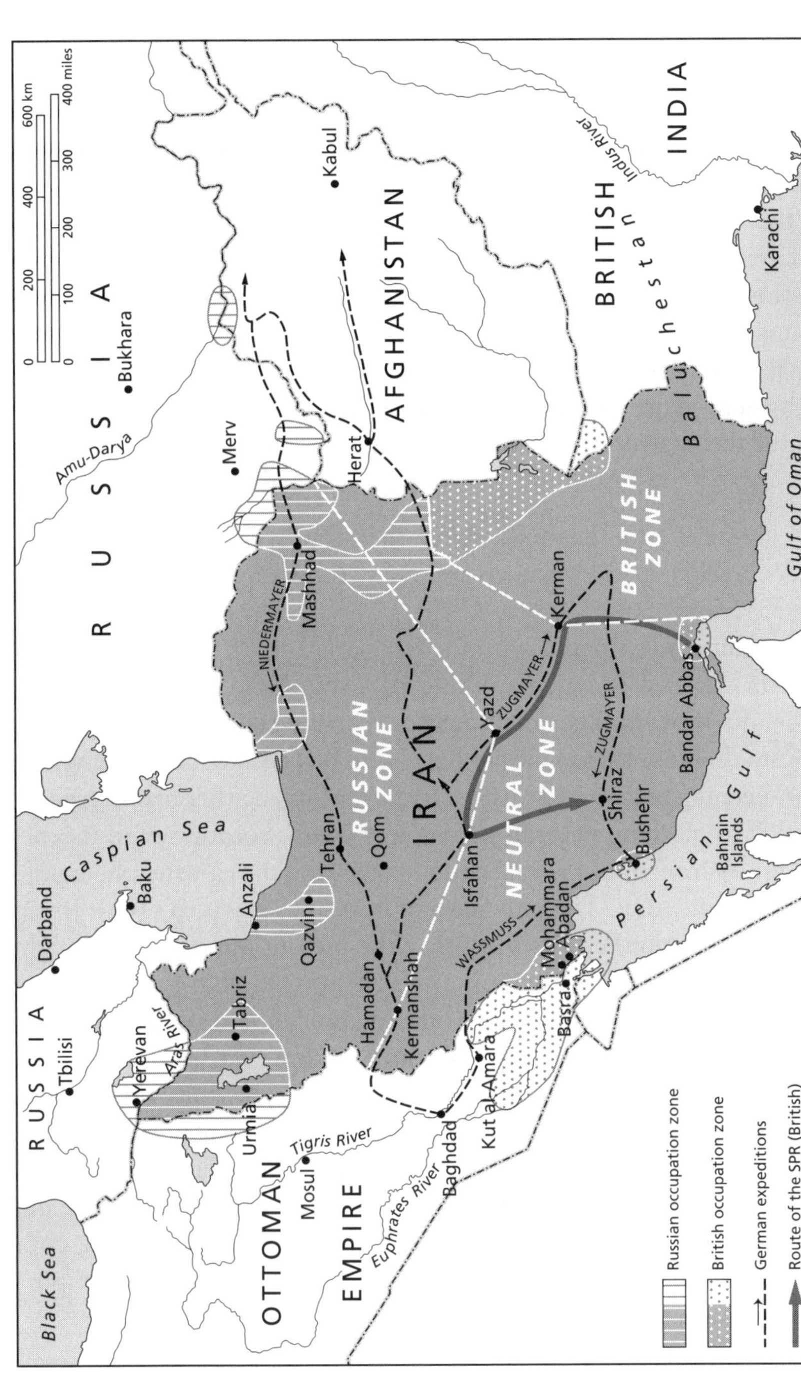

M3 Iran in World War I

Germans about the nomadic tribes, among which they hoped to find logistical and military support.

As early as 1915, Taqizāde anonymously published a work, *Persia and the European War*, criticizing the neutrality of his country; it was quickly translated into French and English. Shortly thereafter, still in Berlin, he began to publish a monthly magazine, *Kāve* (named after the hero blacksmith of Persian mythology). Over five years, from January 1916 until December 1921, the magazine tried to remodel the national identity of its Persian readers through articles praising the Germans and Ottomans as well as praising the literature and history of classical Persia. The editorial of the first issue, published anonymously – though there is little doubt that it was written by Taqizāde himself – presented the view of the nationalists of Berlin on Iran's neutrality in the war:[6]

> Some … for example think that Iran's national duty at the current time, like Romania, Bulgaria and Greece, is a complicated question where there are arguments for and against the alliance with the Russians and British or neutrality. In our view these are nothing but absurd and vain pipe dreams, and even frankly ridiculous for sensible people. What Iran has to do is as clear as the sunlight. Iran has been left nothing worth keeping that would justify any hesitation, neither fear nor hope. By remaining neutral, or worse, by collaborating with its enemies Iran would fall into their claws and the catastrophe would become total. The only dash of hope that exists to save it [from annihilation] consists in using the present opportunity to fight its enemies. The Russians and British would have neither compassion nor respect for Iran and will not leave it with any security. Doubting this truth and hoping that Iran will survive in case of an Anglo-Russian victory is to deny the evidence, it is pure and simple stupidity … Rise up, O illustrious fatherland with a great destiny, O land of prophets and realm of kings, land of grandeur and nobility, region of price and courage. Rise up! Because the losers have insulted you, and traitors among your children want to soil your face with eternal shame. The impure want to take your domain.

---

[6] *Kāve*, n°1, 24 January 1916, p. 2.

Taqizāde also indirectly gave his support to the German missions to Iran and India. It was the Ottomans who came up with the idea of sending an expedition to Afghanistan via Persia to destabilize the northern frontier of the Indian Empire. From the beginning of the war the Germans were involved in this plan and sent a preparatory group to Baghdad on 6 September 1914. Three highly qualified men belonged to this group: Wilhelm Wassmuss (1880–1931), later called the "German Lawrence"; the geographer Oskar Ritter von Niedermayer (1885–1948); and the Austrian zoologist Erich Zugmayer (1879–1938). A second mission was tasked to destroy the oil installations in the south of Persia, which were in British hands, and at the same time to instigate a Shiite uprising in southern Ottoman Iraq. But out in the field, operations led to rivalry over who was in command; the Ottomans wanted to be in charge on the premise that it ought to be Muslims in command in Muslim territories. The Germans and Ottomans were unable to reach an agreement during a historic meeting held in Istanbul on 11 February 1915, the only result of which was the formal Ottoman commitment not to annex Iranian territory in Azerbaijan so as not to cause a hostile reaction among Iranian nationalists.[7]

Wassmuss left Iraq for the south of Persia where, as agreed, he began stirring up anti-British sentiments among the tribes. In many places, the Germans – particularly when they brought money – were received as liberators. The mission to Afghanistan led by Niedermayer arrived in Kermānshāh in April 1915, despite obstacles created by the Ottomans. For a leg of the journey it accompanied the caravan of the Prince von Reuss (1868–1929) who was about to take up his post as plenipotentiary minister in Tehran. On May 6 Niedermayer arrived in Isfahan, where he was joined by a second German expedition, led by von Hentig (1886–1984), a diplomat tasked by Berlin to submit a proposal for an alliance to the Emir of Kabul in the form of a personal letter from the Kaiser.

In Isfahan, despite their rivalry and their different methods, the two German expeditions were able to convince the Shiite clergy to preach holy war against the Russians and the British. Nierdermayer

---

[7] Apart from Enver Pasha, Minister of War of the Young Turk government, the German and Austro-Hungarian plenipotentiaries posted at Tehran also joined the meeting together with the Persian plenipotentiary minister in Istanbul, despite the official neutrality of his country.

used his radio-telegraph station to spread fresh news – filtered and interpreted to suit his negotiations – about the European front to convince the chiefs of the Bakhtyāri tribe to break their alliance with the British. The Germans also employed the services of Nāyeb Khān, a bandit, who paralyzed trade in the region of Kāshan. On 1 September, the British consul Thomas Grahame (1861–1922), who had been in Persia since 1899, was forced to leave Isfahan, taking with him the subjects of the allied nations.

The joint expedition of Niedermayer and von Hentig continued toward the south-east to Kermān. There the Germans clashed with the city's governor, who had 400 armed men and the backing of the Russian and British consuls. Zugmayer, benefiting from the complicity of the clergy, was able to hire 300 men and established a consulate. In December 1915, the allied consuls fled, and the Germans remained the sole masters of Kermān. Yazd saw the same course of events. Gradually, the Germans took control of the telegraph and plundered the branch offices of the Imperial Bank. In return, Niedermayer and von Hentig's caravan suffered heavy losses during the crossing of the Kavir desert and at a military roadblock established along the Afghan border, the East Persia Cordon. Having left Isfahan with 140 men and 236 animals, the mission arrived in Herāt with only 37 men and 79 animals, and further losses were suffered on the road to Kabul. What is more, the alliance that the Kaiser hoped to secure with Emir Habibollāh was not the success the Germans had counted on, as the Afghans demanded aid and guarantees that the Germans were unable to provide.

Meanwhile, in the south, Wassmusss had made progress thanks to his contacts among the Iranian tribes.[8] He knew the region well, having been consul in Bushehr in 1910. Arrested by the British, he managed to flee; among his papers were documents written in Urdu and five other languages, proving that he was charged with a mission to go as far as India.[9] In mid-July, Wassmuss launched a skirmish between a local tribe, the Tangestānis, and an Indo-British detachment, which lost several men including two officers. The British sent for reinforcements from India to occupy Bushehr militarily.

---

[8] See the memoirs of Mahdi-Qoli MOKHBER OS-SALTANE HEDĀYAT, *Khāterāt va khatarāt*, pp. 242–80.

[9] C. J. EDMONDS, *East and West of Zagros*, p. 68.

In Shiraz, the German consul Kurt Wustrow, who had Marxist sympathies, had arranged with the Germanophile governor of the city, Mokhber os-Saltane Hedāyat (1864–1955), for a pro-German nationalist committee "for the protection of Iran's independence" (*Komite-ye hāfezin-e esteqlāl-e mamlekat-e Irān*). After the assassination of the British vice-consul, of Indian origin, on 7 September 1915, Mokhber os-Saltane, who had made an effort to maintain the official neutrality and to protect the British consular staff, was recalled to Tehran. He was replaced by a powerful landowner, who was openly described as "British," Qavām ol-Molk (1869–1916). The tide changed in November, when the nationalist committee and the gendarmerie of Shiraz, led by Major Ali-Qoli Khān Pasyān, gave the British consulate, which was besieged by the gendarmes, an ultimatum. Consul O'Connor was forced to surrender along with his staff and was held as a hostage by the nationalist tribes loyal to Wassmuss.[10]

In Kermānshāh, the Germans maintained a solid position, forcing the Allied consuls to withdraw to Hamadān, from where they were also expelled in November 1915. The German mission was reinforced by the one sent to destroy the British oil installations near Ābādān, which was making its way back having failed to do so.

By the close of 1915, a large part of central Iran was under the control of the Germans. Their strategy only failed in Tehran, where the exodus of the government with the nationalist deputies met with effective resistance by the Allied legations. The German minister finally refused to return to his post in Tehran. From Qom he went to Kermānshāh, whence he was recalled to Berlin.

Russians and Ottomans

At the beginning of hostilities, Russian troops still occupied the north of the country which they had invaded in December 1911. The government had tried in vain to convince the Russian legation that the Ottoman Empire might take this as a pretext to violate, in its turn, the Persian border in order to dislodge its enemies. With the

---

[10] The archives of the British consulate that proved the many violations of Persian neutrality and the collusion of the local elite such as Qavām ol-Molk or Sheykh Khaz'al of Mohammara with the British, were published in Berlin in 1917 under the title *Englische Dokumente zur Erdrosselung Persiens* (French and English translations were published the same year in Amsterdam).

outbreak of war, the Czarist troops arrested the Austrian and Ottoman consuls of Tabriz, who were sent to Tiflis; the German consul Wilhelm Litten (1880–1932), who had taken the side of the nationalists, was able to escape. They also arrested dozens of German citizens who were deported.

In 1914 the Ottomans launched an offensive, relying on Kurdish units established on both sides of the border. The Russians attempted to mobilize the Armenian and Assyrian Christian population. They escorted to Persia Sho'ā os-Saltane, the brother of the deposed Shah, who had met with unanimous hostility in Shiraz before the revolution. The prince fought the Kurds on behalf of his new protectors but was defeated and returned to Tiflis. The Russians wanted to charge the cost of his military campaign to the Persian treasury. The Ottomans entered Tabriz on 9 January 1915. The population received them warmly. The Iranian historian Ahmad Kasravi, who witnessed the events first hand, wrote:

> After five years of grief and humiliation, this was the first time that a sign of enthusiasm and of joy was seen among the population. That the Russian army should leave Tabriz! One did not dare to believe it … The people believed that the Russians had left for good and did not think about their return, like people who leave prison they congratulated each other.[11]

The Ottoman contingent only numbered 600 men, and the Russians retook the city on 30 January.

During the summer, the Russians, who had chased the Ottomans from Iran, used Persian territory to send troops to the Ottoman front via the Caspian Sea, and by land through Anzali, Qazvin, and Hamadān. They made an incursion into Vān and then advanced toward Anatolia after May 1916 via Qasr-e Shirin (between Baghdad and Kermānshāh). However, the Ottomans had the upper hand in the south of Iraq, forcing the British to withdraw to Kut al-Amara. In the fall, they gave chase to the Russians and invaded the region of Kermānshāh (Iranian Kurdistan), which they occupied in February 1917. But the British, thanks to troops having arrived from India, retook Kut al-Amara; in March 1917 they entered Baghdad and from then on were masters of the strategic route linking Mesopotamia with Hamadān.

11 A. Kasravi, *Tārikh-e hejdah sāle-ye Āzarbāyjān …*, pp. 603–04.

In 1917, after the Bolshevik Revolution, Russian soldiers withdrew from Tabriz and the entire region. Formed into soviets and starving, they pillaged villages along their route. After their departure, many scores were settled: Persians who had collaborated with the occupiers were summarily executed, and a rebellion led by Sheykh Khiābāni seized control over the region, in an echo of the revolutionary ecstasy that ended the Russian Empire. The revolt collapsed between June and October 1918, when Ottoman troops occupied the region after having been dislodged from the Mesopotamian front and redeployed to the rear as far as Baku.

The last Ottoman occupation of Azerbaijan was a kind of annexation. In a sense, since the 1890s, the Iranian Pan-Islamists and the nationalists who had fought the Russians and the British had hoped for, if not a political union, then at least a rapprochement with the Ottomans. Pan-Turkish propaganda, to detract from the undisciplined state of the military forward advance and to compensate for the withdrawals in the Middle East, contributed to the myth of Greater Turkey among the committees of Union and Progress created by the Young Turks. The libertarian dreams of the democrats of Tabriz gave way to the nightmare of an occupation even more brutal than that of the Russians. Education in schools was Turkified and the administration reorganized, effectively imposing annexation in advance of the anticipated international negotiations. The repression was brutal and the economy of the province of Azerbaijan was systematically plundered. The costs of the occupying troops was levied on the population, who had worthless paper money imposed on them; whoever refused it was subjected to humiliating corporal punishment. On the announcement of the Ottoman surrender and of the withdrawal of the occupation forces to the Turkish border, a triumphant euphoria that could not fail to strengthen nationalist sentiment in Persia swept through the population.

The British in the South, and the South Persia Rifles

In early 1916, the official government was barely in control of the region around Tehran. Public opinion favored the Germans, as did the clergy, and they were received as victors and liberators. The Allies were in a desperate situation, and the Russian and British consuls had left most of the cities in the center.

The British were only able to protect the region of Ahvaz and Ābādān and the coast of the Persian Gulf, the sites of the vital oil installations whose security was ensured throughout the war thanks to the collaboration of a majority of the Bakhtyāri – most of the wells were in their territory – as well as the Arab tribes of the Banu Ka'b – whose territories included Ābādān and Mohammara, the location of the refineries and export terminals. The Chief of the Banu Ka'b tribe, Sheykh Khaz'al (1861–1936) had tied his fate to the British, who repelled an Ottoman attack in the fall of 1914, and then faced acts of sabotage supported by Wassmuss, including the dynamiting of a pipeline which halted production for several months in 1915. During the years 1912–18, oil production rose tenfold growing from 80,800 tons to 897,402 tons.[12] Some of the crude oil was sent to be refined in Cairo, the rest in Ābādān. The Iranians only enjoyed a percentage of the benefits from the oil industry; for practical reasons (a lack of transportation facilities), they still imported their kerosene and gasoline from Baku. The management of the Anglo-Persian Oil Company and its finances were controlled by the British, who deducted the cost of their own military occupation in Iran and, after 1917, that of the Cossack Brigade, from the Iranian share of the revenue.

To re-establish order and the authority of the central government in their zone of influence and in the neutral zone, the British could not count on Persian forces. In that vast region, which stretched from Isfahan to Bandar Abbās and Zāhedān, the gendarmerie's attitude to the British was hostile, and they typically offered their services to the Germans and the nationalist government in Kermānshāh. The Persian Cossack Brigade was too weak – although there were plans to increase it to 10,000 men – and commanded by Russian officers. The idea to create a force similar to that of the Cossacks was put forward by Marling, the British minister plenipotentiary in Tehran. An Anglo-Russian force was already deployed in the East Persia Cordon to prevent German agents entering Afghanistan, but it only became effective after the passage of the Zugmayer mission. In accordance with formalities, in particular Persian neutrality, it was necessary that the new armed force be placed under the command of the Persian government, as, in principle, was the Cossack Brigade. For the duration of the war, British diplomats tried in vain to convince Iranian politicians to legitimize such a force.

[12] R. W. FERRIER, *The History of the British Petroleum Company*, p. 262.

Marling and the Viceroy of India appealed to General Sir Percy Sykes (1867–1945), an uncommon man, whom we came across above (Chapter 3) when he was consul in Kermān. After having occupied that same post at Mashhad, he had carried out a spy mission in Central Asia where he still remained. Sykes arrived in Bandar Abbās in mid-March 1916 and began to recruit Persian volunteers who were trained by Indian instructors. Conceived as a British initiative to maintain their interests against German agitators, nationalist Persians, and the gendarmerie, this army had to be financed by the Persian government because it was supposed to maintain the state's sovereignty within its borders. The Russians and the British agreed, in exchange for this supplementary effort, to a moratorium on debt repayments until the end of the war. Thus Persia, which had not formally agreed to the plans, found itself in a double bind. In vain Iran demanded, by way of compensation, that the allied powers give up certain privileges linked to the capitulations, such as the fiscal exemption of foreign citizens, and the extension to Persian subjects of consular protection and capitulary rights, two demands that seemed to be obviously justified according to international law.

It was intended that the South Persia Rifles (SPR) should number 11,000 men. According to Sykes, the unit was founded "to create a force for the restoration of law and order in the interests of the Persian and British Governments."[13] Originally composed of six officers, three British and three Indian, and twenty Indian non-commissioned officers (NCOs) escorted by twenty-five mounted guards, it was scantily supplied with arms, having only two mountain guns and no machine guns, and its number did not exceed 8,000 men.

After the initial success of founding the militia, Sykes received reinforcements, at the same time that Qavām ol-Molk, the anglophile governor, returned to Shiraz; events which contributed to the weakening of the German position. On 17 May, Sykes set off, leaving the Persian Gulf for Kermān, improvising a caravan of pack animals and the organization of supplies in temperatures averaging over 40 degrees Celcius (104 degrees Fahrenheit). In Kermān, he met up with some acquaintances and was able to rest his troops, before the SPR column continued their march to Shiraz. To benefit from the telegraph line and to revictual, he travelled via Yazd, which he reached on 14 August.

---

[13] P. SYKES, *A History of Persia*, II, p. 452.

There, Sykes decided to push on to Isfahan, where the commander of the Russian force had requested his help against an attack by Bakhtyāri elements trained by the Turks and the Germans. The Russians had retaken the city from the Germans on 16 March. To allow Isfahan to fall again into enemy hands would in any case have paralyzed the advance of SPR troops to Shiraz. On 11 September, Sykes reached Isfahan where he shared bread and salt with the Cossacks of Baratov. To open up trade and ensure reinforcements from British positions in Khuzestan, he opened the Lynch Road, through the Zagros passes, which had been cut off by bandits.

Once the Russian positions at Isfahan had been secured, the SPR continued the march to Shiraz where they arrived on 11 November 1916. The city and its environs were held by the gendarmerie, but there were no Swedish officers. Sykes proposed that the gendarmes enter into Persian service under his command. Most of them accepted, attracted by the regular pay and good equipment. Sykes used his forces to secure the access roads to Shiraz and make ready, by any makeshift means, about 1,500 km (950 miles) of road suitable for motor vehicles, which allowed the first cars to drive between Kermān, Yazd, and Shiraz.

Sykes' mission was an undeniable military success. After the war, the continuation of the SPR seemed likely, as it had integrated existing forces and as their role was in principle to consolidate the Qajar state. In reality, Sykes acted outside the control of central government and had no legitimacy that would have given him official recognition.[14] Under the guise of promoting reform to the Persian administration, the British actually contributed to discrediting what remained of the central government in Tehran.

The Bolshevik Revolution left Persia even more vulnerable, because, among other consequences, it put an end to the counterbalance against British meddling. Progressively, various zones under Russian control, such as Khorasan and Isfahan, passed to British control. The Persian Cossacks were still, for their part, commanded by Russian officers loyal to the Czarist regime – under the orders, after 1918 of a very anti-British officer, Colonel Starosselski – but it was the British who paid their wages and maintained the division's upkeep with funds levied from the Khuzistan oil revenues.

---

[14] On 21 March 1917, Vosuq od-Dowle agreed to give the SPR official status, but this measure was annulled three months later by the government of Alā os-Saltane.

Before the sovietization of the Caucasus, to channel urgent military aid to the government in Baku, then threatened by Turkish troops, the British sent an elite corps across Persia, the Dunsterforce. Behaving as if they were in a conquered country, they did not even consult Tehran about the operation.[15] This was also the impression that emanated from the negotiations in 1919 between the British and a seemingly anglophile Iranian government, to such an extent that the Anglo-Persian Agreement which they arrived at, placed the entire country, its resources, its institutions, and its future under the tutelage of Great Britain. Without waiting for the creation of the League of Nations, through which the victorious powers decided the fate of the provinces detached from the former Ottoman Empire (with Palestine, Jordan, and Iraq assigned to British control; and Syria and Lebanon to French administration), the British tied the government in Tehran to their aid, provided exclusively for the reorganization and financing of the army and the administration.

This agreement, negotiated in secret, sparked an outcry in the French press once it became public knowledge, and the French fanned the smoldering Iranian opinion which raged against the British and the leader of the government, Vosuq od-Dowle. The French and the Americans described the Agreement of 1919 as an "Anglo-Persian arrangement," thereby emphasizing its difference from a formal "agreement," which would have to be ratified by Parliament; they considered it illegitimate and not to be enforced in any way. Lord Curzon (1859–1925), on the other hand, declared it "a great triumph as I have done it all alone."[16] As secretary of the Foreign Office, Curzon, who had only spent a few months in Persia in 1888, prided himself on knowing Persia better than anyone else. Curzon insisted that the various points of the accord would be applied prior to the elections. In fact, it was known that no deputy was about to risk approving the "agreement," because of the hostility of public opinion in Persia; in any case, an election was near impossible to organize as the state was on the brink of collapse.

Did an alternative solution exist? In October 1920 the British ended the contract with the Russian Cossack officers, after they lost credibility against the Jangalis in an operation that turned into

---

[15] On Caucasus, see S. AFANASYAN, *L'Arménie, l'Azerbaïdjan et la Géorgie, de l'indépendance à l'instauration du pouvoir soviétique, 1917–1923*. L. C. DUNSTERVILLE, *The Adventures of Dunsterforce*; A. H. ARSLANIAN, "Dunsterville's Adventure: A Reappraisal."

[16] L. MOSLEY, *Curzon the End of an Epoch*, p. 202.

a fiasco.[17] Public opinion was manipulated by the fear of Bolshevism, and Western diplomats were under British pressure to evacuate Iran with their compatriots. Only the British army, stationed in Qazvin, offered a safeguard against a Bolshevik advance on Tehran. Given the drastic budgetary reductions and rebellious troubles that the British faced in Iraq, the general staff announced the decision to withdraw the garrison of Qazvin after the winter of 1920/1.

The Role of French Diplomacy

French interests in Persia were insignificant compared with those of the British and Russians, and primarily concerned the promotion of French language and education, including the teaching of law at the School of Political Science, and archeology, with the French having the monopoly on excavations since 1900. But the situation had evolved, even before the sudden eclipse of Russia. The 1916 Sykes-Picot Agreement, which negotiated the division of the Middle East between France and Great Britain, stipulated that the Mosul region bordering Iran in northern Iraq had to be included, at the end of the war, in the French zone of influence. In Paris a committee of the Franco-Persian Union, close to the "Colonial Party," which for a number of years had participated in Parliament, argued to uphold French ambitions in Asia. It comprised a few dozen politicians hoping to respond to the wishes of many Francophile Iranians to balance British interests in their country with a more active French presence.

Throughout the war, French diplomacy endeavored to coordinate and organize the Allied efforts in Persia. Raymond Lecomte (1858–1921), who had previously been posted to Berlin and spoke German well, was minister plenipotentiary in Tehran from 1908 to 1919. During that long period, of all the foreign diplomats, he was probably the man with the most coherent overview of events. From November 1915, thanks to his wisdom and sound contacts in Iranian political circles, he was aware of the plans to move the capital to Isfahan. He induced the Russians to march on Qazvin, threatening to occupy Tehran, which had the effect of forcing the most troublesome nationalists and the German minister plenipotentiary to leave for Qom. Ahmad Shāh, who also was ready to leave, was dissuaded in exchange for the

[17] On the Jangali question see Chapter 7.

promise that the Russian soldiers would stop at Karaj, 50 km (30 miles) from the capital.

The Bolshevik Revolution and the Russian withdrawal left a vacuum. From December 1917, the French and British began to discuss an agreement to divide tasks and benefits in the reorganization of Persia, that would replace the Anglo-Russian Agreement of 1907, which had become null and void.[18] This new agreement included in the first clause an article that was quasi-identical to the original and that repeated Persia's sovereignty and integrity. The remainder proposed, instead of dividing the Persian territory into zones of influence, a defined protected domain for each of the two powers, who would share the exclusive rights to loans and jointly provide administrative expertise and assistance in developing both the military and economic infrastructure. But the agreement was not concluded, because Clemenceau, who returned to government in November 1917, refused any expansion of imperial power and concentrated his efforts on the victory and the reconstruction of France.

The French attitude was in continuation to what had prevailed during the nineteenth century with the annulment of the Treaty of Finkenstein. Persia was not its domain, and Paris left the region to the British, who, concerned about the security of their Indian Empire, had solid reasons to be in Persia. Apart from promoting the teaching of French and engaging in archeological excavations, two activities that had been suspended during the war, France was nevertheless also anxious to maintain its traditional image as protector of Christian minorities. It is true that this role had become somewhat paradoxical since the separation of Church and state (1905) and the ban that followed concerning the subsidizing of missionary operations. In reality, the most secular-minded diplomats (often Freemasons) were not reluctant to help Christian francophone schools spread the French language and culture to the minorities, the provinces, and the smaller towns where the Alliance française did not operate. In Tehran, between 1919 and 1921, the military attaché Georges Ducrocq (1874–1927) was both a fervent member of the colonial party, a friend of the deputy Louis Marin. and a Catholic critical of the "secular" spirit of some of his diplomatic colleagues. The special relationship between France and the

---

[18] See M. Habibi, *L'interface France-Iran, 1907–1938 ...*, p. 156 sq.

Oriental Christians of Iran became apparent during the tragic events of Urmia.

The Decline of the Christian Minorities of Azerbaijan and the Ambulance of Urmia

The outbreak of war offered the opportunity for centrifugal forces to either seek foreign protectors or to liberate themselves from the grip of central authorities and seek new political forms. The European powers had no common strategy for Persia, but all forces, notably the minorities, became the levers for their actions and the protection of their own interests.

The Armenian and Syriac Christians of the Eastern Church had lived in Iran since before the arrival of Islam. Even when the Russian thrust in the nineteenth century had weakened their loyalty to the Iranian monarchy, these Christians were not worried. Grouped in entirely Christian villages or in districts where they had their churches, they observed their own customs and segregation was such that, apart from cases of Kurdish razzias, intercommunal marriages and religious conflicts were rare. Tensions began at the beginning of the Qajar period when Iranian princes feigned protectorship over the Muslims in the Caucasus, and the Russian princes likewise claimed to be the protectors of the Christians of Azerbaijan. After the first Ottoman persecutions of Armenians (1894–95), and then the great massacres of 1915–16, large numbers of refugees arrived in Iran. Many held anti-Ottoman, anti-Turk, and even anti-Muslim sentiments and proved a destabilizing presence for relations between Christians and nationalist Persians. The view of Persian nationalists, especially in Tabriz, became more critical. The European missionaries, who found it difficult to accept the traditional communitarianism, were rejected by the Armenians, who did not want the Gregorian Church to be weakened by conversions to Catholicism or Protestantism. The arrival of Russian troops in Azerbaijan had the potential to politicize these communities, transforming them into a potential threat to the local populations who had initially welcomed the Ottomans as allies against the Czarist threat.

In the climate of disorder and misery under the Ottoman occupation (1907–12), then under the occupation of the Russian troops

(1912–15), and then once again under the Ottomans, the Assyro-Chaldean suffered even more than the Armenians because they had no link with the Caucasus and no refuge in case of violence. On the eve of war, they numbered about 50,000, and they felt vulnerable. In January 1915, during the first Ottoman occupation, some 10,000 took refuge in the region of Tiflis, while others went to Urmia, claiming asylum at the American and French missions.[19] Among those who stayed behind, many died of sickness or were executed by the Turks. At the end of 1915, these local Christians were joined by 40,000 "Nestorians" (Eastern Christians) chased from the Ottoman Hakkari province by the Ottoman army and Kurdish militias. Mountain people, these semi-nomadic Jelo Christians found it difficult to gain acceptance by their hosts. They had fled with their flocks but did not have land to pasture them, and they stole because they were hungry. The solidarity and humanitarian aid, provided in particular by the American missionary Dr. Shedd and under the aegis of an international committee presided over by the Russian consul Basile Nikitine, were insufficient.

In September 1917, French military physicians arrived at Urmia with the "Ambulance Alpine du Caucase" sent by the French Minister of Foreign Affairs and financed by donations from towns and villages across France. Its mission was to assist Russian troops, who were by now in full revolt, and the physicians, after a brief residence in Tiflis, settled in Urmia, that Iranian border town, with their modern medical equipment. The "ambulance" included an electric generator, an X-ray machine, an operating room, and a laboratory among other items. While tending to the sick and wounded, irrespective of religion or ethnic origin – in the manner of the NGOs of today – the French found themselves becoming involved in local conflicts.

Faced with the Ottoman threat after the departure of the Russian troops, the Christians had formed militias to ensure their survival. Even if their initial mission had not foreseen this new situation, the French military doctors assisted with the formation of Chaldean militias. The Assyro-Chaldean Christians expressed their ambition, verbally encouraged by the British, to create an independent Christian kingdom – such was, it seems, the main motivation of Mar Shimun XIX

---

[19] H. DE MAUROY, *Les Assyro-Chaldéens dans l'Iran d'aujourd'hui*, p. 8; on the question see now Fl. HELLOT-BELLIER, *Chroniques de massacres annoncés. Les Assyro-Chaldéens d'Iran et du Hakkari*.

Benyamin, the Nestorian patriarch who arrived in Urmia with the Jelo in 1915. The Muslim nationalists of Tabriz, who were generally poorly informed about the situation in Urmia, saw the Assyro-Chaldean Christians as agents of a foreign power. They held them responsible for the acts of violence that tore apart the communities of the city after the fall of 1917, which the French witnessed without being able to bring any relief. On 17 March 1918, Mar Shimun, who, according to the Iranian historian Kasravi wanted to extend his power over the city and environs of Salmas and attract the Kurds in an alliance to conquer the entire region, including Tabriz, was taken in an ambush set up by the redoubtable Iranian Kurdish chief Esmāil Āqā Simko, who most likely acted at the instigation of nationalist Persians from Tabriz. Following an apparently cordial meeting in Kohne-Shahr between the patriarch and the Kurdish chief, the latter signaled his men to massacre his guest and his escort of 140 men in military uniform. Only a few men were able to flee; on arriving at Urmia they spread the news and launched a full-blown civil war between Christians and Kurds, or rather between Christians and Muslims.[20]

The French physicians withdrew with some difficulty to Qazvin, from where they accompanied the Dunsterforce to Baghdad, which was now in British hands. The latter, by dropping messages from an airplane coming from Qazvin, incited the Christians to organize themselves into a column of dozens of thousands and head for Hamadān where British troops would escort them to Baghdad. But many died of exhaustion en route or were killed by Ottoman attacks. The survivors continued on foot to Baghdad. About 40,000 Christians arrived in October 1918 and were soon settled by the new occupiers in a refugee camp at Bakoubah, near Baghdad. Only a small number returned to their country after 1921 when it was evident that the British promise of the formation of a national Assyrian homeland would not be realized.

Some thousands of Christians remained in Urmia. Among them, the apostolic delegate Mgr Émile Sontag was murdered on 31 July 1918 by a Muslim who had sought refuge with him for a few weeks and who had wanted to steal the money entrusted to the priest by fleeing

---

20 G. Bohas & Fl. Hellot-Bellier, *Les Assyriens du Hakkari au Khabour*, pp. 71f; Fl. Hellot-Bellier, *Chronique de massacres annoncés*; A. Kasravi, *Tārikh-e hejdah sāle-ye Āzarbāyjān*, pp. 725f; R. Motamed ol-Vezāra & K. Bayāt, eds., *Orumiya dar mohārebe-ye ālam-suz*.

Christians. The Ottomans arrived in the town and took revenge on the remaining Christians for the defeats they had suffered in Iraq.

The Christians had lost their intellectual and political status and did not play a major role in Iranian history after the Mongols. Huddled within their identity and drawn to the West by the foreign missions, they lost during World War I the tranquil life they had enjoyed in rural Azerbaijan. The evolution of the Iranian nation, which had involved them in the Constitutional Revolution (Armenians from the Caucasus played a significant role in Tabriz and Rasht, both as socialist militants and militia-trained fighters, as illustrated by Yefrem Khān), would continue without them. Those who went to live in the cities of Tabriz and Tehran were but the vestige of a great history.

"The End of an Era"?

The collapse of czarist Russia and the weakening of European powers after five years of a pivotal and destructive war were about to profoundly change the international perspective. With a peace treaty signed in Versailles and the League of Nations emerging to mitigate the threat of such violence in the future, was Iran to remain on the outside? Or would this ancient nation take up the challenge to enter a new international world?

Progressive European encroachment on the economy and the Europeans' interference in the political life of Persia since the beginning of the Qajar period had made Iranians aware of the extent to which their survival as a nation depended on radical change and sacrifice. But World War I was even more effective in this. Although Western armies had imposed many sacrifices, none of the foreign military campaigns on Persian soil were motivated by an urge to defend either Persia or its people. Rather, the armed interventions in Iran by Europeans were to safeguard European interests. Because of its strategic position and resources, Persia was used as a base to either repulse the Ottomans or to protect the Indian border. Routes were secured against the German missions to prevent the threat of a German infiltration into British territories that could spark any uprising among those colonized by the British; the oil supply for the British Admiralty had to be guaranteed or, conversely, destabilized by the Axis powers; and the safety of the routes had to be guaranteed to supply troops in the field. The goal was never – except in the nationalist propaganda circulated by Berlin – to protect Iran and its people, who on the contrary were trampled upon and whose leaders were despised.

The Ottomans considered the annexation of Azerbaijan; the British behaved in the south as if the oil were not under the sovereignty of Iran; and the Christians of Azerbaijan were manipulated with the promise of territory for a new kingdom, removing their chance of identifying themselves as Persian (or Turkish) subjects. It is not an exaggeration to imagine at this stage that Iran might have been purely and simply dismembered like the Ottoman Empire eventually was. In the next chapter we will see that this perspective was firmly established by regional insurrectionists, particularly in Gilan and Azerbaijan.

But did these revolts not have precisely the objective of ridding Iran of foreign armies and corrupt elites? The insurgents wanted to escape from the shame of foreign tutelage. The depth of national sentiment revealed itself to be stronger than foreseen. Even the political leaders whom historians have often hastily condemned showed themselves to be shrewd and inventive politicians who contributed to the renewal of the Iranian state.

7 THE END OF THE QAJARS

With their ambition – and the cruelty they meted out to their enemies – the first Qajar kings brought Persia, a region already coveted by hegemonic powers, firmly under their control. Little more than a century later, internal divisions and rivalries as well as the external conflicts that had escalated on the international stage, the secessionist attempts, and the revolts of the provinces all endangered the unity of the kingdom. After Nāser od-Din Shāh's long and eventful reign, degeneration and decadence followed under the rule of a sickly king, then a despot deposed by the people, and finally the libidinous and greedy adolescent who would attempt to pass off his egoism as wisdom. Ahmad Shāh personified the absence of any political direction in Iran. To resolve that lethal crisis, many Iranians were ready to do anything, even sell out their country and deliver it to a dictator, a Garibaldi or a Bismarck. But the traditional politicians, recruited from among the major landowners or the relatives of the royal family, were unable to do any better than the reformers, idealists, and other forebears; they were not statesmen.

Iranian Diplomacy at the End of World War I

The collapse of the Iranian state became more marked during World War I. Most Iranians, like the nationalist democrats, wanted an end to the Anglo-Russian domination enshrined in the 1907 agreement. But those who courageously spoke out for rupture, many of whom eventually decided to flee to Qom, Kermānshāh, and some even into exile in Baghdad and Istanbul, probably did not make the best political choice. First, by abandoning the existing institutions, they lost the instruments of legitimization that would have allowed them to take back authority within the country and regain credibility from abroad. Secondly, by allowing the political elite to become accustomed to daily compromise with the allied powers, they maintained the feeling of indifference concerning the achievements of the 1906 revolution. After the war, when anti-British paranoia replaced antipathy toward the Russians, neither the Parliament nor the government nor the monarchy clearly represented the expression of the will of the people. The political elite resigned themselves to a submissive approach, while hoping for a national renewal that would be produced with the intervention of an exterior event, such as the Bolshevik Revolution.

The role of the Iranian elite of that period has for many years been overshadowed by the dominant historical narrative in Iran that glorified persons of renown who lacked any concrete political direction, such as Sattār Khān and Bāqer Khān, the popular heroes of the revolt in Tabriz. In the Pahlavi period it was fashionable to blacken the reputations of the men that came before the coup d'état of February 1921, which brought the new dynasty to the throne. In their correspondence with the Foreign Office, British diplomats in Tehran aired very harsh judgments on the Iranian politicians of the time. To justify their necessary and "benevolent" assistance they had an interest in demonstrating that the local elite was incompetent and corrupt, and that it had betrayed the hope that the victors had placed in their alliance. Underlining, even with elements of caricature, the weakness of royal power and the absence of a countervailing power in the political system or in the press, it was very easy for them to submit concrete evidence of the venality of high officials. They used the same arguments with their allies to justify their supremacy over Persia – notably during the peace negotiations at Versailles which saw the founding of the League of Nations – the stated discourse was concern about preserving peace, but oil exploitation was a central objective. With open access to British archives, western and Iranian historians easily find arguments and evidence to discredit the vestiges of political pride among the elite. Concerning the Iranian archives of that period, which are poorly organized and often dispersed among private collections, they are at pains to reverse the common historical vision, that of salvation – or imperialist (the result is almost the same) – intervention by London. Here, we must correct this view and refrain from generalizations, even though the study of Iranians' bitter historical awareness, whether or not based on false perceptions, is itself a subject for historians.

The Role of Vosuq od-Dowle

Hasan Vosuq od-Dowle (1872–1951) was the most vilified politician of this period. According to Bāmdād, an Iranian historian from the end of the Pahlavi period, Vosuq started out with little at the time of the 1906 Constitution, and had enriched himself throughout his career:

> This person, writes Bamdad, was an educated and intelligent man, a good writer, an orator, and an active and energetic man, but all this in the sense that he was a traitor and bent. "When the thief has a lantern inside, he chooses his loot better," the expression of the poet Sana'i perfectly fits that individual. Those who became chancellor, vizier, head of government, prime minister were in most cases talented persons, but, unfortunately, as there was no nation to hold them to account and to punish them when they committed crimes or acts of treason, and as the nation and the Iranian state were then still caught between the two powerful and duplicitous powers like grain between two mill-stones, these people were only interested in seeking honors, appointments, and money and only sought the road of their success through their commitment to foreigners.[1]

This severe judgment is silent about Vosuq od-Dowle's diplomatic activities as prime minister in 1916–17 when he gave, as we have seen above, signs of accommodation to the British by officially recognizing the SPR, a decision that was later annulled. The government that followed him was very much aware of the real interest of Persia and continued to prepare for negotiations after the war. To that end, it formed a preparatory compensation commission (*Komisyon-e ta`yin-e khesārāt*) that was charged with listing the damage local populations had suffered throughout the region due to foreign troops that had passed by and who had demanded lodgings, wheat, animals, fodder,

---

[1] M. Bāmdād, *Tārikh-e rejāl-e Irān*, I, p. 351. On Vosuq see O. Bast, *Die persische Außenpolitik und der erste Weltkrieg*, to which this section is much indebted.

and so on, so that Iran might submit its complaints to the victors when the war was over. The country was unable to prove its active participation alongside the Allies, despite a late entry into the war supporting the British in 1918. Thus the government listened with great interest to the speech of President Wilson in that same year, quickly grasping the benefits Iran might obtain from his proposal for a League of Nations.[2]

In August 1918, a new government led by Vosuq od-Dowle was put in place under British protection. Exceptionally it lasted almost two years, until July 1920, and therefore, it was he who had to list the Persian demands to the Allies: (1) affirmation of the national independence of Persia; (2) maintenance of the territorial integrity of Persia; (3) the right to reparations for the damage suffered caused by the belligerent powers; (4) economic independence; and (5) receipt of international aid to put reforms in place. Availing himself of the unanticipated opportunity that the Versailles conference offered to the Persians to make themselves heard, on 17 December 1918, Vosuq sent a mission to Paris led by the Minister of Foreign Affairs, Moshāver ol-Mamālek (1868–1940).[3] The British and French were against the inclusion of the Persian delegation in the negotiations, because Persia had remained neutral and, moreover, it had lent more to the German side than to that of the Allies. The Iranian delegation contented itself with making political contacts on the fringes of the conference.

In parallel, and implicitly disowning the stunning initiative of that delegation, with which he was in permanent contact by telegraph, Vosuq secretly negotiated with the British on the Agreement of 1919, as though he was anticipating the inevitable failure of his Minister of Foreign Affairs. The Agreement, discussed in the previous chapter, seemed to endorse the removal of his country from the major international postwar settlement, because Great Britain alone committed itself to "the absolute respect of the independence and integrity of Iran." But Vosuq considered this to be only "the second best solution," a solution whose definite conclusion could only be sealed with the convocation and the agreement of Parliament, two stages which were at the time impossible to contemplate. Vosuq also turned to the French to ask them

---

[2] In particular, see Point 14 of this famous speech that foresaw: "A general association of nations must be formed under specific covenants for the purpose of affording mutual guarantees of political independence and territorial integrity to great and small states alike."
[3] On the choice of Moshāver and the work of the Persian mission, see M. Lashgari, "Dar nime-rāh-e konferāns-e solh-e Pāris."

for aid, in what appears to be a means to get out of the implementation of the treaty with the British that he himself had signed.[4] The head of the government in fact preferred any solution obtained within a multilateral framework.

This Anglo-Persian Agreement attracted violent criticism, and detractors accused Vosuq and his ministers of corruption. In fact, Vosuq reimbursed the money that he had received to undertake this mission. He had taken it in order to bribe his opponents and to obtain the support of the press. In receiving this money from the British, he offered them pledges to obtain from them basic concessions; according to the perverse law of credit, which the Agreement fully illustrated, lending money gives the lender power over the receiver, and refusing the bribe would have alerted the corruptors. The two Iranian partners in this operation, Nosrat od-Dowle and Sārem od-Dowle, who also received gratuities, most likely did not share the same moral principles.

To prevent the British from reducing Persia to a satellite state, Vosuq opened up a second line of communications. In November 1919 he decided to send a delegation to Baku and Tiflis on a mission led by an anglophile journalist, one of the few to sincerely approve of the signing of the controversial Anglo-Persian Agreement, Seyyed Ziā od-Din Tabātabā'i (1889–1969). The envoy's purpose was to ensure that the Azari and Caucasian nationalists would not adopt the annexation slogans of Pan-Turkism in Azerbaijan, and move toward a confederation of the republics of Azerbaijan (Baku), Georgia, and Armenia, which had not yet sovietized, with the Iranian kingdom.[5] Seyyed Ziā could not evade British detection on this, because he was in contact with Major Stokes, based in Baku, and was followed by another British expert in the region, Major Edmonds. But the Iranian government succeeded to make contact with the new neighboring states without Great Britain being able to oppose this. Shortly after Ziā's mission to Baku, the town and all the Caucasus fell into the hands of the Bolsheviks, rendering his efforts useless.

Vosuq undertook a third initiative, which would prove longer lasting, because, after the fall of his government, it would result in the

[4] As evident in the telegram of the French minister in Tehran, Charles Bonin, of 14 September 1919, Ministère des Affaires Étrangères (MAE), Asie 1918–1940, Perse-Iran 33.

[5] See R. ĀZARI-SHAHREZĀ'I, ed., *Hey'at-e fowq ol-ādde-ye qafqāziye*; C. J. Edmonds, *East and West of Zagros*, ch. 22.

Irano-Soviet Friendship Treaty, which remained in force until 1979, according to the Iranians, or until 1990, according to the Soviets. During the conference at Versailles, Moshāver's envoy had demanded the return to Iran of the Caucasian territories ceded to the Russians by the treaties of 1813 and 1828; a short time later, in Moscow, a delegation led by Moshāver ol-Mamālek entered into discussions, suggesting that Iran was ready to give up its territorial claims if the Soviet Union undertook to respect the integrity of Iranian territory, if it returned all concessions and monopolies purchased by Russia from Iran during the nineteenth century, and if it cancelled Persian debt. This debt, calculated in rubles, had little value after the consecutive devaluations following the revolution. To show their respect for Iranian nationalism, the Soviets agreed to give up the capitulation privileges of the Treaty of Torkamanchāy. The Friendship Treaty signed on 26 February 1921, in some ways responded to the cynicism with which the British, during the fall/winter of 1920/1, used the fear of a Bolshevik invasion and their move toward Tehran to push the Iranians to implement – prior to ratification – the clauses of the Anglo-Persian Agreement of 1919. One clause of the Irano-Soviet Treaty, often cited in Moscow, gave the Soviets the right to intervene militarily if any military force launched operations against the Soviet Union from the Iranian border.

In short, did Vosuq not act as a skillful politician, inspired by a real patriotic concern, when confronted with a particularly complex and unmanageable situation? To pass him off simply as corrupt and a traitor is to gloss over the novel initiatives he had undertaken, though without great success, to free Iran from its isolation and its underdevelopment.

The Jangal Movement

The Jangalis and the Russians

The government in Tehran was confronted with a long rebellion in the north of the country, in Gilan, which threatened to discredit it and cause its collapse. At first the rebellion took the form of a movement against the Russians before transforming into a campaign against all foreign occupation. Its chief made an oath to cut neither his beard nor his hair for as long as the British remained in Persia. The movement received its name from the forest (*jangal*) that covers Gilan, a vast expanse situated below sea level, along the Caspian shore, which has a humid subtropical climate. Social unrest spread much faster in this densely populated area than in the isolated valleys of the Iranian plateau, and its proximity to the Caucasus, then in full revolutionary uproar, made it the gateway to and birthplace of new ideas.

As of December 1911, the Russian occupation had resulted in a nationalist reaction in the region, which grew more violent as central authority continued to weaken. Since the government in Tehran was but a marionette in the hands of foreign powers, the rioters decided to liberate the province, not to obtain autonomy that would deny Gilan's ties to the nation, but in the name of liberty and national pride and so that the entire country could regain its independence.

The insurrection began in 1915 under the leadership of an unusual molla, Mirzā Yunes, or Mirzā Kuchek Khān (1878–1921). A man of impressive stature, despite the fact that his nickname means "small," with reference to his father, Mirzā "the big" (*Bozorg*), he was a scribe in the service of a wealthy local proprietor. He had taken his first steps into politics during the "minor dictatorship" of Mohammad-Ali Shāh (1908–09). In 1910, he was wounded in a fight against adherents of the Shah's restoration, and he was treated in Tiflis. At the beginning of the war, he mobilized peasants who favored Pan-Islamism and urged them to rise up against the Russian occupier by procuring arms by any means; his men, the *Jangalis*, sourced weaponry from Iranian soldiers who had deserted, bought them from Russian soldiers, or took them from victims; they also procured them from the Ottomans. To finance their movement, they collected a revolutionary tax from the population.

The insurgents first launched guerilla attacks, disappearing as quickly as they appeared. In August 1915, some sixty rebels managed to defeat 500 well-armed men that the Russians had sent against them at Makhlavān, killing most of them – only forty-five Cossacks survived. The Russians swore to finish off the Jangalis, but they were nowhere to be found after each attack even though they captured a large number of prisoners.

The prestige of such a determined peasant army that defied a mighty occupier continued to grow. At the end of the year, the government in Tehran, then headed by Mostowfi ol-Mamālek, tried to open negotiations with the Jangalis, whose patriotic intentions he acknowledged. He appointed a governor to Gilān who favored dialogue, but the prime minister was replaced before an agreement could be reached with the leader of the rebels. The Russians, for their part, launched several campaigns against them, all without success.

The collapse of the Czarist regime did not end the rebellion. On the contrary, the *Jangalis*, encouraged by the success of the revolution, now demanded the departure of the British and the liberation of the central government. Established in Rasht in June 1917, they increasingly organized themselves as an independent state with its own administration, schools, postal system, and so on. Kuchek Khān then contacted the Kerenski government. He committed to ending the harassment of Russians – some of their troops were still stationed in Iran due to the lack of means to repatriate them – in exchange for their permanent withdrawal and the annulation of all concessions and monopolies that the Czars had extracted from his country. This is precisely what the government of Tehran would demand from Moscow in 1920.

The Jangalis and the British

The leader of the rebels expressed his demands clearly in the first issue of the newspaper *Jangal* on 10 June 1917, which, according to its motto only wanted "to defend the rights of Iranians, to enlighten the thinking of Muslims." He did not claim any autonomous status for Gilan, but stressed the urgency to organize new elections and the necessity of making Iran's neutrality a reality recognized unreservedly:

> The Russian and British governments assert: "We will not leave as long as the Ottomans are there." The Ottomans state: "We only remain in Persia to chase away the Russians and British, we will leave when they have left." This history may drag on until the Day of Judgment, it is a vicious circle of which we are the victims … We say to all of them let us breathe in peace in our ruined house … may they leave us the inheritance part of one of their sisters [half according to Islamic law] and may they not sterilize our desire for reforms. May they put in practice their friendly words.

In the spring of 1918, the patriotism of the insurgents was not in doubt; even General Dunsterville, then present in the region, emphasized it. The Bolshevik revolutionaries showed themselves very quickly to be friendly toward the *Jangalis*; they bowed to the tombs of the victims of Czarist repression in Gilan and asked for forgiveness from their families. The *Ettehād-e Eslām* (Islamic Union) committee made a first step toward reconciliation by organizing a mixed police force to maintain order in Rasht and Anzali, the region's major towns. Even if the ideology of the Jangalis remained based on Muslim patriotism, henceforth the Russians and Jangalis had a common enemy, Great Britain.

The rebels boycotted British products and asked all Gilan merchants to demand payment in coin for the Imperial Bank's paper money. On 18 March they arrested a spy returning from the Caucasus, Captain Noel, who worked for General Dunsterville. The latter had established his headquarters at Qazvin, where the troops were stationed, and had, with the collaboration of a White Russian general, Bicherakov, begun to contact the Jangalis to request permission for his troops to pass through Anzali to go to Baku by sea. The leader of the rebels agreed to let the White Russian general, who stated that he wanted to return to his country, pass freely, but not the British. He was steadfast and refused to allow himself to be bribed during the negotiations led by Colonel Stokes and Basile Nikitine, two Persian speakers: In essence he told them: "Give the money to those who made you come to Iran and if you want to go to Baku take another route." The Bolshevik military units stationed in Anzali, and mostly composed of Armenians, were ready to serve as intermediaries because it was a matter of dislodging the Turks who had advanced as far as Baku. But, at that time, their relations with the Jangalis had deteriorated, even if they continued to supply them with arms. Finally, after two months of fighting, the aerial bombardment of Rasht, and the intervention of armored cars, the British concluded an agreement with the Jangalis on 14 July 1918. They accepted to use only the corridor linking Qazvin to Anzali and committed not to interfere with the rebellion, thereby ignoring such principles as the integrity of Iranian territory.[6] This agreement showed British pragmatism in dealing with Iranian politics and the limit of Mirzā's stubbornness. During the few months that the Dunsterville mission lasted, it ensured a relative ceasefire and allowed the British, for a second time, to impose on Tehran the nomination of Vosuq od-Dowle as the head of the government.

---

[6] To this W. Floor remarks that they had permission from the Persian government to be there; they were not there to suppress local rebellions.

In his turn, Vosuq od-Dowle attempted to negotiate with the Jangalis, and, when this failed, decided to send in the Cossack Brigade against them. But the campaign against the insurgents, commanded by a White Russian officer, Colonel Starosselski, after some initial success, ended in fiasco. British troops, stationed at Qazvin, did nothing to help; their inaction hinted that they wanted to reveal the weakness of the Russian officers in command.[7] After this defeat, Great Britain, who financed the Brigade, demanded that the Russian officers depart, to be replaced instead by Persian officers with British training and supervision. We will return to this episode, which is crucial to understanding the events leading upto the 1921 coup. But let us first turn to the complicated relations between the Jangalis and the Bolshevik Russian troops.

The Jangalis and the Bolsheviks

Although, steadfast Pan-Islamists, the Jangalis – weakened by the defection of some of their leaders and by the impoverishment that resulted from their isolation and the heavy tax burden levied on merchants and landowners in the wake of the revolution – were not insensitive to Bolshevik propaganda.[8] Some were of the opinion that Iran had to be "sovietized" like the Caucasus nations, a process already developed in some Central Asian Republics. The Communist Party of Iran was created. The Leninist doctrine that prevailed among communists advocated collaboration with national liberation movements against the colonialists, notably in Iran where, to put an end to the traditional relationship of domination over the peasant class, communists had to help "bourgeois-democratic liberation movements in their struggle against the clergy and other reactionary and medieval elements."[9]

---

[7] Such is the interpretation given in the informal report of Starosselsky to Georges Ducrocq, on 29 October 1920, in Y. RICHARD, ed., *Regards français sur le coup d'état de 1921 en Perse.* Gh.-R. AFKHAMI, *The Life and Times of the Shah*, p. 13, states that the Cossacks of Starosselski were bombed by British airplanes. Although Ironside had prohibited his men from militarily supporting the Cossacks, there is no evidence to prove he wanted to destroy them. See further B. PEARCE, *The Staroselsky Problem*, p. 68

[8] A proletarian Marxist party, *Adalat* (Justice) had been formed in the Caucasus in 1916 among Iranian migrants from the ruins of the Social Democratic Party. In harmony with the Bolshevik Revolution the party created an Iranian "Red Army" that consisted of volunteers.

[9] C. CHAQUERI, *The Soviet Socialist Republic*, p. 164.

Until then, Mirzā Kuchek Khān had rejected Bolshevik proposals because they gave no assurance as to the independence of his fight. The leader of the Jangalis knew that he was unable to dislodge them in the case of victory over the British-dominated government of Tehran. During the winter of 1919/20, to gain time, and rest his forces, he let Vosuq od-Dowle know that he was ready to lay down his arms with honor, as Vosuq had proposed to him. But, shortly thereafter, he joined forces with the Bolsheviks who had taken power in "Soviet Azerbaijan," and intended to disembark at Anzali to demand the departure of the British, who still held the port. The pretext of the landing was the recapture of General Denekin's fleet and ammunition which belonged to the Russian people. In the spring of 1920, the British were forced to withdraw to Rasht, and then to Qazvin, under superior firepower. It was a heavy psychological defeat for their army, which wanted to show that it could ensure order in the country. The government of Tehran protested to the newly created League of Nations about the Russian aggression. The Jangalis rejoiced at the British departure, but the property owners started to panic and fled to the interior of the country.

The objective of the Jangali and Bolshevik leaders was not in fact to remain in Gilan, but was, in their eyes, to liberate the Iranian state and transform it into a "republic of councils" (*jomhuriyat-e shur-avi*), the Persian term designating the "soviet" republics.[10] A historic meeting took place between them on the warship *Kursk* – Kuchek Khān was reportedly able to talk with Lenin by radio. In talks concluded on 20 May 1920 they reached agreement on several issues:[11] (1) communist principles regarding property rights would not be applied and communist propaganda would be proscribed in Gilan; (2) a provisional revolutionary republican regime would be established; (3) the people would determine the nature of the regime through a constituent assembly after the seizure of Tehran; (4) the Soviets would not interfere in the affairs of the revolutionary government, which would alone be in charge; (5) no Soviet troops should enter Iran beyond the existing 2,000 without authorization by the revolutionary regime; (6) expenses of the troops stationed in Iran would be covered by the revolutionary regime; (7) any

---

[10] C. CHAQUERI, *The Soviet Socialist Republic*, pp. 147, 194.
[11] C. CHAQUERI, *The Soviet Socialist Republic*, p. 192, translating the notes of Mirzā Esmā'il Jangali, nephew of Mirzā Kuchek Khān published by E. RĀ'IN, *Qiām-e Jangal*, p. 139.

arms and munitions requested by the revolutionary regime would be delivered on receipt of payment; (8) Iranian merchandise confiscated at Baku would be handed over to the revolutionary regime; and (9) all Russian commercial enterprises in Iran would be handed over to the republican regime.

This declaration brought consternation in Tehran where the rebels were considered dangerous seditious communists. Kuchek Khān clearly demanded the abolition of the monarchy and justified this on the grounds that the decadence of the Qajar state had made it a playground for foreign interests. Some days later, on 4 June, the Red revolutionary committee of Persia proclaimed, according to the terms used by the Jangali leader, the abolition of monarchy and the creation of a republic of councils; the formation of a provisional government; the cancellation of all previous treaties with foreign powers; "that [to] all peoples of humanity unanimously having the ideal of a republican government, the government will act with fairness to all and will observe the obligation to maintain the practices of Islam."[12] This last restriction was certainly aimed to reassure Muslims who were concerned about the revolutionary phraseology. The Jangalis sent telegrams to France and the USA, the "two revolutionary republics" of the free world, who had openly condemned the Anglo-Persian Agreement, to inform them of the abolition of the monarchy, and to express their independence from Moscow. They sent two other messages to Lenin and Trotsky requesting help to topple the regime of Tehran, which had reduced the population to slavery. Kuchek Khān was unaware that negotiations were continuing both between London and Moscow, on the one hand, and, on the other hand, between Tehran and Moscow to establish official political and commercial relations with the Soviet Union. The presence of Bolshevik troops in Gilan gave Tehran a solid argument to refute those favoring a compromise with the Jangalis; negotiating between state and state was something entirely different from military intervention.

Soon thereafter, the Jangalis disarmed the Persian Cossacks stationed at Rasht and confiscated their arms. Some Russian officers of that brigade preferred to return to the Soviet Union, while others went to Tehran, where they participated in new operations against the Jangalis. Kuchek Khān also had to contend with the landing of

---

[12] E. RāʾIN, *Qiām-e Jangal*, p. 147; C. CHAQUERI, *The Soviet Socialist Republic*, p. 194.

Bolshevik reinforcements, which he disarmed in turn, arguing that they violated the agreement signed on 20 May. Other causes of dissent placed the Jangalis in opposition to the Iranian Communist Party, in particular, the land reform that for the communists was a matter of principle. On 9 July 1920, Kuchek Khān left Rasht to show his disagreement. He soon met with an emissary from Tehran who proposed advantageous conditions for surrender; the Jangalis would submit to the government, he would be appointed governor of Gilan, and his men would be integrated into law enforcement. Kuchek Khān replied with an unequivocal condemnation of the Qajar dynasty, denouncing the feasts and drinking sessions to which the Shah devoted himself. "I will not lay down arms [until] Iran [is] delivered from the foreigners and the traitors."[13]

Benefiting from Kuchek Khān's eclipse, the communists formed a radical government in Gilan led by Ehsān Dustār (1883–1938). They only formed a single command with the Jangalis in 1921, after the failure of their extremist policy and the confiscation of properties which earned them the population's hostility. In October 1921, the new Soviet plenipotentiary minister in Tehran, Rothstein, asked the communists forces to leave Iran to sustain the Irano-Soviet Treaty of friendship signed in February in Moscow.

The government troops would crush the Jangalis in the fall of 1921; it was one of the first great military victories of Rezā Khān, then Minister of War, the future Rezā Shāh. Kuchek Khān, found half-dead on 6 December in the mountains due to exposure to freezing weather, was taken to Rasht where he was beheaded. One of his Kurdish lieutenants who had defected, Khālu Qorbān, brought his head to Tehran as a trophy and received the title of *Sālār Mozaffar* (Victorious Commander) from Rezā Khān.

The Jangalis hold a profound and enduring place in the Iranian psyche, thanks, undoubtedly, to the exceptional personality of its leader. Kuchek Khān was at the same time a Pan-Islamist, nationalist, and close to the people. For Iranian progressives, this was a paradox; the Soviet Republic of Gilan was proclaimed on 20 May 1920 and seemed to function for more than a year, but its uncontested leader was not a communist, and the Soviet Union caused it to fail.[14] For Muslims, the

---

[13] Md-H. Saburi-Deylami, *Negāh-i az darun be enqelāb-e mosallahāne-ye Jangal*, p. 158.
[14] See C. Chaqueri, *The Soviet Socialist Republic*, pp. 276f.

Jangalis were an example of resistance to secular ideologies in the national liberation. For the nationalists, Kuchek Khān did not betray the ideal of an Iran free from imperialist intervention, but he had attacked the sacrosanct principle of territorial unity.

The Khiābāni Revolt in Tabriz

The revolt that broke out in Tabriz in 1920 lasted only six months and caused few casualties, but its memory remained engraved in the counsciousness of the inhabitants of the province as a dream of liberation that was quickly smothered. Nationalist mobilization factors were not lacking in Tabriz, an important center of political movements since the beginning of the century, but its successive occupations by the Russians and then by the Ottomans did not leave them any space where they could be expressed.

Sheykh Mohammad Khiābāni (1880–1920) came from a family of Tabrizi traders, who had immigrated from the Caucasus. He learnt Russian and modern science and prepared to take over from his father, when, having returned to Tabriz, he began studying theology and Islamic law. Having become a preacher at a mosque in Tabriz at a very young age, replacing his father-in-law, he went on to be elected deputy to the second Majles, where he drew the attention of the Democrats. After the dissolution of Parliament in December 1911, he fled to the Caucasus out of fear of the Russian repression that gripped Tabriz. He quietly returned later, but only became an active militant after the war. Advocating a nationalism that was more regional than Iranian, he managed to get hold of an arms cache left by the retreating Russian army and organized aid to the victims of the famine. The Ottomans exiled him to Marāqe during the short but pitiless occupation of Tabriz. On his return, Khiābāni began denouncing the Anglo-Persian Agreement of 1919 and stood for the legislative elections to the fourth Majles.

In March 1920, with the connivance of the military commander of Azerbaijan, Khiābāni took control of the police and administration of Tabriz in the name of the Democrats. Having founded the newspaper *Tajaddod* (Renewal) with some friends, on 9 April, they published a manifesto signed by an "Executive commission of associations" which summarized the substance of their thinking. The text was published in both Persian and French for the benefit of foreigners and

Christians. The Persian word *āzādikhāhān,* translated as "liberal" in the French version, means "those who want (are ready to struggle for) freedom," where "freedom" could be also translated as "liberation."[15]

> The liberals of the city of Tabriz, moved by the reactionary tendencies that are clear from a series of anti-constitutional acts committed by the local authorities and which have just been clarified in a disquieting manner in the capital of Azerbaijan, have risen up with the objective of a lively and energetic protest. The liberals of Tabriz declare that their program consists entirely in the obtaining of full and complete satisfaction as to the respect by the people in charge of the government of the liberal regime of this country and the loyal observation on its part of the constitutional laws that define its character. The liberals, appreciating the exceptional delicate nature of the current situation, have decided to maintain at all cost the public order and peace. In two words, here is the program of the liberals: – Maintenance of public order – Realization of the constitutional regime. Tabriz, 9 April 1920.

In fact, the insurgents wanted to implement a comprehensive program of reforms, that were agricultural, educational, social, fiscal, and even linguistic, since they wanted Azari Turkish to be recognized as an official language on the same footing as Persian. They also demanded the government apply the Constitution by convoking Parliament to debate major reforms, notably the Anglo-Persian Agreement, but also to organize elections for regional and local assemblies as stated in the Constitution (Supplement, article 92).

Against the advice of some Democrats, Khiābāni decided to change the name of Āzarbāyjān to Āzādestān, "land of freedom," not to signal that the province wanted to cut ties with Tehran, but to put forward the example of its freedom. It was also intended to politically distance the region from the Republic of Azerbaijan, recently created in Transcaucasia, which usurped the ancient name of their province. The central government had several reasons to keep an eye on the province: apart from Pan-Turkish propaganda in Tabriz (as discussed in Chapter 6, Khiābāni had defied the Turks who had expelled him from

---

[15] A. ÂZARI, *Qiyām-e Mohammad Khiābāni dar Tabriz,* p. 344; C. J. Edmonds, *East and West of Zagros,* p. 285.

the city, which shows that the Democrat movement was not at all attracted by Istanbul) and the risk of extending the Jangali rebellion to Azerbaijan, the insurgents had dismissed two Swedish officers of the Persian gendarmerie accused of spying on the Democrats in order to reverse the situation and restore the authority of the state.

What were Khiābāni's motivations? According to a British officer, Major Edmonds (1889–1979) who met with him on 1 May 1920: "Indeed his manner was almost shy, but for all that he spoke with an evident conviction that he held Tabriz in the hollow of his hand, and that his decisions could admit of no discussion."[16] Khiābāni told Edmonds, in categorical fashion, that "there was nothing of a separatist nature in their movement. They considered Azerbaijan as an integral part of Iran."[17] This he had told the Turks explicitly, after their propaganda campaign favoring annexation. Khiābāni felt more Turkish than Persian, but more Iranian than Turk. He admitted that voices had been raised at Tabriz with cries of "Death to the British! Death to Vosuq od-Dowle!" but these had ceased to be heard.

In fact, Khiābāni did not like the Bolsheviks any better than the Ottomans. He fought the German consul Kurt Wüstrow. Wüstrow, who committed suicide in Tabriz on 3 June 1920, was a Marxist sympathizer and fiercely anti-British. Khiābāni also condemned the Jangali movement when it allied itself with the Bolsheviks. The British were happy to find in Khiābāni an adversary with whom they had much in common. But the central government succeeded in bringing the revolt to an end before it managed to use all of its trump cards.

In an attempt to negotiate, Vosuq od-Dowle's successor sent Mokhber os-Saltane, a politician who was the closest in ideology to the Democrats, to Tabriz. At first, he accepted all the conditions stipulated by Khiābāni and arrived in the city without a military escort. What began as a conciliatory declaration descended into an impasse. Khiābāni hardened, prompting Mokhber os-Saltane to request law enforcement troops. Khiābāni preferred to take his own life on 14 September 1920 than to give himself up.[18] Iranian intellectuals saluted his heroism, but they were divided as to his patriotism. His regional orientation and his

---

[16] C. J. EDMONDS, *East and West of Zagros*, p. 288.
[17] C. J. EDMONDS, *East and West of Zagros*, p. 290.
[18] This is MOKHBER OS-SALTANE's version (*Khāterāt va khatarāt*, p. 318). A British report says he would rather have been killed by the Cossacks, see T. ATABAKI, *Azerbaijan. Ethnicity and Autonomy*, p. 199, n. 102.

closeness to the masses worried those who favored the Jacobin ideal of a centralized and unified state, or even one made uniform on the basis of more universal concepts and nationalist ideology.

The 1921 Coup d'État

Persia found itself in a desperate situation. The agreement of 1919 began to be applied timidly, but public opinion was so dead set against it that no politician dared to contemplate ratifying the preliminary reports of the mixed commissions. Rebellion raged in the north, with Bolshevik support, and in Tabriz. The country was exhausted. To add further to the misery, Spanish flu did not spare Iran, where the pandemic, worsened by the famine that resulted from bad harvests and the paralysis in transportation, claimed the lives of tens of thousands. To these hardships was added the constant insecurity. Caravans were regularly plundered by groups of bandits, some of whom (Nāyeb Khān and his son) presented themselves as the Robin Hood of social bandits, taking from the rich to give to the poor.

The Iranian army was in total collapse: the soldiers were ragged and the lack of discipline was amplified by the absence of pay. The only exception was the Persian Cossack Brigade, which had thought it would achieve a final victory over the Jangalis. Ahmad Shāh had tried to retain the Czarist Russian Cossack officers, to whom he entrusted his personal safety, but he was forced to give in (as we have already seen) in October 1920 after the humiliating defeat of Starosselski against the Jangalis. The British, who now financed the Brigade, had sought for a number of months an opportunity to get rid of the White Russian officers, of which certain elements had defected to the Soviet Union. Thus they forced the Shah to replace them with Persian officers, some of whom had graduated from prestigious European military schools, that the British would train. The Cossack Brigade (of about 4,000 men) was stationed in Qazvin in 1920 under the provisional command of the North Persia Force (Norperforce), which provided the necessary training. The Norperforce was the remnant of Dunsterville's army. It had given up its positions at Anzali and numbered about 10,000 men at Qazvin.

Colonel Henry Smyth (1866–1943), also stationed in Qazvin, arrived in Iran under the framework of the 1919 agreement and was charged with the creation of a national army. The project was of great importance to the nationalists and a pressing need since the Constitutional

Revolution. It had been more concretely defined by the mixed-military commission as one of the main programs of the agreement. This unified army was to put together the draft army, the Cossack brigade, and the gendarmerie, an agenda that would be later realized by Rezā Khān.

General Edmund Ironside (1880–1959), who was charged with the dismantling and repatriation of Norperforce whose men were needed in Iraq, arrived in Qazvin in October 1920. The Briton had another secret mission: to provoke a coup. The plan was not to take over the government but to entrust it to a group that the British could rely on. Under the advice of two of his officers, friends of Seyyed Ziā, he noticed Rezā Khān (1878–1944), a Cossack with an imposing presence who, it seemed to him, was held in high esteem among his men. This Persian soldier would assure the success of the military operation. The political management was to be manned by Seyyed Ziā, who did not hide his intention to put an end to corruption and advocated radical methods to this end – it would appear that Ironside didn't know Ziā; he does not mention his name in his diaries. This journalist, whom we have seen above as a politician during his 1920 mission to the Caucasus, enjoyed friendly relations with several Britons in Tehran. Great Britain hoped that he would become head of government after the coup d'état. The only condition, which was explicitly demanded of the two conspirators, was that they would not touch the Qajar dynasty: the prospect of a republic seemed dangerous and untimely.

The conspiracy was organized in Qazvin with the complicity of the War Office, though the British legation in Tehran was left as if it were unaware of the developments. The new British plenipotentiary minister Herman Norman (1872–1965) certainly had been forewarned, though he claimed ignorance. The British implication in the organization of the putsch itself is important, because the official Iranian propaganda, up to 1979, maintained the fiction of a purely patriotic movement that distinguished itself from the political customs of the Qajar dynasty by its total independence *vis-à-vis* Russian and British imperialist pressure. The only solid Iranian report of the event, which was broadly critical of Rezā Khān, was that by the poet Mohammad-Taqi Bahār, but it does not offer any significant details.[19] According to Major Edmonds, Rezā Khān would regularly visit British headquarters to use their telephone line to talk to General

---

[19] Md-T. Bahār, *Tārikh-e mokhtasar-e ahzāb-e siāsi-e Irān*, pp. 61f. There are contradictions in almost all reports of the coup, see Y. Richard, "Le coup d'état de 1921 et les sources historiques," pp. 69f.

Dickson, a Persian speaker who was then in Tehran. Some days before the coup, Rezā Khān asked Edmonds to remind Smyth to be discrete. The latter moved to make ready the Cossacks who had been designated to intervene in Tehran. Rumors about the plans began to circulate, and Rezā Khān presumed that Edmonds was aware of them; in fact, he did not yet know the precise details of what was brewing, despite his friendship with Seyyed Ziā.[20]

Rezā Khān's move to Tehran was duly scheduled, but with fewer troops. Asked by emissaries to stop their march, they disobeyed, worrying the government and some diplomats. On 21 February 1921, Reza Khan's men, almost without a fight, took the capital. Seyyed Ziā was immediately appointed prime minister, replacing Sepahdār Rashti (1860–1921) who had led a short interim government.

Significantly, Rezā Khān's march from Qazvin with 2,000 smartly dressed and well-shod Cossacks immediately inspired in Tehran the rumor of a conspiratorial link with London, and while Seyyed Ziā did not hide his anglophile sentiments, Iranian official sources are silent about British complicity. However, it was an open secret that there was a common consensus not to look too deeply into where the funding had come from. The official version that prevailed until the fall of the Pahlavis spoke only of the patriotic reawakening. A particularly interesting version by Seyyed Ziā himself, released more than fifty years later, reveals the strong patriotic commitment of the young journalist, without any mention of any initiative on the part of Rezā Khān or any involvement of the British officers.[21]

The coup d'état put an end to months of uncertainty and was welcomed by many. The British could finally leave Iran with the assurance that the political reforms, which had been agreed upon with Vosuq od-Dowle, would be realized, even when the agreement itself was not formally kept. As for the nationalists, they were satisfied with the spectacular steps that Ziā had taken: the swift arrest of dozens of members of the oligarchy in order to extract from them the financial contributions they had for many years refused to pay to the government; the official cancellation of the 1919 agreement; the signing of the friendship treaty with the Soviet Union; the reorganization of the army and the administration; and the convocation of Parliament. For the first time in

---

[20] C. J. EDMONDS, *East and West of Zagros*, p. 313.
[21] Md-A. JAMĀLZĀDE, "Seyyed Ziā va *Ketāb-e siyāh*-e u."

many years, Iranians felt they now governed themselves. Ahmad Shāh was afraid, but he had no choice other than to acquiesce to the change of government imposed by force.

The British had deftly orchestrated the unfolding of events: they had created a political and military vacuum for the conspirators, and to ensure the utmost support among the population, they pretended to be afraid of a greater danger and fueled the Persian public's fears of a Bolshevik influx, like the Mongol incursions in the Middle Ages. The plan had worked perfectly. The most insignificant protagonist was Ahmad Shāh who did little to slow the power grab by the two parvenus, and whose sense of urgency to normalize the situation was inspired only by his desire to head back to the French casinos as quickly as possible. Dispossessed of the Russian officers of his Cossack Guards, he had no defense against the revolutionary initiatives put forward by his new prime minister, who, as he was well aware, was supported by Great Britain.

8 REZĀ KHĀN TO REZĀ SHĀH: DEFENDER OF THE NATION

Promoted to minister of war in the government reshuffle that followed in the weeks after the coup d'état, Rezā Khān, taking the title of *Sardār Sepah* (commander of the army), succeeded in deposing his first contender and former ally, Seyyed Ziā, whose activism upset too many interests. Ziā had sought British support to reorganize the army. The minister of war considered such a plan – that consisted of under-handedly applying the main chapters of the 1919 agreement which had allegedly been revoked – unacceptable. On any other chapter of the agreement Rezā Khān was less touchy, but the army was *his* domain, and he did not want to see it taken over by either Britons or Russians, despite any likely general agreement with Ironside.[1] Rezā Khān found an ally in Ahmad Shāh who was concerned at seeing Qajar princes in prison and ransomed by this young anglophile revolutionary. On 25 May – three months after the coup – the Seyyed, whose life was spared for fear of the British reaction, was put in a car headed for Qazvin and Iraq, accompanied by his friend Gaspar Ipekian, an Armenian journalist whom he had chosen as mayor of Tehran. Ahmad Shāh immediately nominated as prime minister Vosuq od-Dowle's brother, Qavām os-Saltane (1873–1955) who had been imprisoned by Ziā; he was a member of the oligarchy but politically

---

[1] In his diary (12 February 1921) Ironside writes: "I made two things clear to Rezā Khan when I agreed to let him go: i) That he must make no attempt to shoot [me] up behind as he goes or as I go … ii) That the Shah must on no [account] be deposed. Rezā promised glibly enough and I shook hands with him." In Y. RICHARD, "Le coup d'état de 1921," p. 102; E. IRONSIDE, *High Road to Command,* p. 160.

a reformist, and he enjoyed the trust of the British without being subordinate to them (he had studied in Russia).

The *revolutionary* project concocted by Seyyed Ziā consisted in reforming Iran from top to bottom, to free it from anarchy and the domination of social parasites and to give it an efficacious administration. Ziā's dismissal immediately changed the social dimension of that artificial "revolution." Reza Khān made a deal with Ahmad Shāh to get rid of his accomplice and to free the aristocrats whom Ziā had imprisoned. Moreover, the new prime minister was an eminent member of the Qajar elite. For sure, numerous intimidation measures were taken by Rezā to oblige the old aristocracy to collaborate. Many eminent politicians of the Qajar era went over, at least temporarily, to Rezā Khān's service: as well as Qavām and his brother Vosuq, these included Mosaddeq os-Saltane, Hasan Mostowfi ol-Mamālek, Prince Firuz Mirzā Nosrat od-Dowle, and Mokhber os-Saltane Hedāyat.

At this stage, one may say with certainty that Rezā Khān did not know what direction to take. When Iranians were obliged to register their families at the registry office, to be identified like Europeans by first name and family name, he chose Pahlavi as surname, which went back to the Parthian dynasty and to the language of the Sasanids, a nationalist allusion. Of low-class origin, he literally rose through the ranks of the Cossack Brigade. Extremely strong, almost two meters (6′ 6″) tall, he spoke with a soft and self-assured voice. His fits of anger were proverbial, which meant his interlocutors had a tendency to never tell him the plain truth about any issue. In general, Rezā Khān did not tolerate naysayers or opponents, and in certain cases he chased them away with a lash of his whip. Known for his austere lifestyle, Rezā Pahlavi wanted to rebalance his humble origins and amassed landed property and accounts abroad.

His trajectory at the head of Iran shares little in common with his counterpart, Ataturk, who founded the Turkish Republic in the same period. Mustafa Kemal (1881–1938) received an advanced education – he had read the philosophers of the Enlightenment in French – and had traveled in Europe, which served as a model for him. A hero respected by his enemies, he took power while fighting against the foreign armies that occupied Turkey, by mobilizing the Turkish population. It was this patriotic act of liberation that allowed him to overcome, by a heightened collective pride, the trauma of the Ottoman defeat. Conversely, Rezā Pahlavi had only received a rudimentary education;

apart from Persian and a Turkic dialect, he spoke no more than a few words of Russian that allowed him to understand the orders of his superiors and could only just decipher the headlines of the Persian newspapers. Having never left Iran, except for a short pilgrimage to Karbala and a trip to Ankara (1934), what he knew of Europe had been gleaned from the Russian and British officers and through distorted echoes of Kemalism. Finally, to conquer his throne, he merely had to fight domestic enemies; the threats of Europeans and the Soviets were but secondary crises, even though he took care to dramatize them to enhance his image as defender of the nation. Rezā Khān feared the will of the nation and the various expressions of this will: the press, the intellectuals, and the Parliament. An Iraqi Shiite cleric exiled to Persia in 1923, who met the future Rezā Shāh several times, evoked the contrast in this respect with Ataturk, the words of whom he cited: "I have always foreseen, since I observed its emergence, the need for a forum where the will of the nation might be expressed and take charge of the country's affairs. Therefore, it is quite natural that I have supported the formation of the national Grand Assembly [of Ankara]."[2] Rezā Khān, however, defied any national expression. He systematically organized sham elections where candidates were designated beforehand and took care to prevent parliamentary debates. This caricature of the Constitution was repeated from legislature to legislature with the exception of the 1942–53 period until the revolution of 1979.

Rezā Khān hesitated as to the most suitable way to establish the political order of which he dreamt. First, he accommodated a decadent and often absent monarch. Had he not promised General Ironside not to touch the monarchy? Nominated prime minister before Ahmad Shāh's departure for London, it was the *Sardār Sepah* who really exercised executive power. But the situation was tense. In 1923 he organized, with the help of his followers throughout the country, a major campaign to establish a republic. As we will see below ("The Marginalization of the Clergy"), the clergy would be the main obstacle, frightened by the Kemalist and Bolshevik examples. The only other option was to replace the Qajars, which Rezā Khān did without violence, Ahmad Shāh not having the courage to return to Iran to oppose it. Before its dissolution in October 1925, when Rezā Khān returned victoriously from his campaign against the Sheykh of Mohammara (see the section on "Sheykh

---

[2] Md-Mahdi al-KHALISI, *La vie de l'ayatollah Mahdi al-Khalisi*, p. 371.

Khaz'al" below), the fifth Parliament voted for the removal of the Qajar dynasty, and Rezā Khān sent an emissary to Ironside to terminate his promise of 1921. Only five deputies had the courage to oppose the change of dynasty, the cleric Modarres and four secular democrats. A constituent assembly elected especially for this occasion, in which many ulama were seated, entrusted the Crown to Rezā Pahlavi and his offspring. The coronation took place in April 1926.

Return to Order: Jangalis, Pasyān, Khaz'al

Rezā Khān conquered his kingdom by crushing one by one the rebellions that threatened the interests and the unity of the country. In Tabriz, the very brief uprising by Khiābāni had been smothered in 1920, leaving in its wake much bitterness and local frustrations. As for the Jangali revolt in the north, the fear of its spread to Tehran was only definitively extinguished with Kuchek Khān's death in December 1921. Rezā Khān personally participated in the operations and closely supervised their implementation. He crushed, with just as much brutality, the local revolts by Colonel Pasyān in the north-west of the country, by Simko in Kurdistan (1922), and, by staging an impressive campaign in the south, he put an end to that of Sheykh Khaz'al, a wealthy Arab tribal chief ruling over Khuzestan and part of southern Iraq, and an ally of the British.

Mohammad-Taqi Pasyān

Mohammad-Taqi Khan Pasyān (1892–1921), a young gendarmerie officer, had stood out during the war in the ranks of the army of the nationalist movement in Kermānshāh and was at Taqizāde's side in Berlin. On his return to Iran he was appointed the commander of the gendarmerie in Khorasan in 1920 and accused the governor, who was no other than Qavām os-Saltane, of appropriating the wages of the troops. After the coup d'état he was charged with arresting him and seeing him escorted to his prison in Tehran. With the support of his 200 gendarmes, he seized control of Mashhad, the capital of Khorāsān, where he decreed martial law and had the elite arrested, as Seyyed Ziā had done in Tehran. With Seyyed Ziā's approval, he tried to have the rich pay taxes and to clean up the finances of Imam Rezā's sanctuary. The fall of the prime minister in May led to his dismissal and Qavām, now freed, was nominated head of government. Pasyān gave orders to block the telegraph so that the province would not know about the nomination, fearing retribution by his former prisoner. Under the illusion that there was strong popular support, he threatened to take Tehran. Rezā Khān, whose troops were occupied in Gilan, preferred to reach a compromise with him. At the end of June, Pasyān agreed to let the governor appointed by Tehran do his job and free the prisoners. In exchange, he would remain the head of the armed forces in Khorāsān. In response, Qavām encouraged the tribes of Khorāsān to rise up against Pasyān and, to replace him, he appointed the Bakhtyāri chief Samsām os-Saltane, whose tribal force could serve as reinforcement to the government. On 22 August, Pasyān officially announced his rupture with the capital and formed a revolutionary committee with the rebel gendarmes. This time Rezā Khān decided to use force and to send in the Cossacks, who quickly routed the gendarmes. Pasyān died during the fighting and was elevated to the status of martyr for having wanted to defend the constitutionalist ideal. The Khorāsāni gendarmes were the first to be dismantled and reintegrated in the new army, where they were under the command of former Cossacks.

Is it possible to detect Moscow's hand, or London's, or both, behind this local rebellion? At the beginning of June, Pasyān had consulted the British consul at Mashhad, who had tried to dissuade him from overtly breaking away from Tehran, in the fear that such a move would play into the Bolsheviks' hands, setting Iran ablaze. But, at the same time, the minister of the Soviet Union in Tehran, suspecting the British of supporting the revolt in Khorāsān, offered Rezā Khān the assistance of Bolshevik troops from neighboring Turkestan. In any case, this double confusion shows that the two powers both tried to make good use of Iranian national sentiments to weaken the ambitions of their rival.

Sheykh Khaz'al (Sardār-e Aqdas)

Of a different nature was the rebellion of Sheykh Khaz'al (1881–1936) in the south-west of the country, where the British, to protect their interests in the region, covertly supported Rezā Khān. Khaz'al, chief of the Arab tribe, the Banu Ka'b, whose territories straddled Iran and the Ottoman Empire, was based at Mohammara (now Khorramshahr), an important strategic position for the British, even before the extraction of oil, because it allowed them to penetrate into the heart of Persia by navigating the Karun up to Ahvāz and the Lynch Road that since 1897 linked Ahvāz and Isfahan. In this region, which was not part of their zone of influence, they had signed an agreement, recognized by Tehran, with the Bakhtyāris and had established direct contacts with the tribal chiefs to maintain security for their merchants and keep the rival Russians at a distance. In 1902, they had signed an alliance with Khaz'al with the objective of getting rid of the Belgian customs officials, whose allegedly pro-Russian actions they feared; above all the new customs duties would slice into Khaz'al's income from local imports.

The British had even more need of the tribal chief after the discovery of oil in 1908 and the construction of an oil pipeline to Ābādān. It was with him and not with Tehran that APOC negotiated the location of the refinery. The Sheykh was honored with the Cross of the Indian Empire, received arms, and was given responsibility for the security of the oil installations during the war, which implied his allegiance at a time when the Germans and Ottomans, in vain, encouraged the tribes to turn against the British. After the war, in recognition of his services, the British thanked him and gave him a steamship as well as 3,000 rifles and ammunition to protect the oil company and to cover the withdrawal of their troops.

In 1923, the Sheykh rebelled when Rezā Khān demanded that he pay taxes he owed to the public treasury and, to show how serious he was, sent troops to Mohammara. The British minister in Tehran, Sir Percy Loraine, tried to gain time. He gave Khaz'al the assurance of his protection if he followed his advice and paid the taxes; at the same time, he requested that Rezā Khān recognize the Sheykh's autonomy. When the troops advanced to the south, the British hesitated. Some, doubting that Rezā Khān had the capacity to remain in power for long enough to reconstruct the Iranian state, remained of the opinion that local allies should be defended, even at the expense of Iranian national unity. Others, such as Loraine, believed Rezā Khān had to be supported and were ready to cut their local alliances, because thereafter they might be able to exercise some measure of control over him and in this way use him as buffer against the Soviets.[3] Moreover, defying the central

<hr>

[3] "To support Minister of War means the almost certain lapse of our local friendships of which the most important and difficult case is that of Sheykh Mohammerah; but support

authority would mean encouraging rebellion and favoring communist propaganda.

According to this line of thinking, disarming the tribes protected British interests in the long run. Benefiting from Loraine's vacation in Europe, Rezā Khān let Sheykh Khaz'al know that he would spare his life on the condition that he was to surrender without delay. Loraine returned immediately from his holiday and asked the Sheykh to submit to the demands, stating that the occupation of the province would be temporary. A few months later, in April 1925, Khaz'al was arrested and taken to Tehran. Under house arrest, he died, or was killed, in 1936. Rezā Khān's popularity was immense after his bloodless victory in Khuzestan, a triumph that he once again owed to the indirect support of the British.

Bandits and the Nomads: Enemies of the Central State

Aside from the suppression of local revolts, the central authority of the state acted as guarantor of the free circulation of people and goods, bringing an end to the prevalence of banditry and securing the submission and disarmament of the tribes.

The most well-known bandit of the time, Nāyeb Hoseyn Kāshi, had been arrested and executed with his two sons in 1919 on Vosuq od-Dowle's orders. According to contemporary chronicles, the Nāyeb's gang, the *Nāyebiān*, plundered and killed indiscriminately between Tehran and Isfahan, instiling terror and insecurity in travelers and local populations. A recent historian has drawn an alternative and more romantic Robin Hood-type portrait, that of an enemy of the exploitative British and local feudal oligarchy, a Pan-Islamist militant and partisan of Jamāl od-Din and of constitutionalism.[4]

The alleged knight of justice, taking from the rich to distribute among the needy, in any case went against the Jacobin national unity of which Rezā Khān was the executive arm. Rezā clearly stated in a declaration during the first anniversary of his coup d'état:

might enable us to control Reza Khan to some extent and perhaps tie him down to definite assurances as regards Sheykh's position. Support would also strengthen bulwark against Russia," Loraine, Tehran, 5 May 1923, FO 371/9024, in M. P. ZIRINSKY, "Imperial power and dictatorship: Britain and the rise of Reza Shah, 1921–1926," p. 654.

4 Md-R. KHOSRAVI, *Toqyān-e nāyebiān dar jariān-e Enqelāb-e Mashrutiyat-e Irān.* (Review of this book by Sd A. Āl-e Dā'ud, *Nashr-e dānesh,* 18, 3 (1380/2001), p. 318.)

It had become intolerable for me that this nation each year collects five million tumans from poor old women of Kermān and Baluchestān to spend them on maintaining the law enforcement force, while a thief engages in banditry, cutting all routes for ten years around Qom and Kāshān as far as the gates of Tehran by using the complicity of some officials in the capital.[5]

Rezā Pahlavi spoke of the nomads in almost the same terms, even when he began to use the military force of the tribes, for example, against Pasyān, before bringing them rudely to heel. He demanded total loyalty from the Qashqā'is, a large Turkic-speaking tribe in the Shiraz region, arranging that their chiefs, among them Esmā'il Khan, be elected to Parliament. But once in Tehran, they were assigned a residence and Esmā'il Khān was poisoned (1933). A Bakhtyāri chief, Ja'far Qoli Khān (Sardār As'ad III, 1880–1934), in turn was imprisoned without any form of trial, shortly after having been nominated minister of war. The Qashqā'is twice rebelled, in 1929 and 1939, dragging some sedentary peasants along with them.

The nomads' way of life and their tribal structure stood in opposition to the modernization imagined by Rezā Pahlavi. They not only represented a local power, but their seasonal migrations, their adaptation to environmental conditions, and their temporary camps were to him the opposite of "civilization." In his eyes, civilization was only that which left permanent traces of its culture, thus urban society. Based on Ataturk's model, he wanted to put an end to outmoded traditions and impose industrialization to vanquish the constraints imposed by nature itself. Moreover, the tribal order, which relied on particularly strong kinship connections, stood in opposition to modern practices. Had not the Qajars ruled the country since the end of the eighteenth century in the same manner, with members of their kinship the only ones to obtain executive functions?

More than their nomadic way of life, their refusal to submit to central rule created a major obstacle for the man who wanted to consolidate a centralized state.

To disarm the tribes and settle the nomads, Rezā Shāh used the full force of the state's military might. Until his abdication in 1941, operations against the tribes required an impressive mobilization of

---

5 H. Narāqi, *Tārikh-e ejtemā'i-e Kāshān*, p. 318.

forces, and airplanes dropped bombs on the mountain camps. The migration routes were severed, and the nomads were confined to areas that were very hot in summer, where their flocks had nothing to eat and died. But as soon as the military pressure ended nomadic customs resumed.

The Marginalization of the Clergy

In 1921, among his "revolutionary" reforms, Seyyed Ziā ordered liquor shops and bars to be closed and alcohol during official banquets to be replaced by *dugh* (a savory yogurt-based beverage). This was more to impose a populist reform of customs than to please the demands of the clergy, although Ziā had himself donned clerical dress and the turban until the coup d'état.

The clergy were partisans of order and preferred Rezā Khān's martial law to the anti-religious destruction that would result from a Bolshevik victory. Three traumatizing events in fact obliged the ulama to proceed with great caution: the violence of the Leninist repression of Christianity and Islam in Russia and Central Asia from 1917; the crushing of the Shiite revolt in Iraq by the British in 1920; and the slow and inexorable rise of a secular republic in Turkey (1923).

The Shiite Uprising in Iraq and Its Consequences

The creation of Iraq and the Shiite revolt against the British Mandate that followed had consequences in Iran. Political violence in the region that had already suffered considerably from military campaigns during the Great War, induced the ulama to move away from the traditional Shiite religious centers that Najaf, Karbalā, Samarrā, and Kāzemeyn had been since the end of the Safavid period. In the holy places in Iraq (*Atabāt*), the Iranian ulama had developed prestigious theological seminaries that were entirely independent from Iranian political authority and had served as centers of open political contestation against royal power since the end of Nāser od-Din Shāh's reign. From Iraq, the eminent Iranian clerical families spread their authority over the Shiite clergy in India, Bahrain, Syria, and Iraq, and they enjoyed relative freedom. But, henceforth, political power in Iraq, under the British Mandate, was perceived as a direct enemy. Increasingly, the ulama chose to avoid confrontation, following the example of Sheykh

Abd ol-Karim Hā'eri (1860–1937), who was resolutely apolitical or "quietist":[6] he did not return to Iraq after the war and finally, in 1922, he accepted a proposal to revive the theological schools in Qom. Paradoxically, the establishment of a secular state in Tehran also led to the creation, near the Iranian capital, of a center of counter-vailing power, where the ulama, despite anti-religious measures by the government, felt better protected than in Iraq. In Qom, they depended on an authority led by Muslims, where the submission to British power was not as obvious as in Baghdad.

The arrival of the Iraqi ulama in Iran (July 1923) reinforced this sentiment. Banned from Iraq for having advocated the boycott of the elections organized by the British and having taken the side of Ayatollah Mahdi Khālesi (1855–1925), who was deported to Aden, a group of half a dozen renowned Shiite dignitaries went to Qasr-e Shirin and were triumphantly received in Qom. The son of Ayatollah Mahdi Khālesi, Mohammad Khālesizāde (1880–1963), was the first to reach Iran, where he waged a campaign to denounce British intervention in Iraq.[7] In Qom, Tehran, and Mashhad he climbed the pulpit, met ulama and politicians, and notably tried to convince Rezā Khān to help the ulama dislodge the impious regime that had been installed in the Mesopotamian province of the former Ottoman Empire. Soon, Khālesizāde noticed (or claimed to) that his contacts were under surveillance, that the British censored the press, and that Rezā Khān did not in fact have the much-vaunted freedom of action he believed he had.

Thus the intrepid son of Khālesi witnessed the British takeover of Iraq, and the diversion of Iranian patriotism behind the screen of the minister of war whose nationalist slogans, according to Khālesi, concealed British domination. During the winter of 1923/4, Rezā Khān, then prime minister, organized a major campaign for the establishment of a republic. The failure of the movement had nothing to do with any sentiment of loyalty toward the Qajar dynasty; Ahmad Shāh himself was more interested in the spas of Europe, where he was tending his obesity and boredom, than in the fate of his kingdom. Nevertheless, the clergy feared the repetition in Iran of the anti-Muslim wave that they saw in Kemalist Turkey.

---

[6] A term coined by the historian Nikki Keddie. (In French, *quiétisme* refers to a specific trend of mysticism among Catholics in the seventeenth century.)

[7] Md-M. al-KHALISI, *La vie de l'ayatollah Khalesizadeh*; Y. NAKASH, *The Shi'is of Iraq*, p. 82.

Khālesizāda relates with a certain self-satisfaction the role he played in the failure of the republican complot. There were a few ulama, such as, for example, the young Abol-Qāsem Kāshāni (1882–1962), who, exiled from Iraq, approved of Rezā Khān's plan and whose followers sent telegrams from all over Iran to demand a republic. Even Sheykh Abd ol-Karim Hā'eri in Qom was ready to join the cause.[8] But, typically, the clergy, although favorable to the return of central authority, saw protection in the institution of the monarchy. The majority did not support the demands despite the determination of some politicians. Hasan Modarres (1870–1937), a very popular religious nationalist, was manhandled in Parliament after opposing the change of regime. A widespread reaction, which the prime minister had not anticipated, broke out against him. With theatrical pomp, upon seeing that the republic was not going to be adopted before the parliamentary holidays for the New Year (21 March 1924), he resigned, making a volte-face while courting the ulama: Rezā Khān issued a public statement stating they were right and abandoned the call for a republic. He withdrew to Rudehen, 50 km (30 miles) east of Tehran, and Ahmad Shāh, from Paris, nominated Mostowfi as head of government. Conveniently, Lorestān province was on the verge of rebellion – or, most likely, pro-Rezā Khān officers had threatened to withdraw their protection from this mountainous region where tribal unrest was a permanent feature. An avalanche of telegrams begged Parliament to recall Rezā Khān. Fickle public opinion did its best to forget the concerns that it had about *Sardār Sepah*. To allow the Iraqi ulama to return to Najaf without losing face, Rezā Khān, reinstalled as prime minister, arranged with the Iraqi government of King Faisal that an official emissary from Baghdad would come to invite the dignitaries taking refuge in Qom to return to the holy sites. Once returned, where they were received by the king, the most eminent among them, Mirzā Hoseyn Nā'ini, sent as a thank-you a sword reputed to be blessed by Abbās, the half-brother of the third Imam, martyr of Karbala, and a portrait representing the first Imam to the Iranian prime minister. In a letter to Sardār Sepah, Nā'ini described all enemies of the prime minister as enemies of Islam. To crown his return to grace in religious circles, Rezā Khān took the opportunity of his military campaign to Mohammara for a pilgrimage to Karbala (December 1924).

---

[8] A.-H. HAIRI, *Shiism and Constitutionalism in Iran*, p. 142.

This homage paid to the clergy clearly had a political motivation; it gave the ulama, until the fall of 1925, the feeling that Islam was protected under the new political authority. Such was the price to pay for the coming change of regime – no longer a change to a republic, but a change of dynasty. Despite the denunciations of Khālesizāde, who was able to dissuade the Tehran ulama to participate in the ceremony that publicized the gratitude of the Iraqi ulama, Rezā Pahlavi had offered sufficient guarantees, and a large number of ulama participated in the vote that deposed the Qajars and gave him the right to accede to the throne.[9] Many turbans can be seen in the photo of the official coronation ceremony that took place on 25 April 1926, notably Abol-Qāsem Kāshāni, a refugee from Iraq and an enemy of the British.

Rezā Shāh's relations with the clergy were defined by a succession of conflicts, both symbolic and structural. The political elite of the constitutional period recalled the resistance of a large part of the ulama to the application of democratic values, in particular, to consider people as equal citizens and no longer solely as members of a community of believers. The ulama adopted a defensive position, almost a siege mentality, because the model of a modern state put forward was that of a secular, Europeanized regime that drifted too far from their dogma and threatened their religious tenets.

Education

The main traditional branches of clerical influence were progressively entrusted to officials who had to prove their loyalty to the state and whose nomination was based on criteria of competence (at least in theory) in their field. Thus a system of primary and secondary education was established based on the French system, with teachers educated in training colleges. Religion was still to be taught by ulama but only had a secondary place in the program. When a university was established in Tehran in 1934, in addition to the faculties of humanities, science, medicine, and law, a faculty of theology was established, called the "Sciences of Intellect and Tradition" (*Olum-e ma'qul-o manqul*), which aimed to compete with the traditional system of religious education in the *madrase*-s of Qom and Mashhad.

---

[9] On the negative reaction of the ulama of Qom and Tehran, see A. HAIRI, *Shī'ism and Constitutionalism in Iran*, pp. 144f.

Many teachers had received a classical Islamic education in the *madrase*, but now they had to dress in civilian clothing and submit to the control of state examinations.

The Judiciary

Civil (*orfi*) justice had existed at least since the Safavids, and was extended and placed under state control by Nāser od-Din Shāh; it was entirely reorganized in 1911 under the supervision of the French jurist Adolphe Perny, who was in charge of writing a civil code. Rezā Pahlavi's reforms were a systematic continuation of previous advances: justice was henceforth exclusively controlled by the ministry of justice, and judges were requested to have a modern judicial training (not theology and *fiqh*).[10] From 1928, a new civil code, written under the guidance of Ali-Akbar Dāvar (1887–1937), was enshrined and defined the law, separating it as much as possible from religious law (*shari'at*), except where it concerned personal status (marriage, heritage), where the particularities of Shiite Islam were maintained, among them the right to polygamy, the right to repudiation exclusively given to the husband, and the right to the "pleasure marriage" or temporary marriage (*mot'a*, commonly called *siqe*), which was a less formal marriage than permanent marriage and which the two contracting parties may decide to enter into for a limited period. The registration of business or real-estate transactions and of marital status was henceforth no longer entrusted to the clergy but to sworn-in public notaries.

The Secularization of the Clergy

The economic marginalization of the clergy following these measures was accompanied by the lowering of clerical status and much humiliation. Wearing a turban and an *abā* (clerical garb) in fact became subject to official authorization. Only theologians had the right to dress in this way, those who had agreed to sit an examination on behalf of the public authorities. Submitting to an exam, moreover one that was organized by the ministry, meant deferring to a superior power.

---

[10] See W. Floor, "The Secular Judicial System in Safavid Persia"; "Judicial System from the Advent of Islam through the 19th Century"; "Changes and Developments in the Judicial System of Qajar Iran (1800–1925)."

Presenting a permit to wear a turban to the police did not mean it was not necessary to go to the police station to find a police officer capable of deciphering it. For example, tired of harassment, Mohammad-Taqi Shariati (1907–87), heir of a long line of clerics of Khorāsān, ceased to claim his clerical status, dressed in civilian clothing, and taught at a public school. Conversely, the father of the essayist Āl-e Ahmad, a mollā at Tāleqān, lost his income as a traditional notary by refusing to join the ministry of justice and was ruined.

The vexations experienced by the clergy also included conflict over military service. As of 1922, a law established obligatory conscription for all men aged twenty-one. The mollā-s, also being citizens, had to enlist, but a compromise was agreed upon, exempting young clergymen who could justify their theological competence (again a state control on Islamic studies). In reality, this law was shaping a new definition of the individual vis-à-vis the state. There was no longer communal recruitment, by village community, but recruitment by name, based on the civil registry. The systematic census of all citizens, the establishment of family names and the rational definition of parentage and identities broke with customs that had entrusted exclusive control over personal status to the clergy, according to the rule of the *shariat*.

Dress Code, Unveiling of Women

A further step in anti-clerical measures was taken when, to standardize – in an expression of imposed solidarity – the outward appearance and dress of the Iranians, a national dress was imposed upon all male citizens. Instead of the turban or traditional headwear, cap or regional hat, it included in particular, the wearing of a ridiculous kepi, of which the visor, rigidly positioned at the front, in principle prevented the ritual prosternation at prayer unless one bared one's head (which is shameful in traditional society) or turned the kepi around (even more ridiculous). After his trip to Turkey, Rezā Shāh wanted to remedy the grotesque *kolāh-pahlavi* (or Pahlavi hat, the name given to the kepi) and replace it with a soft European hat, instructions for the use of which had to be distributed by means of incredible administrative circulars: one had to, it was said, bare one's head to greet another or when entering a house and so on. Religious circles put up strong resistance to these measures, the adoption of Western dress being considered as an outward sign of submission to the infidels.

In July 1935 a nonviolent demonstration was organized in Mashhad against the dress reforms. Although the unveiling of women was only decreed in January 1936, it was already at the forefront of people's minds, and this transgression of tradition prompted the demonstrators in the Gowhar Shād mosque (mausoleum of the Eighth Imam), at the provocation of vociferous preachers, notably Sheykh Bohlul, to denounce the rulings on dress.[11] The police fired at the crowd, causing many casualties (several dozen, or even hundreds according to some reports). This violence inside a sanctuary was ignored by the press, a silence which accentuated, in the informal transmission of the information, its dramatic character and entrenched a deeper rift between the secular state and the clergy.

The law prohibiting women to wear the veil in public spaces transferred the problem to the most private area of life. In fact, women in many traditional societies, as in the south of Europe, for example, are the carriers of the reputation of the family that is jealously defended by men. An attack on the dignity or honor (*nāmus*) of a sister or a wife has immediately to be countered with an honor crime. Thus unveiling women was a form of rape more deeply felt than an ideological attack against Islam. Some women, who had received an education in girls' schools established since the end of the nineteenth century, started to express themselves in the public sphere and to attend meetings that until then had been the preserve of men; the phenomenon became more widespread thanks to secondary female education becoming increasingly common, but the shocking legal restrictions on the wearing of the veil, far from facilitating this evolution, tainted it with a diabolical character. Traditional families tried to keep their girls at home instead of educating them in public schools. Some women only went outside at times when the police would not see them. It could be said that the obligatory unveiling, far from contributing to the emancipation of women, actually slowed it down. Although the ulama took many adversities in their stride, even the most conciliatory, such as Sheykh Abd ol-Karim Hā'eri, on this point voiced their protests to Rezā Shāh.

"Emancipated" from the veil, wives and relatives of officials were obliged to show themselves in public, strangely dressed and ill at ease. In official ceremonies, some used the service of "temporary" wives so as not to dishonor their spouse through exposure. The mechanical

---

[11] S. Vāhed, *Qiyām-e Gowhar Shād.*

application of a reform that claimed to liberate women – against their will – from a constraining tradition resulted in replanting a mistrust of modernization in the population.

Clerical Resistance

The ulama did not lose all their resources. Despite the confiscation or the diversion – or state control – of a large part of the endowments (*vaqf*, pl. *owqāf*) that allowed the clergy to maintain their educational service (in the *madrase*) and their charitable and pious deeds (pilgrimage, help to the needy, the funding of hospitals etc.), Islamic taxes continued to be paid by believers to the agents of the grand ayatollahs, such that the Shiite institutions were relatively well maintained. Contrary to the radical secularization measures taken by Ataturk, Rezā Shāh, who never abjured Islam, maintained important symbols: prayers and the call to prayer were retained in Arabic, a language that continued to be taught in all secondary schools, and the Persian script (with a slightly modified Arabic alphabet) was not abandoned, although one of the tasks of the Persian Language Academy was to find Persian neologisms to replace scientific or technical terms borrowed from Arabic and European languages. Finally, despite the attempts to create a state-controlled religious education separate from traditional Islam, the clerical institution was maintained at Qom and Mashhad.

Two attitudes prevailed among the Qom ulama. The first was to make no concessions at all, whether ideological or political, but to keep their heads down so as not to provoke a run-in with the authorities. For ulama such as Ruhollāh Khomeyni (1902–89), who had started their theological program after the coup d'état, bitterness and a thirst for vengeance only grew. Rezā Pahlavi proved to them the failure of the policy of compromise that the constitutionalist ulama had tried to maintain to preserve their influence despite the modernization of institutions and minds. The second, more pragmatic, attitude was to use the authoritarian secularization measures as an opportunity to reform their religion in ridding it of superstition and instead presenting Islam to the intellectuals as the solution to the problems of their time.

This stance was expressed in *Homāyun*, a journal published in Qom in 1934 (eleven issues); the editor Ali-Akbar Hakamizāde (d. 1985) had decided to look for the positive aspects in Rezā Shāh's reforms – with the exception of the case of women's unveiling. He took the side of Shariat Sangalaji in a theological dispute in which this young audacious theologian was denounced as a heretic. Although these reforming ulama did not have a political role, they were taken to task after 1941 by the radicals. Thus when Hakamizāde published – after having left his religious career toward 1940 – a pamphlet to ridicule the "millenary mysteries" of clerical Islam, he became the main target of a virulent piece published by Khomeyni in 1943, the future revolutionary leader's first piece of writing, in which he speaks openly about societal phenomena without questioning the institution of monarchy at that time.[12]

Sangalaji (1890–1944) went far in his religious reform, since, without giving up Shiism nor the turban, he even sought ideas among Salafists. (These reformers of Sunnite Islam were fascinated by the example of Wahhabism, in which they believed it was possible to see the purity of Islam in its essence, freed from the superstitions of the cult of saints and the rituals that burden Shiism.)

Despite the profusion of teachings and the intellectual and ideological legacy of this atypical theologian, it was the other tendency that apparently triumphed, belatedly, in the revolution of 1979: the clerical tendency. Among the radical clerics of Khomeyni's generation who studied at Qom during the worst times of anti-religious repression, the refusal to concede to secularization prevailed. Retrenched at Qom in a kind of counterstate, over which Rezā Shāh had no power, they had sown among their students the seeds of a counterbalance to the European model of modernization. Yet between these two extremes – on the one hand the secularization by the state and on the other the clerical bond to Islamic tradition – following on from the participation of the clerics in the constitutional revolution, there flourished an intermediary fringe of Muslims, who, in the name of patriotism and national solidarity, agreed to go much further in their political commitment, including participating in the secular system. This tendency was evident in political life particularly after World War II, and especially in the fight for the nationalization of the oil industry in which numerous Muslims

---

[12] Hakamizāde asked me never to mention his name until after his death. He said he was proud to have spent the second part of his life engaged in an activity that was more useful to his compatriots than theology, the raising of chickens. See V. MARTIN, "Religion and State in Khumaini's *Kashf al-asrar*"; A. RAHNEMA, *Shi'i Reformation in Iran: The Life and Theology of Shari'at Sangalaji*.

participated, including the ulama. Their heritage was the implantation in Iran of a political modernity defined as "Islamic government," which was nothing other than parliamentary democracy dressed in religious colors. They didn't reject the core ideology of the constitutional revolution, despite their wish to keep in check the very principles of equality, secularity, liberty, and human rights. In the dictatorship of Rezā Shāh, these beautiful words had been turned into a repulsive caricature, inciting citizens to seek the achievements of political participation and social justice in other ways.

The Communists, Going Underground

As early as the Constitutional Revolution, several Social Democratic movements emerged in Iran, sometimes linked to revolutionary movements in the Caucasus. During World War I, they founded the anti-imperialist Adālat Party that had allied itself with the Bolsheviks to fight the Czarist army. The Adālat activists tried to rally the progressive militants in the large Iranian cities to their cause, but they gained little success beyond the Caspian coastal plain. After the landing of the Bolsheviks and the proclamation of a socialist republic in Gilan in June 1920, the Adālat Party met in Anzali and decided to create a Communist Party of Iran. The famous revolutionary Heydar Khān Amugli (1880–1921), who had stood out during the Constitutional Revolution was absent, although he had organized a conference of Adālat at Tashkent. The congress of Anzali advocated a rapprochement with progressive forces of the national bourgeoisie, because "Persia is not ripe for communism." The first objective was to expel the British from Iranian soil. Another tendency advocated working toward the dictatorship of the proletariat and the nationalization of factories, banks, and so on, and redistributing the land to the peasantry, including that of religious endowments.

Shortly thereafter, in September 1920, the Congress of the Peoples of the Orient met at Baku, where they decided to fight for a revolution which would be national before it would be socialist. Heydar Khān then returned to Gilan to work on establishing a revolutionary regime with Kuchek Khān. Meanwhile, Moscow negotiated, on the one hand, with Tehran (with a friendship treaty signed soon after the coup d'état in February 1921) and, on the other hand, with the British. It was some years before the Soviets could build up a coherent foreign policy: local alliances with the Jangalis or with

Pasyān signaled some hesitation. The Soviet minister in Tehran asked the revolutionary Jangalis to lay down their arms, and Heydar Khān was killed, perhaps by a Soviet agent. The purely communist revolution was abandoned in favor of a "proletarian direction" for the national liberation movement that supported Rezā Khān, considered as the representative of the Iranian national bourgeoisie, and praised his fight against the landed aristocracy. After *Haqiqat* ("Truth"), a newspaper banned in June 1922, the communists published another newspaper named *Kār* ("Work"). Despite the repression, they tried to develop trade-union activities and to sensitize public opinion to the working conditions of the proletariat. Their successes were insignificant (relative to the receptivity of the Persian working classes of that time). After the change of dynasty, communist support for Rezā Pahlavi ceased. The Second Congress of the Communist Party of Iran, today called the Congress of Urmia (but held in the Ukraine, in the of fall 1927) appealed for the overthrow of the monarchy and radical agrarian reform.

Dr. Arāni and His Group

In the secret clauses linked to the signing of the Irano-Soviet Treaty of Friendship of 1921, article 3 stipulated that "the Iranian government will agree to the diffusion of socialist ideas and trade union organization in Iran on condition that they are not hostile to the state, in accordance with a law that will be approved by the National Assembly." The article, first suppressed at the request of Iran, was apparently retained at the request of the Soviet Union.[13] The surveillance of all propaganda activities that might have been considered an interference in Iranian affairs rendered the strict application of that freedom very difficult. To that end, after the strikes in the oil industry of Khuzestan (1929)[14] and in the textile industry in Isfahan (1931) a law of June 1931 imposed heavy punishments on Iranians who propagated socialist opinions.

---

[13] See B. Navāzeni, *Ahd-nāme-ye mavaddat-e Irān va Shuravi*, p. 134. On the history of communism in Iran, see C. Chaqueri, "Communism, I," *Encyclopaedia Iranica*.

[14] J. H. Bamberg, *The History of the British Petroleum Company*, 2, pp. 76f; W. Floor (referring to Lāhuti's memoirs), in *Labour Unions, Law and Conditions in Iran (1900–1941)*, p. 53 minimizes the disturbance: "the Abadan strike was a great to-do about nothing, which nevertheless had great propaganda value." The importance of the Abadan strike has been generally overstated, as in E. Abrahamian, *Iran Between Two Revolutions*, p. 162.

Pressure was exerted on Germany, which allowed total freedom to Iranian communists such as Mortazā Alavi (1905–41), the brother of the novel writer Bozorg Alavi, who also was a communist. Alavi published in Berlin the journal *Peykār* ("Combat") which was eventually closed down. The Communist Party of Iran was dissolved. A chemist who had studied in Germany, Taqi Arāni (1902–40) founded *Donyā* ("World"), a small magazine published in Tehran in 1933 apparently to diffuse modern scientific knowledge, and the group later known as the "Group of the Fifty-Three" or the Arāni group.

Contrary to members of the Communist Party, who for the majority were Azaris and many of whom had lived or studied in Russia, the members of the Arāni group were Persian speakers, and the intellectuals among them who had studied abroad came from Germany and France. Abd os-Samad Kāmbakhsh (1904–71) was the only one of the group who had lived for a long time in the Soviet Union. It was he who denounced Arāni and the other members of the group and had caused their arrest in 1937. In the survivors' accounts of that adventure, who wrote their Memoirs much later and published them after the fall of the Pahlavi regime, the communist movement was virtually divided into two: those who defended social justice inside the borders and who wished to invent a kind of socialism adapted to Persian culture, and those who defended Soviet policies and Stalinian propaganda. This dichotomy was underlined when the fifty-two survivors were freed from prison in the winter of 1941/2 after the overthrow of Rezā Shāh; many of them founded the Toudeh (*Hezb-e Tude* "Party of the Masses"), a popular party that first tried to realize the policy defined for it by its large sister party in Moscow. Very rapidly, to oppose their loyalty to Moscow, Iranian Marxists organized a party of the Third Force: they denounced the attempt by Stalin to create an autonomous Azerbaijan under Soviet control in Tabriz in 1946.

The law of 1931 de facto prohibited not only communist propaganda but any trade union activity. In reality, most industrial enterprises, including those created by the voluntary development policy of Rezā Shāh, had a limited workforce. In 1930, none had more than 500 salaried workers; ten years later, there were only seventeen companies, employing a total of 15,000 workers. This industrialization did not, properly speaking, create a proletariat united by social demands. The oil sector, the only one where such movements were possible, was closely supervised by the British, above all after the 1929 strike. The fall of Rezā

Shāh and encouragement from the Soviets, who occupied the north of the country in 1941, allowed for the creation of a major mass movement, capable of organizing spectacular strikes and demonstrations. The awareness of social inequity, the feeling of being exploited by unscrupulous industrialists, and the quasi-absence of labor legislation fanned the flames for the radical rejection of the existing government, a position that only communism could fully articulate as soon as it was given the freedom to do so.

A New Man for Iran

Rezā Pahlavi had neither a particularly elaborate doctrine of power nor a firm grasp of the principles of government. Was there a "national plan" of which he was the grand executor? If one compares the radical and systemic reforms implemented by the new "strong man" of Iran with the discourse of some intellectuals disappointed by the drift of the constitutional institutions, one is struck by their convergence.

Taqizāde

Until Rezā Khān's campaign for the change of dynasty, Tehran had known a few years of relative freedom of expression. Several periodicals featured persuasive articles defending the Constitutionalist Revolution while demanding a return to national sovereignty after the humiliations of the campaigns of foreign troops. More than anywhere else, Berlin had become a center of modernity during World War I for nationalist intellectuals; there, the magazine *Kāve* set the tone.[15] Taqizāde restarted the publication in 1920 thanks to funding from some Iranian donors, mostly merchants, and made himself the advocate of the modernization of Iran:

> First, without reserve or condition, we have to adopt and promote European civilization, a total submission to Europe, the assimilation of culture, of habits and customs, of organization, of science, of art, of life, of the entire lifestyle of Europe, with the single exception of the language, by getting rid of any kind of self-satisfaction, any objection that might become an uncalled

---

[15] J. BEHNĀM, *Berlani-hā. Andishmandān-e irāni dar Berlan 1915–1930* ; T. EPKENHANS, *Die iranische Moderne im Exil*.

for or false patriotic sentiment ... Iran has to Europeanize in appearance and reality, body and soul, that is all (*Irān bāyad zāheran va bātenan, jesman va ruhan farangi-ma'āb shavad, va bas*).

For the nationalists, the Persian language became the precious refuge of Iranian identity. After four centuries of Turkic dynasties (Safavid, Qajar), Persia in the person of Rezā Shāh finally had a monarch whose main language was that of the nation. This idea was far from self-evident in 1920. At that time, centralism had not yet been enforced in Iran, and Persian was only spoken in some provinces and in the big cities. Moreover, Taqizāde and the nationalists witnessed with some anxiety the regrouping of heterogeneous nationalities across Persia: Turkey withdrew to Anatolia where it crushed the Kurds in the name of an imagined Turkish identity, but not without having attempted to attract the Iranian Azaris and the Turkic speakers of the Caucasus. The new Iraq encompassed a mosaic of disparate ethnic groups: Arab Bedouins and sedentary Arabs, Kurds, and Circassians. The Turkic Caucasus was united in a single entity that took the name of Azerbaijan. For those who were Iranian nationalists but Turkic speakers, like Taqizāde and Kasravi, the Persian language was the only means to defend a homogeneous national entity: education, administration, the army, trade – all depended on a national language for unity and modernization.

Some months later, on 15 December 1921, Taqizāde summarized his reforming ideas in the last issue of *Kāve*: (1) the generalization of public education and sports; combatting opium, alcohol, and syphilis;[16] (2) the construction of schools, the sending of students abroad, and the hiring of foreign advisers to reform the administration; (3) the security of public life, political stability, and the pacification of the provinces at whatever cost (repression is a priori a justified means); and (4) the moderation of demands from radicals (*āzādikhāh*, literally, "those who want freedom") so that the state would have the means to act.

---

[16] The obsession with syphilis is found all over the press of that time, amid fear about the degeneration of the Iranian race. It reflects the fact that about 40 percent of the urban population was affected by venereal disease. See W. FLOOR, *Public Health in Qajar Iran*, pp. 33f and C. SCHAYEGH, *Who Is Knowledgeable Is Strong*, index *s.v.*

Farangestān

In the early 1920s other intellectuals, often strongly anti-clerical, sought a powerful authority to impose reforms and national unity. In Berlin, too, *Farangestān* ("Europe"), a magazine published in 1924–25 by some of the collaborators of *Kāve* – by then no longer in existence – regrouped around much more virulent themes against Islam and for modernity, started by inviting young Iranians to rid themselves of the obstacles to freedom:

> Come, let us prepare Iran for a moral revolution that will see us evolve from medieval man into man of the twentieth century! said the editorial of 12 April 1924 of *Farangestān* ... We want to Europeanize Iran, we want to guide the current of civilization toward Iran. While preserving the moral advantages of our Iranian identity, we want to apply this famous watch word, *Iran has to Europeanize in appearance and in reality, in body and soul, that is all.*

Somewhat further, the magazine editor, Moshveq Kāzemi,[17] defined the lengths the nation would have to go to in order to bring about the type of social revolution in Iran he aspired to: "Blood has to be shed, revolution has to be made, at least 100,000 people of a population of 9 million have to be sacrificed." As long as the majority of the population was composed of ignorant turbaned men and simple people, continued Moshveq Kāzemi, one could not do anything through law because the masses will always line up behind a preacher who will tell them to reject the reforms, as had been seen during the constitutionalist revolution.

> Are there only four or five of the deputies who have any academic education? Their mutual dissent renders them incapable of understanding anything and they make us ashamed ... In a country that knows the problems of Iran, only the thought of an individual may save society, the thought of one individual, the action of one individual.

But who? The government of a majority of ignoramuses, as the parliamentary monarchy had shown since the Constitution of 1906,

---

[17] Mortazā Moshveq Kāzemi (1902–77) became a novelist and diplomat and for a time he was the head of the protocol department of Rezā Shāh.

was unable to bring about a single reform, writes Moshveq Kāzemi. "In my opinion," he continues, "such a person has to rise up from among people who have engaged in modern studies, above all those who know what happens in Europe," he has to be the equivalent of Mussolini, an educated and determined man. Among Iranians of his day, the editor already sees changes in Parliament, where short-lived coalitions have ceased, because there is an iron fist behind the deputies. Nevertheless, the elections have sent a considerable number of obscurantist deputies to the Majles. At present, Iran has a need for this enlightened dictator who will give, as in Europe, real freedom:

> We don't have any choice other than placing our hope in the strong hands of an experienced individual. He has to begin with actions that prepare the nation for the real revolution, he has to become the guide and distinguish between traitor and servant to the state and give back to the people the pleasure of real life. Think, if you see somebody around you who has these qualities, support him and give him that function, because finally he has to be the new man of Iran, he has to bring new thoughts and open a new era for the inhabitants of this old country of Iran.

Only fifteen years after the Constitutional Revolution, this text illustrates the resignation of Iranian intellectuals and the shift toward the theory of an enlightened avant-garde, the need for a guide, and the impossibility of the people governing themselves wisely without being constrained by force. Implicitly, Moshveq Kāzemi approved beforehand all the coercive measures that Rezā Pahlavi was to take. But the journal also argued with conviction for a modern education to be given to Iranian women, and for the promotion of a universal education in the arts, music, sport, and so on.

Mahmud Afshār

Meanwhile in Tehran, Mahmud Afshār (1894–1983), a lawyer who had studied in Switzerland, founded a monthly journal called *Āyande* ("the Future") where he also showed himself to be an ardent defender of national unity. He compared the difficult gestation of this unity with what he observed in the history of Europe: Germany, Italy, and Yugoslavia, inter alia. Iran had to preserve the political, moral, and social unity of the peoples that lived within its borders, he wrote. All the particularities of dress, customs, and the like had to be suppressed, local feudalists were to be extirpated, and the ethnic cleavages between Kurds, Arabs, Lors, Turks, Turkmen, and so on overcome so that all Iranians would speak the same language and dress the same.

> As long as Iranian national unity is not realized through language, customs, dress and such, political independence and territorial integrity are constantly in danger ... Those who are interested in the history of Iran, who feel they are linked to the Persian language and literature, who are attached to the Shiite religion, have to know that nothing will remain of this country if the link that connects them is undone.

Afshār goes on to list a series of measures that he advocated to realize that unity, measures that Rezā Shāh in fact did realize, which more than likely would also have been implemented under any other regime, though with a different pace: the construction of schools, roads, railways to link the south to the north and the east to the west; the publication of books in Persian; the requirement for non-Persian speaking tribes to sedentarize in Persian-speaking areas; the systematic change of geographical names and of ethnic groups, following the example of the French revolutionaries of 1789 who broke up the traditional provinces to reorganize the country into "departments"; and a ban on using foreign languages in the army, in the administration, and in the courts. The lines of economic, political, and diplomatic action as defined in the journal would be the guiding principle of Rezā Shāh's monarchy.

Between Patriotic Culture and Authoritarian Nationalism

Education and Literary Achievements

In contrast to the ambitious attempts of industrial development, the creation of a unified system of education from one end of Iran to the other, and from primary school to university, is an undeniable achievement of Rezā Shāh's legacy. Even though education in rural areas where the majority of the population was living remained underdeveloped and girls' education remained very limited, the network was created. The writing of textbooks mobilized many teachers who created a new culture, strongly shaped by a classical education but combined too with a focus that was oriented toward modern science. The attempts at educational reform which had begun in the mid-nineteenth century were finally established. Education was no longer left to Christian missionaries who came to diffuse an off-center culture; it was led by intellectuals moved by patriotic feelings, and aware of their sacred mission in preparing Iranian youth for entry into the modern world. This new culture was not entirely secular; Islam continued to be taught, often by mollas, even when it was considered secondary to the learning of other subjects. Iranian secularism was born from these worthy educational reforms, which produced big names in twentieth-century literature and in Iranian scholarship.

To crown the new culture, after the establishment of colleges and the university of Tehran, a Persian Language Academy (*Farhangestān*) was created in 1935, the year of the construction of an archeological museum, right after the grand celebration of the millenary of the epic poet Ferdowsi.[18] One of the tasks assigned to the academicians was to create Persian words to replace the vocabulary borrowed from the Arabs and more recently from the Europeans. Many of their created words have remained anchored in the Persian language, even though the assimilation of foreign neologisms, which has been one of the strengths of the Persian language for centuries, has not ceased. Some Iranian intellectuals such as Taqizāde criticized the systematic elimination of Arabic words by nationalist Kemalists in Turkey and by the Academy in Iran. Taqizāde believed that this lexical treasury, common to Muslim peoples, allowed for much easier communication between neighboring countries, and he was of the opinion that its elimination brought with it more difficulties than those it was supposed to solve. Although the Iranian Academy made a central issue of this linguistic problem, the tendency to Persianize language dates from the time of Nāser od-Din Shāh, notably by Mirzā Āqā Khān Kermāni, and continues to this day. The Academy also had the task of preserving the heritage of classical literature and supporting the efforts of the great traditional scholars, such as Badi oz-Zamān Foruzānfar (1900–70) and Mohammad Qazvini (1877–1949) to produce critical editions of the great monuments of Persian culture. An entire generation of Iranian scholars aided by the work of European linguists and orientalists, discovered the wealth of the Persian cultural patrimony, learned Middle Persian and, with Ebrāhim Pur-e Dāvud and the poet

---

[18] On the conference in October 1934 see A. Marashi, "The Nation's Poet: Ferdowsi and the Iranian National Imagination," pp. 105f.

Mohammad-Taqi Bahār, started to read the works of the pre-Islamic period.

Finally, in the domain of literature, the period between the two world wars saw the development of a new style of poetry and prose. In the domain of fiction – mainly short stories, but also novels – we must mention Mohammad-Ali Jamalzāde (1893–1997), the son of Jamāl od-Din Vā'ez, who was executed in 1908 on Mohammad-Ali Shāh's order; a great innovator and a companion of Taqizāde in Berlin, he spent most of his life outside Iran. Above all, there was Sādeq Hedāyat (1903–50) whose novel *The Blind Owl* (*Buf-e kur*, 1937) gained an international reputation. In the field of poetry, in the 1920s, Nimā Yushij (1897–1960), a young student of Collège Saint Louis in Tehran, invented, by reconnecting with his local culture of Māzandarān, in the north of Iran, the concept of "new poetry"(*she'r-e now*) inspired by French symbolist poets but strongly marked by the rhythm of classical prosody from which the poet tried to free himself. These three authors alone suffice as evidence of the vitality and richness of Persian culture and the favorable conditions which allowed it to flourish during Rezā Shāh's period.

The nationalism that Rezā Shāh imposed by repression had the consequence of delaying the beneficial effects of patriotism. How could one expect national loyalty from nomads when they were pinned to a territory where their flocks wasted away? How could conscripts who were humiliated and bullied for two years in the barracks be integrated in an ideological entity, given the continual fueling of their resentment for an army that represses their fellows and brings them no benefit, failing even to teach them discipline? How could nationalism be given an attractive face when in many of its realizations the regime proposes only superficial xenophobic measures, scarcely concealing a congenital link with British power? One might extend this catalog of contradictions to many fields. During the sixteen years that Rezā Shah ruled Iran, the freedoms so dear to intellectuals were trampled upon, the newspapers gagged, political parties non-existent, and elections reduced to nominations by the Ministry of the Interior. The worst deformation of the constitutionalist ideal consisted in preserving quasi intact the founding texts and the appearance of institutions such as Parliament, justice, fundamental rights but reduced to a sinister caricature.[19]

[19] See A. GHEISSARI, *Iranian Intellectuals in the Twentieth Century*; particularly ch. 3 "Intellectuals and State Nationalism, 1921–1941."

Iranians have not abandoned nationalism despite their aversion for a regime which used it as a means to power and mobilization, but they have lost faith in democratic institutions. Mistrusting the achievements of the Constitutionalist Revolution dragged the nation into a dramatic setback. Political participation, the criterion of modernity, has lost its attraction and significance. Women, incited by forced emancipation to leave their home and take off their veil against their will, were generally the losers in this unsuccessful modernization, and many rejected it.

Trans-Iranian Railway

A symbolic realization of Rezā Shāh's nationalism in the economic field is the construction of the Trans-Iranian Railway. At the time when India, Turkey, the Caucasus, and Central Asia were linked by effective networks, Iran could not continue transporting its goods on camels. A railway linking Khorramshahr to Tehran (later to the Caspian plain), allowed the capital to be connected with a big sea port and with the oil-producing region. The Caspian plain was thus opened up to passengers and goods. Oil products from the Caucasus would now be replaced by Iranian oil products from the south. The nationalists really were committed to this project. Foreign companies that until the 1920s held concessions for the construction of railways had mutually neutralized any new railway project. The Germans and Russians each wanted to link their network to that of Tehran, the Baghdadbahn from Baghdad, the Russian network from the Caucasus, but the British desperately did not want these lines, fearing that their rivals would one day use them to transport their troops and their goods to the heart of Persia (their own line did not go further than Zahedan close to the Indian border).

Work on the Trans-Iranian lasted eleven years, from 1927 to 1938. Construction of the line spanned 1,400 km (840 miles), included 4,700 bridges and 224 tunnels, and monopolized many of the fiscal resources of the Iranian state, notably a special tax on sugar and tea, so that Iran did not have to borrow a single rial to finance it. It was an entirely Iranian enterprise. Certainly, the engineering was entrusted to foreign companies, Swedish–Danish, American, German, and Russian, but it was above all a matter of national pride. Ninety percent of the personnel was Iranian, which gave a strong boost to industry and to the training of skilled technical workers.

From its inception, the project was severely criticized; the financial adviser Arthur Millspaugh showed that its cost-effectiveness was doubtful, since no road network would link with the railway and the latter only linked two cities, Ahvaz and Tehran. The road network was created after the railway, which served as a magnet. The rolling stock did not keep pace with the laying of rails. In 1941, only one train a day used the single track of the Trans-Iranian. The infrastructure existed; that was what was essential for the Allies who put it back into working order and used it to supply the Soviet Union during World War II – a sad fate for a prestigious achievement that in origin was a matter of national pride but that was first of use to foreign occupiers.[20]

Sometimes we try to characterize the achievements of politicians through a particular social model. Paradoxically, the army was not at the center of Rezā Shah's social model. We have already said that it was not a real factor in national integration, and Rezā Shāh spent a great deal to provide it with modern arms, to build military schools, and to have an intervention force that was totally independent of any foreign power. But recalling the manner in which he, a Cossack, had pulled off a coup d'état in 1921, Rezā Shāh constantly kept watch over his senior officers, permanently suspecting them of hatching plots, and he did not hesitate to dismiss them at any opportunity. The rifles were kept in one barracks, the ammunition in another. As a result, the army, despite its excessive organization and modern arms, was itself the cause for much concern.

The King Falls, the Nation Celebrates

The social emergence of Rezā Pahlavi resembles a fairy tale. Having become colonel, then minister, prime minister, and finally king, this illiterate soldier remained coarse. Nevertheless, he took as his third wife a Qajar princess, Turān (Qamar ol-Moluk) Amir-Soleymāni (1904–94) thus establishing his ascent to the highest echelons of society. Through his acquisitions, he himself became a large landowner. In 1939, his eldest son, Crown Prince Mohammad-Rezā (who had

---

[20] J. Bharier, *Economic Development in Iran*, pp. 206f., gives a comparison between railway and road construction costs and benefits.

spent several years at Le Rosey boarding school, in Switzerland), at the age of 20 married an Egyptian princess, Fawzia. The ceremony was a fiasco from the point of view of protocol and court customs which greatly upset the Egyptians; the Iranian women did not know how to dress or how to behave. Fawzia did not remain for long at Tehran where she languished far from the chic salons of Cairo and Alexandria. The Pahlavi family had gained an international reputation even if it was not entirely convincing.

The end of this king who came from nothing is in itself an incredible story. As we will see in the next chapter, Iran, in not choosing sides, wishing to repeat the equivocation of World War I, had made a bad choice. For fear of German retaliation if the Nazi army won the battle for the Caucasus, Rezā Shāh delayed in dismissing, as the Allies had demanded, the many German experts in Iran, among whom there were evidently many political agents.[21] The British decision to invade Iran was followed by a very short military campaign. The mighty army that was the pride of Rezā Shāh did not fight for long, and there were few victims to mourn. Thus, the dictator who terrorized his people was swept away without regret, with the collaboration of his prime minister – Mohammad Foruqi thereby exacting his revenge for the many humiliations he had been subjected to by the Shah. Intellectuals started to debate again; newspapers discovered freedom of expression; women went around in veils and the mollas in turbans; Iran found itself again at last while under the domination of foreign troops.

To replace the fallen king, the British flirted with the idea of placing a Qajar pretender on the throne, who did not speak Persian, but finally agreed to the succession of Mohammad-Rezā Pahlavi (1919–80), a sign that they held the fate of that arrogant dynasty in their hands.[22] Such was the paradox of a reign that raised nationalist ambition to such a height.

---

[21] R. Āzari-Shahrezā'i, ed., *Dowlat-e Irān va motakhassesān-e mohājer-e ālemāni*, p. xxv; Y. P. Hischfeld, *Deutschland und Iran im Spielfeld der Mächte*, pp. 252f.

[22] D. Wright, *The Persians*, pp. 213f.

9 FROM PERSIA TO IRAN: FOREIGN RELATIONS

In 1935, Rezā Shāh ordered foreign chancelleries to no longer call his country Persia. As of then it was to be *Irān*, a name that was not used at all in the West except by geographers to denote the high plateau between the Zagros and the Alborz. For Iranians, the name of their country had always been Irān, a name that originally meant "land of the Aryans." The change in name perfectly symbolized their declared willingness to present themselves in a new way to the world. Westerners knew the country by a term that was used in antiquity, associated in the collective imagination with carpets, poetry, literature, architecture, and exotism. Imposing a different name meant drawing attention to its modernity, as an oil producer and an industrialized country, open to the world.

The change also reflected the king's willingness to take the initiative in his relations with the rest of the world, contrary to the state of affairs under the Qajars. This authoritarian nationalism was implemented along two converging paths of reform.

The first path was the process of the 1919 agreement that defined the framework for modernization assisted by one or more foreign powers. Persia needed foreign aid to shore up public finances, to form a national army, and to roll out a program of national public and higher education. More and more Rezā Shāh wanted to hide this assistance, which mainly came from the British, but also from France (army, education), Germany (industrialization, banking), and the Americans. Efforts to create an independent and self-sufficient industrial base were often thwarted by low productivity in the domestic industries; for example, the proportion of sugar produced locally rose from 5 percent to 20 percent of consumption between 1933 and 1940, but the price of sugar produced in the Marvdasht mill in 1936 was 200 percent higher than that of imported sugar. However, the fostering of economic development through a voluntary policy (taxation, investment) produced some results. "Iran was partly successful in realizing its economic policy objectives, and in pulling itself up by its bootstraps."[1]

The fury with which he threw the oil dossier into the fireplace in 1932 expresses Rezā Shāh's deep resentment at not being able to modernize his country because of a lack of control over revenues particularly from the oil industry; he immediately renegotiated with APOC a concession that was hardly better and which left a painful thorn in the Iranian nationalists' side.

The second path of reforms, based on total independence, was taken by Rezā Shāh when he decided that the railway would be constructed without any foreign aid and that the European or American companies contracted to work on it would be obliged to only use local labor.

The Iranian inclination for an authoritarian government without doubt encouraged Rezā Shāh to impose his rule when faced with domestic tensions. But the covetousness of the foreign powers could only increase with the industrialization of Europe, which brought with it an increasingly huge consumption of oil products. How did Rezā Shāh react to such external challenges as the destabilizing growth of the Soviet Union, the imperial greed of the British, the world economic depression of 1929, and the rise of Nazi power in Europe?

Soviet Ambiguity and Inconvenient British Support

Rezā Shāh, the patriot, wanted to wipe from national memory the decisive aid that London had given him in the coup d'état of February 1921; each gesture of support from that inconvenient ally was for him an impediment. Moreover, because of their cautious relations with the Soviet Union, the British, for whom Iranian oil was becoming more and more important, had no interest in weakening the Shah by protecting him too obviously. The xenophobic measures that

[1] P. CLAWSON & W. FLOOR, "Finance and Foreign Exchange for Industrialization in Iran, 1310–1319 (1931–1940/41)," pp. 125f.

Rezā Shāh had increasingly applied in a stricter manner seemed to them acceptable compensation for the preservation of their economic supremacy. In January 1933, during difficult negotiations with the British, the Shah suddenly ordered the arrest of the powerful minister of court, Abd ol-Hoseyn Teymurtāsh (1880–1933), who in practice had guided Iranian foreign policy since 1925, because he suspected him of conspiring with Moscow. Teymurtāsh was killed in prison without trial.[2] The fear of complots was boundless with Rezā Shāh, who prohibited his subjects from having personal relations with foreigners living in Iran.

The Soviet Union tried, to all appearances, to maintain good relations with the new monarch and banned all hostile propaganda. In reality, relations were often tense. From 1926, without warning, the Soviet Union broke off bilateral trade and the transit of goods to Europe for eighteen months, the time needed to negotiate a provisional trade agreement.[3] Ultimately, the Caspian fisheries, which produced caviar for export to Western Europe, remained half Russian, managed by a mixed company (it was only nationalized in 1952 by Mosaddeq). A substantial shadow was cast on the relations between the two countries after the defection in 1929 by a Russian agent of the GPU, Agabekov, because he revealed the existence of an intelligence network and communist propaganda in Iran. Their relations worsened in 1938–39 when Tehran gave commercial advantages to Germany (including the air link between Tehran and Mashhad, not far from the Soviet border). In response, the Soviets decided to close their consulates in Mashhad, Tabriz, and Isfahan and not to renew the bilateral trade agreement; they also expelled 3,500 Iranians from the Caucasus, among whom were numerous undetectable political agents, who infiltrated Iranian territory.

As for the British, their economic interests in Iran became more sensitive. APOC, whose profits continued to rise, reinvested a large portion of its profits, such that the British Treasury enriched itself twice: through the increase of capital, since it was the main shareholder, and through taxation. Conversely, the royalties paid to Iran, calculated on the basis of the net profit after reinvestment, were lower than the taxes sent to London. They were also subject to fluctuations that made

---

[2] M. Rezun, *The Soviet Union and Iran*, pp. 64f, 242f; B. Āqeli, *Teymurtāsh dar sahne-ye Siāsat-e Irān*, pp. 295f.

[3] A. or-R. Hushang-Mahdavi, *Siāsat-e khāreji-e Irān dar dowrān-e Pahlavi*, p. 28.

any forward planning impossible, in both the short and the long term. Moreover, the Iranians, who represented about 70 percent of the work-force were systematically excluded from high-ranking positions at the production sites; the staff were British or Indian. The foreigners working for the Company lived in Ābādān and Ahwaz, in protected enclaves where they had their own network of services (electricity, water, telephone etc.) and their own police, forming a state within a state. The Iranian authorities were well aware of this situation and used anti-British feelings in public opinion to demand a renegotiation of the concession.

Iran's means of exerting pressure were limited, however. Despite the irregularity of oil revenues and the slow but real industrial development of the country, more and more, the Iranian economy became dependent on that income whose suspension would have been a catastrophe. In 1914, the country only produced 273,000 tons of crude oil; in 1920 its production reached 1,385,000 tons. On the eve of World War II it reached 10–11 million tons per year.[4] The Company's annual revenues increased by the same proportion: £1,333,000 in 1914; £1,590,000 in 1920 (with a supplementary payment); and about £4 million in 1939 (the figures don't match with the value in real terms, because of inflation). To this was added 20 percent dividends, which rounded off the sum. The government of Iran quietly arranged the manipulation of the Company's local rate of exchange and collected taxes on salaries, which increased the oil revenues. Toward 1925 the royalties represented about 10 percent of the state's revenue; they rose to 30 percent between 1929 and 1932, and then stabilized at 25 percent. At the same time, local consumption increased. Iran imported about 85 percent of the oil it consumed from the Soviet Union in 1923, and 70 percent in 1929. Thanks to the construction of roads and above all of the Trans-Iranian Railway, the country stopped importing oil products at the end of the 1930s. Finally, the oil company was the model of a modern company – it employed about 30,000 people at the time of the outbreak of World War II – and any major crisis would have led to unemployment of a large number of workers that local industry could never absorb.

Iranians were forced to conclude that this national wealth was to a large extent appropriated by the British, who relied on a purely

---

[4] J. Bharier, *Economic Development*, pp. 157f.

capitalist concept of management, taking the formal concession agreement as a right to rule over production and export as if they were beyond the sovereignty of Tehran.[5] (At the time of the d'Arcy concession, nobody could foresee how oil production was going to grow.) Apart from a better distribution of the top jobs with decision-making power, Tehran demanded to have political control over APOC, to decide the quantities to be produced and an increase from the previous 16 percent to 20 percent of the royalties on exported oil with an annual guaranteed revenue. The British company itself did not want to alienate Iranian public opinion, but the economic climate during the Great Depression, after the crash of 1929, was not favorable to great generosity. In June 1932, when an agreement between the British and Teymurtash was in sight, it was learnt that the royalties for the year 1931 would not exceed £306,872, or a quarter of the revenues for the preceding year (about £1.3 million). This sparked a violent press campaign against APOC and the Iranian government demanded to examine the accounts. On 26 November 1932, during a cabinet meeting, Rezā Shāh demanded to see the oil company dossier himself and threw it into the fire, demanding that the ministers obtain an immediate cancellation of the concession. Hasan Taqizāde, who was minister of finance, signed the cancellation. Iran negotiated again for a few months.

The British turned the dispute into an international affair, taking the case to the Permanent Court of International Justice of The Hague and to the League of Nations (LoN). The LoN sent Edvard Beneš, then the Czechoslovakian minister of foreign affairs, to bring the two sides together but without demanding international arbitrage that would have allowed Iran to access the company's accounts. As the negotiations dragged on in Tehran, the director of the company, John Cadman, played on the terror that the Shah inflicted on his ministers and threatened to break off negotiations.[6]

The monarch ordered his ministers to sign APOC's proposal: geographical extension of the concession was reduced to 100,000 square miles (259,000 km²) or a reduction of 80 percent compared with d'Arcy's concession that included the whole of Iran except the northern provinces. In exchange for that reduction, the length of the

---

[5] Nobody was willing to invest either when d'Arcy lost money. Also, all medical care in the concession area, normally a government function, was paid for by APOC (W. Floor).

[6] J. H. BAMBERG, *The History of the British Petroleum Company*, vol. 2, *The Anglo-Iranian Years*, pp. 33f.

concession was extended to sixty years instead of thirty as demanded by Iran. "Beginning on 1 January 1933 the royalty was to be 4s [shillings] per ton of oil consumed in Iran or exported, plus a sum equal to 20% of the dividends paid to the Company's ordinary shareholders in excess of £671,250."[7] The royalties were retrospectively increased from 1931. APOC agreed to create public health facilities, dispensaries, and hospitals and to pay medical doctors in the concession area, a facility which was already provided for the company staff, but was extended now to Iranian as well as foreign workers, on "all the lands of the Company."[8]

The signing of the agreement took place on 29 April 1933. Iran obtained the right to exploit part of its oil and to build a refinery at Kermanshah so that it did not need to import oil products: minor benefits in view of the long-term security that APOC was gaining. Cadman's own report about the way Rezā Shāh humiliated his ministers to impose the signing of the new concession deserves to be cited:

> [Rezā Shāh] gave a little homily to his Ministers, who, he said, were down on the ground and could not see very far beyond their noses, whilst he was placed on a pinnacle and could see the great world around him ... The Ministers sat in almost subdued silence listening to his lecture like small schoolboys, occasionally putting in a word or two in answering questions when spoken to by HM.[9]

This poorly chaired meeting is a reflection of the weakness of a despotic system. The absence of discussion allows decisions to be arbitrary and prevents ministers from exercising the least responsibility. How do we explain the fact that intelligent, cultured, and experienced politicians such as Taqizāde, Teymurtāsh, Dāvar (minister of justice), and many others, accepted such constraining conditions? Neither corruption nor weakness nor ignorance explains their submissiveness. Their protests of helplessness before the violent and badly informed dictator suggest that they had the feeling that the Shah, despite his brutality, was averting worse disorder and that clerical obscurantism,

---

[7] *Ibid.*, p. 50.

[8] L. P. Elwell-Sutton, *Persian Oil. A Study in Power Politics*, p. 96; see W. Floor, "A Neglected Aspect of the Social History of the Iranian Oil Industry," p. 240.

[9] Cadman's diaries (from the archives of the British Petroleum, BP96659, quoted by J. H. Bamberg, *The History of the British Petroleum Company*, vol. 2, p. 46.

the greedy blindness of the landowners, and the population's apathy would have frozen any social and political reform.

In 1946, during famous debates in the Majles, Taqizāde was taken to task by nationalists who reproached him for having put his signature on the oil agreement of 1933 without defending Iran's interests; it would have been advisable to nationalize the oil then. Would a more equitable distribution have avoided the serious crises after the war? The Arabian American Oil Company (Aramco), which exploited Saudi oil from 1938 onward, distributed the profits equally right from the start, thereby circumventing passionate local reactions like those of the Iranians.

The oil rent that the Iranian state received had several perverse effects. The state's affluence, no longer depending on the nation's prosperity, transformed a mercantile economy into a redistributive economy. Moreover, oil revenues were not integrated in the normal state budget but in a budget reserved for the arbitration of the monarch. Rezā Shāh reserved the right to buy arms to supply his army and undoubtedly used part of the revenue to this end. But the oil money most likely facilitated his personal enrichment. He refused to submit to financial and parliamentary control. Arthur Millspaugh (1883–1955), an American financial adviser hired in 1922 to continue Shuster's work, was dismissed precisely because he wanted to put an end to this practice. Did Rezā Shāh divert important sums which he asked the British to send to his private accounts in Europe? A rather laudatory work about him underlines that, at the time he was deposed, he had 68 million tumans in the bank (the equivalent of £3 million in 1941) and that he owned some 12,000 km² of agricultural land.[10]

Rapprochement with Iraq and Turkey

Iranians could not remain indifferent to the political situation of their Iraqi neighbors. Iraq was geographically too close and too dear to their religious and historical consciousness. Rezā Khān had succeeded in reassuring Iranian public opinion in 1924 by returning the exiled ulama to Najaf and Karbalā. However, he did not establish political relations with this spurious regime, which was under British mandate from 1920 and thus lacked full international credibility. Border conflicts between

[10] D. N. WILBER, *Riza Shah Pahlavi: The Resurrection and Reconstruction of Iran*, pp. 243f.

the two countries persisted, notably concerning navigation of the Shatt ol-Arab, that broad river formed by the confluence of the Tigris and Euphrates, which Iranians from the time of Rezā Shāh, to make their divergence clear, call the Arvand-rud. At the Treaty of Erzurum (1847), when commercial navigation was unimportant, the border was fixed at the eastern bank so that, to go between the neighboring cities of Ābādān and Mohammara, boats had to pass through Ottoman waters. The situation improved in 1932 when Iraq became independent. As of April, King Feysal was received in Tehran accompanied by his prime minister and his minister of foreign affairs. But it was only in 1937 that Iran and Iraq signed a border treaty thanks to tireless Turkish mediation. The treaty gave sovereignty of the river to Iraq, except for a zone of 5 km (3 miles) around Ābādān where the border passes through the middle of the river (thalweg). Freedom of navigation was granted to the two countries' military and commercial ships, a totally theoretical freedom since it was an Iraqi river. British intervention was a determining factor in making Iran give in.[11] This retrograde move would have serious consequences since the border conflict was one of the causes of the Iran–Iraq War in 1980.

In 1934 Rezā Shāh made a historic journey to Turkey. A mutual understanding came out of the meeting of Ataturk and the Shah, who spoke to each other in Turkish, and who agreed to extend the visit for additional engagements. From this country, which had an evolution parallel to that of Iran, Rezā Shāh took back ideas to give a new élan to his westernization policy. He most likely hoped for an alliance, integrating the two countries that had for generations been confronted by similar problems, even though Persia had not experienced a dismantling comparable to that of the Ottoman Empire.

This meeting moved forward the idea that the three major non-Arab states of the region, Afghanistan, Iran, and Turkey – joined later by Iraq after the signing of the border treaty – could conclude a regional alliance to "contribute to the general peace," in the spirit advocated by the LoN. On 8 July 1937, the representatives of the four countries met in the Shah's summer palace, north of Tehran, and signed the Pact of Sa'dabad, named after the palace. Ratified the following year, the pact had the main goal of ensuring the security of the borders and

---

[11] A. ol-R. HUSHANG MAHDAVI, *Siāsat-e khāreji-e Irān*, p. 40; A. FLEURY, "Le pacte de Saadabad comme contribution à la sécurité collective dans les années trente," pp. 8f.

establishing a permanent Council of the four powers that would meet at least once a year.

The Soviet Union supported the rapprochement between Turkey, Iran, and Afghanistan, three countries with which it had entered into bilateral treaties. But the pact also suited the aspirations of the British, who thought that through their influence on Iraq, it would help to neutralize Soviet propaganda in the Middle East (originally, it was also to include the Hejaz and Egypt). The pact proved worthless when Iran was invaded by the Soviets and the British in 1941, and one may, therefore, see it as the result of a kind of non-aggression pact between the Soviet and British empires. In Iran, it was understood as demonstrating the will of the four independent countries to affirm their regional autonomy outside of the big blocs. It also showed the regional foothold of the country, at a time when the escalation in nationalist discourse might lead one to forget the need to maintain good relations with the neighbors.

The Germans, a Third Force

Weimar Germany, returning gradually to a policy of economic expansion, naturally turned to the close allies which Berlin had had in the Middle East until 1918. For the nationalists in Tehran who wanted to free themselves from the heavy tutelage of the two neighboring empires, Germany was a third force whose support remained relevant. But the British slowed down the return of their rival, notably, until 1922, by barring entry to those whom they had blacklisted and by limiting access to commercial German companies to Iran. France likewise wanted to fill the void left by those defeated in World War I, in sectors such as maritime links between Europe and the Persian Gulf, heavy arms, and new technology, such as the aeronautical industry.

From the 1920s, the Germans redoubled proposals to return to the Persian market. The first success was achieved by Junkers, which opened several air links, first in 1927 between Anzali (renamed Bandar Pahlavi), Tehran, and Bushehr, and between Tehran and Qasr-e Shirin, and then in 1929 between Tehran and Mashhad. In the financial field, it was a German, Kurt Lindenblatt, who was entrusted with the management of the National Bank of Iran (*Bānk-e melli-e Irān*), when it was created in 1928. After the departure of the American Arthur Millspaugh the previous year, Iran wanted to show that Germans enjoyed their full confidence. Lindenblatt began an unequal competition with the Imperial Bank, the British bank, which soon lost its monopoly and saw its privilege to issue money withdrawn. The British saw Lindenblatt as a "snake in the grass."[12]

A new monetary unit was created in 1932, the *riāl*, which replaced the *qerān*. Shortly after having suppressed the capitulations in 1928, Rezā Shāh was able to resume that regalian function that the Qajar kings had given up. The crash of 1929 destabilized the carpet and oil markets and very rapidly the rial depreciated. The financial crisis hampered the construction of the railway undertaken by Rezā Shāh, who prided himself on not having to borrow from abroad. He compelled the population to carry this burden by paying new taxes, notably on sugar and tea. To support the rial, a drastic control of the exchange rate was established, and the official rate was made compulsory; merchants had to sell their foreign currency at a loss to the Bānk-e Melli. As a consequence of this policy, which inhibited importers, from July to November 1930, the price of imported goods rose by 100 percent to 150 percent. Count von Schulenburg, the German minister in Tehran between 1922 and 1931 had a much more cooperative attitude with the British than Lindenblatt. He advocated the repatriation to Iran of all blocked Iranian assets in Europe (Great Britain and Germany) and to collaborate more directly with the British bank, but he did not have any authority over the Germans who managed Iranian finances.

At that time, Tehran put pressure on Iranian communists living in Germany to invite them to cease their activities, which led to a wave of protests in the German press. In October 1931 an article in the *Münchner illustrierte Zeitung* mentioned the past of the Persian Cossack Rezā Khān, recalling that he had received a slap from a diplomat who had been exasperated by his impertinence when he was standing guard in front of the German legation. Tehran immediately threatened to break off diplomatic relations to obtain the expulsion of the opponent Mortazā Alavi, and the closure of the communist newspaper *Peykār*. The new German minister in Tehran, von Blücher, who was finally authorized to present his credentials, wrote to his government: "I have the impression that we are facing here an act of

---

[12] Imperial Bank's chief manager E. Wilkinson, quoted by G. Jones, *Banking and Empire in Iran*, p. 218.

despotic absolutism by the quick-tempered Shah. If Teymurtash had been there, this would not have happened."[13] Until his dismissal, it was Teymurtāsh who conducted foreign affairs, always hiding behind a ministerial front man. Rezā Shāh by intervening in a passionate manner, in the name of his own ego, weakened Iran's place in the international community. A genuine leader with the backing of his nation would have received stronger support abroad, noted Iranian diplomats who had to deal with the complaints of their monarch abroad.

The Germans ran into obstacles, despite their involvement in the industrialization of important sectors of the economy such as sugar, textiles, and explosives. Junkers decided to discontinue its flights to Persia because of its permanent deficit. Trade across the Soviet Union was subject to the erratic goodwill of the Soviets. In March 1932, Germany lost large military orders to Great Britain, despite the higher cost (twenty training planes were ordered from the British). The Germans were no longer a counterweight to the dominating British influence. In June 1932, Taqizāde, the minister of finance, ordered an investigation into the accounts of the Bānk-e Melli to look for evidence of corruption by Teymurtāsh, who advised Lindenblatt to take a holiday in Europe. After the discovery of two sets of books and of traffic in foreign currency as well as numerous embezzlements, Lindenblatt was held responsible for improper conduct. His German assistant director committed suicide.

Another German succeeded Lindenblatt at the head of the Bānk-e Melli. At the time of the cancellation of the British oil concession, a favorable wind began to blow once more on Irano-German relations. Lufthansa replaced Junkers, and a German industrial syndicate obtained an important contract for the railway in the south. But the arrest of Teymurtāsh (22 December 1932) slowed down this trend considerably, and the British rapidly obtained a new concession for APOC.

The following year, when the National Socialist Party came to power in Berlin, Soviet-German relations improved and commercial transit across the Soviet Union became regular. Conversely, the situation of Germans in Persia did not improve because, although Iranian nationalism had symbolically entered the Aryan Nazi propaganda, there

[13] Quoted in Y. P. HIRSCHFELD, *Deutschland und Iran*, p. 117; W. VON BLÜCHER, *Zeitenwwende im Iran: Erlebnisse und Beobachtungen*, pp. 165f.

was no political communication between the two countries. Repeated incidents in Germany made Iranians think that their citizens were treated by Germans as *Untermenschen*, a category in which Hitler classed Asian people. The Führer was not interested in Iran: he seems never to have talked about it. Moreover, the first finance minister of the Reich was ready to cut all trade relations with Persia because of the commercial deficit that Germany had. The two countries were on the brink of severing all ties in April, when a newspaper in Jena published an article on the humble past of Rezā Shāh, which the despot did not like at all.

Nevertheless, Iran made an effort to renew its relations with Germany, as it was unwilling to depend exclusively on the Czechs and Danes for armaments and railway equipment. Having returned to Iran to be judged, Lindenblatt was finally allowed to leave the country after the case was dismissed. An Iranian consulate was opened in Hamburg in 1934. On the day of the anniversary of Rezā Khān's coup d'état (22 February 1934) an article in the newspaper *Shafaq-e Sorkh* expressed the Iranians' admiration for the cult of the Führer in Germany. The ideological trend corresponded with Iranian nationalists' rejection of references to Islam because of the Semitic origins of the Koranic message, while, conversely, the Zoroastrian religion was seen by them as a purely Iranian contribution. This trend crystallized with the official name change of Persia to Iran, in reference to the Aryan origin of the Iranians.

German industrial hopes led to the visit of Thomas Brown, an Irish-born German official in charge of industrial financing, but he was disappointed to see that the rank of Iranian commercial orders in Germany was much lower than expected.[14] Cultural links developed rather quickly between the two countries; study scholarships attracted Iranian students to the Reich, while several prestigious publications glorified the modernizing work of Rezā Shāh. A strong delegation of German orientalists was invited in 1934 for the celebrations of the thousandth anniversary of the great poet Ferdowsi and received many presents, particularly books. But the political relationship was much cooler, and the Shah declined an invitation to visit Germany.

---

[14] Hirschfeld, *Deutschland und Iran*, p. 147. Brown had worked previously in the Gulf ports for Woenkhaus & Co.

The Iranian government tried to improve its relations with Berlin, while fearing that the Soviet Union would use this as a pretext for an invasion, based on the treaty of friendship of 1921, since article 6 authorized the sending of Soviet troops to Iran should forces hostile to the Soviet Union operate from Persia. Only British protection could preserve the country from an invasion by its mighty neighbor, not a distant German promise. (The example of the Italian attack on Ethiopia in October 1935 brought this home to them. Moreover, Iran was one of the most virulent countries in condemning Italy in the LoN and imposing trade sanctions on it.) Thus recourse to British industries was a priority in Rezā Shāh's eyes. The agreement on *clearing* in the trade regulations signed between Berlin and Tehran, which the Majles only ratified in 1936, did not imply an alignment with Germany. Iran watched warily the first approaches of the Nazis to annex the Memel Territory from 1935.

As of 1936, Germany redoubled its efforts to win markets in Iran and to develop political relations with it. The minister of foreign affairs encouraged and financed the publication of laudatory books on modern Iran (Herbert Melzig, Walther Hinz). The minister of economy, Hjalmar Schacht (1877–1970) extended to Iran his visit to Turkey, but Rezā Shāh made no effort to meet him and even left Tehran shortly after his arrival. Schacht offered to help the Iranians to exploit their mineral and agricultural resources and wanted to increase the purchase of raw materials. He not only envisaged the extension of Lufthansa's services but the development of the road, rail, and maritime network, and the creation of radio stations. His country would assist with oil drilling, construction of refineries and oil pipelines, in exchange for oil deliveries. Moreover, Schacht offered to build the Iranians a modern hospital and a chancellery for the German legation in Tehran. Finally, he proposed the sale of modern arms to Iran and showed that the Germans wanted to participate in the industrialization and development of the country.

These proposals were tempting, but Iran dreaded upsetting its mighty neighbors by too obvious a rapprochement with Germany. Ali-Akbar Dāvar, then minister of finance, dodged the issue in his reply to Schacht. Even in the military domain, where Iran was tempted by German planes, no decision was taken before Rezā Shāh's fall, Dāvar hoping instead for the arming of a commercial fleet to facilitate Iranian exports. For Germany that meant opening Iran up somewhat more to other industrialized countries and competition with its own maritime company. Schacht's visit gave a new impulse to bilateral trade, but it did not have the spectacular consequences expected of the German proposals.

In this complicated game in which Iran repeatedly gave trade advantages to the Soviet Union, Germany, and the USA (oil drilling), it is difficult to see a resolutely constant policy. In 1937, after having granted the exploitation of a mine at Anārak, near Nā'in in the center of the country, to the German company Ferrostahl, Iran ordered from this same company 65 locomotives and 1,300 railway cars for the transport of goods and passengers, a deal that the British had recently abandoned because they refused to engage in barter. By not choosing Czechoslovakia, whose proposal was supported by the Soviet Union, Iran made a strategic choice. Tehran agreed an even bigger deal (£2.3 million) with Demag and Krupp for the construction of a steel mill, payment for which was planned over eight years.

In other areas, negotiations were at a standstill, in particular with Lufthansa which expected a concession for five years. The Iranians demanded that the Germans not only build an airport but finance the training of five mechanics over two years as well as of five pilots and two military personnel who would protect them during training and so on. Without counting the oil sold directly by the Anglo-Iranian Oil Company (AIOC),[15] Iranian sales did not balance German sales, as foreseen by the payment agreement. The different means of compensation proposed by the Germans were rejected, and the supply of cotton, skins, tobacco, and other raw materials did not increase. The Iranian deficit (27 million Reichsmark) was left on the account of the payment agreement, so that Demag and Krupp had to wait years before being paid. Deals by the Iranian army for the purchase of arms were made in Switzerland, Czechoslovakia, Sweden, and in Great Britain rather than in Germany.

Official visits realized the double aspect of German-Iranian relations. The president of the Majles, Hasan Esfandyāri (1862–1945) was received in Berlin with full honors and even had an audience with the Führer. A few months later, in December 1937, the president of the Reichsjugend, Baldur von Schirach, was received with great pomp in Tehran. But the measures expected from these meetings did not follow. Nazism seems to have been perceived by Iranians as a way to suppress the

---

[15] Anglo-Iranian Oil Company, APOC's new name after 1935.

communist contagion, which did not mean that they adhered to its ideology. The Germans, who tried to carry along the British in their alliance against the Komintern and tried to cooperate with them in Iran, notably with AIOC, presented themselves as a better defense against the spread of communist ideas. They were accepted as business associates or as technicians, but propaganda inside the country was restricted even though Hitler had a certain popularity because he was anti-communist and anti-British, and because of a latent anti-Semitism among the Iranians.

In September 1938, when the Soviets boycotted Iranian products to exercise additional pressure, Iran was still able to turn to Germany to find a new market for them. Between 1938 and 1939, its deliveries of wheat, skins and pelts, wool, and dried fruit doubled, rising from 28 percent to 42 percent of total Iranian exports (in value), while its export to the Soviet Union dropped from 34 percent to 5 percent . In 1939, Iran's exports to Germany exceeded the most ambitious forecasts by 20 percent, and the balance of payments was reversed, Germany becoming the debtor.

Things changed in March 1939 when Hitler occupied Czechoslovakia, because Iranian dependence on Germany became too restrictive, particularly for the purchase of arms. Even before the start of World War II, the Iranians feared that the presence of numerous German experts and technicians on their soil would give the Soviet Union a pretext for invasion. The British could have given the Soviets free access to invade Iran as token of a new alliance.

Contrary to a discourse often repeated, Iran did not fundamentally change its policy on Germany after the Nazis came to power. Even though the two countries shared the same extreme nationalism, the same anti-communism, Tehran kept its distance from the Nazis, a caution dictated by its need not to worry its British and Soviet neighbors. The traditional skill of its diplomats, who had learnt how to juggle several powers to preserve the independence and sovereignty of their country, allowed Iran to do rather well out of what had looked to be a desperate situation. The start of World War II would upset this equilibrium all over again.

The French

After Rezā Shāh's rise to power and his accession to the throne, France did not abandon its role as a disinterested observer generally resigned to assist the British while criticizing their hegemony. The traditional domains in which it exerted influence – language, culture, education, and archaeology – continued to assure francophone cultural supremacy and to attract the near-natural sympathy of the Iranian elite for French civilization and literature, and for its rationalist spirit and anti-clericalism. The education system put in place in Iran emulated the French one, crowned by the baccalaureate (*diplom*). The first Iranian university, that of Tehran established in 1935, was a francophone institution and several French professors were invited to teach there.

Victorious in World War I, whose bloodiest battles were fought on its land, France benefited from its immense military prestige. Was Rezā Shāh not like Napoléon, a soldier who had risen through the ranks? It was to the French military schools that young Iranian officers turned henceforth. This attraction would have been neutralized if the agreement of 1919 had been ratified and applied. Article 3 would have assigned Great Britain to put the military experts and trainers needed to reorganize its army at Iran's disposal. On this sensitive point, Rezā Khān came into conflict with Seyyed Ziā who, despite the cancellation of the 1919 Agreement, had planned to hire British officers in Iran. As of 1921, when he became minister of war, Rezā Khān sent officer-trainees to the schools of a nation that did not represent a danger to Iran, despite his aversion to the excesses of French socialists. He reminded the students whom the government sent to extend their studies in France that he sent them

> to a country that not only has the largest and the best organized army in the world, but whose deeds set an example to any other country as to indestructible national feelings, loyalty, and patriotism ... You are sent by a monarchical state to a republic only to take the model of patriotism of the French and to make it take root in your heart, so that your efforts are guided toward courage and love of the fatherland.[16]

In 1923, sixty student-officers thus joined the schools of St. Cyr, Saumur, and Fontainebleau. But the sending of several waves of student-officers did not erase the project of a true national army.

---

[16] A. Sādeqipur, ed., *Yādegār-e gozashte: Majmu'e-ye sokhanrāni-hā-ye a'lā-hazrat-e faqid Rezā Shāh-e Kabir*, pp. 45f.

The financial cost of these students as well as the risk of having senior officers who were too close to foreigners did not escape Rezā Khān. As of February 1922, after the merging of rival army groups, i.e. the Cossacks and the gendarmes, he decided to create an officers' school that regrouped the training centers of these two institutions. In 1925, the French military attaché was approached to test the French reaction to the appointment of high-ranking French military trainers. The first French instructors did not arrive in Tehran until 1933. As of 1935, they were commanded by a general in active service. The Quai d'Orsay in fact did have a clear interest in conducting a more ambitious policy in this country that was not traditionally subject to French influence. Training officers also meant selling to Iran heavy and light arms which the French knew better how to use and which they demonstrated to their students. Moreover, Paris feared that – if not the French – the Nazis would benefit from such large contracts. In fact, lucrative heavy artillery contracts negotiated by Schneider were eventually cancelled in favor of orders from Krupp.

Negotiations between France and Iran were blocked by matters of principle: Were the trainers "professors" or "technical advisers"? The negotiated contracts anticipated hiring each officer "to serve in H.I.M.'s army as a professor at the military school of Tehran. He will potentially take on, as technical adviser, all other military missions, … everything that concerns organization, administration, management, training, equipment, and preparation for war."[17] The Iranians wanted to remain in control of each contract and to be able to oversee all the activities and private relationships of the military sent to their soil. They demanded that personal contact between Frenchmen and Iranians be subject to special authorization, as was the case for other foreigners. Moreover, to be more discrete, they had to wear uniform of the Iranian army; the Quai d'Orsay considered this to be unacceptable, particularly since a French military mission in Turkey had adopted civilian dress. However, the French gave in on this symbolic point, which shows that this mission, for Paris, was of a more political than a military nature.

Lt. Col. Caldairou, who first led the mission, arrived in Tehran in December 1933 and other officers followed. Very quickly, Rezā Shāh thought about creating a higher-education war college. Caldairou, who

---

[17] Archives diplomatiques, *Asie 1918–1940*, subseries Perse/Iran, 99, f°101, quoted from M. HABIBI, *L'interface France-Iran, 1907–1938*, p. 314.

was not involved in all the preparatory meetings, objected that such a project required preparation a long time in advance and that it would be impossible to put French generals at the disposal of the Iranian general staff to provide assistance. Caldairou was sent back to Paris, Tehran accusing the French of being British allies.

During his trip to Turkey, the Shah had seen the efficacy of German military instructors and the great prestige that they enjoyed among Turkish officers. He also wanted to have senior officers, a project that Pozzi, the new French minister in Tehran supported so as not to compromise France's edge in relation to other powers. Even before Caldairou's dismissal became known, the Iranian legation in Paris insisted that in three months the French would designate senior officers, including at least one general, to take charge of the training of the general staff college. The army was not enthusiastic about the idea to see a general hired under such conditions, all the more so because he might be dismissed without reason and without appeal. But as of September 1935, a new group of seven officers, one of them a general, Francois Gendre (1873–1939), reached Tehran.

Gendre gave himself the role of military attaché, overstepping the terms of his contract and antagonizing the actual military attaché at the legation. He soon became the enemy of the whole legation. Albert Bodard, the new French minister considered him to be a "mentally unbalanced person." For his part, Gendre denounced the latter's authoritarian character and addled-brain, calling him "the missions' gravedigger." Other problems involving people and relationships with the Iranian administration complicated the work of the military mission. The French generally blamed the cooling of French-Iranian relations on the rapprochement between Tehran and Germany. In reality, the French-Soviet pact (May 1935) and, above all, the Popular Front taking over the government (June 1936) frightened Rezā Shāh, who saw the Bolsheviks already in the republic.[18] In June 1938, General Gendre, who retired, was replaced, but the other contracts were not renewed.

A greater difficulty would rise in the French press. Freedom of expression was incomprehensible to the Shah, who did not tolerate being criticized by European newspapers. His extreme nationalism and his xenophobia made it difficult to make any comment without

---

[18] M. Habibi, *L'interface France-Iran, 1907–1938*, p. 353; Fl. Hellot-Bellier, *France-Iran*, p. 278.

resorting to the sycophancy into which he forced his subjects. One of the first articles critical of Iran appeared in November 1936 in the *Revue de France*; it described a dirty and miserable country, hoping for the status of a colony or protectorate for Iran. The Iranian minister was called back from Paris. The Shah announced that he would not even give £100 to finance Iran's participation in the World Exhibition of 1937. Ongoing contracts with France were immediately cancelled and students called back from France. To reply to the article that had given rise to the royal fury, the French minister in Tehran published a eulogy disproportionate in its praise of Rezā Shāh in the same magazine:[19]

> This officer of pure Iranian race who has delivered his country from foreign domination has ensured its absolute civil and penal autonomy through the suppression of capitulations, has reestablished its finances, given it a modern administrative organization, built banks and factories, crushed religious fanaticism, and is at last founding a dynasty ... A tourist traveling alone and unarmed through it at present in total security and in a comfortable car ... who complains about not finding asphalted roads and comfortable hotels ... forgets that a traveler in the time of Loti or of Claude Anet, some 20 or 30 years ago, had to make these long journeys on the back of a donkey, accompanied by guards, and that one was often attacked by bandits at the very gates of Tehran.

This defense did not succeed in silencing caricaturists or opponents, who launched a campaign in the press, the wording of which the Shah considered to be intolerable. "This monarch who boasts of being modern does not want it to be said that if one scratches the Shah, one finds the Cossack," wrote A. de Montgon in the *Petit Bleu* of 21 January 1937. The efforts of the Quai d'Orsay to obtain apologies and complimentary articles ended in collapse. Diplomatic relations were interrupted for several months in 1938–39. This rupture led to the weakening of French influence and the uncertainty of Iranian strategic choices on the eve of World War II. Shortly thereafter, a law prohibited educational activities at all foreign schools, a measure that hit French interests and the schools of Catholic missionaries hard.

[19] M. Habibi, *L'interface France-Iran, 1907–1938*, pp. 369f.

In international relations, Rezā Shāh had great difficulty in establishing an equilibrium between his exaggerated nationalism and the sense of reality that forced him to be pragmatic and to set aside ideological preferences. A stabilized Iran became once more a commercial and strategic target, all the more so because its oil revenues assured great financial solvency. But the absence of any political dialogue between the king and his closest collaborators, and his mistrust of any minister who might be tempted to replace him with the help of a foreign power, brought more than one beneficial alliance to an end. Handicapped by his limited education and his ignorance of European languages, Rezā Shāh lived on the defensive, even in areas where Iran had an advantageous position. This irresolution became fatal when the conflicts of World War II neared the Iranian borders in June 1941.

10 THE DEMOCRATIC AWAKENING (1941–53)

In 1939, Iran proclaimed its neutrality. As experienced during World War I, Iranian opinion had pro-German sympathies, above all as a reaction to British hegemony. But more so than in 1914, its neutrality was unacceptable to the belligerent nations because of its strategic position and the importance of its oil. The Soviets and British agreed to occupy it, in the first place to stop the German advance toward the Caucasus and, secondly, to supply the Soviet Union with food and arms. On 25 August 1941 Allied troops entered the country. The Iranian army, on which Rezā Shāh had focused much of his efforts over twenty years, resisted for one week.

The monarch's days on the throne were numbered. The common understanding is that Britain both brought him to power in 1921 and also deposed him. This assertion, however, is only partially true. The Shah's abdication on 16 September 1941 was not simply the result of a foreign complot, but also the expression of a national political will.

One may recall that the initiative for the coup d'état came from Seyyed Ziā. His Cossack acolyte was a military branch which few suspected at that time would have been used to alter royal destiny. Twenty years later, we see an inverse scenario. In August 1941 the Shah recognized that the Soviet-British military invasion, having weakened Iran, called for a man who was both respected within the country and an expert interlocutor in negotiating with outside forces. Rezā Shāh recalled the services of Mohammad-Ali Foruqi (Foroughi), a learned Freemason, who had been removed from government in 1935, after the riot in Mashhad.[1] This time, in a context as dramatic as that of 1921, it was the politician who prevailed.

He had barely been nominated prime minister when Foruqi demanded an end to the hostilities and the surrender of the Iranian army. Taking his revenge for his earlier dismissal, which had forced him to live in great poverty for several years, he entered into secret negotiations with the British to request the BBC and diplomatic channels use all means at their disposal to push forward propaganda with the aim of forcing the Shah to abdicate.[2] In reality, Rezā Pahlavi was deposed. Officially, the Pahlavi dynasty continued, with the British allowing the twenty-two-year-old son of the fallen king, Mohammad-Rezā, to take the throne, in the belief that he would best serve their interests.

Occupation

Since 1939 the Allies had applied pressure on Tehran to oust the German personnel who were distributed across Iranian soil. They did not have a precise list of how many were involved and in what capacity – estimates place the number between 1,700 and 2,000 – but they suspected that many of them were assessing the terrain in preparation for a German invasion or, at the least, to forge the way for a German-Iranian alliance.[3] Their expulsion became urgent on 22 June 1941, when Germany declared war on the Soviet Union. Stalin knew that the Soviet Union alone was unable to endure for any length of time, despite its patriotic surge, because it lacked arms, wheat, and oil. The advance of the Wehrmacht into the Caucasus risked destabilizing the fragile equilibrium in the region. Germany would not only take the oil at Baku, but, quickly afterwards, take Iran. Therefore, in the final days

---

[1] In August 1935, after the massacre of the demonstrators at the shrine of Mashhad (see Chapter 8), Mohammad-Ali Foruqi Zokā ol-Molk (1866–1942), who was prime minister for the second time, begged for mercy for the manager of Imam Reza's shrine's endowments, Mohammad-Vali Asadi, his daughter's father-in-law, who had been made the scapegoat unquestionably because he was a rival of the governor of Khorasan, Fathollāh Pākravān. Foruqi was then dismissed. See S. Vāhed, *Qiām-e Gowhar-Shād*, pp. 57f; M. Bāmdād, *Tārikh-e rejāl-e Irān*, IV, pp. 16f.

[2] A. Varedi, *Muhammad 'Ali Furughi Zukā al-Mulk (1877–1942)*, p. 101.

[3] Figures given by A. Lambton, cf. Sir Reader Bullard, *Letters from Tehran*, p. 31. Another estimation, 690 Germans, is given in the newspaper *Ettelā'āt*, 17 tir 1320/9 July 1941, p. 1. Soviet propaganda gave the estimation of 5,000 to 10,000 Germans, but the number of persons deported to Australia (including women and children), did not exceed 1,000. See Y. P. Hirschfeld, *Deuschland und Iran im Spielfeld der Mächte*, pp. 275f.

M4 Occupation of Iran 1941–46

of July 1941, Churchill and Stalin agreed to invade. On 25 August, the same day that their troops entered the country, while proclaiming their respect for Tehran's neutrality, they delivered to the Shah and the Iranian government an ultimatum, giving them three days to expel the Germans. Rezā Shāh was worried about upsetting Berlin before gaining a clearer idea about the military operations. Thus Tehran delayed in responding to the Allies' demands, explaining that there was no list detailing the Germans to be expelled and that the German personnel were needed for the functioning of the recently established industries, that they were simply innocuous advisers. A few days later the Shah abdicated.

The expulsion of German personnel was a simple pretext. In reality, the Soviets and British had decided to invade even before ascertaining the extent to which the Germans were planning to encroach on the Caucasus. The British, who were determined to prioritize the protection of their oil installations, were not averse to helping the Soviets in an attack against Germany.[4]

The occupation of Iran was followed by a formal commitment by the Allies. In Tehran, on 29 January 1942, between Iran, the Soviet Union, and Great Britain a tripartite alliance treaty was concluded, which resulted in Iran becoming one of the first signatories of the Atlantic Charter, a prelude to the creation of the United Nations (UN). The occupiers recognized Iran's sovereignty and territorial integrity; they also committed to evacuate their troops from Iranian soil within six months of the cessation of hostilities and to indemnify Iran for any damage caused by the foreign armies. For its part, Iran broke off diplomatic relations with Germany and Vichy France. Shortly afterwards, encouraged by the British, the government appealed to the Americans, demanding assistance to reorganize their police force.

During 1942, the threat of a German occupation of the oil sites in the Caucasus became more serious, raising the fears of an invasion of Iran and the defeat of the Allied armies. The Americans decided to send 30,000 men, commanded by General Donald Connolly, who established his general staff near Tehran. Their mission was to safeguard the transport of arms and food via the Trans-Iranian Railway to the Soviet troops, many of whom were engaged in the defense of Stalingrad, where the Nazis capitulated only in February 1943. American assistance also ensured the return to Tehran of Arthur Millspaugh as a financial adviser. During his first mission (1922–27) the American expert had been able to make useful inroads, although he remained contemptuous of the Iranian administration. This time, older and in poor health, and still not having learnt Persian or French, Millspaugh failed to bring about reforms to the increasingly complex political apparatus, whose reach had burgeoned. Other American advisers were assigned to facilitate food and sanitary aid. General Clarence Ridley from the army and Colonel Norman Schwarzkopf in the police were the most durable

---

4 See F. Eshraghi, "Anglo-Soviet Occupation of Iran in August 1941"; "The Immediate Aftermath of the Anglo-Soviet Occupation of Iran"; H. Elāhi, *Ahammiyat-e esterātezhik-e Irān dar jang-e jahāni-e dovvom*.

elements of the American set-up in Iran, tasked with the reorganization and arming of the branches of law enforcement, a commitment that would pay off in the future.[5] President Roosevelt stood firm in his guarantee of the Allies' commitment to Iran, but the USA, after their entry into the war, had not formally signed an alliance with Tehran.

After the hard-won and painful Allied victory at Stalingrad, several international conferences convened to draw up plans to end the war and to consider the repartition of the territories freed from Nazism. At the beginning of December 1943, Stalin, Roosevelt, and Churchill chose to meet in Tehran. The leaders of the Allied powers renewed their formal recognition of the independence and sovereignty of Iran, whose territorial integrity they guaranteed. During the Tehran Conference they decided on the general plan of the Normandy landings, the moving of the Polish borders, and the annexation of the Baltic states, decisions from which de Gaulle was excluded, and the latter two of which were confirmed at Yalta in 1945.

Paradoxically, many Iranians experienced the Soviet-British occupation as a liberating force. Censorship was ended, people began to talk openly, and criticisms of Rezā Shāh could be heard. The clergy were permitted to wear the turban again as well as preach and engage in public activities, and women put on the veil to go out into the streets. It was at that time that young clergymen, hostile to the anti-religious reforms of Rezā Shāh, founded the first radical Islamic movement, the *Fedāiān-e Eslām* ("devotees of Islam"). A tide of change swept across the country. The communists of the Arāni group who, in 1937, had been arrested and sentenced, were released from prison, and several political parties were created. One of the first was the Toudeh Party (*Hezb-e Tude-ye Irān*, or "Party of the Masses of Iran"), founded in 1942, and while ostensibly socialist and nationalist, it was in reality controlled by Moscow. The Toudeh attracted popular support, particularly among the intelligentsia. Nevertheless, two difficulties arose from the occupation of Iran: the autonomous movements in Azerbaijan and Kurdistan, both of which were encouraged by the Soviets, and the oil crisis.

---

[5] M. H. Lytle, *The Origins of the Iranian-American* Alliance, 1941–1953, pp. 27f. See A. or-R. Hushang Mahdavi, *Siāsat-e Irān dar dowrān-e Pahlavi*, pp. 82f. This General Schwarzkopf is the father of the general who headed the Desert Storm operations in the Kuwait War in 1990–91.

M5 Secessions 1946

The Short-Lived Secessions of Azerbaijan and Kurdistan

In the early twentieth century, Azerbaijan experienced large-scale revolutionary unrest. The Ottoman, then Russian occupation, followed by the short-lived Khiābāni revolt in 1920, had left a feeling of unfinished business due to its internal divisions. The Khiābāni movement (see Chapter 7) was more nationalist and socialist, in reaction to the domination of foreign powers and powerful landlords, than separatist, but Iranian nationalists had severely condemned it in the name of national Iranian unity.

After the German surrender, US and British troops swiftly left Iran. However, the Soviets refused to move, letting it be known that their protection had been requested by the local movement based in Tabriz. They effectively used the irredentist feelings of the Azaris, the Turkic ethnic group whose links with the Caucasus were long-established, to arouse new separatist demands. Playing on their pride, Russian propaganda asserted that the agricultural and commercial wealth of Azerbaijan went directly to Tehran, which only sent crumbs in return, and that the Azaris had to fight to demand the recognition of their rights. The Toudeh Party created a local branch under the name of the Democratic Party of Azerbaijan (*Ferqe-ye Demokrāt-e Āzerbāyjān*). At its head was a deputy, Ja'far Pishavari (1802–1947), whose election the Majles had not wanted to recognize, because of his participation in the Jangal movement which came to end in 1921 (see Chapter 7).

From 1945, militants of the party attacked government buildings in Tabriz, demanding autonomy and the recognition of Azari Turkish as an official language. They had more difficulty in rallying the troops, but a compromise allowed the officers who did not want to swear an oath to the separatists to withdraw on the condition that they leave their arms behind. Two barracks in Tabriz and Urmia had to be subdued by force. On 12 December, they proclaimed a national autonomous government of Azerbaijan and announced the creation of a "national" army. Tehran sent an armed detachment, but it was stopped by Soviet troops before reaching Zanjān.

Tehran, vigorously supported by the Americans, sent a protest to the UN, where it became the first major case to be discussed by the Security Council. Simultaneously, the Soviet Union sent a mission to Tehran, stating that it refused to withdraw its troops as long as the British kept their garrisons in Iraq and in their empire in India, and for as long as the Americans themselves had bases along the Soviet border. Nevertheless, Moscow proposed to withdraw from the north-east of the country in return for an oil concession in the Caspian plain, where, since 1918, it had planned to prospect for oil, as a reserve was believed to exist similar in scale to that of Baku; they also asked for Tehran's respect for the democratic rights of the inhabitants (*ahāli*) of Azerbaijan – the Soviets deliberately avoided the word "nation" (*mellat*) so as not to clash with the patriotism of a large number of Iranians. The Soviets finally recognized that the solution to the Azerbaijan question was an internal Iranian matter and that they should not intervene. Despite this precaution, several communist intellectuals left the Toudeh, breaking ranks with a party that supported Pishavari's separatist movement. Finally, Qavām os-Saltane, who returned to government in February 1946, succeeded in making Stalin back down with the promise that the new Majles would examine the Soviet demand for the grant of an oil concession in the north, but specifying that the assembly, according to the Constitution, could not be elected as long as there were foreign troops on Iranian territory. The prime minister knew that once the Majles met, it would reject any new concession because there were already talks planned to cancel those granted to the British.

For the time being, the government of Tehran proposed a compromise to Pishavari. The senior officials of Azerbaijan would be appointed by the representatives of the provincial council, an entity that was foreseen in the Constitution, and primary education would be given in Azari Turkish, but Persian would remain the official language. Without waiting for the results of the negotiations that had begun in Tehran, the government of Tabriz decided on several radical social measures: the large domains belonging to the state would be redistributed among landless peasants; and the right to vote and to stand for election would be given to women, a particularly progressive step for that time. To appease the worries of the clergy, a series of declarations officialized the cancellation of the anti-religious measures of Rezā Shāh; in particular, it ended the prohibition of the wearing of the veil for women and that of the performance of the *ta'ziya*, a religious play that commemorates the Imam Hoseyn's martyrdom.

To the west of Azerbaijan, the Kurds also claimed their autonomy. In Kurdistan, dissidence was less marked by communist ideology, even when the Soviets present there encouraged the movement and gave their support in 1942 to the formation of *Komela-ye Jiyān-e Kordestān* (Organization for the Renewal of Kurdistan). In 1945, Qāzi Mohammad, a polyglot intellectual clergyman and author, a supporter of dialogue, remolded the party into the *Ferqa-ye Demokrāt-e Kordestān* ("Democratic Party of Kurdistan"), in a situation similar to that in Azerbaijan. The Kurds demanded administrative autonomy, the teaching of Kurdish in schools and the election of a provincial council. Its role, "in conformity with the Iranian Constitution" would be "to supervise and control all government and social affairs," notably the collection of taxes and their use. A Kurdish republic was proclaimed at Mahābād on 22 January 1946. It received the support of Mostafā Bārzāni's troops, a Kurdish chief who had been expelled from Iraq with 2,000 armed men, and who thus showed the transnational character of Kurdish irredentism. This alliance gave rise to fierce criticism by nationalist Persians against Qāzi Mohammad. Relations between the two young republics of Azerbaijan and Kurdistan were not good; the authorities in Tabriz had initially considered Kurdistan to be part of their territory, in particular the cities of Urmia and Khoy, west of the lake.

From the viewpoint of Tehran, where the move caused a surge in nationalism, the autonomy of these two entities was unacceptable. In London, the issue was seen differently. From 1943, an official in charge of the Middle East in the Foreign Office had discussed the possibility of an annexation of parts of the Iranian territory by the Soviets and recommended that it be prepared for what it expected to be inevitable rapacity. "If the Allies win the war we will owe the Russians a great deal, and whatever happens, we owe the Persians nothing. If therefore the Russians are determined to protect their southern frontiers by acquiring further territories in north Persia, it would be advisable to put the best face we can on the matter."[6]

The British minister in Tehran, Sir Reader Bullard (1885–1976) could think of only one alternative: Iran's return to a dictatorship similar to that of Rezā Shāh's. While, from the spring of 1946, the British were satisfied with American defense of Iranian interests in line with the UN agreement, they also knew that Washington wished to limit the progress of Moscow's foreign interests. They were ready to give way to Soviet demands, since the grant of an oil concession to the Russians would also offer them a means of consolidating their own concessions in the south. The Iranians were sensitive to their inalienable sovereign right to the exploitation of the oil. To refuse this advantage to the Soviet Union was to challenge the very foundations of AIOC. British oil installations in Khuzestān were the scene of fierce strikes, encouraged by Toudeh activists; in response, London pragmatically sought to foster unrest among the region's tribes so as to create an autonomous zone

---

[6] FO371/31413, 22 April 1942 and FO37131488 17 January 1943, quoted in L. Fawcett, *Iran and the Cold War*, p. 153.

under their influence, to safeguard against any eventuality of the Toudeh seizing power in Tehran.[7]

Soviet troops, in conformity with an agreement signed on 24 March 1946 left Iran in May of that year. Some months later, the Iranian government invaded Azerbaijan without significant resistance by launching a campaign that resembled a punitive expedition. On 13 December 1946 the Iranian army entered Tabriz where it was received with enthusiasm by the city's population, who were exhausted after months of tension and worry about the measures that aimed to socialize the lifeless economy of the region. Numerous summary executions took place, but Pishavari managed to flee to the Soviet Union with around 5,000 separatist militants. Four days later, the force from Tehran took Mahābād, the capital of the autonomous Kurdistan. Bārzāni fled, but Qāzi Mohammad was arrested and hanged on 31 May 1947.

The dismantling of Iran had been avoided. The young Mohammad-Rezā Shāh claimed victory for this regained unity, the anniversary of which continued to be celebrated every year, until the end of his reign. On 5 November 1978 in a historic speech, while the demonstrations and strikes proliferated, he raised the specter of the transformation of Iran into *Irānestān*, that is, a puppet republic of the Soviet Empire. When, in 1991, after the Gulf War, the Islamic republic abstained from supporting the revolts of the Shiites and the Kurds, it was to a great extent out of fear that any dismantling of its Iraqi neighbor might reawaken the prospect of a dismantling of Iran. The trauma of the separatist movements of 1946 had not been forgotten.

Birth of Political Parties

Thanks to the paradoxical vacuum of political freedom that the Soviet-British occupation guaranteed, popular political parties were formed, both left- and right-wing. It was the friends of the Soviets, as discussed, who founded the Toudeh Party to extend the reach of Soviet policy, but the party's slogan, "Bread, health and education for all," did not reference the Marxist influence directly. The first secretary of the party, Mohsen Eskandari (Soleymān Mirzā, 1862–1944), was himself a Qajar prince whose socialist sympathies had been known for many

---

[7] L. FAWCETT, *Iran and the Cold War*, pp. 155, 171.

years. In 1925, he had refused to vote in favor of the transfer of the monarchy to Rezā Shāh.[8]

Many Iranians thought that the fatherland of communism was an ideal state and the envy of all European countries, all the more because very few among them had had the opportunity to visit the Soviet Union. The success of the Toudeh Party can be partly explained by the pressures of the Russian occupation, but it was also aroused by the economic difficulties of occupied Iran. Bread was scarce in the capital during the war years, when essential supplies, such as wheat, were requisitioned by the Allies to supply the Soviet Union; however, other reasons such as hoarding for the black market and disruption to transportation after the seizing of trucks by the occupying forces may explain the grain shortage and the bread crisis more convincingly.[9] In the elections of 1943–44 (the 14th legislative) the Toudeh Party presented fifteen candidates in the northern provinces and in Isfahan. It had nine of the 120 deputies, with about 200,000 votes out of a total of one million.[10] The success in Isfahan was owed in large part to the dominance of the textile industry, which was concentrated there, and industry strikes had resulted in substantial wage increases.

In opposition to Toudeh, whose ideas were diffused to a broad public by an anti-fascist organ, *Mardom* ("the People") and by the weekly *Rahbar* ("the Guide"), were numerous small parties, or often – to be precise – groups loyal to a leader, who tried with varying success to define a common political line. It was only after the war, from 1946, that Qavām, the prime minister, organized a popular party to support his policies, which he mischievously called the Democratic Party of Iran (*Hezb-e demokrāt-e Irān*), exploiting the confusion with the Democratic Party of Azerbaijan (*Ferqe-ye demokrāt-e Āzarbāyjān*). With his model of a loyalist party, Qavām garnered support from the landed proprietors from the north, who were concerned about the influence of communism, as well as support from the intelligentsia. Its reach was comparable to that of the Toudeh, and it too had branches all over the country and influence in the country's newspapers.

---

[8] See N. RASTEGĀR, "Majles-e mo'asessān-e 1303 va mokhālefān-e ān." In his memoirs, a historical communist militant describes Soleymān Mirzā: "Until the end of his life, he opposed any collaboration or reconciliation with the English and their agents, and as long as he could he prevented the Toudeh party from blindly following Soviet policies," A. KHĀMA'I, *Khāterāt*, II, *Forsat-e bozorg-e az dast rafte*, p. 24.

[9] W. FLOOR, *History of Bread in Iran*, pp. 148f.

[10] S. ZABIH, *The Communist Movement in Iran*, p. 79, quoting H. Carrère d'Encausse.

The Democratic Party included, above all, those politicians who wished to settle accounts of the heritage of Rezā Shāh's dictatorship, because many had been imprisoned under the first Pahlavi. Some, misled by a social and even progressive rhetoric, suspected that Qavām was a vassal of Moscow and that he wanted to bring back the Soviet cause to those whom the Toudeh had either repelled or discarded. The prime minister had indeed included some Toudeh Party members in his cabinet in 1946, most probably to both neutralize any opposition from the Soviet Union and reduce political rivalry from within the country. From its perspective, the British embassy avoided any clear-cut statement, or the suggestion of any approval that might have tarnished the nationalist image of the new party. Benefiting from the retaking of Azerbaijan, the Democratic Party obtained eighteen seats during the elections of 1947 for the 15th legislature, forming the most important group in the Majles, but Mohammad Mosaddeq, the aristocratic lawyer who had been dismissed from politics when he opposed Rezā Shāh, denounced the electoral manipulations that would tarnish Qavām's success. The latter was soon replaced as head of the government and left the country for Europe. His party no longer had a raison d'être and quite rapidly ceased to exist.[11]

Before his departure, however, Qavam secured Parliament's decision to refuse any oil concessions to the Soviets, and an agreement with Washington was made for the purchase of arms. But he also managed to awaken British hostility when he attempted to reassert Iranian sovereignty over the Bahrain peninsula, a matter that was only resolved in 1970.

Consolidation of Royal Power

A new actor occupied the political stage, the Shah. In September 1941, the British considered the young Mohammad-Rezā Pahlavi (1919–80) a benign figure and recognized his legitimacy as his father's successor. Psychologically crushed by the latter, the young monarch was dominated by his twin sister, Princess Ashraf, and, moreover, visibly influenced by his intimate companion from his days at Le Rosey School, in Switzerland, Ernest Perron, the son of the gardener of that famous institute. Perron, who had arrived in Tehran before his first marriage,

---

[11] R. Kauz, *Politische Parteien und Bevölkerung in Iran: Die hezb-e Demükrât-e Irân*, pp. 263f.

and had access to the private apartments of the court, played an obscure role until 1954 when the Shah was forced to dismiss him.[12] Despite this relationship, the Shah was also attracted to women.

The Shah gradually emerged from the shadows after having received recognition for the reintegration of Azerbaijan and Kurdistan into the national territory. Above all, he had secured the confidence of the USA. During the summer of 1948, he made his first official journey to Europe. The following year he went to the USA.

His popularity was considerably strengthened by an assassination attempt, the origins of which are obscure. In February 1949, during an official ceremony at the University of Tehran, a journalist working for the radical Islamic movement *Fedāiān-e Eslām*, oddly also affiliated with the Toudeh Party, shot at the monarch, lightly wounding his face. Rather than overpowering the would-be assassin in order to take him into custody and proceed to investigation, the guards riddled him with bullets. The media coverage of this event raised questions whether this was a real attack. Whatever the truth, the assassination attempt strengthened support for the monarch and consolidated further royal power, with the Toudeh Party banned and the leaders of the *Fedāiān-e Eslām* arrested or sent into exile, including Āyatollāh Kāshāni.

In that same year, the Shah undertook to amend the fundamental law to reinforce his role as constitutional monarch. He began by establishing the Senate, an assembly defined in the Constitution of 1906 (art. 43f), but which had so far never been convened – half of its members were appointed by the monarch. He then had himself granted the right to dissolve Parliament, whose legislative period was henceforth changed from two to four years. In the fall, during the elections of the 16th legislature of the Majles, he arranged things such that opponents were not elected.

In Tehran, fraud was evident. In the face of the magnitude of electoral manipulations a group of politicians, representing different parties, among whom was Mohammad Mosaddeq (1882–1967) led a peaceful demonstration in front of the royal palace. Nineteen politicians joined them and occupied the palace garden where they decided to

---

[12] On him, see General FARDUST's memoirs, *Zohur va soqut-e saltanat-e Pahlavi*, in particular pp. 187f; Wm R. LOUIS, "Musaddiq and the dilemmas of British imperialism," p. 234; M. Zonis, *Majestic Failure: The Fall of the Shah*, pp. 116–20; A. MILANI, *The Shah*, pp. 49f.

form the National Front (*Jebhe-ye melli*),[13] a coalition of parties which first demanded the cancellation of the elections in the capital, press freedom, and an end to the martial law that had been decreed after the assassination attempt. Soon there was a new election, and several leaders were elected, presenting themselves as champions of the defense of freedoms. Among the new deputies was Āyatollāh Abo'l-Qāsem Kāshāni (1882–1962), the mentor of the *Fedāiān-e Eslām*. On his return from exile in Lebanon, on 10 June 1950, the clergyman made a triumphal entry into Tehran.

Immediately after having been installed as a party in Parliament, the National Front was threatened by a split due to the divergence of its constituents. The most radical elements demanded a return to Islamic law, while its leader, Mosaddeq, like many members of the Qajar aristocracy, was Muslim, but without particular conviction. One day in Parliament, during Ramadan, he shocked Muslims by pausing in the middle of a speech to drink a glass of water. Convinced of the necessity to secularize political life in the manner of European democracies, he replied to the radicals who demanded the Islamization of public life that the essential question, his priority, was the nationalization of the country's oil, because it would give true independence to the Iranian nation.

Ayatollah Kāshāni was very anti-British and unflinchingly prepared to support Mosaddeq's fight for oil nationalization. This man of the cloth was one of the most modern and most progressive of his time. He had been on the side of the "republicans" in 1924 and had supported Rezā Shāh in his ascendancy to the throne. Committed to politics, he stood in sharp contrast to the ulama of Qom who preferred to adopt the "quietist" attitude of Ayatollah Hoseyn Borujerdi (1875–1961), the "model to imitate" (*marja-e taqlid*) for the majority of Shiites at that time. His audience, particularly because of his open opposition to the British, went far beyond radical Islam.[14]

Young politicized ulama such as Ruhollāh Khomeyni, or the *Fedāiān-e Eslām*, naturally turned towards Ayatollah Kāshāni. Protected by the Ayatollah, the *Fedāiān-e Eslām* destabilized political life and became famous for several assassinations. They had been founded during World War II by Seyyed Mojtabā Mir-Lowhi, also

---

[13] H. KATOUZIAN, *The Political Economy of Modern Iran* translates this as "Popular Front."

[14] Kāshāni had participated in the struggle of Iraqi Shiites against the British in 1920. He had been arrested by the occupying British forces in 1942 for pro-German propaganda. See Y. RICHARD, "Ayatollah Kashani: Precursor of the Islamic Republic?".

known as Navvāb-e Safavi (1924–56), a young molla who railed against the infidels and apostasy. He went after Ahmad Kasravi (1890–1946), a nationalist judge from Tabriz, who had significant influence among young intellectuals. This humanist and rationalist lawyer had become known through his works on contemporary history, notably about the constitutionalist revolution, and his essays on morality, in which he condemned the depravity and decadence into which, according to him, clerical Shiism and mystical poetry dragged Muslims. Seeing Kasravi preaching a kind of new religion, Navvāb, charged with a fatwa, undertook to make this apostate of Islam return to true faith, and then, after his refusal, wounded him during an attack. Eventually one of his accomplices killed Kasravi in 1946 in the office of the examining magistrate. Henceforth famous, the *Fedāiān-e Eslām* thereafter committed several spectacular assassinations, including that of the Minister of Court, Hazhir, and most notably of General Razmārā, the then prime minister.

Ali Razmārā (1901–51) was head of the government for nine months. A former student of the French military school of St. Cyr, he had a brilliant military career and commanded the Iranian army when it retook control of Azerbaijan in 1946. He feared that his country might fall into chaos if it ever proceeded to oil nationalization. "We are not capable," he declared to the Majles in December 1950, "to make a sewer for our toilets nor to operate a cement factory, how can we pretend to manage an oil industry?" Nobody knew with any certainty for whom Razmārā was "performing." He effectively resisted the battering of the National Front by negotiating directly and in secret with AIOC to redefine the oil concession so that the revenue would be shared in equal parts, which would silence the demands of the nationalists. Some accused him of collusion with Moscow because he had set free the Toudeh militants who had been arrested after the failed attack of February 1949. But the American press appreciated this energetic and modern man and reproached President Truman for not having supported him.

Was the Shah complicit in the assassination because he could not bear to see his prime minister's popularity grow – not only in Iran but internationally? Several indications suggest that he was not displeased to be rid of this man who may well have himself attempted a coup d'état, as the Shah's own father had successfully done in 1921. The general was not hindered by much care for democratic functions and at one point stated: "I will let the dome of the royal mosque fall on Kāshāni's head and the ceiling of the Parliament on that of Mosaddeq."[15] The exact circumstances of his assassination by a carpenter adherent of the *Fedāiān-e Eslām*, on 7 March 1951, during a ceremony in a mosque, have not entirely been clarified, although a recent study published all available archival materials.[16] It appears that there were two separate shots, as though a second killer was in place to make sure that Razmārā would not survive the bullet of the Islamists, whom it was convenient to hold responsible for this crime.

The First Postwar National Crisis

Razmārā's death removed the last political deadlock that prevented the National Front from passing the oil nationalization law; it was adopted by Parliament on 15 March 1951. The Shah, who wanted to avoid nationalization for fear of the British reaction, did not believe that the game was over. He sought to recall to government the anglophile Seyyed Ziā, who had led the coup d'état of 1921 and whom Rezā Khān had later removed. But he named instead a "transitional" government (headed by Hoseyn Alā), and very soon popular pressure forced him to give in and appoint Mosaddeq.

"Doctor" Mosaddeq tasked himself with firmly implementing nationalization, against which the British raised all kinds of legal argument. For almost three years, Iran made the headlines of all the world's major newspapers. Not long after Ghandi's achievements and Indian independence, the lawyer Mosaddeq dared to attack the dominance of a European power through peaceful and legal means. The fight, supported by a large mobilization of public opinion, was a great moment in the genesis of the Iranian nation.

Contesting the legality of the nationalization, the British demanded arbitrage under the International Court of Justice at The Hague and decreed an embargo on the export of oil while awaiting the verdict of the judges. In July 1951 the court in The Hague provisionally ruled in favor of AIOC. Mosaddeq reacted by rejecting a limitation on Iranian sovereignty and repeated the reserves made by Iran to bring the Company's position before the Court, which was not

---

[15] Abd-e Khodā'i, *Ettelā'āt*, 27 dey 1359/16 February 1981, "Navvāb-e Safavi's Memorial," p. 3.

[16] Md Torkamān, *Asrār-e qatl-e Razmārā*.

competent in matters of private ownership.[17] The British then took the case to the Security Council. Mosaddeq, who was demonized by the British press, surprised everyone by going to New York himself – making it a point of honor to pay for the cost of the journey out of his own pocket. Feigning poor health, he spent part of his time in hospital to slow down the hearings, which allowed Iranian experts to better prepare their defense. On his return, he stopped in Cairo where the man who had stood up to British imperialism received a triumphal reception.

Mosaddeq was adept at attracting the attention of the media and putting on a performance. In Tehran, he received journalists at his house, where he lay in his wrought-iron bed in his pyjamas. In October 1951, when he was preparing for an important speech before the Majles, opposition deputies left the room to prevent the session from continuing, as a quorum had not been reached. He went out into the streets into the throng of the crowds and repeated: "Parliament is there where the people are," showing his distrust of representative democracy.

Mosaaddeq had barely taken office when, claiming that he was under threat from the *Fedāiān-e Eslām*, he refused the bodyguards offered to him by the Shah (whose inefficacy in protection has been made clear with Razmārā's death) and obtained authorization to reside in the parliamentary precinct. The *Fedāiān-e Eslām* had many grievances against Mosaddeq. In June 1951 he had ordered the arrest of their leader, Navvāb Safavi, who nevertheless benefited from relatively good treatment in prison, where he received visitors and published political statements. Several other members of the group also had been imprisoned. The government seemed to be indifferent to their appeals for freedom and, above all, did not want to give in to their demands to Islamicize the law. In the beginning, Kāshāni himself agreed with Mosaddeq, from whom he expected a more concrete acknowledgment, hoping that he would nominate people close to him for important posts.

After the elections of spring 1952, where he obtained a stronger majority, Mosaddeq demanded that he himself would be in charge of the war ministry. The Shah, who wanted to nominate himself for the position – a prerogative inherited from his father – refused to comply and the prime minister resigned. But the crowd demanded his return with shouts: "Mosaddeq or death!" Faced with these popular riots, on

[17] See L. P. ELWELL-SUTTON, *Persian Oil*, p. 220.

21 July (*Si-e tir* in the Iranian calender and in Persian) the monarch had to yield, and Mosaddeq returned to the head of government. Kāshāni believed, and not without reason, that he had played a decisive role in the mobilization of the people to make the Shah acquiesce and, in turn, demanded the privilege to nominate several ministers. Scornfully, Mosaddeq rejected this request, believing his popularity was such that nobody, neither the Shah nor the Ayatollah, could contest the absolute power that he needed to win the fight over the nationalization of oil. Kāshāni immediately threatened to go into exile to show publicly his disapproval of the prime minister's conduct. Mosaddeq turned the threat on its head, writing to him: "Why does Your Excellency speak about leaving Tehran? Allow it to be your humble servant who abstains from any political activity." Kāshāni yielded.

Despite their attempts at reconciliation in the spring of 1953, the divide between the two men only became more marked when Mosaddeq made overtures toward the communists of the Toudeh to find popular support. Several tragic episodes worsened their conflict. The fake departure of the Shah, encouraged by Mosaddeq's hypocritical deference in February 1953, appeared to be a trap to set a mob against the prime minister who, managing to escape, denounced a failed coup d'état; and the kidnapping and murder of the police commissioner of Tehran by Kāshāni's partisans destabilized the government. Moreover, numerous demonstrations, some of which erupted into violence, created a climate of insecurity; and the oil embargo deprived Iran of external revenues. The economy went from bad to worse. Mosaddeq counted on Washington to agree to loans that would allow him to prop up the economy. But the Americans, obsessed by the specter of communism, could no longer rely on him, and the CIA, in agreement with British secret services, who were using the *Fedāiān-e Eslām* against the National Front, made plans to instigate a coup.

The coup d'état unfolded in two phases. In the evening of 16 August, an officer loyal to the Shah, Colonel Nasiri, was commissioned to inform Mosaddeq that he had been dismissed and replaced by General Fazlollāh Zāhedi. But Mosaddeq, forewarned, had countered the coup by having the colonel arrested before he had accomplished his mission. The Shah, afraid, fled by plane to Baghdad and from there to Rome. In Tehran, a wave of panic gripped the population when they witnessed the Shah's and his father's statues being pulled down. The communists, apparently, controlled the streets and Iranian bank notes were returned with a hole in place of the monarch's effigy. There was mass confusion. Were these demonstrations incited by fake rioters disguised as communist militants to bring about a popular reaction in favor of the Shah's return? According to some historians, the CIA financed and led the operations in which popular spontaneity and political ideals only played a minor role. But one scholar has contested the veracity of a secret CIA report released in 2000 claiming responsibility for the coup. He emphasizes that the call to the communist demonstration was an error later confessed by the Toudeh Party and that the spontaneous reactions of the crowd had followed the assertion allegedly attributed to Ayatollah Borujerdi demanding the Shah's return to curb the danger of Sovietization: "The country needs the king" (*mamlekat Shāh mi-khāhad*).[18] It was in Italy, and hardly gloriously, that on 19 August Mohammad-Rezā Shāh learnt that the army group commanded by General Zāhedi had left its barracks and, warmly cheered on the streets of Tehran, re-established order and the legitimacy of the monarchy.

Mosaddeq was arrested and his house plundered and destroyed, making it impossible to access government archives on the crisis, since he had governed the Iranian state from his home for two years.

After the revolution of 1979 the Islamists published a series of polemical works denouncing the political errors of the nationalist leader, in particular his alliance with the enemies of the popular movement, such as General Zāhedi (1888–1962), who had been arrested by the British for pro-Nazi activities during the war, and whom he had made his minister of interior in 1951 in his first government. But these criticisms have not tarnished the prestige of the patriot Mosaddeq, who forced the British to take a step back when faced with a vast popular movement.

The Smothering of Democracy

In the grip of the anti-Soviet paranoia that had taken hold of Washington, the Americans decided to ward off the communist threat in Iran by lending their support to democratic and liberal tendencies,

---

[18] The first interpretation of the coup, the most common, presenting it as entirely organized by the CIA, is argued by A. RAHNEMA, *Behind the 1953 Coup in Iran*; it is contested and refuted by D. BAYANDOR, *Iran and the CIA: The Fall of Mosadeq Revisited*.

disregarding patriotism. Mosaddeq knew how to monopolize this US irrationality and hoped to receive American financial aid to dig the country out of the financial crisis. In 1953, when he realized that the Americans had finally aligned themselves with British intransigence he ostensibly tried to strike up closer relations with the communists, an indication of his limitated freedom of action and the urgency of external aid. It was too late, and the Americans, unnerved, refused to lend the $10 million that would have allowed Iran to cope with the embargo. The more Mosaddeq wanted to provoke a US reaction by allowing the communists to speak out, the more determined they became to topple him.

Internationally, the coup d'état of 1953 marked a major victory in US strategy. Since 1942, Washington had made immense strides in conjuring up the danger of communist infiltration in Iran. The USA, without political or economic compensation, had sent personnel, distributed food aid, and provided military assistance. Zāhedi's victory had finally secured them a strategic stronghold on the southern borders of the Soviet Union, to keep an eye on air and ballistic activities of their great rival throughout the Cold War.

Politically – and to some lesser extent, economically – the Americans filled the role the British had occupied. As of 1954 oil flowed again; it remained nationalized, but European and American companies formed a consortium to share its exploitation. European hegemony over the world, already weakened by independence in India and Pakistan, undermined by the Chinese revolution and the war in Indochina, and soon to be further eroded by the Suez Crisis and the war in Algeria, was eclipsed in favor of American influence. The Iranian elite's fascination with French culture and European civilization gradually gave way to a focus on another model – that of economic success. It was no longer a paracolonial domination, but a plurinational theater whose center came to be the USA, from where it ignited the ambitions of Iranian developmentalists who, in turn, would enjoy the fruits of international growth.

The fall of Mosaddeq marked a painful end to a national process. Certainly, Mosaddeq, the liberal aristocrat, did not share the features of a political leader in the modern sense, but for some months he had managed to garner strong popular participation and given Iranians hope that finally they were to achieve sovereignty within their own borders. The economic difficulties that arose as a result of the oil embargo even sparked industrial and commercial inventiveness. Anything that could be produced domestically mitigated the need to import from abroad. For the first time since the Constitutional Revolution, Iranians had the feeling of actively participating in their own national destiny. This democratic awakening, however, was smothered by the meddling of Western powers whose political and moral dictates appeared suddenly absurd to Iranians.

The Shah's return "in an American carriage" was reminiscent of the collusion of the Pahlavi dynasty with foreign interests. Mohammad-Rezā Shāh's nationalist, modern, reforming, and sometimes revolutionary rhetoric henceforth had the aftertaste of puppetry and mimicry. A question of illegitimacy hung over this haughty and misunderstood monarch. His short-lived reconciliation with the Shiite clergy of Qom, notably with Ayatollah Borujerdi, on the back of the Bahāi community that was thrown to the clergymen, was not sufficient to reconcile him with the population, nor to suppress the communist complots that culminated in 1955 with the annihilation of the Toudeh Party. Economic recovery offered hope to the urban bourgeoisie, and the early unwavering support of the USA allowed them to undertake ambitious and spectacular reforms. These reforms imposed from above were often rejected by the Iranians because they were misunderstood.

As for the clergy, any outside support, whether Russian, British, or American, was questionable to them. The majority of the ulama had remained distant from the popular (or "nationalist") movement (in contrast to 1906) so as to avoid being dragged further into secular politics than traditional Islam allowed. They drew numerous lessons from the nationalist defeat. Mosaddeq was wrong to expect aid from Washington, and Iranians, therefore, had to rely on themselves. Kāshāni's line of thinking seemed to be a losing one; with his ability to work with Mosaddeq reaching an impasse and by favoring the instigators of the coup d'état (he was in contact with Zāhedi) he placed himself in an untenable position in terms of Iranian opinion. But the Ayatollah had made the choice of political action. Despite his mistrust of parliamentary politics, he had accepted the honorary chairmanship of the Majles and made extensive use of the Iranian media, granting them numerous interviews. Faced with a timorous clergy, he offered, almost thirty years earlier, the model of the committed man of the cloth, as would develop from 1979. He relied in particular on militants willing to do anything in the name of Islam, a revolutionary avant-garde whose ideal ran counter to political modernization, the *Fedāiān-e Eslām*. Though hardly anchored in public opinion, the latter would continue to haunt the consciousness of politicized Muslims. Clerical dress would one day be replaced by the modern revolutionary uniform – the parka and sport shoes.

Mosaddeq's defeat created a crucial dilemma. Should the progressive and resolutely anti-imperialist supporters of reform wait for the necessary political change to bolster Iranian sovereignty, social justice, and unity through the classic parliamentary model? Such means could be diverted in demagogic and populist excesses by those whose interests were contrary to those of the Iranian people. Or should they fight for a radical, revolutionary schism, led by an aware and pro-active avant-garde? The last remnants of Iranian communism, energized by nationalist nostalgia, and even sometimes by Islamic radicalism, were about to produce an explosive device.

11 THE LAST REIGN OF AN IMMORTAL KINGDOM, MOHAMMAD-REZĀ SHĀH

The toppling of Mosaddeq's nationalist government was the leading story in the international press. Despite his role in this confrontation with a popular government, Mohammad-Rezā Shāh still had many assets to make his country a model of political and social success. The Iranian nation had been awakened to democratic aspirations since the Constitutional Revolution. Thanks to its oil wealth, the country could hope to transform its economy, which was still essentially an agrarian one, into an industrial power with means that few Third World nations had. Because of its outlier position in the Islamic world and its vicinity to the Soviet Union, it could hope to play a regional role. For the first time in Iran's history it was governed by a monarch who was familiar with European culture and who seemed to be ready to be inspired by it to modernize his country with less brutal methods than those of this father. Paradoxically, despite this favorable environment to development and reform, and despite the assistance of numerous international experts and the formidable growth of oil revenues after 1973, the Shah gradually began to lose his people's trust, before being toppled by a revolution that few had anticipated. How should we account for the failure of the 'King of Kings' who governed Iran for a quarter of a century?

The Royal Vocation of the King of Kings

The Pahlavi dynasty had barely been in power for fifteen years when Mohammad-Rezā Shāh ascended to the throne in 1941, after his father's abdication. The young monarch was the beneficiary of an immense fortune. He had not spent his early years in a palace, but rather in a working-class neighborhood, where he lived in modest circumstances with his mother and his brother Ali-Rezā;[1] thereafter he was schooled in Switzerland at Institut Le Rosey.[2] His first marriage was to an Egyptian princess, Fawzia, who only bore him a daughter; he divorced her in 1949. Was a nice amorous adventure going to give sparkle to this family of parvenus? In 1951, during the oil nationalization crisis, he married the beautiful Sorayā Esfandyāri, whose father belonged to the Bakhtyāri tribe and whose mother was German. But the happy couple were unable to have children, and protocol demanded a new marriage. Promoting a monogamistic image that was at odds with his habits, the Shah was forced to repudiate the unfortunate Soraya to marry, in 1959, the young Farah Dibā; she was twenty years old; he was forty. The following year, Farah secured the dynasty's future by giving birth to a boy, Rezā, soon followed by three other children.

The Shah's familial difficulties were a delight for the romance-reporting press and made him a well-known figure in the West though it did little to bring him closer to the Iranian people. The Shah continued to make the headlines in all Iranian newspapers, which was both reassuring and obsessive. But could political life be reduced to the glitter of the monarchy alone?

Behind his superficial appearance, Mohammad-Rezā Shāh made use of Iranian traditions to strengthen his image as a monarch elected by God. In a book published in 1961, where he defined the "mission that he had received for his country," he relates several significant anecdotes about his religious experiences. With unfeigned naiveté he did not hesitate to write that he owed his life to Abbās, Imam Hoseyn's half-brother. He was still a child and was on a family outing in the mountains when, after having fainted because of a bad fall from a horse, he regained conscience "thanks to the hand of Lord Abbās who took me when I fell to prevent that I would wound myself." On another occasion, he had a vision when awake during which he met the Hidden Imam in person bathed in a glorious light, while his companions did not see anything.[3] He described

---

[1] Ali-Rezā was killed in 1954 in a plane accident. If the attempt on the Shah's life in 1949 had succeeded, only his brother would have succeeded him, as the other Pahlavi princes were born to a Qajar mother.

[2] Md-R. Shāh PAHLAVI, *Ma'muriat barā-ye vatan-am*, p. 82.

[3] Md-R. Shāh PAHLAVI, *Ma'muriat barā-ye vatan-am*, pp. 88–89.

similar experiences concerning failed assassination attempts against him and a plane accident from which he escaped alive. These mystical encounters gave him an enormous trust in himself.

> When I measure my will against that of God All High, I am very worried and ask myself whether my will is constrained or whether I am free in my decisions. The eternal will and divine force have protected me every time. This will is necessarily founded on a cause, on a reason. These beliefs will seem strange to those so-called free thinkers or rationalists, but, as for me, the Supreme Lord has protected me and has helped to overcome the dangers and perils. That is why I believe in his uniqueness and his justice. Other evolved nations share that same belief. The British are not ashamed by their formula *God save the Queen* and the Americans inscribe *In God we trust* on their money.[4]

In relating such episodes Mohammad-Rezā Shāh certainly wanted to distinguish himself from the agnostic or indifferent attitude of his father. He presented himself as a believer, whom God protected because he had a sacred role. A poster presented him in a staged hieratic image with the traditional formula establishing the legitimacy of monarchs in classical Islam: "The king is the shadow of God" (*Shāh, sāye-ye Khodā'st*). Moreover, in the kingdom's motto: "God, Shah and Fatherland" (*Khodā, Shāh, Mihan*), the three terms were placed in such a way that one might wonder whether God had been relegated to second place.

In 1967, combining the advantages that his male offspring conferred on him as well as his mystical aura, the Shah decided to organize a formal ceremony for his coronation. It was above all an opportunity for a procession in his carriage through the streets of Tehran, to show himself to his people with a crown and to have himself photographed next to the queen and the crown prince. The photo of that new priestly trinity was put up in all government offices, in shops, and in sitting rooms. Not having in one's home the monarch's icon dressed in his golden vestments, with the royal scepter in his right hand, was to rebel against the royal order. In the press, the solemn king could only be called by his fawning title: "King of Kings, Sun of the Aryans, Supreme Commander" (*Shāhanshāh, Āryāmehr, Bozorg-e arteshtārān*).

---

[4] Md-R. Shāh PAHLAVI, Ma'muriat barā-ye vatan-am, p. 90.

God's shadow on earth suddenly radiated an immemorial light that, to make one forget his modest origins, harked back to nothing less than the establishment of the Achaemenid Empire. In October 1971, to mark the imaginary 2,500th anniversary of the revived Persian Empire, royalty from all over the world and the presidents of orphan states that no longer had royal heads of state, were invited to attend a parade worthy of an epic Hollywood production on the plains of Persepolis, the site of the Achaemenid ruins, in a profusion of luxury that no parvenu could ever have dreamed of. From Paris, planes brought luxury tents, furniture, napkins, colossal quantities of wine and meat, not to mention numerous servants. Launching this media ritual in front of the tomb of Cyrus, Mohammad-Rezā Shāh spoke these historic words not knowing to what extent the sublime would turn into the ridiculous: "O Cyrus, you may sleep in peace, because we are awake" (*Ey Kurosh āsude bekhāb, ke mā bidār-im*).

At the time of the royal festivities, to which the Iranian people had not been invited, the Shah did not yet know that thanks to the quadrupling of the price of oil in 1973, his resources were going to grow so much so that all his ambitions would be within reach. At that time, Iran had already helped the American military efforts in Vietnam by sending a squadron of F-5 fighter-bombers and, in Oman, by participating in the suppression of the Marxist-Leninist rebellion in the south of the Sultanate. Considered the "policeman of the Gulf," the Shah began to speak as an equal to leaders of the industrialized world. He denounced in his press conferences the permissiveness of western societies and soon adopted the ambitious rhetoric of Iran's access to the "Great Civilization" (*tamaddon-e bozorg*), according to the title of his book published in 1977 and widely distributed in Iran before the Islamic Revolution. He announced that Iran not only had to become the Switzerland of Asia, but the fifth global power.[5] "Within 10 years, we will have the same standard of living that you have now, you Germans, French and British," he told *Der Spiegel* in 1973. One might compare these arrogant statements by the Shah about the West of that time with some of the statements made by Khomeyni and other leaders of the Islamic Republic. Both express the same contempt for the success of western societies, which without a doubt exerted on them the same fascination, and contrasted it with the desire to find new resources for

---

[5] Md-R. Shāh PAHLAVI, *Be-suy-e tamaddon-e bozorg*, see for example, p. 255.

the country in Islam and Iranian civilization; the Shah himself did not reject a return to religion, in fact quite the opposite.[6]

Security at Home

Confident that he had been charged with a great mission, the Shah was also convinced that all means were permitted to make this clear to his adversaries. As of 1953, when he had his hands free to act, since America was providing Iran with financial and food aid until the resumption of oil exports, he decreed martial law and prohibited any public political activity. The Shah detested anything that resembled communist ideology. He relentlessly had members of the Toudeh Party persecuted and dismantled its network that had infiltrated the army; 28 militants were executed, more than 500 were given long prison sentences, and 3,000 were exiled to Khārk island in the Persian Gulf. The communist leaders who had been able to flee mostly ended up in East Berlin from where they continued to issue publications and present radio programs. Their influence in Iran became more and more insignificant, but it continued to justify the repression inside the country.

As for the ulama, Mohammad-Rezā Shāh liked them as long as they preached submission in their mosques, but he did not hesitate in curbing, and with force, their attempts to get involved in politics.

The takeover of Iran that began in August 1953 was a blow to the networks of parties and the various solidarity groups, who then went underground. The young monarch did not forgive Mosaddeq either for having tried to oust him. In this old liberal aristocrat, he saw the symbol of an ineffectual and ambitious politician, and from then onward it was forbidden to refer in a positive sense to the government of the National Front, though it had been a key player in the construction of the Iranian nation. The former prime minister was arrested, dragged before a military court, sentenced to three years in prison, and thereafter kept under house arrest in his residence at Ahmadabad, near Tehran. Several groups tried to carry on his work, in particular the Movement of National Resistance (*Nahzat-e moqāvemat-e melli*). This included above all the religious wing of Mosaddeq's loyalists, among whom were Ayatollah Mahmud Tāleqāni (1912–79) and Ing. Mahdi Bāzargān

---

[6] Md-R. Shāh PAHLAVI, *Be-suy-e tamaddon-e bozorg*, pp. 309f.

(1907–94) and several other members of the movement who would resurface in 1979. Other groups, under the name of National Front II, brought together those who remained nostalgic about the Mosaddeq period; often belonging to the westernized bourgeoisie, they were easily neutralized by the Shah who banned them from any political expression.

Among more peripheral groups, the *Fedāiān-e Eslām* – who had turned against Mosaddeq – had apparently been successfully manipulated when the Shah needed clerical support to compensate for his diminishing popular legitimacy. Over the years 1953–55, the newspapers reported every day on religious events in Qom, on the pilgrimage of this or that ayatollah, and the declamations of another. Ayatollah Hoseyn Borujerdi (1875–1961), champion of non-intervention by the ulama in political life triumphed. He was the guiding religious leader, the "model to imitate" (*marja-e taqlid*) of Iranian Shiites, and the Shah visited him several times, a significant mark of respect with no equivalent in the reign of Rezā Shāh. In 1955, when Iran reestablished its diplomatic relations with Great Britain and negotiated the organization of the Baghdad Pact, through which the strategic allegiance to the Americans became explicit (see below), this new link with the West needed to be balanced in some way: the Shah turned to the clergy and encouraged them to track down the Bahāis, whom they consider as heretics and apostates. The ulama launched a violent campaign against their community, and the dome of their temple in Tehran was destroyed with pick-axes, with the collusion of police. Then the *Fedāiān-e Eslām*, who refused to join the ranks of the apolitical clergy, were persecuted in their turn, and four of their leaders, among whom was Navvāb Safavi, were executed without any reaction from the leading theologians.

In 1957, the Shah, judging that the pacification of Iran had been sufficiently achieved, lifted martial law. He authorized the formation of two loyalist parties: the *Melliun* ("nationalists"), which defended government policies, and the *Mardom* ("the people"), which acted as the opposition. To consolidate his power, the Shah created the *Sāvāk* (the Persian acronym for "Organization for intelligence and the security of the country"), the well-known political police established by General Teymur Bakhtyār. The latter was a former student of St. Cyr, but to organize the Sāvāk he turned to Washington and Israel for assistance, who were only too pleased to lend the Shah their experience and support against destabilizing entities when the region was troubled by the

Palestinian question, the rise of Nasserism, and soon the Iraqi revolution (1958). The Sāvāk made overwhelming use of espionage and delation, such that Iranians had the impression of being under surveillance at all times. Torture was frequently used. The Shah implicitly acknowledged this on 8 October 1971 when he told Eric Rouleau, who interviewed him for *Le Monde*, that his country no longer needed to use physical torture, because psychological torture often led to the same results.

For opportunistic reasons, no Sāvāk official dared inform the political leaders, let alone the Shah, about the real feelings of the nation when these were negative. Criticism was only made with endless circumspection. The reports of the Sāvāk therefore, did not reflect the reality of public opinion, but the Americans relied on them, having given up on the duplication of domestic intelligence gathering, which explained why they understood so late the divide between the Shah and his people. No political actor had such an intelligence network, but, paradoxically, the formidable means that the Shah mobilized prevented him from gauging the smoldering fire of discontent. At the end of the 1980s, an Iranian sociologist, Ehsan Naraghi, who had the opportunity to speak with agents of the royal regime as well as with Marxist militants, having on two occasions spent several months with them in the prisons of the Islamic Republic, explained:

> The Savak have lost the Shah because it was obsessed by the idea of a conspiracy directed from abroad ... The kind of religion of intelligence propagated by the secret services simply prevents governments from thinking. They are over-informed. And this excess of information makes them arrogant and isolated from their people. They take leave of their senses. They no longer know the meaning of political wisdom.[7]

Security Abroad

Israel and Egypt

Iran's de facto recognition of Israel – that is, without an exchange of ambassadors – was not only because of its allegiance to

---

[7] E. NARAGHI, "Dans les prisons de Téhéran," interview with Ph. Simonnot, *Esprit*, Aug.–Sept. 1987, p. 61.

Washington, but because it presented an opportunity to weaken Arab nationalism, of which Gamal Abdel Nasser liked to think of himself as the leader.[8] In reality, although, out of solidarity with Arab countries, Iran had voted against the UN resolution that created Israel, Tehran did not in any way want to be drawn into this conflict. Irano-Israeli relations dated back to 1950 and represented an Israeli initiative to avoid isolation; after the establishment of relations between Tel Aviv and Ankara (1949) the Israelis wanted an embassy in Tehran. At that time there were about 100,000 Jews in Iran, who did not suffer a direct backlash during the 1948 war but whom Zionist propaganda wanted to attract to Palestine. A relatively small number of that ancient community left at that time.[9] The Aliyah branch in Tehran facilitated the emigration of Jewish Poles, and later those of Iraq, who passed through Iran. Mossad agents established a branch office in Tehran as of 1950. Apart from the organization of the Sāvāk, Israeli experts helped Iranians with development schemes, including irrigation and agricultural projects.

The Israelis also knew how to benefit from every opportunity to secure allies. At the beginning of the 1960s, the Shah and Israel found themselves in the same position, supporting the Kurds in Iraq against the Baathist regime in Baghdad. Years later, in October 1973, during the Ramadan (Yom Kippur) War, Iran was to play an important role: the Shah had kept the diplomatic mission of the Zionist state open in Tehran and did not stop oil deliveries to Israel, while providing logistical support in the delivery of supplies to the Syrian front and the evacuation of injured Arab soldiers. The rapprochement between Anwar Sadat and the USA naturally led to a reconciliation between Egypt and Iran. These new relations were not tarnished by Yitzak Rabin's trips to Tehran in 1974. Here Mohammad-Rezā Shāh played the role of essential intermediary, allowing the radical reversal of the Egyptian position. He himself went to Cairo where he was warmly received. The Egyptian President Anwar Sadat who had become a personal friend of the Shah,

---

[8] See U. BIALER, "The Iranian Connection in Israel's Foreign Policy – 1948–1951"; A.-R. HUSHANG-MAHDAVI, *Siāsat-e khāreji-e Irān dar dowrān-e Pahlavi*, pp. 151f.

[9] This is notably the case of the Israeli President Moshe Katsav (Musā Qassāb, 2000–07), born in 1945 in Yazd, who emigrated in 1951 with his parents. An interesting anecdote is that when, for alphabetical reasons, he was placed near the Iranian President Khātami during the funeral of Pope John Paul II (2005), he shook hands with him and greeted him in his provincial Persian. Khātami, who is also from Yazd, replied that he wished that one day the two nations would be reconciled. Later the Iranian president denied this story.

signed the peace treaty with Israel after having gone in person to Jerusalem (1977).[10]

Baghdad Pact: The Central Treaty Organization

The Anglo-Soviet occupation of 1941 had rendered null and void the Sa'dābād Treaty signed in 1937 between Iran, Turkey, Iraq, and Afghanistan – with Great Britain in the background. At the time of the Cold War, an alliance between the four countries was even more pressing. Mosaddeq had refused any alliance with a great power on account of the "negative equilibrium" defined in the mid-nineteenth century by Amir Kabir. But the Shah was hostile to the idealization of independence, arguing that it isolated Iran internationally and would increase British interference. In 1961, he advocated a "positive nationalism" in foreign affairs, seeing in it

> the method to guarantee maximum political and economic independence for the country, in agreement with the country's interests. For us Iranians, positive nationalism does not have the sense of a withdrawal and isolation, it means that without preoccupying ourselves with the wants or policies of other countries, we sign the treaties that serve the interests of our own country, and we will not yield to the threats of those who would like to choose our friends in our place.[11]

In reality, the Shah had clearly committed himself to the American strategy by signing, in 1955, the Baghdad Pact, a defensive alliance between Turkey, Iran, Iraq, Pakistan, and Great Britain; it was later renamed Central Treaty Organization (CENTO), when Iraq withdrew in 1959, and the office moved from Baghdad to Ankara. Even if the USA was not formally associated with it until one year later, the Baghdad Pact had as its objective – like the Sa'dābād pact – to halt Soviet influence on their southern border. More and more it looked, despite the civil chapters of the treaty, like a link between NATO and Southeast Asia Treaty Organisation. This alliance came at a high price for Iran when it tried to find a regional leading role, because no Arab country wanted to join. CENTO did not allow the settlement of

---

[10] A.-R. Hushang-Mahdavi, *Siāsat-e khāreji-e Irān dar dowrān-e Pahlavi*, pp. 440f.
[11] Md-R. Pahlavi, *Ma'muriat barā-ye vatan-am*, pp. 231–32.

conflicts in which member states were involved, neither the Cyprus crisis in 1964, nor the conflict of Iran with the Arab Emirates concerning the Persian Gulf in 1971, nor the war in Bangladesh in that same year. The oversupply of arms, to which we will return, and the technical and military assistance that the USA provided was going to accentuate the divide between Iran and its Arab neighbors, whether linked to the Soviet Union or not.

The American alliance and friendly relations with Israel had tarnished Iran's image among its Arab neighbors. Mosaddeq succeeded temporarily in redressing the situation by freezing relations with Israel, but, after his fall, the American grip on Iran and political radicalization in the Arab world only made things worse. After the Suez Crisis (1956) the Arab countries demanded that the 'Persian Gulf' now be known as the 'Arabian Gulf,' a name only attested on some seventeenth-century maps but that had been abandoned and of which modern geographers were completely unaware. Iran's interest in that zone was revived when the British in 1971 ended their protectorate of Oman and abandoned their strategic position on three islets situated near the opening of the Persian Gulf onto the Indian Ocean: the Greater and Lesser Tunbs and Abu Musa. The Shah's army immediately occupied them on the basis of old agreements. This occupation facilitated military surveillance of oil traffic, vital for the Iranian economy. The Arab countries were unanimous in condemning the Iranian operation, arguing that the people of these islands were Arabs. They redoubled anti-Iranian propaganda. The strategic importance of these islets has disappeared at the time of the Islamic Revolution with the emergence of satellites and long-range missiles, but patriotic feelings run high whenever one encroaches upon a state's territorial integrity. The Iranian sovereignty of these islets, although since then governed by condominium agreements, has several times been reaffirmed whenever the leaders of the Islamic Republic have needed to unite the nation behind them in the wake of political crises.

During the last years of the monarchy, Sadat allowed the Shah to appear as a leader in the region by reestablishing relations that had broken down during Nasser's reign. The signing of the Algiers Agreement in 1975 put an end to a long period of hostility between Iran and Iraq, and established a return to a better understanding of Iran among Arab states at a time when Iran's interests as an oil producer came closer to those both of Arabia and of Kuwait.

The White Revolution

In 1960, the election of a Democrat as President of the USA, J. F. Kennedy, somewhat modified Iran's priorities. Henceforth, the anti-communist strategy took the path of social and economic reforms, aiming to reduce the immense disparity between the landed proprietors, who dominated the political scene, and the peasants. Urbanization was still in its infancy and industries were small-scale. In the spirit of American consultancy firms, Iran's modernization could only happen via industrialization and by the development of modern media that conveyed the model of political participation, and with entrepreneurial economy replacing the passive domination of the masses in traditional rural society. In 1960, more than half of the population, or about 20 million people, worked in agriculture, but 56 percent of the land belonged to just 1 percent of the population.

Rezā Shāh had accumulated landed property. His son was preoccupied with breaking away from this image of a latifundista, which had defined the old Qajar aristocracy. After his return to power in 1953, he began to sell a large number of the villages he had inherited to the peasantry. Although this operation was not a philanthropic one, it met with great success – even when many of those who had contested Rezā Shāh's methods of acquiring these lands rather expected their restitution. It served as a test for land reform. In 1960, a new law prohibited the possession of landed property of more than 400 hectares (about 1,000 acres). Ayatollah Borujerdi, usually uncommunicative on social or political issues, objected through a fatwa that this law was contrary to Islam. It was adopted by the two Chambers, but remained on the shelf, because it was practically impossible to enforce it in the absence of any cadastral data.

In the spring of 1961, at the request of the Americans, the Shah named a new prime minister, Ali Amini (1905–92), a Qajar aristocrat, himself a large landownder, who not long before had been ambassador to Washington. This government worked to restore the state's authority in the most remote villages. To begin with, he asked the Shah to dissolve the two Chambers. The Majles that had just been elected,[12] was composed of a majority of landed proprietors and could only impede real

---

[12] The elections of summer 1960 had been so heavily manipulated that they were cancelled and launched again in early 1961. Losing any credibility the Melliun Party disappeared.

reform. To get out of the impasse due to the absence of a cadastre and to put an end to the rule of the big feudalists, the 1960 law was amended by the Minister of Agriculture, Hasan Arsanjāni (1922–1969), a fervent partisan since the 1940s of a redistribution of the land. Ayatollah Borujerdi's death spared long deliberations, putting an end to the validity of his fatwa against land reform. According to the new wording of the law, landed proprietors were prohibited from owning more than one village. Escaping the structures of the law were lands worked with modern machinery by the proprietor himself, as well as, in a first stage, the lands of pious endowments (*vaqf*).[13]

This reform emancipated peasants from quasi-feudal relationships that tied them to their land – until then, they were sold together with the villages – and allowed them to benefit from advantageous loans to purchase their land and immediately become landowners. But one of its objectives also was to transform family subsistence farms into agro-industrial enterprises endowed with the means to purchase agricultural machinery and to invest in irrigation works; the farmers themselves would become wage-earners. The government hoped that the old latifundia owners would invest the liquid assets obtained through the sale of land in industrial activities and would employ the poorest peasants who had not been able to become landowners. But the money earned from the sale of land was used instead in real estate speculation, thus contributing to the incoherent urban policy.

In the political arena, the Amini government was unable to convince Mosaddeq's supporters to return to parliamentary life and approve his reforms. The latter demanded upfront that the Sāvāk be dissolved and that free elections be held. Contrary to all expectations they were mostly hostile to the land reforms, as they were undoubtedly too closely related to the landed aristocracy and above all to the clergy. Mosaddeq himself, when asked in a letter, endorsed the reform and disapproved of the National Front's attitude.

After the success of his land reforms, the Shah had the support to go further. He soon made known the key points of a "revolution" consisting of six sections. In addition to land reform, he proposed the nationalization of the forests throughout the national territory (to prevent deforestation); the sale of the state's shares in industry to financially cover the land reforms; profit-sharing for workers in their enterprises (a

---

[13] A detailed study of land reform is given by A. K. S. LAMBTON, *The Persian Land Reform*.

measure inspired by similar reforms by de Gaulle in France at the time); a new electoral law giving women the right to vote; and the creation of an Army of Knowledge (*Sepāh-e dānesh*), an organization that was to eliminate illiteracy with the help of young recruits. This "White Revolution" (*Enqelāb-e sefid*) was expected to make him the most progressive monarch to date, but in fact turned him into the most misunderstood. The Shah explained his intentions in a book:[14]

> This is the only way that can secure the future of my country, in accordance with the ancient traditions of our history and with the spiritual and universal mission of this nation. I'm grateful to God that – precisely at the moment when, thanks to the historical conditions and the international situation, the implementation of this program was made possible – the command of this country's policies, this nation which I love with all my heart and which I deeply respect, was entrusted to me. Today, my people and I have a strong mutual bond, both sentimental and spiritual – there has probably never been such a bond in any place of the world. The root of this bond is not limited to my own firm will to devote my existence entirely to the progress and flourishing of my country, nor to the trust which the thankful and noble people of Iran have put in the sovereign who has, for 26 years [since the beginning of his reign], suffered so many trials and tribulations, but this bond is based mainly on the nature and the spirituality of the royal function and the person of the Shah in Iran, an institution which goes back to very ancient traditions.

In the same book, the Shah announced his intention to free Parliament from the influence of powerful landowners. In the absence of Parliament, once again imitating de Gaulle, he took the initiative to have his reforms directly adopted by the people through a referendum – this type of consultation would be copied later by the Islamic Republic. The vote took place on 26 January 1963, and women were called upon to vote, even though their ballot papers, placed in separate urns, were not officially counted, because the first protests and the absence of a prior law authorizing women's suffrage risked undermining the value of the referendum.

---

[14] Md-R. PAHLAVI, *Enqelāb-e sefid*, p. 2 of the introduction to a 1967 edition.

This fine reform resulted in immense social disruption. In general, it was very popular in the rural areas where it put an end to centuries of oppression. At the same time, it displaced peasants without land (*khoshneshin*) or those indebted and unable to honor new repayment obligations. It led to the formation of a subproletariat of "uprooted peasants," removed from their villages and not integrated into the economy – ideal conditions for the ulama, who put forward another way for this group to be integrated into society, based primarily on religious criteria.

In September 1963, the elections for the Majles (21st legislature) were boycotted by the opposition but proved the Shah right by drawing deputies to the ranks of the Assembly who, for the first time, were not mostly landed proprietors. Women took part in the elections, and six were elected. The real popularity of the Shah, both within and outside the country, where he became the model reformer king, had as its counterpart his isolation from the political class of his own country. Any opposition, any criticism, led to persecution and intimidation.

The White Revolution, later called the Revolution of Shah and the Nation (or "People," *Enqelāb-e shāh-o mellat*), was extended by other social reforms, but these consisted more of slogans and developmentalist programs that were imposed more or less skillfully than demands emanating from the people or effective measures to reform the country. These reforms came up against an increasingly determined opposition.

A Divided Opposition

The nostalgia for Mosaddeq's popular government, who had inspired the second and then the third National Front, had been redoubled by the Shah's nationalist rhetoric and by his progressive reforms. Opponents criticized first the authoritarian methods, the electoral manipulations, and the repression of freedoms, without themselves proposing a real program. Among them was an increasing number of intellectuals who, understanding that any political opposition of the parliamentary type had become impossible, got involved either in leftist movements, including paramilitary action groups who were partisans of armed struggle, or in fundamental reflection to criticize the developmentalist model.

An Intellectual in Opposition: Jalāl Āl-e Ahmad

Typical for that period and very popular among intellectuals, who circulated his writings in manuscript form, the fiction writer and essayist Jalāl Āl-e Ahmad (1923–69), a former communist militant from a clerical family, published two studies that were immediately banned: *Weststruckness* (1962) and *About Good Services and Betrayal of the Intellectuals* (1965).[15] In the former, reinterpreting a concept coined by the philosopher Ahmad Fardid (see below), he denounced Iranian intellectuals and politicians who imitated the West, explaining that by aping his master, the dominated Iranian was but a caricature of his own identity. Despite the exaggeration of his arguments, Āl-e Ahmad planted an idea about identity that Iranian intellectuals have had difficulty in uprooting even at the beginning of the twenty-first century. Alienated by development and by the glitter of western societies, they seek the "essence" of what they once were, without accepting the idea that this search is bound to be in vain.

In his second book, more sociological in tone, Āl-e Ahmad denounced the way in which the Iranian elite since the Qajar era had been stripped of their own social and national character by the desire to reproduce the western model. On the other hand, he unexpectedly and paradoxically praised the ulama, who, according to him, had courageously defended the national identity and had remained in the service of the people, although their role had not been acknowledged. He cited the example of Sheykh Fazlollāh Nuri, the theologian who was hanged in 1909 by the revolutionaries for having refused to follow the model provided by European political institutions, and whom the Iranian intellectuals had always denounced as the paragon a reactionary obscurantism because he sided with the anti-constitutionalist Mohammad-Ali Shāh.

Āl-e Ahmad also cited the example of Ayatollāh Ruhollāh Khomeyni, unexpected praise from a former communist militant. In 1962, Khomeyni then still unknown beyond the theological circles of Qom, started to lead the religious resistance against the Shah's reforms. Āl-e Ahmad quotes at length his brave speech on the return of the capitulations in October 1964 (see below).

---

[15] See Bibliography under Āl-e Ahmad. On Āl-e Ahmad see further A. Gheissari, *Iranian Intellectuals in the Twentieth Century*, pp. 88f.

Before the referendum, Khomeyni had opposed the new electoral law which gave women the right to vote and which foresaw that the elected would swear an oath "on the holy book."[16] In the name of Islamic traditions raised to the rank of dogma, the ulama could not consider including women among the electorate; and the loose concept of "holy book" opened up the possibility of Bahāis being recognized as citizens, a sensitive issue.

On the issue of women's suffrage, other political opponents were less reactionary. The Movement for Liberty in Iran (*Nahzat-e āzādi-e Irān* – of Mosaddeqist Islamic tendency) of Mahdi Bazargan explained that, given that the government does not respect the freedom of elections, extending the right to vote to women did not make any sense. For the clergy, the oath on the "holy book" on which those elected to the provincial and municipal assemblies had to swear seemed to indicate that minorities that had not been officially recognized would be allowed to participate in political life, choosing their own "book." The ulama were clearly concerned here about the Bahāis to whom they could not consider giving the status of full citizen. Since the persecution of 1954–55 the Bahāis had slowly re-emerged; they were again authorized to visit their temple in Tehran, without its dome, and some had made major fortunes in industry (Habib Sābet). One of them, Amir Abbās Hoveydā (1919–79) would be nominated prime minister in 1965 and remained in place until 1977. The ulama's protests against the new electoral rules also concerned the announcement of a new phase in land reform, which they opposed because it would oblige them, once eventually enforced, to sell the pious endowments managed by the clergy for the benefit of theological schools and religious institutions and to give up their comfortable financial autonomy.

The Rise of Khomeyni

The government made concessions. Notably, it revised the electoral law, postponing the right to vote for women to the legislative elections of 1963 – it is for this reason that the ballot boxes reserved

---

[16] On the ulama's opposition see W. FLOOR, "The Revolutionary Character of the Ulama, Wishful Thinking or Reality," pp. 73–97; A. DAVĀNI, *Nahzat-e do-māhe-ye ruhāniun-e Irān*. Khomeyni's telegrams to the Shah justified, in the name of Islam, the setting aside of women in public life. The ayatollah tried to get the Shah onto his side by addressing his vehement criticisms to Alam.

for women during the referendum were counted separately and women's votes deprived of any legal value. But the theological schools still opposed the referendum and openly protested. On the eve of the referendum, in January 1963, the Shah visited Qom to distribute land ownership certificates to peasants. He used the opportunity to clumsily improvise a speech in which he vehemently denounced the "black reaction," (*ertejā'-e siyāh*), designating, without naming them, the ulama who, he alleged, belonged to society of the time of the beginning of Islam.[17] This provocation led to demonstrations in the theological schools, and the police intervened with force. On 21 March, at the time of the Iranian New Year festivities, when many police forces were still in Qom, Khomeyni benefited from the presence of many pilgrims, addressing the faithful gathered inside the Feyziye school and replied to the Shah's words: "Don't fear the rusty old bayonets, because soon they will break. The state cannot use bayonets to resist the will of a great nation (*mellat-e bozorg*), sooner or later it will fail."[18] Thus the theologian clearly involved himself in political affairs with concrete vocabulary. When using the term *mellat,* often translated as "nation," he probably meant it in the traditional sense of "religious community" rather than the people constituted in a nation and politically organized. The police, having arrived in force, did not hesitate to unceremoniously beat the ulama. The official press reported on the demonstrations as a clash between supporters of the reforms and the reactionaries who opposed them.

Shortly thereafter, on 3 June 1963, demonstrations organized at Qom on the occasion of the ritual mourning during the month of Moharram broke out in the form of a riot against the government, but the police could not intervene because of the size of the crowd. Khomeyni obstinately refused all attempts at reconciliation, he addressed the Shah sharply in a sermon and predicted his demise. Two days later (5 June; in the Iranian calender 15 *Khordād*), he was arrested, which provoked demonstrations across Iran.[19] To set him free, the main religious leaders let it be known that they acknowledged Khomeyni as a grand ayatollah, who may be chosen by believers as a "model to imitate" (*marja-e taqlid*) to succeed Borujerdi, while the Shah, who

[17] Sd H. Ruhāni, *Bar-rasi va tahlil-i az nahzat-e Emām Khomeyni dar Irān,* I, pp. 263f.
[18] Sd H. Ruhāni, *Bar-rasi va tahlil-i az nahzat-e Emām Khomeyni dar Irān,* I, p. 289.
[19] See, for example, J. Erfān-Manesh, ed., *Khāterāt-e 15-e khordād-e Shirāz.*

tried hard to de-Shiitize Iran and de-Iranize Shiism, applied pressure to ensure an apolitical Iraqi residing in Najaf, Mohsen al-Hakim, be acknowledged as *marja*. The spontaneous demonstrations in support of Khomeyni were suppressed by force of arms, and martial law was again imposed. The repression claimed several hundred victims, the exact number being impossible to know with any certainty. The trauma caused by the events of 1963 signified the rupture between the royal regime and the clergy.

Once acknowledged as *āyatollāh* (literally, "miraculous sign of God"), Khomeyni had become virtually untouchable. Despite this, he was imprisoned as though he were to be judged and executed. In prison he received a visit from General Hasan Pākravān, then director of the Sāvāk. Pākravān, who favored dialogue, told the Shah that he had been unable to find the slightest trace of a foreign conspiracy behind the ayatollah and asked the latter to withdraw his attacks against the monarchy. Following a compromise between the two men, which the ayatollah categorically denied later, Khomeyni was assigned to a villa in Tehran for about ten months, before being entirely and quietly released on 7 April 1964 thanks to a change in government.

The tension had ebbed, and the Shah believed he had permanently halted the politization of the ulama. But, the following October, Parliament adopted a law granting diplomatic immunity, that is, judicial extraterritoriality, to American military personnel in Iran. This measure reminded nationalists of the sad memory of the capitulations, abolished in 1928. Khomeyni, alone among Iranian politicians, openly denounced this law in a sermon on 27 October 1964, on the occasion of a pilgrimage that had attracted a large crowd in Qom:

> I cannot express the sorrow I feel in my heart. My heart is constricted. Since the day I heard of the latest developments affecting Iran, I have barely slept. I am profoundly disturbed, and my heart is constricted. With sorrowful heart, I count the days until death shall come and deliver me ... A law has been put before the Majles according to which we are to accede to the Vienna Convention, and a provision has been added to it that all American military advisers, together with their families, technical and administrative officials, and servants – in short, anyone in any way connected to them – are to enjoy legal immunity with respect to any crime they may commit in Iran. If some

American's servant, some American's cook, assassinates your *marja* in the middle of the bazaar, or runs over him, the Iranian police do not have the right to apprehend him! Iranian courts do not have the right to judge him! The dossier must be sent to America, so that our masters there can decide what is to be done! ... They passed it without any shame, and the government shamelessly defended this scandalous measure. They have reduced the Iranian people (*mellat*) to a level lower than that of an American dog. If someone runs over a dog, belonging to an American, he will be prosecuted. Even if the Shah himself were to run over a dog belonging to an American, he would be prosecuted. But if an American cook runs over the Shah, the head of state, no one will have the right to interfere with him ... We do not regard as law what they claim to have passed. We do not regard this Majles as a Majles. We do not regard this government as a government. They are traitors, guilty of high treason![20]

One week later, on 4 November, Khomeyni was seized by agents of the Sāvāk and exiled to Turkey from where he went to Najaf a few months later. In the holy Iraqi city, he found fuller independence as an authority over the faithful. His communications with the Iranian people were hindered, but ulama close to him continued to correspond with him, and some went to see him clandestinely from Europe. He himself sent messages each year to Iranian pilgrims who went to Mecca.

At Najaf, Khomeyni had a small core of theology students who served as his secretaries and as a sound board. It is there that he wrote, in Arabic, a juridical-theological tract on transactions, in which he condemned, without appeal, more explicitly than before, the idea of democracy.[21] He developed the same idea, in a simpler style for Iranians in lessons that he gave in Persian in Najaf. Grouped together

---

[20] Sd H. Ruhāni, *Bar-rasi va tahlil-i az nahzat-e Emām Khomeyni dar Irān*, I, pp. 716–26. The translation is quoted from B. Moin, *Khomeini, Life of the Ayatollah*, pp. 122f. The term *mellat* might be translated here as "religious community," the ambiguity, probably on purpose, is significant. It is interesting to recall that this sermon was published for the first time in the book of Jalāl Āl-e Ahmad, *Dar khedmat va khiānat*, II, pp. 84f; nevertheless with vexed comments by Āl-e Ahmad when Khomeyni denounces the emancipation of women.

[21] R. Khomeyni, *Ketāb al-bey'*, vol. II, pp. 459–63. See the analysis by N. Calder, "Accommodation and Revolution in Imami Shi'i Jurisprudence: Khumayni and the Classical Tradition."

in a book with the title *The Islamic Government* (*Hokumat-e Eslāmi*), these lessons were a clear systematization of his theory of "the governance of the jurist-theologian" (*velāyat-e faqih*), a concept that would become the keystone of the Constitution of 1979.

According to this theory, during the Occultation of the Twelfth Imam, the ulama received the task, inherited from the Prophet to take charge of government of the terrestrial city. In it, Khomeyni acknowledges the universal competence of the ulama, extending it notably to the political sphere, their legitimacy being confirmed by their co-optation among believers, according to the criteria of wisdom and integrity. One might make a comparison between Mohammad-Rezā Shāh, who sanctified the royal function and tried to distance Iranian society from its religious points of reference, and Ayatollah Khomeyni, who, at the same time, gave an increasingly political definition to the clerical role, by denying the legitimacy of universal suffrage and even condemning the idea of secularism or indeed of any separation between religion and politics. Few Iranians had read *Islamic Government* before 1979, although the book had already been made available the year before during the large demonstrations, when the name of Khomeyni became known on a wider scale. They saw the ayatollah as their liberator from the Shah's dictatorship, without understanding that his political system was potentially more dangerous to democratic liberties.

Armed Movements

Apart from Āl-e Ahmad, few westernized intellectuals had understood the force of the political impact of Ayatollah Khomeyni's message in the defense of a national identity when faced with American imperialism. The most moderate opposition politicians, supporters of the Movement for Liberty in Iran, had been dragged before the courts for having dared to criticize the White Revolution. Prophetically, at the end of his defense in the military court of appeals in 1964, Mahdi Bāzargān declared: "We are the last to rise up to fight with constitutional means. We expect the president of this court to bring this point to the notice of the authorities."[22] The young, impatient to see action, in fact drew their conclusion from these events:

---

[22] M. Bāzargān's speech for his defense in the military court, quoted by Q. Nejāti, *Tārikh-e siāsi-e bist-o-panj sāle-ye Irān*, I, p. 373. On Bāzargān and his movement, see H. Chehabi, *Iranian Politics and Religious Modernism*.

The massacres of 1963 were a historical turning point. Before, the opposition tried hard to only fight against the regime with street demonstrations, worker strikes and covert activities. The killings of 1963 showed the failure and uselessness of these methods. Henceforth, the militants abandoned the ideology and posed the question "What is to be done?" The reply was clear: armed struggle.[23]

These young Iranians, who acknowledged the uselessness of parliamentarianism, turned more spontaneously to modern and "progressive" forms of struggle inspired by the guerilla wars in Vietnam and in Latin America. Their hero was Lenin, the intransigent and anti-religious man, or Mao, the theoretician of the popular army, or even the romantic figure of Che Guevara, the revolutionary hero of the Third World. For them, it was not time to seek refuge in the mosques but to get training in Palestinian camps so as to wage a relentless war against the Shah's regime. Among these youngsters, several rival groups splintered, mainly over the question of their allegiance – or the lack of it – to Islam and on the priority given either to armed struggle or to the awakening of the people.

Marxist Guerrilla

The first to organize and present themselves as a militant group were the Marxist-Leninist guerillas (*Sāzemān-e cherik-hā-ye fedāi-e khalq-e Irān*, the Organization of fighting guerillas of the People of Iran, commonly known as *Fedāiān*), a movement stemming from the fusion in 1971 of two parallel groups. One was led, until 1968, by Bizhan Jazani (1937–75), a militant jaded by the pro-Soviet position of the Toudeh Party; he was arrested and summarily executed, after having been tortured without giving up the names of his comrades. The other group had formed around Mas'ud Ahmadzāde, a theorician of armed struggle, who had come to militancy through the National Front and the Movement for Liberty in Iran. The *Fedāiān* were organized into small cells of three militants, any larger scale was impossible because of police repression. "The mission of each group was simply to provoke armed clashes to strike at our enemy, to break the political

---

[23] From *Mojāhed*, 2, Fall 1353/1974, pp. 5–6, quoted from Q. NEJĀTI, *Tārikh-e siāsi-e bist-o-panj sāla*, p. 375.

stranglehold and to show our people that the only possible fight is armed struggle."[24]

The *Fedā'iān* began to plunder banks to finance the purchase of arms and to fit out hideouts. In 1971, for their first combined military action, they chose a mountain village in Gilān, in the north of Iran. After one of them had been taken prisoner they gained control over the gendarmerie of the village of Siyāhkal with all its arsenal on 8 February (9 Bahman 1349). They resisted for almost one month strongly undermining the self-confidence of the security forces, who had to call for military reinforcements to finish the job. One of the causes of their failure was that they had not been able to convince the local peasants to support them. The survivors of this heroic adventure could only place a bomb in the American Cultural Institute or kill American and Iranian officers. They resurfaced after the revolution of 1979, believing they would then have the opportunity to launch a vast offensive on Iranian public opinion.

Islamic Guerilla

For their part, the Mojāhedin, that is, members of the Organization of Mojāhedin of the People of Iran (*Sāzemān-e mojāhedin-e khalq-e Irān*), came from the religious wing of Mosaddeq's nationalist partisans, the "Movement for Liberty in Iran" of Mahdi Bāzargān. After the revolution, Bāzargān, who was reproached for his liberal ideas, tried to understand the filiation of this guerilla, somewhat similar to that of a chick having brooded a duck egg. He called on his spiritual children, on the one hand the leaders of the Islamic Republic and on the other the Mojāhedin, to reconcile with him around the idea of social justice and loyalty for a progressive Islam. But the Mojāhedin from the start also had Marxist leanings. Driven by competition with the Fedāiān, they wanted to do better; with the Koran in hand they wanted to build a just society on earth free from any enslavement, but also to guarantee access to paradise on the other side. The founders of the Mojāhedin were, like Bāzargān, engineers and were not yet twenty years old in 1953 when Mosaddeq was toppled. Their true political initiation was the revolt of 1963 and the repression that followed. Coming from a middle-class background, they

[24] H. ASHRAF, *Jam'-bandi-e se-sāle* [Results of three years' action], Tehran, 1358/1979, quoted by Q. NEJĀTI, *Tārikh-e siāsi-e bist-o-panj sāl*, p. 384.

had links with certain ulama notably with Ayatollah Mahmud Tāleqāni (1912–1979), an atypical personality attuned to political problems and a friend of Bāzargān. Tāleqāni saw in them "jewels that shone in the darkness."

For a time, the Mojāhedin were also close to Ali Shariati (1935–77), a revolutionary thinker who, in France, had become friends with militants of Algerian independence and who hoped to draw inspirational themes from Islam. Shariati spoke as follows about Mohammad Hanif-Nezhād one of the three founders of the Mojāhedin, an agricultural engineer: "O enemy of the tyrant! Friend of the oppressed, O Moslem combatant! O you of the race of prophets, who returns from the circumabulations of love, the ordeal of water, the stage of awareness and of self-consciousness."[25] The amity between the Mojāhedin and Shariati was short, the latter criticized their haste for action and developed instead a theory of a revolutionary awareness-raising among the masses before resorting to armed militancy.

From the beginning, the Mojāhedin added to their religious references theories inspired by Marxism. "Our first intention is to combine the supreme values of Islamic religion with the scientific thought of Marxism ... We think that true Islam is in agreement with theories of social change, of historical determination and of class struggle."[26] At the beginning of the 1979 revolution the new leaders demanded that the Mojāhedin, whose publications were then freely distributed in Iran, explain their ideology. In response, this statement was given in one of their manifestos: "We say no to Marxist philosophy, in particular on the subject of atheism (*elhād*), but we say yes to its social ideas, in particular to its analysis of feudalism, capitalism and imperialism."[27]

The Mojāhedin were preoccupied with the world of the peasant, but, more realistic than the Fedāiān, they quickly recognized that the Shah's land reforms, which had transformed peasants into landowners, had seriously diminished their revolutionary potential. Deciding to turn

---

[25] Cited by Q. Nejāti, *Tārikh-e siāsi-e bist-o-panj sāl*, p. 394. *Hanif* means "pure and pious" like the family of the prophet, *nezhād* means "race," hence Shariati's allusion. Hanif-nezhad (1938–1972), was executed after a trial held behind closed doors, see E. Abrahamian, *The Iranian Mojahedin*, pp. 87f, 135. Abrahamian fails to understand the rupture between Shariati and the Mojāhedin.

[26] *Peykār*, 79 (3rd November 1981), interview with Hoseyn Ruhāni and Torāb Haqq-Shenās, quoted by Q. Nejāti, *Tārikh-e siāsi-e bist-o-panj sāl*, p. 397.

[27] Quoted in Q. Nejāti, *Tārikh-e siāsi-e bist-o-panj sāl*, p. 397.

to the cities, they contacted the armed wing of Fatah, the liberation movement of Palestine, and sent eight of their militants to undergo military training in a camp in Lebanon. Six of these militants were arrested in Dubai, but the Mojāhedin diverted to Baghdad the plane that should have taken them to Tehran where they were to be judged. Thus they ended up joining training camps without the Sāvāk being able to detect where they were.

Upon their return to Iran, they were hastened into terrorist action by the echo of the Fedāiān operation at Siyāhkal. They, too, had to build up a revolutionary reputation. They wanted to blow up the high-voltage lines that enabled the interconnection of the electrical power grid during the Persepolis festivities (October 1971), but their operation failed due to imprudence: to obtain explosives they had contacted a Toudeh militant who had been turned by the Sāvāk. In a few days, thirty-five of the most active members of the Mojāhedin were arrested, of whom eleven were leaders. During their trial behind closed doors (the text of their defense was published abroad), they claimed responsibility for the plan to topple the constitutional monarchy by inciting urban rebellions. Twelve were sentenced to death, sixteen to life imprisonment. Two of the condemned, Bahman Bāzargāni and Mas'ud Rajavi, whose brother, in Switzerland, had mobilized academics to intervene publicly with the Shah, were eventually pardoned and imprisoned. To tarnish their reputations, it was announced that they had agreed to collaborate with the police.

The survivors reorganized into smaller, better-insulated groups, and like the Fedāiān, they mounted attacks aiming to destabilize the authorities but also to frighten the Americans. In May 1972, a few minutes prior to President Nixon's arrival in Tehran, they detonated a bomb in Rezā Shāh's mausoleum in Rey, an obligatory place to visit for all foreign guests. The also fired at the car of General Harold L. Price, who commanded the American officers providing military assistance between 1969 and 1972, but only wounded him. But they killed Iranian officers as well as Col. Lewis Hawkins, assistant director of American military aid. Several dozens of Mojāhedin, of whom three were women, were killed in street fights. Their terrorist activities were immediately reported in the international press and caused a feeling of insecurity, which was alleviated by closer police surveillance in a climate of general suspicion.

In September 1975, the Mojāhedin published a communiqué announcing that henceforth Marxist philosophy would be the only true benchmark for their action. "In the beginning, we believed that one might mix Marxism and Islam and accept historical determination without dialectic materialism. Now we have understood that this is not possible; we have chosen Marxism, because it is the right road to liberate the exploited working class." Following this ideological turnabout linked to thoughts about the struggles in the Third World, China, Cuba, Vietnam, and Algeria, the Mojāhedin split. The majority group, opting for Marxism, later took the name of "Organization of combat to liberate the working class" (*Sāzemān-e Peykār dar rāh-e āzādi-e tabaqe-ye kārgar*), usually called *Peykār*.

The split of the Mojāhedin had three causes, according to Abrahamian:[28] their deception vis-à-vis the ambiguous attitude of the ulama who were hostile to the royal regime, such as Khomeyni; the difficulty in attracting the young, utterly de-Islamized intellectuals to political struggle in the name of Islam; and finally, the attraction exercised by organizations that had exclusively opted for Marxism, such as the Fedāiān, who offered a clearer and more revolutionary answer to the problem of repression. In fact, Khomeyni, and with him a large part of the clergy who fought against the regime, felt a radical hostility to the influence of the traditional clergy in the Mojāhedin doctrine, and this mistrust increased after the split, suggesting that those who maintained Islam as a point of reference only did so out of opportunism. The division was not simply an ideological dispute; it caused trouble for all those who sought an alternative to the royal regime in political Islam. The hatred that it aroused would lead to killings among the Mojāhedin and their renegade brothers.

Despite their strong mobilization in November 1978, after the liberation of political prisoners, the Mojāhedin have never succeeded in being admitted to the leading ranks in the Islamic Republic. They only obtained a weak result during the first elections and were eliminated as "dividers" (*monāfeqin*, often translated as "hypocrites"). "The dividers are worse than infidels," Khomeyni stated in June 1980, one year prior to the systemic elimination of the Mojāhedin. Their failure was

---

[28] Iranian historian Qolāmrezā Nejāti follows Abrahamian here without acknowledging his borrowings. See E. Abrahamian, *The Iranian Mojahedin*, pp. 149f. The subject of the Mojāhedin is very sensitive in Iran. Its treatment by Nejāti, although borrowed, seems to be honest and without hatred for the prerevolutionary part.

unexpected because, as Bāzargān had said, the Mojāhedin had maintained direct links with certain historical leaders of the Movement for Liberty in Iran and, since 1971, had promoted the image of a modern militancy acting in the name of Islam. The dress adopted by the Mojāhedin – parka, flat-fronted canvas trousers, collarless shirt without a tie, and moustache – was taken over (with the addition of a beard), by the militants and militia of the Islamic Republic, who in some ways made it the new conformist dress, replacing the suit and tie of the previous regime. This is even more the case with women, where a dress code that conformed both with Islam and with active militancy was completely lacking. Rejecting the chador as too old-fashioned and reactionary, the young militant women of the Mojāhedin wore headscarves of a single color, generally blue, and a simple light coat over trousers; this was more comfortable and did not restrict their movements when demonstrating or at work. Such has been the costume of many Iranian women since the Islamic Republic gave the order prohibiting them from showing uncovered hair or bare legs. The immense attraction that Mojāhedin ideology exercised on young college and university students concealed their lack of social basis. Their strategy had been much smarter than that of the Fedāiān, but their success was just as short.[29]

Debates on Iranian Identity

These insurrections revealed the tremendous turmoil of some particularly determined young militants. Others, those who had studied enough to resist indoctrination, aspired to an ideal other than the material benefits offered by the Pahlavi society to its loyal agents; they were seeking their identity. This artificial society fascinated some but frightened others. The Shah's immense ambitions and extravagant development projects became realizable thanks to the oil profits, but the educational, economic, and political infrastructure lagged far behind. Many Iranians of the 1970s, torn between national or religious traditions and contradictory economic and political programs, were worried about seeing their country invaded by models of consumption imported from the USA. No longer recognizing themselves either in

---

[29] Among witnesses from inside the Mojāhedin organization, see M. BANISADR, *Memoirs of an Iranian Rebel.*

their leaders or in their dreams, they questioned their own identity and embarked on many different trains of thought, which constituted a kind of tranquilizing metaphysics, a distraction from their anxiety in the face of the rapid changes to their country.

Renewal in Clerical Thought

The first faltering steps of a debate about globalization and its negative effects, these philosophical reflections on identity thus continued the questioning popularized by Āl-e Ahmad. Some turned to Islam to find an answer, others to a search for the universal through their Iranian existence. Still others even went in search of ways to cross from one to the other, in a healthy dialectic between a generally progressive Iranian Shiite Islam and a philosophical speculation rooted in Persian literature and in metaphysical or Sufi thought, most often outside political commitment and far from any kind of militancy. The question of identity did not seem dangerous to anybody. The Shah's regime understood the necessity to leave space for intellectuals to debate, while trying in vain to channel or even control the intellectual discourse and favoring the secular trend.

The renewal of Iranian Islam began in 1961 with the death of Ayatollah Borujerdi. Desiring to have an Iraqi *marja* recognized at the head of the clergy, the Shah probably contributed – inspite of himself – to the modernizing of religion (or *aggiornamento* as often said of the Catholic Church after Vatican II) because he freed the Iranian Shiites of the obsessive teachings of an aged man of the cloth in a politically vulnerable position. As of 1962, meetings to define the role of the clergy in Shiism took place in Qom and in Tehran, in which young progressive ulama (Mahmud Tāleqāni) or disciples of Khomeyni (Mohammad-Hoseyn Beheshti, Mortazā Motahhari) participated, but also non-clerical personalities such as Mahdi Bāzargān. In the book in which they published their discussions they affirm that the complexity of modern life no longer demanded a single *marja*, but a "guidance council" (*shurā-ye marja'iyat*).[30] Removing some of the distant mystique from the clerical role, they advocated solutions which were better suited to preaching in the modern world and recommended, for example, that

---

[30] *Bahs-i dar bāre-ye marja'iyat va ruhāniyat*. A study of this debate in A. K. S. Lambton, "A reconsideration of the Position of the *Marja' at-taqlid* and the Religious Institution."

young mollas learn English to better understand the outside world, while a few years earlier Ayatollah Borujerdi, in his own school of theology, had to give up such an innovation which had caused scandal among the rich bazār merchants who financed the clergy.

In Khomeyni's movement, Ayatollah Beheshti himself offered the example of a clergyman who had adapted to modernity. He had studied French at school and knew enough English to teach it; later, during a spell as leader of the mosque of Hamburg, he learnt German. He busied himself, at the request of the Ministry of Education, with the editing of Shiite religion manuals for Iranian school children. As for Motahhari, he agreed to teach theology and philosophy at the state faculty of religious science in Tehran. He read and commented on western philosophers (in translation) and did not hesitate to debate social subjects with feminist editors of the magazine *Zan-e ruz* ("Today's Woman"), markedly justifying the wearing of the veil and temporary marriage.[31] If he did not manage to convince the readers of that magazine with its wide audience, at least he made the effort to present Islam with modern arguments. Motahhari and Beheshti were two of the main architects of the regime that was put in place after the revolution. Their violent deaths, on 1 May 1979 and 28 June 1981 respectively, deprived the Islamic Republic of two personalities who might perhaps have been able to avoid many of the excesses that have handicapped the new regime.

Ali Shariati

The killing of Motahhari was linked to the critical positions that this theologian had taken at the beginning of the 1970s to warn against the immoderation of an agitator of ideas, Ali Shariati (1933–77). After his university studies in Mashhad, where he was a member of the religious wing of the National Front, this young intellectual from an open-minded clerical family spent five years in France (1959–64) at the time of the end of the war in Algeria. Returning to Iran with a doctoral degree and simmering with revolutionary ideas, he remained faithful to the Islam of his youth; he had trouble finding a job where his influence on young people would not worry the authorities. He finally became the

---

[31] On this typical Shiite institution, the temporary marriage, see Sh. HAERI, *Law of Desire: Temporary Marriage in Iran*; Y. RICHARD, *Shiite Islam*, ch. 6, pp. 148f.

main organizer of the *Hoseyniye Ershād*, a religious institute founded in 1963 in Tehran by Muslim bazaaris and some modernizing theologians. His ambition was to break with Shiite dolorism. While the Hoseyniye is the traditional religious theater where the mourning of the Shiite Imams (*taziye*) is celebrated and where the public joins in with the weeping and tears of the actors, the public of the Hoseyniye Ershād applauded the orators, who were more lecturers than preachers. Shariati believed that Islam had to educate so as not to be smothered by modern culture, and he wanted to de-clericalize Shiism, that is, to take control away from the ulama. Within a few years he made the Ershād a place of religious education to rival the traditional theological schools. The Koran and the interpretations were read outside the clerical jumble. He himself spoke there wearing a tie, used the vocabulary of social sciences, with many French words; he referred to Marxist authors, yes, but only in order to return to the great revolutionary inspiration of Shiism, that which had guided Hussein to martyrdom. For Shariati, fighting oppression, freeing the enslaved, being the defender of Islam were one and the same thing.

After the "economy without oil," the slogan launched by Mosaddeq, who, benefiting from the embargo, had wanted to give a boost to the Iranian economy, Shariati went on to launch the formula "Islam without clerics" (*Eslām menhā-ye ākhund*), or "tomorrow's Islam will no longer be the Islam of the mollas."[32] He had immense success as a religious orator, partly owing to his modernity, which allowed him to respond to the Marxist challenge without being reactionary. But the Hoseyniye Ershād was closed in 1972 at the demand of certain ulama, in particular Motahhari, because Shariati, like all ideologues who did not have the background of a classical clerical education, represented a major challenge for them. Accepting that an intellectual had learnt to read and interpret the Koran without the mediation of institutional tradition was destroying the clerical monopoly on legitimate speech. Shortly thereafter Shariati was arrested, at the time when the Sāvāk was worried about all kinds of subversive activities, and remained in prison for two years. When he left prison, the Pahlavi regime saw his potential to counter the communist influence among young students. A text written by Shariati to refute Marxism was published in the semi-official newspaper *Keyhān* on 14 February 1976,

---

[32] A. SHARIATI, *Bā mokhātab-hā-ye āshnā*, pp. 8, 141.

letting it be understood that henceforth there was common ground between him and the regime. Despite this last uncertain point, Shariati fascinated his listeners and his entourage, above all, because of the mystical inspiration that fed and energized all his revolutionary ideology.

Prevented from speaking freely after his release from prison, Shariati finally resigned himself to going into exile and died of a heart problem in London, shortly after having arrived in Europe, when he learned that the police were refusing to let his wife join him. Fearing that his funeral would lead to violent demonstrations, at a time when the Shah's regime had barely started to be liberalized, Shariati's family and Imam Musā Sadr managed to bury him in Damascus near a Shiite mausoleum (Zeynabiya). His works were published after his death thanks to the palpable liberalization that Iran enjoyed under pressure from the newly elected Jimmy Carter, and people stood in long lines to buy copies.

Several non-clerical religious authors tackled subjects that would lead to the revolution, but Shariati was the most popular. The future Guardians of the Revolution (*Pāsdārān*) and most of the young militants who would fill the ranks of the Mojāhedin had come to political Islam via Shariati. His portrait would be carried in all the major processions of the revolution. Later, the Islamic Republic tried to clamp down on the distribution of his works, at least his most anti-clerical texts. Although certain topics have become outdated, he continues to be at the heart of debates about the renewal of Islam and its declericalization.

Identity in the Intellectual Discourse

Amid this Islamic awakening, several discussion groups were beginning to develop a sociology of identity. In his polemical writings, Jalāl Āl-e Ahmad has given this train of thought a strong impetus. Monographs written within the purview of the faculty of social sciences at the University of Tehran – based on in-depth surveys on the population, family (Jamshid Behnām), the feudality of the state (Paul Vieille, Abol-Hasan Banisadr, Mortazā Kotobi), and, finally, education (Ehsan Naraghi) – fueled debates on modernization, the impact of development, and the rootlessness of the modern elite, whose models were systematically borrowed from the West. The underdeveloped Iranian university system, only took in a small proportion of the young people who wanted to receive a higher education, and most of them left for Europe or the USA. Those who remained did not hold stronger national sentiments than the expatriates. Until the mid-1970s, the University of Tehran did not offer any regular teaching of Iranian Islamic philosophy; thus, in Iran, this rich tradition of the Islamic world was only transmitted within traditional clerical circles although at the same time it was read and studied in the West.

The French orientalist Henry Corbin, who since 1946 had spent long periods in Tehran, was one of the first to publish critical editions of a Persian mystic philosopher of the seventeenth century, Mollā Sadrā (d. 1640) and of his successors, whom he did not hesitate to compare with European thinkers. Thanks to him, two brilliant Iranian scholars, Seyyed Hoseyn Nasr and Dāriush Shāyegān, rediscovered the Iranian traditions. Nasr, who studied history of science at Harvard, became the private secretary of Empress Farah in the last months of the monarchy. She encouraged him to found in 1975 the Royal Academy of Philosophy. (The Academy still exists, but the adjective 'royal' has been replaced by 'Islamic'.) Shāyegān, philosopher and Sanskritist, founded somewhat later the Iranian Center for the Study of Civilizations, a distant ancestor of "the dialogue of civilizations" that was dear to Mohammad Khātami.

In the fall of 1977, during a colloquium organized in Tehran in the presence of Empress Farah, Dāriush Shāyegān gathered thinkers from all over the world, among whom was Roger Garaudy, then a regular consultant of the Empress.[33] Some months later, Shayegan resigned from his official institute and joined, in an unexpected manner, Ayatollah Khomeyni, whom he compared to Ghandi.[34] For a number of years, well before philosophical speculation on globalization, Shayegan had been reflecting on the disappearance of the high tradition of Iranian Islamic thought, and he joined a philosophical group that centered around Fardid, a guru who defies classification.

[33] D. SHAYEGAN, ed., *L'Impact planétaire de la pensée occidentale rend-il possible un dialogue réel entre les civilisations?* The Third-Worldist philosopher and ex-communist Garaudy later converted to Islam in its Saudi version and hurled abuse at Shiism, then, constant in his inconstancy, he adopted Khomeyni's Islam and returned to Tehran's ways, praised by the ayatollahs.

[34] *Les Nouvelles littéraires*, 56, 7–14 December 1978, p. 23.

Ahmad Fardid

Ahmad Fardid (1910–94), who, as we have already mentioned, barely published any personal writings during his lifetime, remains an obscure figure for many of his contemporaries.[35] After theological studies in his home town of Yazd, and then moving on to a modern school in Tehran after 1926, Seyyed Ahmad *Mahini Yazdi* was employed by the censorship office of Rezā Shāh where he worked as a translator. He translated the first work of Henry Corbin on Iranian spiritual traditions (1946) into Persian. As of 1945 he called himself Fardid, a name that may be translated as "charismatic vision." Having belatedly received a scholarship to study philosophy at the Sorbonne, he read Bergson and became a disciple of Heidegger, with whom he studied in Germany and whom he introduced to Iran. Fardid, who had himself called *doktor*, most likely never finished his thesis, but he was hired as a professor at the University of Tehran where he tried, using a phenomenological approach, with the help of examples borrowed from Islamic mysticism, to develop an anti-rationalist philosophy and even an anti-western stance, which he made famous through the concept *qarb-zadegi* (Weststruckness). According to Fardid, the West had turned all its thoughts to the negation of God as a transcendent being to deify an entity known as Theos (Deus), which Islamic tradition calls "the carnal soul" (*nafs-e ammāre*, literally "the commanding soul"). Theos in the Koran, explains Fardid, is *Tāqut*, the anti-Allah. Since the Renaissance, this "commanding soul" has reversed all values by taking the form of human rights, faith in progress, and reason. To put man in his proper place, the philosopher proposes to let him roam until his self-destruction, transformed into an idol by his pride, and to return as "Yesterday's and Tomorrow's God, as the God of no one and everyone," that is, as a transcendence irrelevant to the present day. The West, denier of God, is caught in a nihilist whirlwind into which it drags the great spiritual traditions of mankind. The central character of the Universal Declaration of Human Rights is sick. Should one lament this sickness? No, replies Fardid:

---

[35] Some lectures have been posthumously published. On Fardid, see A. Mirsepassi, *Transnationalism in Iranian Political Thought*; Md-M. Hāshemi, *Hoviat andishān va mirās-e fekri-e Ahmad Fardid* [Fardid and the issue of identity].

> Modern man (*bashar*) has a fever. Some think that he may heal, he will perspire and that he will get better . . . God forbid that he gets better! Because it is an understatement to say that he is "sick." One has to pray so that this human history that is now in crisis will not "perspire" (which will heal him). Would that man may die that he may be reborn! It is when he has been reborn that the true Day After Tomorrow's God of grace will come in a time that will be his own. It is then that man will become totally human (*ensān*), then that communion and communication (*hamdeli, hamsokhani*) will really return to history, in contrast with today, when there is neither communion nor communication.[36]

The violence of Fardid's words led him, under the Shah, to approve the most insupportable aspects of dictatorship because the Pahlavi dynasty, by undermining the legitimacy of democratic rights, allowed for belief in its irrational transhistorical legitimacy. Shayegan repeated the same words in his publications where he strongly criticized Christianity as responsible, he said, for the tyranny of historical time and of mortifying nihilism, since the God of the Christians is dead like a slave and he is worshipped in his very suffering.[37] After the revolution, Fardid was to support Khomeyni's religious absolutism in weekly lectures at the Academy of Philosophy, where he denounced Freemason academics. He criticized the humanist pretensions of Shariati and the rationalism of the philosopher Abd ol-Karim Sorush, whom he accused of being an agent of the Intelligence Service. With his teacher Motahhari, Sorush had first sought the paths to liberation within a radical Islam before discovering the virtues of rationality. He replied to Fardid and all the ideologues fascinated by absolute idealism in a public speech in the University of Tehran in January 1988, when Khomeyni was still alive: the appeal to the incarnation of the Absolute in history, according to the process described by Hegel, only led, said Sorush, to awful totalitarian regimes like Nazism.

---

[36] From a (unpublished) documentary film by Kāmrān YUSOFZĀDE (1980). See how D. SHAYEGAN presents Fardid in his interview with R. JHANBEGLOO: *Sous les ciels du monde*, pp. 90f, 114f.

[37] D. SHĀYEGĀN, *Bot-hā-ye zehni va khātere-ye azali*, pp. 96, 220; *Āsyā dar barābar-e qarb*, pp. 47f, 281.

This scathing criticism of the desire for the Absolute in politics was aimed principally, in 1988, at the Islamic Republic of Iran, but it also targeted the political construction of the country from 1975 – what one might call the radicalization of the royal regime into a sort of Iranian fascism.

Political Obstruction and Repression

Despite these ideological movements and the opening up of Iran to the outside world – Iranian money was accepted everywhere in the world at a favorable exchange rate, and Iranians could easily travel abroad – the Shah's regime only became more severe while consolidating power. Thanks to its financial means, the government was able to silence any dissent and buy collaboration. The sporadic activities of guerilla groups, even marginal ones, gave him cause to tighten surveillance of the press and book publishing. In the mid-1970s expressing one's political ideas was prohibited, and, even in family gatherings, Iranians were afraid to speak as denouncements and ideological espionage were oppressive. When foreign journalists asked Prime Minister Hoveydā about political prisoners and torture he inevitably replied that he was not informed about the activities of the Sāvāk, because it was the Shah who was personally in charge.

In 1975, the Shah said that he despaired to see the extent of corruption, for which some said in private, not without reason, that he set the example by collecting the commission on foreign bids. Under the pretext of the population's political apathy, having himself removed all independent leaders, he decreed the end of the two-party system, a decision that contradicted his earlier criticisms of communist systems with a single party. In 1957 he had tried, as we have seen, to renew the parties by creating *Mardom* ("the People") and *Melliun* ("Nathionalists"), two parties whose agendas were identical and that had not led to any membership movement.[38] Henceforth, there would be only one party, *Hezb-e rastākhiz-e mellat-e Irān* ("Party of the Resurrection [Renewal] of the Nation of Iran"), known as *Rastākhiz*. The idea was to involve all civil servants and political actors in governing the country, whatever their ideological leanings, and to launch a major membership campaign that

---

[38] The Melliun Party had disappeared after the disastrous 1961 elections and was replaced by the *Irān-e novin* ('New Iran') Party which had the majority in the Majles until 1975.

would lead to a large number of Iranians becoming actively enrolled. Within the administration there was strong pressure to register new members. The stream of official fawning that poured out through the Iranian press to praise the Shah surpassed what the newspapers of the Islamic Republic would later publish in their praise of Khomeyni when he was at the zenith of his power.

The Shah's popularity gained little from the strengthening of autocracy. In parallel, to calm public feeling – which had become impatient in the face of innumerable instances of misfunction in public services and the dizzying rise of prices, particularly in the rental costs of housing, which was increasingly difficult to find because of the influx of foreigners – the Shah launched a major campaign against the hoarders and profiteers, who did not respect the decreed profit margins. Merchants were put in prison. As a result, a number of goods disappeared from the shops – to buy onions or tires one had to go to the back of the shop and pay double for a product that would be covertly delivered. Daily life became more and more difficult. Electricity was regularly cut three hours a day, due to unforeseen over-consumption, and traffic jams in major towns, because of huge increases in new-car sales, made daily driving a nightmare. The Shah himself practically always traveled by helicopter. Awaiting the Great Civilization that he promised them, the Iranians discovered hell.

Still in 1975, he took another clumsy measure, in the form of the continuation of the idealization of the allegedly 2,500-year-old Persian Empire. He removed the Hegira reference from the Iranian calender. The Iranians are the only nation whose calender refers to the Hegira of the Prophet to Medina (in 622 CE) alongside solar reckoning (365 days and 6 hours) so that their calender, which begins the year at the spring equinox, could be modified by royal decree. The year 1354 of the solar hegira began on 21 March 1975 and ended on 20 March 1976. The next day, was consequently made the first day of year 2535 of the empire, an artificial figure chosen to maintain the same succession of units to make comparison less difficult. The population rejected this change despite the pressure from the media and the bureaucracy and the prohibition to henceforth mention the Hegira year. People only wrote the last figure to be sure not to be mistaken. "It was, an Iranian historian said, the most efficacious propaganda that the regime made against itself by thus officially announcing that the Iranian empire and Islam could not cohabit."[39]

---

[39] Sd J. MADANI, *Tārikh-e siāsi-e moʿāser-e Irān*, II, p. 234.

Other measures, according to rumors, were scheduled to follow, such as moving the weekly day of rest from a Friday to a Sunday (to facilitate international transactions) or even changing the alphabet to adopt the Latin alphabet like the Turks, a system better suited to Persian. These measures would no longer have surprised Iranians who, from then on, saw their leaders as demonic beings seeking to extirpate Islam from their culture. Each day, they noticed the progress of immorality. Cinema posters showed naked women, bars opened in the most remote townships, casinos sprung up in several places, to which was added the immense international brothel that the Shah established on the island of Kish.

In the last days of his reign, the Shah aroused colossal loathing among Iranians. A memory that was shared with me after the revolution by Mohammad-Hoseyn Mashāyekh-Fereydani, a former ambassador of the Shah who remained attached to Islam, reveals its extent. Having himself driven before dawn, to avoid traffic jams, to the mausoleum at Rey where his parents were buried, he was surprised to see people praying in the darkness, murmuring. Bending down to discover what prayer it was that came forth from these gloomy figures, he could clearly distinguish hate slogans and death curses directed at the Shah. It was not a demonstration yet, but a troubling undercurrent which no police, no censorship, no political measure would be able do anything about. For that man who served the Shah, the murmuring was a warning. How many others paid attention only to flattering heralds?

The Shah then bought so much advanced weaponry that the Americans themselves tried to slow him down. In 1977 they refused to sell him AWACS radar-planes whose technology was too sensitive, but he bought 250 F-4D Tomcat at $30 million per plane and two years later 160 F-16 fighter-bombers, for a total of $3.8 billion. As for American personnel stationed in Iran, partly for the maintenance of that arsenal, it grew from 16,000 in 1972 to 50,000 in 1978.[40]

Mohammad-Rezā Shāh's power appeared to impress the entire world. Nevertheless, two events without any relation to Iranian politics would put an end to it: on the one hand, the election of a Democratic President in Washington, Jimmy Carter, and, on the other, the confirmation by French physicians that the Shah had incurable lymphoma.

---

[40] R. K. Ramazani, *The United States and Iran*, pp. 47f.

How Was the "Islamic" Revolution Born?

In November 1976, Jimmy Carter defeated Gerald Ford in the American elections. The Democratic candidate had made, among others, respect for human rights across the globe one of his core campaign themes. Immediately, in Iran, international organizations were permitted to visit prisons and attend political trials. Former prisoners unanimously recall the softening of their detention and the near disappearance of torture. Nationalist liberal intellectuals of the opposition, among whom were Mozaffar Baqāi and Shāpur Bakhtyār, dared to publish copies of open letters that they sent to the Shah to demand a radical change of his policies and to criticize his government. Soon the distribution in bookstores of Shariati's and other thinkers' works, until then on the blacklist, indicated a new political climate.

The moderation of the regime, although slow and progressive, seemed inevitable. In November 1977 the Shah visited Washington on an official visit to meet with the new Democrat administration. A speech on the podium in front of the White House was on the agenda, but students of the Iranian opposition, having come from all over North America, were so numerous that the police had to use tear gas to dispel the crowds, and the Shah and his wife wept in front of the cameras.

That image of the Shah, broadcast on Iranian television, suddenly revealed a monarch no longer the invincible epic hero that the Iranian media had always presented but a vulnerable man. Carter continued to press for the liberalization of Iran, until, in December 1977, he realized that rocking the Iranian regime would be prejudicial to American interests. From Jordan, where he was on a visit, the American president traveled to Tehran to celebrate 1 January 1978 with his friend, the Shah.[41] It was a clumsy and counterproductive gesture. Neither the Baptist president nor the sick Shah probably drank the glass of champagne that they held in their hand in the photos published the next day across the world. According to Iranian opinion, it was yet another illustration of the Shah's illegitimacy. Carter's inhibiting support precipitated the Shah's disgrace, until the attack on the American embassy in November 1979 and the American embassy crisis, when the kidnappers, showing no gratitude toward Carter, who had indirectly provoked

---

[41] Iranian new year's day is the first day of spring, usually 21 March. This 1 January celebration was thus questionable in Tehran.

the revolution, handed the US hostages to Ronald Reagan. In his American policy, the Shah had always favored the Republican Party; the Islamic Republic continued.

Hoveydā was replaced as head of government (September 1977) and already the finger was pointed at him as being responsible for corruption. As Minister of Court he was still able to advise the Shah. The latter sacrificed his devoted politician by having him arrested on 8 November 1978. Hoveyda refused to benefit from the confusion of the insurrection to flee to Europe and was executed after a fake trial shortly after the revolution.

An Article in a Newspaper

Meanwhile, seeing the Shah's weakness clerical opposition revived. Some high-ranking politicians thought they could stamp it out by publishing in the newspaper *Ettelā`āt*, on Saturday, 7 January 1978 at the end of the Shiite month of mourning (*moharram*), an article with the title "Iran and red and black colonialism," which denounced the enemies of the revolution of the Shah and the people.[42] Its author said that he was astonished to see that the communists had allied themselves with reactionary clerics, which he called "black colonialists" because historically they were linked with British imperialism. The feudal lords who were dispossessed of their right to exploit the peasants by the land reforms had turned to the clergy. To attempt to have the acquisition of properties through that reform declared illegal, they needed an opportunistic religious leader and one in the pocket of the big colonial cities. They found the one who was the most deprived of any conviction, the most reactionary, and who, his science and virtue having failed to earn him any distinction among the clerics, thought that he would acquire the fame of which he dreamt by intervening in politics.

> Ruhollāh Khomeyni was the best prepared agent for this task; the red [i.e. the communist] and black [clerical] reaction have seen in him the individual who is the best placed to oppose the Iranian revolution [the White Revolution], he who was known

---

[42] Ahmad Rashidi-Motlaq, "Irān va este'mār-e sorkh va siyāh" [Iran and red and black colonialism]; on the history of this text, directly emanating from the imperial palace, see A. Milani, *Eminent Persians*, pp. 390f.

as the agent of the shameful event of 15 *Khordād* [5 June 1963 when the ayatollah openly opposed the Shah].

The article further insinuated that Khomeyni had lived in India before independence where he had been a British agent in Kashmir. Furthermore, the ayatollah was accused of having received from an Arab adventurer, Mohammad-Towfiq al-Qisi, a sum of 10 million rials in cash to overturn the White Revolution. "Fortunately, the Iranian revolution has been victorious and the last resistance of the latifundistas and communist agents have been broken. Fortunately, the road to progress, the flourishing and the realization of the principles of social justice have been smoothed."

The next day, when the newspaper reached them, the theologians of Qom were furious at reading these few provocative lines. The army opened fire on the demonstrators and the news of the repression was passed on by word of mouth. To commemorate the mourning of the victims there were popular demonstrations forty days later in Tabriz, and then forty days later in another city to commemorate the victims in Tabriz. These mournings were not the cause of the revolution but the trigger. Sentences of the article could have been reused some months later to denounce abortive plots against the "Islamic" revolution, of which Khomeyni, this time, was indeed the prime instigator: did he not indeed mobilize the communist forces at the same time as those of the radical Muslims? In the fervor of the revolutionary movement, the leftist forces saw no other issue than to rally behind the ayatollah.

Revolutionary Demonstrations

In the short term, this article, far from neutralizing tension, increased it tenfold. Having seen that the Shah was weak (he shed tears in Washington) and harbored hatred for a defenseless enemy (Khomeyni), despite the small extension of liberties that he had undertaken to please the Americans, the Iranians felt his weakness even more and sensed his illness. Even the bloody repression of 1978 did not appear to result in a fascist radicalization of the regime nor to its militarization. The movement could develop freely, because the Shah did not react in person, and it appears that he had even given orders to avoid bloodbaths. In spring, he disappeared from the Iranian media for several weeks, a long absence that at the time made people believe that he had died or, according to others, had been wounded by one of his close collaborators. During Ramadan (from 5 August to 4 September 1978), the demonstrations continued to gain in strength. This time, the men of the cloth spoke out and intervened in the political debate. No open letter, no book, nor any speech of nostalgic Mosaddeq supporters ever attained the power to mobilize the population like the leaders of the mosques and the preachers of Ramadan. On 4 September, after the celebration at the end of the fast, the first impressive processions crossed Tehran carrying the portrait of the former prime minister, but it was lost behind that of the ayatollahs and Shariati. Foreign journalists went to interview Khomeyni in Najaf and then almost every day after in Paris, which gave him an unprecedented status justified by the loudening echo of the demonstrators in Tehran.

Trying to escape from the growing pressure of the Iraqi police, the ayatollah had sought to go to neighboring Kuwait, but the border remained closed to him. His only choice was to leave by plane. He first thought was to go to Damascus, but three of his close advisers, Sādeq Qotbzāde, Ebrāhim Yazdi and Abol-Hasan Banisadr, found it more opportune to diffuse his messages in a capital where the world's media would have access to him. He decided to go to Paris, where he arrived on 6 October 1978. President Giscard d'Estaing, worried about the potential repercussions, consulted the Shah, who himself was delighted by this distance, not thinking about the media response that from France sapped his power base. After a short stay in Cachan at Banisadr, Khomeyni took up residence in Neauphle-le-Château, about 40 km (25 miles) from Paris.

Throughout 1978, inexorable revolutionary mobilization was interrupted by acts of violence. On 19 August – the anniversary of the coup which toppled Mosaddeq – the Rex cinema in Ābādān caught fire when the doors were closed as police tried to arrest opponents. Nobody, for weeks, was able to decide what provocation resulted in the death of at least 470 Iranians in that fire, which could have been caused by Islamic militants to cast blame on the Savak. (The culprits, sent from a local mosque, had not foreseen the huge number of casualties.) On Friday 8 September, Black Friday, the army fired on the crowd in Zhāle square who had defied Tehran's curfew, causing several hundred of deaths – it was then that Hoveydā resigned as Minister of Court, disassociating himself from the ferocious repression and putting himself in the position of scapegoat. Several days later, the earthquake at Tabas in Khorasan caused 15,000 deaths within a few minutes, as if the elements wanted to dramatize the pain at the birth of the revolution. The help that religious foundations once again sent immediately showed that the Pahlavi state, with their slow rescue teams, was not equal to the task. Mutual aid among the victims, in the name of Islam, anticipated the seamless transition that would allow no gap to emerge during the changeover between the two regimes; the clerical network covered the entire territory. On 4–5 November, in the capital, where numerous demonstrators set fire to cinemas, banks, and bars, what orders were given to the law enforcement agents who kept an eye on the crowd, as if they were expecting a signal for repression? One will never know. Between these traumatic events, the long processions of protesters, the hard-line strikes in key sectors, oil, education, electricity, all indicated that Iran had had enough and adjured repeatedly for the monarch to go.

On 5 November, the Shah claimed in a historical speech "to have heard the message of the revolution" that the people were sending him. But he was making mistake after mistake. In September a solution with a nationalist liberal leader who would have demanded the Shah's silence and free elections would have probably been able to revive the core of the 1906 Constitution, to re-establish a consensus, and to deprive Khomeyni, when he left Iraq, of that timeless heroic image of the patriarch dictating the end of a kingdom from the shade of an apple tree in Neauphle-le-Château.[43] Instead of having appealed to Mosaddeq's supporters, whom he had so often imprisoned, and to the liberals who had stood up against him, instead of recognizing that political initiative had escaped him, the Shah persisted and named a military man as prime minister, General Azhāri, who, was not only ill but was also a bad politician (November to December 1978). Had he then appointed Bakhtyār, perhaps he might yet have been able to save the throne to the benefit, later, of his son. But he hated all those who reminded him of Mosaddeq, Bakhtyār as much as Bāzargān.

Departure of the Shah, Arrival of the Imam

Except for Bakhtyār and some few liberals who still hoped for a secular solution, with or without the Shah, the great majority of Iranian politicians were destabilized by the assurance and popularity

---

[43] E. NARAGHI published a comments column in *Le Monde* to this sense, 3 November 1978. Reproduced in his book *From Palace to Prison*.

of the patriarch of Neauphle-le-Château who redoubled his intransigence by demanding the Shah's departure. At the beginning of November, when Tehran was set ablaze, Bāzargān had gone to see Khomeyni in France with other nationalist leaders. "I have seen, he said on his return, Āryāmehr [the Shah] with a turban on his head." Their rallying established that which the Shah, for his part, had unknowingly prepared: the annihilation of the liberal alternative faced with the omnipotence of political Islam. Nevertheless, it was during this visit that the future government of Bāzargān (February to November 1979) was discussed.

In reality, this government had begun the moment the Shah nominated Shāpur Bakhtyār, that steadfast friend of Bāzargān, who remained constantly in contact with him over the course of several weeks (January 1979 to 11 February 1979) while he tried to have the legitimacy of his government, appointed by the Shah, recognized by Iranians.[44] Consequently, there was little surprise that the revolution claimed so few victims during the final insurrection, on 11 February 1979. Many regions of Iran, such as Isfahan, were already under a local Islamic government when Khomeyni returned in triumph to Iran on 1 February. Giving in to popular pressure, Bakhtyār finally reopened the airport, after having, because of Khomeyni's categorical refusal, abandoned his plan to make the grand theatrical gesture through which he would have nominally pledged allegiance to the ayatollah who would have confirmed his office.

The Shah had left on 16 January with his wife and personal possessions, weeping on the tarmac; no mosque leader had come to bless his journey, while his people celebrated his departure. The Shah had begun the wanderings of a sick man, as no country, except temporarily for Egypt, Morocco, Mexico, and Panama, was willing to receive him. Where had the guests of Persepolis gone? His short hospitalization in the USA increased Iranian revolutionaries' resentment toward him and did not prevent him from dying miserably in Cairo on 27 July 1980.

The feast on 16 January 1979 was celebrated across the entire press with the headline *Shāh raft*, "the Shah has left." It was followed by an enormous celebration on 1 February, with the headline *Emām āmad*, "the Imam has arrived." The Iranians lived through that intense period – during which the newspapers, emerging after a long strike, believed to

---

[44] H. E. CHEHABI, *Iranian Politics and Religious Modernism*, p. 249.

have conquered forever freedom of speech – in a kind of religious ecstasy.

Calling an ayatollah "Imam" did not come naturally to Iranian Shiites, despite the precedent, in the Arab countries, of Imam Musa Sadr (1928–1978), an Iranian cleric established in Lebanon who disappeared in Libya after having published a resounding rallying call to Khomeyni in *Le Monde* (23 August 1978). The sacred, eschatological character of the Imam's return after his occultation in Iraq would never have attained such a degree of fervor without the value that was unwillingly bestowed on him by Mohammad-Rezā Pahlavi, who played the role of Yazid, the man who ordered the death of Imam Hoseyn at Karbalā. The Shah had made his adversary even more saintly, closer to the imperial legend that in the end would give him entry to the Shiite pantheon.

The government of Bakhtyār ceased to exist on 11 February 1979 (22 *Bahman* 1357 in the Iranian calender) after the revolt in favor of Khomeyni by air force officers and technicians, who took control of the barracks that had remained loyal to the Shah. The days had been full of anxiety, but relatively bloodless. The radio and television were in the hands of the Khomeynists and a government led by Bāzargān, which had hardly any more power than Bakhtyār's, was put in place: Bāzargān constantly had to seek approval from the ulama and Khomeyni in Qom. The Americans, by sending General Huyser to Tehran made certain that their influence and their strategic position would not be affected. The Islamic Republic had been born.

12 AN ISLAMIC REPUBLIC IN IRAN

Chronological Outline

On 1 February 1979 Khomeyni returned to Iran. The revolution had proved victorious over the old order, and on 11 February the new regime of the Islamic Republic of Iran (*Jomhuri-e eslāmi-e Irān*) was ushered in, formally sanctioned in a national referendum held on 1 April. An assembly of "experts" was promptly elected and tasked with writing a new constitution, which was swiftly approved in a referendum in December 1979.

Against the backdrop of this sweeping regime change, amid deteriorating relations with the international community, especially the USA, on 4 November a group of militant students stormed the American Embassy in Tehran, taking its employees hostage. The last hostages were not released until 20 January 1981. This crisis created an enduring rupture in Iran's relations with the international community and stood out as an act of defiance against, in particular, US intervention in the country.

In January 1980 Abol-Hasan Banisadr, a nationalist intellectual, was elected president; and soon after, the Parliament (*Majles*) assembled, with a majority of ulama and under clerical rule. These events, however, were overshadowed by local revolts which erupted in Kurdistan and Torkmansahrā (a northern province next to Turkmenistan), by economic crisis, and by social upheaval. The peasantry were left in a state of great uncertainty, unsure whether the land they had acquired through the reforms of the 'White Revolution' would be taken from them; universities remained closed for two years while they underwent a complete reorganization and Islamicization, known as the 'Cultural Revolution'; censorship was gradually imposed on the press; and the banking system was close to collapse after US sanctions were imposed in retaliation for the embassy hostage crisis. Banisadr, who had liberal tendencies, was swiftly impeached and ousted from power in the spring of 1981 by radical clerics who sought free rein in governing the country.

In September 1980, in a period of growing insecurity, the Iran–Iraq War erupted, called the "imposed war" in Iran (Iraq was the aggressor) and the "Gulf War" in the West. Khomeyni's position was bolstered by this external threat, and Iranian mobilization was spontaneous – certainly at the beginning of the outbreak – in repelling the invasion in Khuzestan. For eight years, industrial investment and political discourse were dominated by the war effort. A ceasefire was declared in July 1988, and, while neither side could claim victory, the Iranian regime had successfully suppressed internal threats, particularly the guerrilla attacks from the People's *Mojāhedin*, an Islamo-Marxist group which eventually sought asylum in Iraq.

Khomeyni died in June 1989 at the pinnacle of his power. Any hope of reform was deceptive under the presidency of Akbar Hāshemi-Rafsanjāni (1989–97), and more so under his successor Mohammad Khātami, both clerics who held a rather pragmatic vision of power. Their actions were curbed by external pressure in the form of further economic sanctions and by the growing power of the Iranian militia group the Guardians of the Revolution (*Pāsdārān-e Enqelāb*). Khomeyni's successor as "Guide" (*Rahbar*) of the Revolution, Ali Khāmene'i, was intended to be a distant leader, but, with the support of the militia, he became more and more intrusive. The presidency of Mahmud Ahmadinezhād (commonly Ahmadinejad, 2005–13) marked a period of tension: Iran was confronted with new sanctions owing to the program of nuclear enrichment, which was made public in 2002, and the country was indirectly involved in two major conflicts, in Afghanistan and Iraq. Ahmadinejad, the first president not to wear the turban since 1980, came from the Guardians of the Revolution. A demagogue, he drew on provocation to crush domestic rivals and to confront external pressures. Yet his power was nevertheless limited even when he succeeded, with the help of Khāmene'i, to secure a second tenure in office in 2009. The revolt of the "Green Movement" (*Nahzat-e sabz*), protesting against this reelection, was crushed with many casualties. No agreement was in sight on the nuclear question.

In 2013 a new reformist president was elected. Hasan Ruhāni promptly engaged in productive negotiations, which resulted in an arrangement on the nuclear issue signed in Vienna, on 14 July 2015. Yet it remains to be seen when Iran will begin to benefit from the economic freedoms that this agreement brought about, as the USA remained reluctant to raise the sanctions. Eventually, in agreement with the aggressive attitude of both Saudi Arabia and Israel, on 8 May 2018 President Trump withdrew the USA from the agreement and decided to raise economic sanctions against Iran to the highest level. The escalating instability in the region, from Afghanistan to Syria and Yemen, offers little hope that a favorable climate will facilitate the return of Iran to the international stage.

Shiism and Foreign Policy

Before the revolution, Iranian foreign policies already had an Islamic dimension. Even when Iran belatedly (1970) renounced any claim to Bahrain, whose population is predominantly Shiite, the attention given by Tehran's diplomacy to countries with a Shiite component was in line with the expectations of the people of these regions. An appeal to the only Shiite sovereign state in the Muslim world seemed natural. The Shiites of Lebanon, even before the arrival of Musa Sadr (1959), had a picture of the Shah in their homes. The ongoing conflicts between Tehran and Baghdad since 1920 and the creation of the state of Iraq heightened Iranians' determination to preserve their pilgrimage rights to the tombs of the Imams and to protect the Iranian minorities who had resided in Mesopotamia for centuries, but also to treat the Iraqi Shiites with the respect that Baghdad had generally failed to show them.

Iranian foreign policy radically changed with the establishment of the Islamic Republic. One of the main slogans of the revolution had been "Independence, Freedom, Islamic Republic" (*esteqlāl, āzādi, jomhuri-e eslāmi*). Why independence first, for a nation which had not been colonized? All the history of Iran since the Treaty of Golestān (1813) comes to a turning point here: after nearly two centuries of decay, humiliation, and manipulation, confrontation with the USA and a long war with Iraq would eventually show how the Islamic republic could withstand major international challenges. Its foreign relations have been marked by confrontations more than alliances.

The Hostage Crisis: November 1979 to January 1981

The Bāzargān government (February to November 1979) wanted to reach an accommodation with the USA. It tried to realize what General Huyser had suggested to the higher Iranian officers before the arrival of Khomeyni to Tehran: the Americans would support any civilian government whether with the Shah or with Khomeyni, to keep Iran as a barrier to Soviet penetration.[1] The Iranian prime minister ended negotiations on the admission of the deposed Shah for treatment in New York with a warm handshake with Zbignew Brzezinski in Algiers (1 November 1979). Mahdi Bāzargān, who himself acknowledged that he was not a revolutionary, had been appointed prime minister by Khomeyni before any elected parliament was up and running and in control of public affairs. His nomination was a means of attracting the approval of nationalists inside Iran and the support of the Americans, who still had some influence among the higher officers of the army. In reaction against this liberal trend and the Algiers handshake, the revolution found its true anti-imperialist dimension on 4 November 1979 with the takeover of the American embassy and the seizing of the diplomats there as hostages. This crisis, which lasted 444 days, gave the ayatollahs an image of militancy that made them popular in many Third World countries and was denounced in the West.

The violation of international agreements – in this case the Convention of Vienna defining diplomatic privileges, which even the Soviet Union and China had constantly respected – made the Islamic Republic of Iran an outlaw. Khomeyni, after some hours of reflection, gave his approval. Iranian public opinion demonstrated with enthusiasm in support of the embassy takeover. The government decided to let things go. The American hostages were not killed but were used with utmost cynicism. In terms of foreign policy, it meant that Tehran definitely severed all its ties with western alliances and brought about the election of a Republican president by the Americans, Ronald Reagan. In terms of domestic policy, it was used to get rid of the last "horrible" liberals whose names were released in reports as friends of the diplomats,

---

[1] See R. E. HUYSER, *Mission to Tehran.*

a hunt that owed much to the model of communist countries. Some have even seen, somewhat hastily, the hand of Moscow in this operation.

The publication of documents found and restored after the attack on the embassy by "Muslim students who follow the line of the Imam" (*Daneshjuyān-e mosalmān-e peyrow-e khatt-e Emām*) allowed Iranians to subsequently justify their violation of international law. Since the beginning of the revolution, the diplomats had been engaged in intelligence operations and political manipulation. They were not the first to trample on the rules of non-interference that theoretically defined diplomatic missions (gathering information in order to improve economic and political relations, the usual activity of all diplomats, can be easily turned into espionage and encroachment on sovereignty – as was understood by the hostage-takers).

In the Tabas operation of 24 April 1980, known as Eagle Claw, the US army tried to establish a temporary airbase in the Iranian desert 500 km (300 miles) from Tehran. They responded in some way to the violence of the Khomeynists with another form of violence, intending to liberate the hostages by force and with the complicity of Iranian officers who had remained in office despite harboring secret hostilities toward the new regime. A series of technical troubles forced the Americans to withdraw their troops in disorder, leaving behind eight dead, who were killed in the explosion of their helicopter, as well as documents allowing the trial of their Iranian accomplices.

The settlement of the American embassy crisis thanks to the mediation of Algeria ended, for the Iranians, in serious litigation. Their reputation as diplomatic hoodlums isolated them in the international arena for a long time, but above all the crisis brought as a consequence the freezing of Iranian assets in the USA (totaling US$10 billion) and the impossibility of legally obtaining the military materials that they had already paid for, which Tehran was forced to import via roundabout routes during the Iran–Iraq War. In 2018, the American embargo on high-tech material continues to handicap Iran in the field of computer equipment and oil exploitation. As of 8 August 1996, under the Clinton administration, the Amato-Kennedy bill heavily penalized firms of any country that invested more than US$40 million in Iran and Libya (of Qaddafi), two countries defined in American political discourse as "rogue states."

Despite its violation of international laws, the hostage crisis fueled a wave of anti-western feeling in the Muslim world. Islamic propaganda pictured Iran for the first time as a leader of a vast wave of protest. Shiites were no longer considered to be a deviant Islamic sect but a Muslim community undertaking historic revenge against former colonial or imperial powers.

The hostage crisis gave new momentum not only to the Iranian revolution but to relations between the Muslim world and the West, and started major confrontations, stimulated by major powers, between Muslim countries. Not only western nations, but also Russia and China are now involved either in energy problems (oil and gas production), in arms export, in curbing the influence of radical ideas on their Muslim minorities, or in the defense of Israel against Palestinians. Even though Iran has not always been directly concerned, the whole region has been greatly destabilized since the Revolution of 1979 and up to the Arab Spring and the Syrian War.

The Iran–Iraq War: 1980–1988

Khomeyni's Iran, after having denounced the implicit recognition of Israel, established relations with Palestine (the PLO) and strengthened its relations with the Islamic world, which had been somewhat neglected by the diplomacy of the Shah. However, the prestige of the Iranian revolution was rapidly lessened by the Iraqi attack of September 1980 and the denunciation by Saddam Hussein of Khomeyni's regime as sectarian.

On 22 September 1980, Saddam Hussein declared war on Iran and claimed sovereignty over Khuzistan, a province rich in oil that was called Arabestān during the Safavid and the Qajar periods. Iraqi troops entered Iranian territory, destroying and plundering the port of Khorramshahr and the Ābādān refinery. In parallel, Iraqi Mirages, breaching the Iranian defenses, made it as far as Tehran's suburbs to bomb an oil refinery. Saddam Hussein stressed his territorial demands with faked maps, ignoring the fact that the Arab population of Khuzistan, predominantly Shiite, have recognized Iranian sovereignty since the time of the Safavids. He also invoked hostility toward the Islamist ideology, radically opposed to the nationalist secularism of the Baath Party.

But would Saddam have attacked Iran without the encouragement of those western countries who found in him the dream agent to rid the world of this revolutionary Shiite contagion? Trips to Baghdad by former officers of the Shah's army close to Shāpur Bakhtyār persuaded the Iraqis that Iran's decimated army would be incapable of resisting a blitz attack. Bakhtyār himself later admitted his reticence in approving this war, but he partly exonerates Iraqi responsibility, for two reasons in particular: "[Iraq] wanted to chase away the big subversive wind that threatened it. – It happened that foreign influences from both sides were pushing the two adversaries to war."[2] Is he suggesting that the Soviet Union, then engaged in a dirty war in Afghanistan, would have pushed Iran to war to divert its attention? In any case, the tone in the western media was clearly in favor of supporting Saddam. In the first months of the new diplomacy with the French Socialists, who had assumed power in May 1981, Claude Cheysson, then minister of foreign affairs, made several explicit statements denouncing the Iranians as enemies of France and implicitly justified military aid to Iraq.

Religious sentiment also played an undeniable role in mobilization. Very soon, the bourgeois middle class, secular intellectuals, and opponents understood the advantage that the Islamic Republic obtained from this war in strengthening its legitimacy and smothering freedoms. The underprivileged, sensitive to the preaching of the clergy, supplied the largest number of volunteers and victims. From then on, the revolution became theirs, since they paid for it with their blood. Propaganda was used to its fullest extent to mobilize the young recruits, who were wound up at the front by exhortations about the Hereafter and their imminent encounter with the Hidden Imam. This perspective prepared them to sacrifice their lives in a spiritual euphoria obtained under other skies with bottles of spirits.

More generally, despite Saddam Hussein's attempts to Islamize his propaganda, the Iranians had little difficulty in showing Baghdad's connivance with the West and the clear impiety of the behavior of the Baathist forces, whose front-line soldiers were plied with alcohol and whose cruelty was unequalled. For Tehran, the continuation of the war had as its purpose the mission to free the Islamic world of such infamy and liberate it as far as Jerusalem, a way to continually drive back the limits of the conflict.

The Iranian desire to defend their country, a fatherland "dearer than our life" (*vatan-e aziztar az jān*) according to Khomeyni, resulted

---

[2] Ch. Bakhtiar, *Ma fidélité*, p. 209.

in an unexpected upsurge that consolidated the regime. Moreover, the continuation of the war, thanks to Khomeyni's stubbornness and refusal to accept offers of Saudi mediation in 1982, allowed the regime to suppress all the leftist groups that had kept up their political activity, mostly clandestinely: the Mojāhedin of the People, the Fedāiān (Marxist-Leninist), and the Toudeh Party (communist), most of whose leaders were arrested or forced into exile. All publications by these groups were completely stopped.

Despite international rules, western nations became involved in the conflict by refusing to condemn the invaders and by supplying offensive arms to Iraq, which folded under Iranian bombardment from spring 1982. In October 1983, France delivered to Iraq five Super-Etendard planes equipped with Exocet anti-ship missiles – with pilots and maintenance teams – "on loan" for two years to circumvent the ban on aiding the belligerents. Henceforth, Iraqi superiority in the Persian Gulf was on the increase; the Iranian oil terminal on Khārk island as well as offshore installations were put out of action. The West only talked about the "Gulf War," thus showing that it did not dare name the Persian Gulf directly for fear of displeasing the Arab countries, and that it feigned to believe that the war had no stake other than oil and its routing through the Gulf in question.

In the last months of the war, under the pretext of assuring safe passage for tankers, American, French, Italian, and Dutch ships patrolled the Iranian coast. The Americans, one of whose ships was targeted by mistake by two Exocet (Iraqi) missiles, reacted brutally by destroying an Iranian platform that was used to attack ships loading oil in Kuwait (October 1987). Iran responded by attacking maritime traffic with floating mines and torpedoes. An American frigate was damaged on 18 April 1988, resulting in immediate retaliation: the destruction of the entire Iranian fleet (an event which the government in Tehran hid so as not to demoralize the population). Finally, on 3 July, an American missile hit a civilian Iranian Airbus in full flight killing 290 passengers, a "regrettable blunder," according to Washington, but most likely a deliberate maneuver to oblige Iran to finally accept the ceasefire that Khomeyni swallowed "like a poison" on 18 July 1988.

This long war broke off Iranian propaganda addressed to the Islamic world, since most Arab countries showed solidarity with the aggressor, painting Tehran as the capital of a community of heretics that they would henceforth call "Persians," or "Mages," alluding to the old

Zoroastrian religion that allegedly turned Islam toward Shiism, a "heresy" assailed by the Sunni ulama. Above all, the endeavor to export the revolution, a Messianic Islamic program doomed to failure, prevented Iranians from establishing friendly relations with their close neighbors. Only Syria, paradoxically, was the exception, since supporting Iran against its rival Baathist regime of Baghdad was to its advantage. Alawite Islam (the religion of Assad and his close supporters) is not Shiism, and the Baathist ideology, a mixture of socialism and nationalism, is the opposite of Khomeyni's political views, but common strategic opportunities prevailed.

Iranian revolutionary propaganda started up again after the war, but this time Shiism gave way to pan-Islamist themes, whether these concerned the holy sites at Mecca and Medina or the defense of Islam against the West. Above all, by supporting Hizbollah and Hamas, Tehran has been in the front row of rejectionist countries: it regarded the Oslo process as little more than a trap by means of which Westerners forced Palestinians to recognize Israel. Neither in Central Asia, where the collapse of the Soviet Union offered hope to Iranians to extend their influence, nor in Islamic countries, Arab or not, was it advisable for the Islamic Republic to promote the Iranian or Shiite specificity, except in Tajikistan, where national and literary symbols prevail, and in Lebanon, where the communitarian links bring Shiites close to one another. In 1997, the hosting of the summit of the Islamic Conference marked a great victory for Iranian diplomacy and the temporary reestablishment of good relations with Saudi Arabia, a rival of Iran and an enemy of Shiism.

Despite the religious and nationalist isolation brought about by the war, Khomeyni tried in vain to resume his hegemonic ambitions over the Islamic world on two fronts: the defense of Islam and the Palestinian issue. The Saudis were denounced as unworthy of controlling Mecca after the massacre that left more than 400 dead during the pilgrimage of 21 July 1987 and were further marginalized when the Imam claimed the integral defense of the Koran in a fatwa against Salman Rushdie (15 February 1989); he accused the Indian–British writer of blasphemy and apostasy in his novel *The Satanic Verses* and called on Muslims to put him to death, a religious measure that rigorously applied the prescriptions of the *shari'a* against apostates and that no Sunni theologian had dared to proclaim with such insolence. Unsupportable for

Westerners, because the religious decree trampled on their sovereignty, the fatwa made Khomeyni popular in most Islamic countries.

As for the Palestinian question, Iranian policy was reversed from that of the Shah's time. The new Iranian regime contests Israeli occupation and supports Palestinian claims to allow refugees to return to their land and villages. Hostility against Israel is not, however, systematic. During the conflict with Iraq, Iran received some aid through the Israelis, notably in the form of spare parts for F-15 fighter aircrafts. Many Iranian leaders, as President Khātami said himself, shortly before the end of his second mandate, would be prepared, on the day the Palestinians make peace with Israel, to recognize this country, which represents a stabilizing presence in the Middle East, counterbalancing Egyptian and Syrian ambitions. Meanwhile, the natural sympathies of the Iranians are with the Palestinians, who are subjected to an unjust fate. Siding unconditionally with the radical Palestinians gives the Iranian regime a means of overcoming the handicap of being neither Arab nor Sunni and of gaining popularity among the various peoples of the region. Iran was the only country in the region to refuse participation in the Annapolis conference on the Israeli–Palestinian peace process (2007), and facts proved that it was right in denouncing discussions where no concessions would be given by either side.

The Iran–Iraq War and the Veterans

The group most determined to maintain the revolutionary zeal of the confrontation with western culture are the militiamen, volunteer veterans of the front; that is, the Guardians of the Revolution (*Pāsdārān-e Enqelāb*) and the *Basiji* (from *basij*, "mobilization"). Their sacrifice, their wounds, and the deaths of their comrades during the war give them a legitimacy that nobody dares to contest. The social and financial advantages – often derisory – that they have obtained are nothing in the face of the power that they hold as militia establishing their solidarity with the Republic.

During the Iran–Iraq War, the *Pāsdārān* army (*Sepāh-e pāsdārān*) doubled the strength of the ordinary army (*artesh*) without doing away with it. For these volunteer militias, the debate on the freedom of the press or political pluralism remains secondary to the fight with exterior enemies (be they *Dāʿesh*, or above all the USA) and their go-betweens (the liberals, westernized intellectuals and the "leftists"). By crystallizing their ideological sclerosis in reference to Khomeyni and supporting the Guide unconditionally, they hinder the evolution of the regime.

The Pāsdārān army professionalized without abandoning its militant origins. It benefits from a priority for military investment and numbers about 120,000 men, including a navy and air force. To ensure its budget allocation, this militia army acquired a growing share in strategic sectors of the economy: oil, gas, petrochemicals, public works (roads, dams, tunnels), telecommunications, port and airport infrastructure, and energy (nuclear technology). According to some sources, its annual revenue could have been as high as US$12 billion before US sanctions hindered all transactions with industrialized countries.

A symbolic example of the growing power of the Pāsdārān was the inauguration by President Khātami of the new Imam Khomeyni Airport planned for 8 May 2004. At the last moment, the airport was occupied and closed by the militias who questioned the contract signed with a Turkish firm. They only accepted the opening of the airport after laborious negotiations that awarded them the benefits of the new installations.

Khātami's planned reforms were generous projects inspired by his liberal culture and were aimed at rationality. He could have realized them with the parliamentary majority that he won in 2002, but he ran into the veto of the Guide. During the last legislative elections of his presidency in 2004, the candidates were strictly screened to avoid a new reformative majority. Khātami threatened to resign, but he finally submitted to the logic of a locked system. Neither his grandiose project of "dialogue of the civilizations," accepted by the United Nations and UNESCO, nor his abortive reforms were able to breach the isolation of the Islamic Republic, whose foreign policy was from 2002 increasingly restricted to negotiations around its nuclear policy. Despised by Iranian reformers who reproached him for having neutralized the hope for change through his inaction, progressively forgotten abroad since his passport was confiscated by the authorities after the end of his second term, and not allowed to speak or have his photograph in the Iranian press, Khātami's legacy leaves the impression of a failure, and clearly demonstrates the power of the Guards of the Revolution.

The political activity of the Pāsdārān peaked during the two terms of President Mahmud Ahmadinejad. Certainly, already before his election in 2005, sensitive institutions such as the police and the regalian ministries were taken over by their networks. But the great popularity that Ahmadinejad enjoyed at the beginning of his first term allowed him to place militia men in key posts in the main ministries and in the governorates of the provinces. He embodied novelty and represented the new military and educated elite – not wearing the turban and holding out the hope of an uninhibited republic and reforming populism.

Nuclear Program

Being one of the first members of the Non-Proliferation Treaty (NPT), Iran had since the 1960s developed a research program in nuclear technology that was oriented toward medical treatment in the framework of the "Atoms for peace" program promoted by the USA. France and Germany had begun the construction of two nuclear plants in Khorramshahr and Bushehr when the revolution broke out, and Chapour Bakhtiār canceled the contracts. Initially the Shah wanted to have twenty-three nuclear power stations. It seems that he accepted not to seek military use of nuclear technology, and the Europeans were flexible with this good client.[3]

Even if the casualties were relatively limited over the course of eight years of war with Iraq,[4] Iran was faced with urban bombardments from long-range missiles and the superiority of its enemy in armaments. Tehran's long isolation certainly hardened its position concerning possible concessions in the dialogue with the West and the nuclear issue. The leaders of the Islamic Republic have not forgotten that, in a position of danger, they were unable to count on international treaties and could only count on themselves. During the war they decided to restart the nuclear program – which had been interrupted in January 1979 – whose strategic objectives took precedence over any energy policies which served as a cover. In terms of an Iranian nuclear program, the country understood very well that there would be no foreign help – aside from that of Pakistan and North Korea. Initially an agreement with Eurodif

---

[3] A discussion on the possible military implications of the Iranian program before the revolution in Gh.-R. AFKHAMI, *The Life and Times of the Shah*, pp. 347–62.

[4] A comparison will better explain. In the four years of the First World War, France, which had fewer than 30 million inhabitants, lost at least 1.5 million lives. In this eight-year war, Iran lost between 350,000 and 500,000 people out of a population of about 60 million inhabitants.

(France) signed in 1974 would have granted Iran the delivery of nuclear fuel, but this was canceled after the revolution. Therefore, during negotiations which took place after 2002, all offers for the supply of enriched fuel seemed to be unreliable.

In March 1988, at the end of the Iran–Iraq War, having launched a campaign to create a vacuum along the border with Iran, Saddam Hussein ordered a chemical bombardment of the Kurdish village of Halabja, causing 5,000 deaths. After their arrival in Iran, the refugees alerted the authorities, and despite the efforts of the Iranian press agencies to denounce the massacre, no western media reported it until several months later – as if it was impossible to contemplate that an ally of the Free World could have played a part in such a horror. This attitude further fueled anti-western hostility among Iranians, who saw themselves faced with blind hatred. They knew that nuclear deterrence was their best protection against annihilation if a new conflict were to start.

Under the cover of finishing the Bushehr plant, which was dealt with by a Russian company, several underground structures, in Natanz and Fordow (near Qom), were secretly equipped to enrich uranium for military use, this being absolutely forbidden by the NPT. As soon as this new program was revealed by opponents in 2002, Iran entered into negotiations first with European countries and agreed to a temporary suspension of enrichment.

Iranians argued that they needed to enrich uranium themselves because no country would sell them the fuel needed for a new heavy water reactor. The fear of proliferation on the part of the six countries who eventually entered into lengthy and difficult negotiations with Iran (the five permanent members of the UN Security Council plus Germany) overplayed the denuclearization policy discourse. In fact, the five permanent members already had atomic weapons and had postponed the dismantling of their own warheads. In the South-West Asia region, three countries that refused to sign the NPT have nuclear warheads: Israel, India, and Pakistan, three new countries that, from their very beginning (1947–48), have been in a quasi-permanent state of war. Nevertheless, these countries were allies of the very powers now trying to deny Iran's access to that technology and were receiving international assistance with their nuclear technology.

The position of the Iranian government initially met with strong public support, which defended the right of Iranians to achieve on their own what the world wanted to forbid. The situation looked very similar to the nationalization of oil in the early 1950s: a national achievement with the aim of full Iranian sovereignty. However, the burden of economic sanctions was on the shoulders of the population at large, and this severely hampered any industrial or developmental project. Oil prices were high but the inflation of the rial rose dramatically; in 2014, an oil barrel was still $110, but it sank rapidly to $30. The situation became intolerable.

The pressure obliged the Iranians to accept direct talks with the Americans. Significantly, negotiations (Iran versus the five UN Security Council members plus Germany) started only in 2013 after Hilary Clinton left the office of Secretary of State in Washington and after the election of a moderate president in Iran, Hasan Ruhāni. Eventually, on 14 July 2015, an arrangement was signed in Vienna under the auspices of the UN agency International Atomic Energy Agency (IAEA). Under this Joint Comprehensive Plan of Action (also called the "Iran nuclear deal") Iran agreed to eliminate its already enriched uranium and to limit further enrichment to 3.67 percent for a period of fifteen years. More importantly for Iranian sovereignty, Iran accepted unlimited inspections and monitoring of its military installations to confirm that it was complying with its obligations.

The feeling of relief on both sides was short lived. Even though the UN sanctions were scheduled to be lifted, American sanctions remained applicable and hindered the freedom of action for international firms wishing to invest in the Iranian economy. Iranian inflation was reduced, but many obstacles prevented the rapid return of international trade despite the country's immense economic potential. In Iran, despite general satisfaction, the acceptance of tough conditions of monitoring was seen, with growing discontent, as a major setback to the principle of national sovereignty. For rival powers in the region, Saudi Arabia and Israel, Iran was once again seen as the target of major investments and development schemes, and therefore as a direct threat. Constant in his policy of canceling the achievements of Barack Obama, President Trump decided, on 8 May 2018, to withdraw the American signature on the agreement, thus jeopardizing a major diplomatic achievement. Consequently, major multinational societies that had signed important contracts with Iran announced their cancelation, to avoid being banned from the American market.

One cannot understand the hostility of Saudi Arabia toward Iran without appreciating the conflicts involving Iran as a neighbor or as the protector of Shiite communities. In Afghanistan, from the time of Soviet occupation, Iran held views that converged with those of the Americans: Islam was *the* right buffer against communism. Then the Taliban, strongly influenced by Wahhābi Islam, revealed their anti-Shiite tendency; Iran saw them as a threat, and when, in 2001, NATO forces invaded Afghanistan Tehran was again on the American side. In 2018, after years of civil war and the failure of military occupation, the Iranian approach seems to be more pragmatic, and some Taliban leaders occasionally find sanctuary on Iranian soil. They have now a common enemy, the "Islamic State," and both want to get rid of a permanent American military presence in Afghanistan.

The situation was different in Iraq, the country which Iran had fought without victory. The majority of the Iraqi population is Shiite, but power, since the creation of the state in 1920, has always been in the hands of Sunni Arabs. The Kurdish minority in the north, mostly Sunni, ignores the border between them and the Kurdish province of Iran. In addition, the Shiite cities of Najaf, Karbalā, and Samarrā attract Iranian pilgrims who, since the 1960s, had been prevented from undertaking this ritual.

Two years after the Iran–Iraq War, Saddam Hussein invaded Kuwait. The territorial claim was similar to the 1980 situation with Iran, but this time the international community reacted swiftly in defense of the wealthy oil emirate.[5] After US intervention (January–April 1991), the Americans left the Iraqi president in power, while encouraging the Kurds in the north and the Shiites in the south to rebel. For Tehran, the Kurdish uprising risked causing a destabilization of Iranian Kurdistan which, given the memory of the 1946 Mahābād Republic, was not acceptable. Did reasons of state hold back the Iranian ayatollahs from helping their Shiite brothers of Najaf and Karbalā who were crushed by the Baathist repression? Their unexpected neutrality shows that religious motivation had given way to political and strategic considerations. A belated victory for Persian nationalism: inaction in front of the crushing of Iraqi Shiites appeared to them preferable in order to maintain the existing borders.

---

[5] The western media called it "the Gulf War," an appellation already used for the Iran–Iraq War.

Iraq Again, Syria, Palestine

When President George W. Bush decided to attack Saddam Hussein with his coalition in 2003, the Iranians were attentive observers.[6] Any democratic consultation after the toppling of the dictator had to give Iraqi Shiites (who are in the majority) the political weight that the various regimes since the Ottomans had refused them. In any case, those who returned to Baghdad under American protection would inevitably unite with the numerous opponents of Saddam who had taken refuge for many years in the Islamic Republic of Iran. Shiism appeared not – as before – a destabilizing factor, but rather an auxiliary in the fight against terrorism. US success in Iraq benefited from the invisible support of the Iranian ayatollahs. Conversely, this benevolent neutrality toward the American occupation weakened Iranian appeal in the rest of the Islamic world. Sunni countries, led by Saudi Arabia, described the supremacy of Shiism over Iraq as the "Shiite Crescent," starting in Bahrain and ending in Lebanon.

Iranian cooperation was still considered essential for a return to normality in Iraq when the American withdrawal began in 2009. In 2017 the military assistance provided by Iranian troops to Iraqi Shiite militias fighting against Dā'esh proved a major factor in their victory, but it prevented Iraqi Sunnis from being able to put their trust in any attempt at nation-building.

To stop the massacre between Shiites and Sunnis and to strengthen its image as a regional power, Iran tried to turn Muslim hostility toward a more neutral target on which they all agree, the state of Israel. This turn concerned, until recently, less a call for genocide or even open war than the instrumentalization of a conflict where, during two major crises, in summer 2006 (Israel's campaign against Hizbollah in South Lebanon) and winter 2008/9 (Israel's conflict with Hamas in Gaza), Iran was the most radical country to support the anti-Israeli cause.

Established initially to fight Israel, the Shiites of Lebanon, whose military force, Hizbollah, receives active support from Iran, were involved from the beginning (2011) of the Syrian civil war, in support of the Baathist regime. The Islamic Republic was thus, together with Russia, a defender of the Assad regime and de facto the enemy of all

---

[6] For a third time the western media named the American war in Iraq "the Gulf War."

the insurgents and their allies. The confrontation with Saudi Arabia continued on a remote field of action.

The Islamic State (*Dā'esh*), a new contender, was inspired by the radical Islam of Wahhābism; however, it has turned out to be the enemy not only of western powers but of all states in the region, including Saudi Arabia, and it has shown particular aggression toward Shiite Muslims. This group has made the situation in the Middle East even more complicated. Iran engaged its special forces under the command of the Pāsdār General Soleymāni to defeat Dā'esh in northern Iraq using ground operations while the Americans used massive air strikes. A concerted effort by those odd allies has once again been necessary.

An unexpected consequence of Iran's involvement in Syria has been the establishment of Iranian forces on the Israeli border. The previous game of verbal imprecations and threats, which was not intended to lead to military encroachment, turned into a real threat, and in spring 2018 Israeli missiles and airstrikes hit several Syrian bases killing many Iranian fighters. After years of ambiguous engagement, a real confrontation was seen to be developing.

A sign of regional ambition, this has been the first time since the collapse of the Sassanian Empire that Iranian soldiers have reached the shores of the Mediterranean. Thus Iran's imperial posture has persisted in the regional role it plays, but what exactly is the nature of this regime?

Power of the Clergy, *Velāyat-e faqih* and Declericalization

The Islamic Republic of Iran first had a government headed by Mahdi Bāzargān, who wore a tie and shared with Shāpur Bakhtyār, the last head of the Shah's government, more than common memories of imprisonment. One made allegiance to the clergy, the other, ultimately, to the former regime, but the political philosophy of both men was similar. Bāzargān was a Muslim but no revolutionary, as he himself admitted. He wanted to make the Islamic Republic a democratic regime, protected by the USA, and to denounce Soviet intentions in Afghanistan.

The proclamation of a new regime on 11 February 1979 was not contentious for anybody. Nevertheless, the new authorities organized a referendum on 1 April to allow the electorate – men and women – to ratify a name that some politicians, in the newspapers, proposed to replace with another. Why not a "Democratic Republic" or a "Republic of the Muslim People of Iran"? The electorate, in an overwhelming show of solidarity, ratified the "Islamic Republic of Iran," with 98 percent of the votes. Khomeyni's new regime made one major concession, namely popular sovereignty expressed by universal suffrage, and in so doing gained democratic legitimacy.

Imām Khomeyni could have decreed that a constitution served no purpose. However, the liberal nationalists expressed the same concern about political legitimacy and demanded a Fundamental Law, preventing any return to tyranny. Khomeyni again gave in to the Constituent Assembly after having initially argued that the country did not need it. Called the "Assembly of Experts" (*Majles-e khobragān*), so that nobody had to lose face, it was elected by universal suffrage. In the Constitution, written in the fall of 1979 and swiftly approved by referendum, democratic controls apparently dominate, since the electorate directly designates three institutions: Parliament, the president, and the "Experts" (*khobragān*), whose council was given the task to control the supreme function, that of the Guide. On this Guide rests the only real measure based on Shiite Islam, which is incompatible with western notions of democracy and republic.

The symbolic protest by Ayatollah Tāleqāni first brought an exotic element to the deliberations of the Assembly of Experts. Rather than sitting down, like the others, on the overstuffed chairs of the Senate of the former regime, Tāleqāni sat on the ground as befitting a non-westernized Iranian. He might have been able to contribute the social touch of a progressive Islam to the Republic, but he died when the Assembly was just beginning its activities, and his example was not followed.

Thus, while moving toward a kind of modern democracy colored by Islam, Ayatollah Beheshti transformed the constitutional draft by introducing a principle that nobody dared contest, as it came explicitly from the writings of Khomeyni on Islamic government. He imposed the adoption, as the keystone of this Constitution, the principle of the "government of the jurist-theologian" (*velāyat-e faqih*), tailormade for Khomeyni himself. He thus covered with theocratic legitimacy a constitution that granted a large role to universal suffrage.

> Article 5: During the Occultation (*qeybat*) of his holiness, the Lord of the Age, [i.e. the Hidden Imam], the regency of the sovereignty [of God] and religious leadership of the community

[of believers] in the Islamic Republic of Iran is the responsibility of the religious jurisconsult (*faqih*) who is just, pious, aware of the situation of his times, courageous, and a capable and efficient administrator, who would be appointed to this office according to Article 107.[7]

Article 56: Absolute sovereignty (*hākemiyat-e motlaq*) over the world and humankind belongs to God. And it is He who has made human beings sovereign (*hākem*) over their social destiny. No one can take this divine right away from human beings or apply it to the interests of a particular individual or group. The nation exercises this God-given right in ways that are specified in the following articles.

Article 57: The governing powers in the Islamic Republic of Iran consist of the legislative, the executive, and the judiciary powers. They operate under the supervision of the absolute authority of the command and religious leadership of the community of believers (*velāyat-e motlaqe-ye amr va emāmat-e ommat*).

The Guide does not have a crown but a turban and is not designated as the heir of a dynasty but by the Experts, according to his virtues and his theological knowledge. His power will not be, as coined in the 1907 formula, "a trust, given by divine grace, on the part of the nation, confided to the person of the king" (Supplement art. 35), but a type of prophetic authority entrusted by the grace of universal suffrage on the part of the nation to the person of an ayatollah.

The clerical power-grab, in a republic which the democratic nationalists had at first believed was theirs, forced all liberals and leftists to face reality: they have been mercilessly reduced to silence, first Bāzargān the prime minister and then Banisadr the first president. In 1983 the Toudeh Party was dissolved, and its leaders convicted of spying for the Soviet Union; Ehsān Tabari, the party ideologue, was destroyed on an ethical plane by engaging in self-criticism on television and in his writings where he praised Khomeyni. In December 1987

---

[7] Art. 107 defines the election of the Guide by the Assembly of Experts (*majles-e khobragān*), and adds "The Guide, regarding the laws, is equal to other individuals of the country." For a detailed discussion on the Constitution and its elaboration, see A. SCHIRAZI, *The Constitution of Iran: Politics and the State in the Islamic Republic*. On the *Velāyat-e faqih* see C. ARMINJON-HACHEM, *Chiisme et état*.

Khomeyni further strengthened his prerogative to settle internal conflicts by stating that the *velāyat-e faqih* was an absolute principle (*motlaqe*), allowing the Guide, if need be, even to suspend Islamic ritual obligations such as fasting and prayer. At that time, the Iran–Iraq War had not yet ended, and its continuation made it possible to weaken any kind of resistance to clerical power.

Succession to Khomeyni

Within Iran, innumerable summary executions in response to attacks against the leaders of the Republic proved Khomeyni's determination to repel any domestic challenge, as he had done with the war with Iraq. In particular, after the ceasefire with Iraq, a nonsensical invasion of western Iran by a small army of Mojāhedin militants from the Iraqi border (in the summer of 1988) provoked cruel retaliations: Khomeyni ordered the execution of several thousand Mojāhedin militants who had been sentenced to prison. This decision resulted in protests by Ayatollah Hoseyn-Ali Montazeri, Khomeyni's designated successor. A few months before his death the "Leader" dismissed the ayatollah from office and had him held under house arrest in Qom. No protest, no sign of regret has ever been heard from the then prime minister Mir-Hoseyn Musavi, even later when he campaigned as a liberal against Ahmadinejad in 2009.

Following his return to Iran, Khomeyni first traveled to his home in Qom, before establishing himself, in January 1980, in Tehran in a modest hermitage, which was difficult to access and the exact opposite of a royal palace. The faithful flocked there to receive his blessing, seated next to ambassadors and journalists, and made their ritual ablutions before appearing in the presence of the saint. The liturgy had changed, but already the sacred see of an imperial leader had been created. Khomeyni died in Tehran on 3 June 1989, amid the people's fervor. The Imam's funeral was the first funeral of an Iranian head of state on Iranian soil since that of Mozaffar od-Din Shāh in January 1907; all the other Shahs (between 1907 and 1989) died despised by their people and in exile. Khomeyni was carried in triumph to his last resting place south of Tehran, an immense mausoleum, situated close to the resting place of several Qajar kings and where Rezā Shāh himself had been buried after his corpse was returned from South Africa.

Upon the death of its founder, the Constitution became inapplicable because the function of Guide had been defined as his alone. After the removal of Montazeri, the possibility of a successor as Guide being found among the ayatollahs qualified as *marja* (model to imitate) was ruled out, because these grand ayatollahs recused themselves, as in 1909 when the *mojtaheds* who had been approached recused themselves from being members of the council of five theologians co-opted by Parliament to guarantee that the laws were in conformity with Islam. In 1989, the Republic attempted to establish permanency by preserving the function and the central role of the Guide. Those who enforced the choice of Seyyed Ali Khāmene'i (b. 1934) are suspected of having forged a posthumous letter by Khomeyni in favor of that succession. The Constitution was scrapped so that Khāmene'i, a militant clergyman, whom Khomeyni had never addressed other than as *hojjat ol-Eslām* ("authority on Islam"), but who was unexpectedly addressed as *āyatollāh*, could be designated as Supreme Guide. Thus the function lost its sacredness, allowing the authority to be imperceptibly secularized and primarily political. At the same time, the constitutional reform of 1989 did away with the function of prime minister, granting executive power to the elected president. The two presidents who followed, Akbar Hāshemi-Rafsanjāni (1989–97) and above all Mohammad Khātami (1997–2005), were clerics, but favored reform. In reality they governed as if they did not wear a turban. Logic followed that the function would go to a non-clergyman, which was indeed the outcome of the elections in June 2005. Mahmud Ahmadinejad (Ahmadinezhād), the next president (2005–13), had come from the Guardians of the Revolution, and did not wear religious dress (he had studied engineering), but his frame of mind was that of devotion of the literal kind, and he was more religious than many of the mollas in politics.

Discussions on the *Velāyat-e faqih*

Many opponents from within the Islamic Republic criticized the preservation of the principle of *velāyat-e faqih* in the Constitution, since it impedes reform and does not contribute anything to Islam or the political system. They most likely were ignoring the royal Iranian tradition that the Guide of the Revolution refashioned in his own style. Shiism has in fact been built, since its beginnings, on the idea of mediation and leadership. The Imam first and foremost is the Guide. It is difficult to radically remove the function of Guide from a society that permanently seeks a leader to follow blindly.

The arguments against the *velāyat-e faqih* have been considered in the manner that republican rhetoric was under the monarchy; that is, as a form of lèse-majesté. They earned heavy prison sentences as well as a "downgrading to non-clerical status" for those who wore the turban, such as Mohsen Kadivar or Hasan Yusofi-Eshkevari. Little could prevent the development of such critics in a country where the institutions were increasingly turning their back on popular (or democratic) legitimacy, transforming it into an Islamic state with a single party. In reality, those who are currently pressing most for a separation between politics and religion are the clergymen themselves, who are worried that the young are increasingly breaking away not only from religious institutions but from religion itself. If clerical authority remains a prisoner to its ties with the political system, the latter's fall or inevitable transformation risks a considerable reduction in clerical influence.

Numerous philosophical reflections continue to germinate in Iran. Typically, they lean toward opposition to clerical dogmatism and contribute to a questioning of the ayatollahs' authority to defend an Islam stripped of its clergy, freed from the authority of the *mojtahed*, and centered around individual spontaneity rather than blind obedience. Following non-clerical thinkers, some ulama do not hesitate to express their thoughts on this premise of individual commitment to the faith. Thus Mohammad Mojtahed-Shabestari, a theologian who lived in Germany and attended seminars in Christian theology and exegetics, redefines adhesion to Islam, contrary to tradition, as a personal decision that each believer has to make with his own free conscience. Quite logically, he develops an original thought that finds resonance among young philosophers of religious pluralism and the pluralism of roads that lead to knowledge of God,[8] dropping a bomb in the quiet garden of clerical Shiism.

For his part, Abdol-Karim Sorush has become famous as a dissident intellectual. This student of Motahhari studied epistemology in Great Britain and has become one of the most radical partisans of the Islamic Republic. A member of the Council of the Cultural Revolution, a radical organization established in 1980 with a view to profoundly

---

[8] Md Mojtahed-Shabestari, *Imān va āzādi.*

reforming the educational system, he assumed, among other things, responsibility for the closure of the universities so as to "Islamize" the programs. Having enthusiastically supported the new regime, he engaged in a reflection on the history of philosophy and tried to reconcile religious thought in Islam with rationalist and liberal ideas from the West. Courageously opposing the absolute politics of Khomeyni, and openly criticizing the function of *velāyat-e faqih* even during the Imam's life, he denounced, as we have seen, this concept as an "absolutization of the [Hegelian] Idea in history" and compared it with the dramatic avatar of the Hegelian ideal in the Nazi state. Without ever having disavowed his attachment to Islam, he henceforth advocated the separation of politics and religion. Expelled, sometimes with physical attacks and insults, from most institutions where he courageously continued to defend his ideas, Sorush paradoxically found more support abroad than in Iran, despite his large number of readers and supporters. He now lives in exile.

Women, from Chador to Emancipation

At the end of the twentieth century, feminist demands took an unexpected turn in Iran. From the time of the Shah, "progressive" laws aimed to promote a modern image of womanhood, to emancipate women by granting them the civil rights that several western democracies were still denying women in their own countries and to guarantee certain rights that went against traditions generally attributed to Islam. Thus women, since the days of the White Revolution, have obtained the right to demand a divorce, a revelation in a country where the *shari'a* was the foundation of the personal statute in the civil code. Polygamy was not prohibited but strongly discouraged by measures that protected the first wife, giving her the right to divorce if she refused her husband's second wife.

Even if the ambitious literacy programs of the former regime were far from being realized, particularly in terms of rural schooling and the schooling of girls, Iranian universities produced a large number of highly educated women. It was often the case that young women became engineers, physicians, and architects, roles that were not just valued for making a good marriage. Among Iranian women who graduated from higher education many were engaged in the 1978 revolution, for the same reasons as men, and also denounced in the name of a humanistic Islam the merchandizing of eroticism in the consumer society that was establishing itself.

After the revolution, women continued to go about town with their heads uncovered, but the steps taken to limit the westernization of customs, concerning dress in particular, rapidly became obsessive. Strict directives on proper female Islamic dress and checks at the entrance of offices were especially humiliating, with women obliged to remove lipstick, nail polish, or even any item of clothing of an attractive color. Rulings to cover one's hair were soon enforced for women in educational establishments and above all in universities where boys and girls were rubbing shoulders, with the requirement to wear the *maqana'a*, a kind of black balaclava that covers the head and neck up to the chin and does not reveal any locks of hair. However, dress restrictions relaxed and became more progressive after the end of the war (1988), and even more so after the election of Khātami (1997). Today, the headscarf slips down from women's heads (in the streets, not in schools or administrative buildings); it is often colored; and it is not uncommon to see some strands of women's hair in public.

A significant reversal of legislation concerning women and marriage returned to men the superiority that Islam grants them: the right to divorce, the right to take a second wife, the inferiority of women in court where their testimony counts for half that of a man's, and so on. Some of these laws, such as that of polygamy, are not in line with the dominant customs of today's urbanized Iranians, whose family model is very similar to that of western societies. Divorce has become progressively more frequent, especially for economic reasons, but nevertheless remains less common than in western countries. As for judicial practice in the protection of women and children, the situation in Iran is clearly not quite so unfavorable to women when compared with many Muslim countries, as shown in a study carried out after the revolution that compares Iranian jurisprudence with that of Morocco.[9]

To only judge the situation of Iranian women by the length of their dark fabric would be simplistic. The obligation to wear the veil is the exact opposite of its violent prohibition in 1936. Since that time, access to higher education has not been prohibited to girls from traditional circles but has been made difficult because of that forced

---

[9] Z. Mir Hosseini, *Marriage on Trial: Study of Islamic Family Laws* (critical review by J. Afary, *Iranian Studies*, 29, 1996).

emancipation which exposed them to the eyes of men, a situation which raised objections in traditional religious families. Today, no young Iranian girl is held back in continuing her studies, the hypocritical "protections" of society having overcome the reticence of most traditional parents. There are more girls than boys in Iranian universities, which can partly be explained by the more rapid need of young men to secure an income and provide for their family. Graduating from universities with higher qualifications than men, women work, marry later, and have fewer children because they more often use contraceptive methods offered by family planning campaigns. At present, an Iranian woman has on average fewer than two children (compared with between six and seven at the time of the revolution).[10] The social reticence that held back the entry of women to professions in some sectors has generally receded. Already, Iranian medicine is largely female dominated, but the progress of women in other professions is even more spectacular. This is also the case for theology, for which there is a need for professors in female establishments (co-education is banned until higher education). To impose unacceptable conditions of judicial inferiority on women who have attained the same status in Islamic theology as the ulama raises serious questions. And these issues are being taken up by many women today who are grappling with the recognition of their rights. A notable figure in the struggle is Shirin Ebadi, an Iranian lawyer who received the Nobel Peace Prize in 2003. The difficulties that she has experienced in her country prove that the rights she defends, particularly those of women, are far from being achieved.

The 2009 Revolt: The Green Movement (*Nahzat-e sabz*)

The repressive logic that dominated after the contested election of Ahmadinejad in 2009 has tarnished the legitimacy and the shine of the Republic. The president wasted the last financial reserves and showed himself incapable of thinking about foreign relations other than in terms of permanent provocation. The appeal to rhetoric regarding the imminence of the return of the Twelfth Imam, which he even mentioned at the General Assembly of the United Nations, to present

---

[10] See M. LADIER-FOULADI, *Population et politique en Iran.*

himself as being vested with a supernatural power, did not deceive anybody and gave rise to many quips in Iran.

However, Ahmadinejad has never been the "dictator" he was so hastily labeled as by western journalists. He only held limited powers and, at the end of his second term, Guide Khāmene'i withdrew his confidence in him.

He was scarcely a danger for Israel. despite his anti-Zionist rhetoric, an improbable threat, which was used by Israelis to justify an extravagant arms program. During this period, Iran exploited the Palestinian cause, strongly demonstrating its solidarity. His refusal to compromise with American mediation brought Ahmadinejād great popularity in the Arab world.

The reelection in 2009 took place in a context of dramatic misunderstandings. To mobilize the electorate, Ahmadinejād agreed to hold free debates broadcast live on television with liberal candidates who sought his post, including a reformer clergyman, Mahdi Karrubi, and a former non-turbaned prime minister, Mir Hussein Musavi. The sincerity of the discussions and the virulence of the criticisms, which were granted equal air time – some denounced the financial chaos, the saber rattling with regard to Israel, and the contempt for individual liberties – encouraged a large number of voters to believe that change was possible. Those who had planned to abstain voted for the reformers, expecting a spectacular change.

The hurried declaration of Ahmadinejad as victor in the first round provoked an immediate reaction and demonstrations in the big cities, particularly in Tehran. The violent repression prompted people to believe that the result had been manipulated. "Give me my vote back," shouted those who were soon known as the "Greens," the color chosen for their campaign banners. In fact, the western media encouraged and magnified the movement, suggesting that a radical change, even the collapse of the Islamic Republic, was possible.

Ahmadinejad's triumph was most probably, as the demonstrators stated, made possible by rigged results that allowed the regime to avoid a new campaign during the second round. The immediate and resolute intervention by Guide Khāmene'i to support him was determinant. In reality, the Green Movement had above all mobilized the youth in the large cities but affected the provinces to a lesser degree; there the Islamic Republic was considered to be a social and cultural rampart and the militias surrounding the outgoing president, its best defenders. Thus the illusion of change proved premature.

The image that struck me at the very beginning of the Islamic Republic, that of a growing religious populism, strong and proud of its cultural uniqueness in the face of liberal nationalism (April 1981), nevertheless seemed to have taken a new turn in 2009, with crowds demonstrating for freedoms and an opening up to the outside world. Even when the regime's resistance showed itself to be effective, strongly established and backed up by the committed and loyal militiamen, political dynamism was no longer on the side of closing doors (rejection of an external enemy, unanimity behind religious leaders) but was looking toward color (green, locks of hair) and political modernity (elections, pluralism, social justice, liberties).

One is tempted when observing the human tide that engulfed the major arteries of Tehran to make a comparison with the popular uprising of 1978. Some photos suggest this comparison. Moreover, in 1978 nobody had foreseen, until the final moment, that such a prosperous regime, so well integrated internationally and also so well policed and armed as the Shah's forces, might so quickly be brought to an end as a result of the people's determination. In 2009, even when prosperity did not offer the glitz of the rentier success of the 1970s and bad economic management accentuated social inequality between wealthy merchants and entrepreneurs and the precarious urban proletariat, Iran's situation, thirty years after the revolution, was far from catastrophic. The country had no foreign debts and had an energy capital that was the envy of emerging countries. Its population, whose growth had stabilized, was no longer illiterate, and many young graduates enriched the whole world by going abroad. On the diplomatic front, Iran's regional prestige, thanks to an independent foreign policy that was defiant toward the West, particularly in the face of the Palestinian question, was immense.

Between the unsatisfied aspirations, the desire for freedom, for pluralism, for political change, for cultural openness and modern politics, and the current leaders' morbid fear of all change, the tension is not yet close to abating. Since the end of the nineteenth century, Iran has been torn between the contradictory forces that tempt it, on the one hand, to join the family of nations and to adopt a European style of life and, on the other hand, to see itself as a threatened community that must mobilize all its forces to repel outside aggression.

The Economy

Traditionally, Islam favors a liberal mercantile economy. However, the shared feelings of some revolutionaries of 1979, inspired by a communist vision, moved toward state control and collectivization of the economy. After the revolution, entire sectors were protected from bankruptcy through state intervention. Others, owing to their strategic importance, were taken over by the Pāsdārān (energy, transport), essentially creating a type of nationalization. Other sectors, such as industrial agriculture in Khorasan and some sensitive sectors, such as the food industry, found themselves in the hands of powerful foundations that often acted like a state within the state, but which operated under a capitalist apparatus. Finally, and rather paradoxically, certain landed estates were returned to their owners with the repeal of the land reform legislation, at the end of painstaking negotiations with mixed local commissions to judge the admissibility of the restitutions.

But the main problem of the Iranian economy, for a century, has been its dependence on oil, an income whose perverse effect is twofold. On the one hand it renders the state insensitive to the real health of the economy, and on the other hand it fluctuates with the vagaries of the international market. The fluctuation has even been accentuated for Iran by the severing of relations with the USA, the main holders of extraction technology, and then by the Iran–Iraq War that destroyed part of its infrastructure (notably the large refinery in Ābādān).

From the beginning, oil revenue has been managed as leased state property. The only objective of the lengthy negotiations between the Iranian state and the British company was to enrich the state more regularly. AIOC was nationalized in 1951. When production started again after Mosaddeq's fall (1953), during the renegotiation of all the agreements with the major oil companies, the National Iranian Oil Company (NIOC, *sherkat-e melli-e naft-e Irān*) represented Iranian interests in front of the international consortium. The nationalization was merely a façade because the major decisions on the volume of production and prospecting were taken by the foreign companies. After the revolution, the NIOC was placed under a Ministry of Petrol, and thus nationalization was achieved.

The share of oil in Iranian exports dropped from 75 percent in 1978 to 25 percent in 2016. Given the impossibility of using certain technologies patented by the USA, the annual quantity produced has never reached pre-revolution levels. In parallel, domestic consumption of refined products has risen with demographic growth, urbanization, and changes in lifestyle (general use of gas heating, cars, industrialization, and so on), thus diminishing the exportable quantity. The dizzying drop in the price of exported crude oil, moreover, has seriously affected the Iranian economy. From July 2014 to January 2016 it fell from US$100 to US$30 per barrel. The embargo imposed since 1996 and the financial sanctions applied by the USA have forced Iran to sacrifice some of its commercial freedom to conclude, in particular with China, disadvantageous barter deals.

As long as alternative energies remain underdeveloped, the advanced economies, and also China and India, will need hydrocarbons; the fact that Iran has a significant share of the global reserves (ranked fifth for oil and second for gas) makes it a very important actor in the twenty-first century. Plans for pipelines to Turkey and India might put Iran back in an enviable position in the world, but material and political obstacles are numerous: first there is the competition of hydrocarbons from Central Asia and the Caspian Sea and, second, the passage through Pakistan, a Sunni state in a permanent tacit war with India. Meanwhile, the maritime route remains primordial, and Iran jealously guards the passage through the Straits of Hormuz while the American Fifth Fleet patrols the Persian Gulf. "The boosting of oil and gas production remains an absolute priority, not only in itself, but because it conditions the development of other sectors of the national economy."[11]

Non-oil-related Iranian industry has remained at a commendable level, notably the production of steel (of which Iran is the prime producer in the Middle East) and cars (production of 1.6 million cars in 2011, dropping thereafter and rising again after the 2015 nuclear agreement). The arms industry, developed during the Iran–Iraq War, exports missiles and light arms. The export of manufactured and industrial goods now exceeds traditional exports (carpets, dried fruit, and so on). Principal clients (including for oil) include China, India, Turkey, South Korea, and, to a lesser extent because of their lower purchasing power, Iraq, Afghanistan, and Pakistan.

No lasting solution in commercial transactions can be foreseen without the agreement of the USA, and on 8 May 2018 (as seen

---

[11] B. HOURCADE, *Géopolitique de l'Iran*, p. 122.

previously in the section on the nuclear program) the American president withdrew his country from the Vienna agreement, thus compelling all international companies to cancel their activities in Iran for fear of financial and judicial retaliation.

From the American perspective, several layers of sanctions and embargo have stacked up, and the process of lifting them will only be undertaken reluctantly. Even if the Federal Government recommends the liberation of Iranian assets and the resumption of banking activities, very complex judicial conflicts still block such a move, and may continue to do so for years. The example of an enormous fine imposed on a French bank in 2014 for having infringed the embargo discourages economic relations, as long as the blocking of certain states, such as Texas, is not clearly discontinued. As for the Iranians, even if they are glad to be courted anew by investors, anti-American dogma has not been extinguished, and it slows down the building of normal relations.

Iran and a Region in Tatters

The positive resolution to the nuclear negotiations has not, however, resolved the problems posed by Iran in the Middle East, where several regional powers are challenging each other with varied strategies in conflicts and power struggles that implicate international alliances.

Since 1979, with the increase in the price of oil, Saudi Arabia has acquired the financial and military potential to intervene and seeks to play a central role in the region. This country was founded in 1935 by a dynasty of Wahhabi Muslims, the most fundamentalist form of Islam and the most hostile to Shiism, which it considers to be the worst of heresies. It has inspired the creation of several movements of radical activists, some of whom have turned against it, such as al-Qaeda, founded by the Yemeni-Saudi Osama bin Laden, and the Islamic State (*Dā'esh*) of the Iraqi Sheykh Abu Bakr al-Baghdadi. Fifteen of the nineteen culprits behind the attacks of 11 September were Saudis.

The Turkish Republic, founded in 1923 and based on an ideology of militant secularism, showed little interest in solidarity with the Khomeynist Islamic Republic. Nevertheless, common interests have obliged it to maintain commercial and political relations with Iran. Their common aversion to Kurdish irredentism and Arab hegemony over the Islamic world has brought them closer. Turkey, a NATO member, with diplomatic relations with Israel, has undergone a dramatic transformation since the beginning of the twenty-first century, and plays its own cards concerning the routing of hydrocarbons from the Caucasus to the Mediterranean. The country is gradually creeping toward a Sunni Islamicization, which in the Caucasus, Central Asia, or in Syria opposes the cultural and political influence of Iran.

The two conflicts started by the Americans in the Middle East, in Afghanistan and Iraq, paradoxically have strengthened Iranian influence. President Ahmadinejad went twice to Kabul to congratulate Hamid Karzai for his election and reelection. Henceforth Iraq is governed by Shiites who are closer to Tehran than to any other Arab country. In reaction to the Shiitization of Iraqi politics, the Islamic State (*Dā'esh*) sought to relocate a sectarian Sunni state. In Iraq and Syria, Iran sent Pāsdārān brigades with Afghan Shiites: they fought in dangerous ground operations while the western-arab coalition air strikes could only destroy limited targets. Thus, when it comes to fighting *Dā'esh* in Iraq, Iran is on the same side as NATO armies, but in Syria it sides with Damascus and Moscow. The sectarian character of this war between Sunni and Shiite Muslims sweeps the real stakes of these conflicts under the carpet.

Despite the Baathist, secular ideology of Hafez al-Asad (the father of Bashar) and the ferocity of the repression of the Muslim Brotherhood, the alliance with an Arab country was precious. Moreover, it allowed Iran to remain in contact with the Shiite militias of Lebanon, Hizbollah. The various rebellious fronts against Damascus since 2011 have been actively supported by Qatar and Saudi Arabia and inspired (like the Islamic State) by virulent anti-Shiite sentiment. In Syria as in the Caucasus (notably Chechnya), Iranian and Russian interests converge, both wanting to reduce or annihilate Sunni domination (and the pro-Saudi insurrectional movements) and to reduce American penetration in the region. On other issues, such as the Palestinian question, both Russia and Iran pursue antagonist policies.

In addition to Syria, Arabia has found in Yemen an area of confrontation with Iran, although Tehran has not directly placed its forces in the service of the Houthi rebellion.

The Islamic Republic, where limited political change through elections allows the renewal of the elite, has been able to adapt its former revolutionary discourse to pursue a regional strategy. On domestic issues, however, it has lost little of its ideological rigidity. The death penalty is applied regularly, and the prisons are filled with journalists and lawyers who made the mistake of demanding human rights and fundamental liberties. Young people, well educated and prepared to take on well-paid jobs in wealthy countries, are still ready to depart en masse from a country in which they are stifled. This desire to migrate to other countries is telling of the fascination the western model holds for Iranian youth, as if the Khomeynist regime's efforts to totally Islamize Iranian culture have been in vain.

Yet one would be mistaken in predicting the regime's end. Since its formation, the Islamic Republic has been expected to experience a rapid demise, but it has proved its strength. Nevertheless, there are many signs of decline: elite corruption; weariness among the population, who would prefer jobs rather than military interventions in Syria; increasing disaffection among intellectuals. The Iranian Republic no longer draws its youth into the dream of a just and prosperous Islamic society; instead its population remains on a neverending quest.

What Is an Islamic Republic?

No one would have dared to predict the emergence of such a regime in Iran at the time the demonstrations against the monarchy began, only twelve months prior to the triumphant return of Khomeyni. The republican dream of the 1978 demonstrators often spontaneously and surprisingly fluctuated between the Chinese and the Western European models. Neither Shariati nor Khomeyni had really defined the Islamic regime. For Shariati, the distant model of an Islamic society governed by the Prophet or by Imam Ali, where social justice was supposed to maintain a perfect equality between believer-fighters, was balanced by the example of revolutionary and anticolonial struggles in the Third World. According to Khomeyni, only clerical power could keep society on the path to justice while awaiting the return of the Imam.

Those who ensured the new regime's victory and inspired the constituents of 1979 are the *mostaz'afin* (disinherited), the common people of the suburb; these "uprooted peasants" looked for protection and representation. Today they owe everything to the revolution: their social and political advancement, and the fact that they have access to schools and universities. The itinerary of President Mahmud Ahmadinejad, born in 1956 to a modest family of a smith in Garmsār,

100 km (60 miles) southeast of Tehran, is exemplary. Driven by militancy and his goal of joining the inner workings of the Islamic Republic, he surprised everybody in 2005 when he outperformed members of the clergy who participated in the presidential elections. He represents the virtuous side of the new elite, naive and populist, while the former President Hāshemi-Rafsanjāni (1934–2017), his rival in the second round, represented the crafty and corrupt clerical face of that same republic.

Islam has an important place in the daily culture of Iranians, whatever the disaffection of the young with the mosque and traditional religion, and whatever their fascination with western cultural outputs that they watch on foreign television channels and the Internet. Islam gives rhythm to their lives and structures their cultural universe, literary or historical. Mosques are not visited often, but pilgrimage sites attract large crowds. The insistence of the authorities on imposing public worship in public places, in offices, or even in educational establishments has led to ostentatious worship, a form of religiosity not particularly popular with Iranians, such as the space reserved for prayer in airplanes, praying in offices, and the recitation of Koranic verses at the beginning of public meetings. But private worship has not ceased with the secularization of customs. The interest in Sufism, the form of mystical spirituality that escapes the attention of the clergy, increases in relation to the diminishment of trust in the mollas.

The forms of intolerance witnessed since 1979 are probably more frequent than in the past. But in the face of the sectarianism of the authorities, the Iranian population sometimes responds with acts of great tolerance, thus making it a point of honor to defy this marginalization. Threats and media campaigns have often convinced non-Muslim communities to leave Iran. As for Armenians, who have never, as a separate ethnic community, had major problems over the last two centuries, they feel all these pressures as a painful reminder of the massacres under the Ottoman Empire. They can now travel to neighboring Armenia with ease, and they know that their economic situation in Iran is not so bad, but they generally aspire to emigrate to western countries which they wrongly imagine as Christendom, a place of salvation.

The Islamic Republic has succeeded in giving the clergy a prominent place in public life. Many believers would undoubtedly be ready to secularize politics and favor a more open republic that is more democratic and more just so as to better preserve religion, faith, and clerical independence from the state.[12] Contrary to the predictions of most analysts since 1979, the Islamic Republic has persisted. But several elements indicate the dynamics of change.

Even though electoral events have led to surprises, they have often been mere palace revolutions. The apparent changes sometimes serve as an alibi for the consolidation of the regime. It is on these grounds that people reproached Khātami for the eight years during which important reforms he had announced never came to fruition, while the repressive apparatus, notably against students, functioned as before.

The Islamic Republic of Iran

Amid the revolution, a French diplomat in Tehran challenged me to offer a coherent rationale for the concept of an "Islamic government." He pointed out the contradiction, or even the oxymoron, which lies in the very concept of "Islamic Republic," a theocratic institution that claims to refer to popular suffrage. After thirty-eight years, the same person, back from a fresh trip to Iran wrote: "This government is not a chimera, but a rare case which no nation but Iran could invent."

Should we stress the final objective of the regime, or, rather, focus on its achievements, even when these are incomplete? Propaganda promulgates idealist objectives and minimizes failures. Yet before we draw any clear-cut conclusions about The Islamic Republic – a subject about which, too often, passions run high – let us outline some connecting threads.

As used in the official denomination, *Jomhuri-e eslāmi* (Islamic Republic), do Iranian leaders understand "Islamic" in a religious or cultural sense? And how can we make sense of the substantive *jomhuri* that is usually translated as "republic"? In classical Persian, *jomhur* means "the crowd, a large number." Is not *democracy* the standard for a republic, a form of political modernity toward which a large number of societies strive as soon as they attain independence? In fact, a constitutional monarchy, whereby a parliament elected on the basis of universal suffrage controls the executive authority, assures the same political participation as a republic; royal control in this case constitutes

---

[12] See H. E. Chehabi, "Religion and Politics in Iran: How Theocratic Is the Islamic Republic?"

a symbolic stability that also guarantees protection by limiting popular power at the outset – out of fear of electoral vagaries or revolution. By adding an adjective to the republic, be it "democratic," "popular" or "Islamic," are we not expressing a similar form of moderation, so as to prevent institutions from self-destruction?

Since the days of contact between Europe and Persia under the Qajars, foreign military and commercial encroachments, along with political and cultural interference, have often weakened the Iranian state from within its own frontiers, in particular in the case of the particularly humiliating "capitulations." From the mid-nineteenth century onwards, Iranian reformers have tried, with more or less success, to reverse this relationship by regaining their sovereignty. It is from this perspective and not exclusively in terms of political modernization that Amir Kabir's and Sepahsālār's reforms must be understood, as well as the conflicts of the Constitutional Revolution and the popular movement that supported, under Mosaddeq, the nationalization of oil. It is also important, therefore, in understanding the birth of the "Islamic Republic" of Iran after the failure of all other forms of opposition. The appeal of this novel, and previously unheard of, political concept discredited the leaders of the Iranian kingdom, who were accused of having abandoned the defense of national sovereignty. By deciding to call themselves "Islamic" – which also means "popular" – this republic forced foreign powers to recognize Iran's sovereignty and discouraged non-Muslim peoples from any kind of interference or encroachment. Its founding slogan, "neither East nor West, Islamic Republic' (*na sharqi, na qarbi, jomhuri-e eslāmi*) rejected Americans and Westerners in general, whose presence had become invasive before the revolution, as well as the communists whom the de-Islamicized intellectuals had been fascinated by since the Bolshevik Revolution.

The Constitution of the Islamic Republic, proclaimed in 1979, is a compromise between the contradictory demands of democratic power and the revenge of the clergy after much humiliation. Persons as distant from each other as Ayatollah Beheshti, the theoretician of clerical power, and Abol-Hasan Banisadr, champion of liberal humanism, were involved in its writing. Moreover, it offers several points of similarity with the Constitution of 1906–07. Despite its theocratic dimension – already present in the

Supplement of the Constitution of 1907 – and contrary to certain fears, it has given in neither to Khomeyni's former distrust of universal suffrage nor to those who opposed the right of women to vote and be elected. On certain points the Islamic Constitution represents progress, even when the practice of universal suffrage remains subject to certain very selective conditions.

In the Constitution of 1979, the Parliament was named *Majles-e shurā-ye melli* (the National Consultative Assembly). One recalls that in August 1906, the first royal edict granting the Assembly had appended the adjective "Islamic" (*eslāmi*), which the revolutionaries had insisted on changing to *melli*, "national." In 1980, the first action – exactly the reverse – of the first Parliament of the Islamic Republic was to call itself *eslāmi*, against the text of the fundamental law that caused it to exist. This mirroring game draws attention to the nature of the Islamic influence with which politics tries to veil itself under the new Iranian regime.

Moreover, the titles of the Guide are ambiguous. They hesitate between the historic "Guide of the Revolution," increasingly less pertinent; the "High Authority of guidance"; the "Very High Authority of governance of the world's Muslims" (*Maqām-e mo'azzam-e rahbari*); and *Emām* Khāmene'i, a fawning appellation that borrows a title that the Twelver Shiites, in principle, should not use for a man who also awaits the return of the Twelfth Imam.

The atypical republic of Iran, which one may compare with an elective monarchy, lost, with the death of its founder in 1989, its sacred character, that for Khomeyni justified the title of Imam. The function of Guide that Khāmene'i obtained without previously having been recognized as *āyatollāh* has little effect in religious matters. Admittedly, it does provide a counterbalance to upheavals in an executive power subject to electoral vagaries, but it also presents above all a constant challenge to any reformist will.

The split of 1979 is undeniable. The references, the goals, and the political motivations of the revolution completely severed any resemblance with the previous regime. Iranians had spilled their blood to found an "Islamic government," that is, on the one hand, to restore the ideological barrier which had been defined in the Supplement to the Fundamental law in 1907, where Islam became the benchmark for laws, and, on the other hand, to return to the theologians the social and political power that had been taken from them by modernization. This "clericalization" legitimized the intervention of the ulama in politics and stands in contrast to the situation that had prevailed since 1909, when the clerics had renounced any direct participation in political reform and modernization.

CONCLUSION: LIES AND TRUTH

Dichtung und Wahrheit, "poetry and truth." Goethe clearly saw in the stories of his childhood and youth how much memory often gives way to imagination. Such is the effect of history, continuously relived and reinterpreted, even for those who have been actors or direct witnesses. Our speculative knowledge of the past, incessantly questioned, relies on documentary evidence, but the documents are not closed to a final interpretation. The main purpose is to use the documents of the past to build up an understanding of our present condition. Historical discourse "incessantly repairs the splits between the past and the present. [It] assures a 'sense' that overcomes violence and the division of time."[1]

The best history never predicts the future, even if it sometimes strays into conjecture. Understanding the past can sometimes lead to an impasse, particularly when documents are missing or insufficient. But predicting the future is impossible because, in addition to the unpredictable effect of emotional factors on political action, natural disasters, such as drought or earthquake, can ruin a city or a civilization without the slightest human action. And interaction between internal and external causes can disrupt a national venture.[2]

---

[1] M. DE CERTEAU, *Histoire et psychanalyse, entre science et fiction*, p. 60.

[2] N. R. KEDDIE, "The Roots of the Ulama's Power in Modern Iran," p. 229 predicted, in the early 1970s, the setback of clerical influence. It was before the oil boom, the strengthening of the Shah's regime, and the Soviet schemes on Afghanistan, and before the American defeat in Vietnam.

At the time of the Iranian revolution, there was a debate between philosopher and historian Michel Foucault, who went to Iran during the upheaval against the Shah and published several lengthy reports in the press, and Maxime Rodinson, a rationalist specialist of Islamic history. Foucault, who was critical of the Shah, raised the issue on the level of a rejection of "a *modernization* that in itself is an *archaism*."[3] He wrote:

> What sense, for the people who live in this small corner of the world whose soil and sub-soil are global issues, to look for, at the price of even their life, that of which we have forgotten the possibility since the Renaissance and the major crises of Christianity, a *political spirituality*. I already hear the French laughing, but I know that they are wrong.

The French version ends here; in the original Italian, Foucault added with somewhat false humility: "I, who know so little about Iran."[4]

Soon after the publication of Foucault's articles, Maxime Rodinson responded in a scathing article in *Le Monde*, in which he predicted that clerical rule, in an Islamic society, would certainly lead to a major setback in societal issues such as freedom of opinion and women's rights. Later Rodinson commented on his response, without mentioning Foucault directly: "As is customary, professional thinkers, quite audacious to rush into the market of militancy of grand ideas, by disdaining the safe-guards that may (sometimes) put in place the facility of positive knowledge, dressed these tendencies of the intelligentsia with impressive references to the grand historic architects of abstraction."[5] Taking the exact opposite view of the enthusiasm that then enflamed the Iranians and of Foucaultian idealism – and of the quasi-general support that western intellectuals gave to the Iranian revolution – Rodinson coldly analyzed the sociological content of political Islam, and concluded by warning people to be on their guard in the case of a return to archaism in a society directed by the ulama. He did not hesitate to propose that Islamic fundamentalism would be unmasked and that

---

[3] M. FOUCAULT, "Lo scià ha cento anni di ritardo," [The Shah is hundred years late], reprinted in *Dits et écrits 1954–1988*, vol. 3, p. 680. Foucault had proposed as a title to this paper: "The dead weight of modernization."

[4] M. FOUCAULT, "À quoi rêvent les Iraniens?"

[5] M. RODINSON, *L'Islam: politique et croyance*, p. 264.

behind the progressive discourse there would be a freezing of women's rights and individual liberties in general under religious authority. Rodinson asked to what Islam owed its success. From the amalgam between religion and nationalism:

> Islam has acquired, even outside the Islamic world, the prestige of being and having been without fail at the forefront of resistance to expansionist Christian, missionary and imperialist Europe or, in other words, the forefront of the anti-European struggle. Henceforth, the enemies on whom the maximum of hate is concentrated are the Europeans and Americans and the Europeanized classes of the periphery societies. Thus, all are identifiable as non-Moslem, anti-Moslem or perverted by blind conformity as regards anti-Islam. One understands that even inside the *Dār al-Islām*, the abode of Islam, one is sensitive to that global polarization, that Islam received with pride the title of universal champion of Good against Evil, without further giving up the banner of the avant-garde to whomever it may be.[6]

This Foucault–Rodinson debate reveals the difficulty in understanding the Iranian revolution from a historical perspective without allowing oneself to be deceived by the rhetoric of political actors and without looking for rigid, or invariant, fundamental tendencies. Societies often claim to adhere to an eternal tradition, even though they themselves break many of the rules of that tradition. The reclusion of women, the condemnation of universal suffrage, the negation of human rights, these are just some of the manifold issues on which the Iranian authorities have not provided the simple answers that one would have expected from reading only Khomeyni. To make a good impression or simply because of social evolution, which inescapably pushes people toward modernity, today's Iranian women study more than men, on average have fewer than two children and demand their share of political power. As for human rights, no human society has yet succeeded in wholly protecting such rights in a satisfactory manner; it is this that was the central argument in a debate that saw the Iranian lawyer Shirin Ebādi receive the Nobel Peace Prize in 2003. Many

---

[6] M. RODINSON, "Réveil de l'intégrisme musulman," *Le Monde*, December 1978, reprinted in *L'Islam: politique et croyance*, p. 279.

Iranians, alongside her, fight to have these rights recognized by the current leaders and enshrined in the name of Islam.

From the very first months of the new regime, to respond to the political challenges of parliamentarism, the program of the very clerical Party of the Islamic Republic, written by Ayatollah Beheshti in the spring of 1981, recognized the legitimacy of free will, pluralism, and democracy, values that undoubtedly would have made Khomeyni shudder a few years earlier.[7]

The manipulation of religion in Iran, as in all societies where a specific religious group dominates, is not something unique to today's political climate. In the Constitutionalist Revolution of 1906–07 we had already witnessed the confrontation of two visions: that of social democracy, of a political radicalism ready to reject any religious authority; and that of a moderate reformism, where the ulama serve as a guarantee for the advancement of political modernity. Nevertheless, from that period onwards, the religious mask has been used by those who reject clerical Islam most vehemently, as Nikkie Keddie has shown particularly well.[8]

Contrary to what Foucault suggests, Mosaddeq, in 1979, was held in contempt by most clerical Islamists who, after the revolution, rejected the last of his nostalgic partisans. After the fall of Bāzargān, who had been one of the occasional collaborators of the nationalist leader at the beginning of the 1950s and had never renounced his loyalty to the National Front, the last Mosaddeqist in the new institutions was Abol-Hasan Banisadr. During the three months Khomeyni stayed in Neauphle-le-Château, France, the man who would become the first president of the Islamic Republic (from January 1980 to June 1981) believed that his interpretation of Khomeynism for Westerners, a progressive humanism, non-violent and anti-imperialist, was the quintessence of the Khomeynist theory of power and did not contradict nationalist heritage in any way.

We have seen that Khomeyni had his own vision of power, of which, incidentally, the Islamic Republic has only ratified the theory of *velāyat-e faqih*. This theocratic principle became the keystone of the 1979 Constitution. Banisadr still believed he could have

---

[7] [Md-H. Beheshti], *Mavāze'-e mā*, p. 35.

[8] N. R. Keddie, "Religion and irreligion in early Iranian nationalism," *Comparative Studies in Society and History* (1962), reprinted in *Iran, Religion, Politics and Society*, pp. 13–52.

the upper hand once he was elected president by embodying this fusion of Mosaddeqism and humanist Khomeynism, when he himself was the only one of the writers of the Constitution who did not sign it. The outbreak of war with Saddam Hussein's Iraq in September 1980 should have given him some advantage over the clerics. Defense of the fatherland, which Banisadr was keen to illustrate by taking up quarters near the front, from where he sent daily articles to the press so as to share his everyday thoughts with his readers, was indeed for him of the utmost priority. Nevertheless, in the middle of the war, impeachment proceedings were started against him.

An event in April 1981 made it clear that the battle for liberal nationalism, even when it was inspired by Islam, as in the case of Bāzargān, had been lost to clerical power: Bāzargān moved closer to Banisadr, whom he saw as the last defender of freedoms under threat. The newspaper *Mizān*, published by the Movement for Liberty in Iran (Bāzargān), had just been banned, and Bāzargān called for a demonstration in support of the president in the name of loyalty to nationalism (or to national values, *melli*) in an attempt to dissuade the deputies from voting for the impeachment. Immediately, Iranian radio broadcast a statement by Khomeyni condemning nationalism as idolatry that was contrary to Islam and appealed for a counter-demonstration. Some members of the middle class and intellectuals lined up on the sidewalks to helplessly witness the multitude of demonstrators who were yelling slogans in an open show of hostility toward Banisadr and liberal policy. On that day it was clear that the political forces were not leaning toward liberal nationalism.

The excessive promotion of political Islam in its most clerical form has finally, more than any authoritarian modernization policy, convinced a large number of Iranians, and among them numerous ulama, that the separation of state and religion is the best form of possible relationship between Islam and power. This outcome of the arduous quest for political modernity follows numerous cultural and political reactions against western interference that pushed Iranians, as Rodinson said, to seek refuge under Islam. Therefore, despite the undeniable differences of a state dominated by turbaned men of the cloth, I still believe that there is a continuity between what was formerly called nationalism and today's Islamism.

Strength of History

Iran's encounter with western societies has entailed passionate debate and significant violence. The hostage crisis, by which a world power, the USA, was humiliated by a revolutionary movement in a remote Asian country, led us to a complete reversal. Yes, the Iranians were retaliating for the humiliation they had endured at the hands of the Russians, the British, and the Americans. They have learnt the limits of western humanitarian discourse and have decided to be independent. Thanks to the immense wealth given to them by oil and gas, they have been able to revive the ambitions of Persian empires of the past: to speak to the world at the highest level.

Iranians, because of the magnificence of their past, are overloaded by history. The Qajars saw themselves as the heirs of the Sassanids and the Safavids; the Pahlavis wanted to link their kingdom to the Achemenids. More realistically, the leaders of the Islamic Republic began with the denunciation of the "return to capitulations," a very sad memory for any nationalist Iranian, and then recalled such struggles as that of Amir Kabir against foreign encroachments;[9] the Tobacco protest and the leading role of Seyyed Jamāloddin Asadābādi; the resistance of Sheykh Fazlollāh Nuri against the imitation of European democracy; and the many confrontations of the ulama with the Pahlavis, from Modarres to Tāleqāni. Khomeyni himself and his close associates were part of a long conflict with the monarchy, and they were rooted in a quasi-mythical history that no media, no official history would dare to mention until the end of the Pahlavi regime; they were put in jail, exiled, reviled.

One major historical event, however, the Mosaddeq movement, was progressively eliminated from official discourse after the revolution, and those streets named after the nationalist prime minister who was execrated by the Shah were later renamed: in Tehran, Mosaddeq Avenue became *Vali-Asr* ("master of the Age," a name for the Twelfth Imam). Mosaddeq's memory and reminiscences of pre-Islamic dynasties remain the weak point of the Islamic Republic. Instead, the turbanned leaders select elements of a religious history, the fight of Imam Hoseyn for justice, the martyrdom of the Imams, the sacred history of the prophetic revelation.

---

[9] In 1967 A. Hāshemi-Rafsanjāni published a book on his "fight against colonialism."

Persian, the language that literacy programs made the common link between all Iranians is, in spite of a rich Islamic legacy, firstly, the language of Iranian mythic history as told by Ferdowsi, a poet of a thousand years ago whose epic poem is still read and loved by all Iranians.[10] Iranians are more comfortable with myths than with history proper, owing to a long series of blurred historical landmarks and the need to juggle with different calenders and chronologies.[11] Ferdowsi, despite his praise of ancient kings, remains the absolute benchmark in the Islamic Republic.

But a time is coming when Iranian schoolchildren will be unable to read Ferdowsi: since the popularization of emails and advertising, they no longer write their correspondence in the beautiful language of Sa'di but in the spoken dialect of Tehran, a misdeed with regrettable consequences for future generations.

Joncy (France), 24 July 2018

[10] A. MARASHI, "The Nation's Poet: Ferdowsi and the Iranian National Imagination," in T. ATABAKI, ed., *Iran in the 20th Century: Historiography and Political Culture*, pp. 93–111.

[11] See Y. RICHARD, introduction to *Regards français sur le coup d'état de 1921 en Perse*, pp. 4f.

CHRONOLOGY

1779–1925: The Qājār dynasty.

1779: Āqā Mohammad Khān.

1786–97: Reign of Mohammad Shāh (Āqā Mohammad Khān).

1797–1834: Reign of Fath-Ali Shāh.

1801: Plundering of Karbalā by the Wahhābis.

1804: First military campaigns in the Caucasus. Abbās Mirzā besieged in Erevān. Russians defeated.

1805: New campaign: Russian troops disembark in Anzali to create a diversion. The Qājārs keep their Caucasian territories, but local princes put themselves under Russian protection.

1807–09: Gardane Mission.

1807: 4 May. Treaty of Finckenstein, soon cancelled through the Peace of Tilsit between Napoléon and the Tsar. In 1810 no Frenchman remains in Persia.

1812: Treaty of Tehrān between Persia and Great Britain (Sir Gore Ouseley).

1813: Persian defeat by Russia. Treaty of Golestān. Persia loses the Caucasus.

1826: Second war with Russia, leading to the Treaty of Torkamanchāy (1828) which was worse than the Golestān Treaty. Beginning of Russian penetration in Iran. Capitulations.

1828–29: Griboyedov, Russian ambassador assassinated in Tehrān.

1833: Siege of Herāt by Persian troops. Crown Prince Abbās Mirzā who had introduced major reforms inspired by the Ottomans (*nezām-e jadid*) dies.

1834–48: Reign of Mohammad-Shāh.

1837–38: Siege of Herāt.

1844: Beginnings of the Bābi movement. Systematic persecutions begin in 1850.

1848–96: Reign of Nāser od-Din Shāh.

1848–51: Amir Kabir prime minister, first important reforms.

1850: 9 July. Public execution of the Bāb in Tabriz.

1852: Failed attempt of the Bābis against the Shah.

1853: Persia recognizes the autonomous status of Herāt.

1857: Herāt has been besieged (1856) then, following the British blockade in Bushehr, evacuated by the Persian troops. A treaty is signed in Paris. British influence over Persia.

1862: English concession for the telegraphic line through Persia.

1864: Pébrine (a disease of silk worms) ruins the silk production in Gilān.

1869–72: Years of drought and famine.

1871–73: Mirzā Hoseyn Khān Sepahsālār supreme vizier.

1872: Reuter concession including railways, mines, irrigation projects, banking, industrial and farming development projects.

1873, 1878, 1889: Three journeys to Europe of Nāser od-Din Shāh.

1879: Creation of the Persian Cossack Brigade with Russian officers.

1883–85: Mirzā Yusof Āshtiyāni supreme vizier.

1885–97: Mirzā Ali Asqar Khān Amin os-Soltān supreme vizier.

1890: Concession of farming and trade of tobacco sold to Talbot. Boycott of tobacco (canceled in 1892).

December: Eviction of Jamāl od-Din "al-Afghani" from Iran.

1896: 1 May. Assassination of Nāser od-Din Shāh.

1896–1907: **Reign of Mozaffar od-Din Shāh.**

1898–1903: Mirzā Ali-Asqar Khān Amin os-Soltānsupreme vizier.

1905: Social unrest, demand for a judiciary court (*adālat-khāne*).

1906: The demonstrations lead to the issuing of a decree convening a Parliament (*Majles*).

1907–09: **Reign of Mohammad-Ali Shāh.** He is sworn in after having signed the Constitution.

1907: Elaboration of the Supplement to the Fundamental law.

May. Amin os-Soltān again head of government.

Summer. Sheykh Fazlollāh Nuri insists in the adoption of art. 2 of the Supplement according to which 5 mojtaheds will supervise the Islamic legitimacy of the laws.

31 August. Signature in St Petersburg of the Russo-British agreement dividing Iran in three zones. Assassination of Amin os-Soltān

1908: June. Mohammad-Ali Shāh cancels the Constitution, sends the troops to shell the Parliament.

1909: Victorious return of the Constitutionalists. Deposition of Mohammad-Ali Shāh. Trial and execution of Sheykh Fazlollāh Nuri.

1909–25: **Reign of Ahmad Shāh.**

1909–11: Second Majles.

1911: December. Under the pressure of a Russian ultimatum, after the dismissal of Treasurer-General Morgan Shuster, the second Majles disbands without convening new elections. Russian troops brutally occupy northern Persia from Tabriz to Mashhad.

1914: Coronation of Ahmad Shāh who has reached legal age. Elections to the third majles. Neutrality of Iran is not respected, the Russians occupy the north, the British the south. Azerbayjan is the ground of bloody confrontations. Pro-Ottoman nationalists boycott the institutions and form a provisory government in Qom, later moved to Kermānshāh.

1916–21: Jangal Movement (pan-Islamist and nationalist) headed by Mirzā Kuchek Khān in the forests of Gilān. In 1920 they make a short-lived alliance with the Bolsheviks.

1919: Anglo-Persian Agreement (also called "Arrangement") signed by the government of Vosuq od-Dowle, unanimously rejected by public opinion. The country is ruined by the war and the government only controls Tehran.

1920: In Tabriz, the nationalist "Democratic" movement of Sheykh Khiābāni is crushed.

1921: 21 February. Rezā Khān, a Cossack officer, and Seyyed Ziā an anglophile journalist, stage a coup d'état. Ziā becomes prime minister. The authority of the state is progressively restored.

27 May. Seyyed Ziā is toppled (and exiled) jointly by Ahmad Shāh and Rezā Khān.

6 December. Death of Mirzā Kuchek Khān, Rezā Khān has definitely defeated the Jangal movement.

1924: Being now prime minister, Rezā Khān seeks to establish a republic. He withdraws after facing general opposition, particularly in religious circles.

1925: A constituent assembly proclaims the deposition of the Qājār dynasty and transfers the monarchy to Rezā Shāh Pahlavi.

1925–41: **Reign of Rezā Shāh.**

1926: 25 April. Coronation of Rezā Shāh.

1928: One of the major reforms of Rezā Shāh is the judiciary system, which transfers the function of judge to civil magistrates (thus ruining the clergy). A civil code is promulgated, and the capitulations are cancelled.

A National Bank (*Bānk-e melli*) is created and controls the national currency system.

1933: New oil concession granted to the Anglo-Iranian Oil Company, with few ameliorations for Iran.

1934: Rezā Shāh's twenty-six-day visit to Turkey.

Laws on clothing:"international" hat for men (instead of the Pahlavi cap).

1935: July. Violent reactions in Mashhad (Gowhar Shād mosque) against clothing regulations.

1936: Interdiction of the chador as a measure for the emancipation of women.

1937: Sa'dābād Pact between Iran, Iraq, Turkey, and Afghanistan.

1941: Great Britain and USSR require the expulsion of German agents of Rezā Shāh, despite the declaration of neutrality.

  25 August. Soviet troops in the north and British in the south invade and occupy Iran. Rezā Shāh abdicates in favor of his son.

1941–79: Reign of Mohammad-Rezā Shāh.

1946: First crisis of the Cold War, the Soviets refuse to evacuate Azerbayjan as previously agreed and scheduled. Azerbayjan and Kurdistan proclaim their autonomy. Eventually the Soviets withdraw, and the Iranian army crushes the autonomists.

1951: General Razmārā, Prime minister, is assassinated by a member of the *Fedāiān-e Eslām*.

  The nationalization of the oil industry is voted by the Parliament.

  Mosaddeq becomes Prime minister.

1952: 21 July. After the elections for the seventeenth Majles, Mosaddeq who has a strong majority, asks the Shah to give him the control over the Ministry of war. The Shah refuses, Mosaddeq resigns. Massive popular demonstrations – partly mobilised by ayatollah Kāshāni – compell the Shah to bring Mosaddeq back to governement.

1953: 19 August. Mosaddeq, weakened by the defection of his religious support (ayatollah Kāshāni) is toppled by a coup reputedly organized by the Americans.

1954: Restoration of diplomatic relations between Iran and the UK.

1955: Wave of persecution against the Bahāis.

  Baghdad Pact between Iran, Iraq, Pakistan, and the United Kingdom; will be named CENTO after the withdrawal of Iraq.

1957: Creation of the SAVAK, a secret police and intelligence service.

1960: The new wife of the Shah, empress Farah, gives birth to a boy, Crown Prince Reza, thus reviving the hope of dynastic continuity.

1962–63: A series of reforms called the "White Revolution," includes a land reform and the right to vote for women. The clergy mobilizes against the new electoral code which suppresses the reference to the Koran (replaced by "sacred book").

  5 June (*15 Khordād*). The police attack the Feyziye theological school in Qom, where Khomeyni teaches, provoking major demonstrations.

1964: 4 November. Khomeyni is arrested and expelled to Turkey after a sermon where he denounced the "new capitulations," the extra-territorial judicial privilege given to the American military personnel in Iran.

1965: Prime Minister Hasan-Ali Mansur is assassinated by an Islamist militant, Mohammad Bokhārā'i.

1965–77: Amir-Abbās Hoveydā prime minister.

1971: February. A Marxist-Leninist group (*Fedāiān-e khalq*) occupies the police station of Siyāhkal in Gilān for a few days.

October. Persepolis celebrations, 2500th anniversary of the Iranian empire.

30 November. Iran occupies militarily three strategical islands of the Persian Gulf previously occupied by the British.

1975: Hardening of the regime, repression, and torture of political opponents. A single party is created, the "Renewal" (*Rastākhiz*).

March. The calender would from now on no longer have its origin in the *hejira* of the Prophet but in the foundation of the Iranian Empire by Cyrus the Great, 1355 becomes 2535.

1977: Jamshid Āmuzgār replaces Hoveydā as prime minister.

November. The Shah visits Washington to meet the new Democrat administration and is confronted with huge demonstrations from opponents.

1978: 7 January. An insulting article against Khomeyni is published by the newspaper *Ettelā'āt*, provoking a series of demonstrations and repression.

August. Regular demonstrations during the month of Ramadhan. Martial law is enforced in Tehrān. Ja'far Sharif-Emāmi becomes Prime minister.

8 September. Black Friday, the army shoots at the crowd of demonstrators.

6 October. Khomeyni arrives in Paris. Soon transferred to Neauphle-le-Château.

6 November. Violent demonstrations in Tehran, Gen. Azhāri becomes prime minister. General strike in most economic sectors all over Iran.

31 December. Chapour Bakhtiar becomes prime minister.

1979–89: Imam Khomeyni, Guide of the Revolution, *vali-e faqih*.

1979: 16 January. The Shah leaves Iran for ever.

1 February. Khomeyni returns from fifteen years of exile in Iraq and France. Mahdi Bāzargān becomes prime minister even before the fall of the monarchy.

11 February. Victory of the Revolution (22 *Bahman*).

1 April. The Islamic Republic of Iran, approved by referendum.

4 November. Taking over of the American Embassy in Tehrān, occupation and hostage taking lasts 444 days. Resignation of Bāzargān.

2 December. The Constitution of the Islamic Republic of Iran approved by referendum.

1980 25 January. Abo'l-Hasan Banisadr is elected the first president of the Iranian Republic.

25 April. Failure of the American rescue operation in Tabas

27 July. Death of Mohammad-Rezā Shāh in exile in Cairo.

22 September. The Iraqis start a war by occupying the southern province of Khuzestan and bombing several oil refinery plants.

1981: 24 July. **Mohammad-Ali Rajā'i** is elected **president** after the empeachment of Banisadr has been voted by the Parliament. Banisadr and Rajavi, the leader of the Mojāhedin-e Khalq flee to France.

30 August. Assassination of Rajā'i and (2 October) election of **Ali Khāmene'i** as **president** (re-elected in 1985).

1982: 24 May. Iran has retaken the territories which had been occupied by Iraq and in turn has penetrated into southern Iraq up to al-Faw, the only Iraqi sea harbour.

1983: October. France *lends* five Super-Etendard fighters to Iraq, with missile equipment.

1987: 31 July. Bloody Saudi repression against a demonstration in Mecca during the pilgrimage, 402 casualties, among them nearly 300 Iranians.

1988: 3 July. A civil Iranian flight is hit by an American missile over the Persian Gulf, 290 casualties.

18 July. Iran accepts UN resolution 598 asking for a ceasefire in the war with Iraq.

1989: 14 February. Khomeyni issues a fatwa asking for the execution of the British writer Salman Rushdie, author of the *Satanic verses*.

28 March. Ayatollah Montazeri, formerly designated to succeed Khomeyni, falls in disgrace.

4 June. Khomeyni dies. Hojjat ol-eslām Ali Khāmene'i is chosen as "Guide of the Revolution."

1989–97: **Akbar Hāshemi Rafsanjāni president** of the Islamic Republic.

1991: 6 August. Assassination of Chapour Bakhtiar near Paris.

1997–2005: **Mohammad Khātami president** of the Islamic Republic (re-elected in 2001).

2002: The enrichment of uranium by Iranians is made known by opponents and becomes a major international issue.

2005–13: **Mahmud Ahmadinejad** (Ahmadi-nežād) **president** of the Islamic Republic.

2009: June. The re-election of Ahmadinejad for a second term leads to huge demonstrations and repression.

2013: June. **Hasan Ruhāni** is elected president of the Islamic Republic. Re-elected in 2017 for a second term.

2015: 14 July. Iran Nuclear deal, officially called Joint Comprehensive Plan of Action, signed in Vienna (Austria); signs of hope for a ruined Iranian economy.

2018: 8 May. President Donald Trump takes back American signature on the Nuclear deal.

BIBLIOGRAPHY

ABRAHAMIAN, Ervand. *Iran between Two Revolutions*, Princeton (NJ), Princeton University Press, 1982.

ABRAHAMIAN, Ervand. *The Iranian Mojahedin*, New Haven, London, Yale University Press /I.B. Tauris, 1989.

ĀDAMIAT, Fereydun. *Amir Kabir va Irān* [Amir Kabir and Iran], Tehrān, Khārezmi, 5th ed., 2535/1976.

ĀDAMIAT, Fereydun. *Fekr-e demokrāsi-e ejtemā'i dar nahzat-e Mashrutiat-e Irān* [The idea of social democracy in the Constitutional movement], Tehrān, Payām, 2nd ed., 2535/1976.

ĀDAMIAT, Fereydun. *Ideoloži-e nahzat-e mashrutiat-e Irān* [Ideology of the Constitutional movement], Tehrān, Payām, 2535/1976.

ĀDAMIAT, Fereydun & NĀTEQ, Homā. *Afkār-e ejtemā'i va siāsi dar āsār-e montasher na-shode-ye dowrān-e Qājār* [Social and political ideas in unpublished works of the Qajar period], Tehrān, Āgāh, 2536/1977.

ĀDAMIAT, Fereydun. *Shuresh bar emtiāz-nāme-ye Reži. Tahlil-e siāsi* [Revolt against the concession of Tobacco. Political analysis], Tehrān, Payām, 1360/1981.

ĀDAMIAT, Fereydun. *Ide'oloži-e nahzat-e Mashrutiat-e Irān. II. Majles-e avval va bohrān-e āzādi* [The first parliament and the crisis of liberty], Tehrān, Rowshangarān, 1991.

ĀDAMIAT, Fereydun. "Sarnevesht-e Qā'em-Maqām" [Fate of Q.-M], *Maqālāt-e tārikhi*, Tehran, Shabgir, 1352/1973.

ĀDAMIAT, Fereydun. *Andishe-hā-ye Mirzā Āqā Khān Kermāni*, Tehran, Payām, 2nd ed., 1357/1978.

ADIB HARAVI, Md-Hasan. *Hadiqat ol-razaviye* [History of Mashhad], 1327/1948.

AFANASYAN, Serge. *L'Arménie, l'Azerbaïdjan et la Géorgie, de l'indépendance à l'instauration du pouvoir soviétique, 1917–1923*, Paris, L'Harmattan, 1981.

AFARY, Janet. *The Iranian Constitutional Revolution, 1906–1911: Grassroots Democracy, Social Democracy, and the Origins of Feminism*, New York, Columbia University Press, 1996.

AFKHAMI, Gholam Reza. *The Life and Times of the Shah*, Berkeley/Los Angeles, University of California Press, 2009.

AFSHĀR, Iraj (ed.). *Ruzname-ye khāterat-e E`temād os-Saltane* [Diaries of E. os-S.], Tehran, 2536/1977.

AFSHĀR, Iraj (ed.). *Owrāq-e tāze-yāb-e Mashrutiat va naqsh-e Taqizāde* [Documents on the rôle of Taqizāde in the Constitutional Movement], Tehran, Jāvidān, 1359/1980.

AKHAVI, Shahrough. *Religion and Politics in Contemporary Iran: Clergy-State Relations in the Pahlavi Period*, Albany, State University of New York Press, 1980.

ĀL-E AHMAD, Jalāl. *Dar khedmat va khiānat-e rowshanfekrān* [On the mission, compromise and treachery of intellectuals], Tehran, Khārezmi, 1357/1978.

ĀL-E AHMAD, Jalāl. *Iranian Society, An Anthology of Writings by Jalal Al-e Ahmad*, compiled & ed. by Michael Hillmann, Lexington, Mazda, 1982.

ĀL-E AHMAD, Jalāl. *Qarbzadagi*, English trans. by J. Green and A. Alizadeh, Lexington, Mazda, 1982. Other trans. the same year by P. Sprachman, *Plagued by the West*, New York, Caravan Books.

ALAVI, Bozorg. *Geschichte und Entwicklung der Modernen Persischen Literatur*, Berlin, Akademie Verlag, 1964.

ALGAR, Hamid. *Mīrzā Malkum Khān. A Biographical Study in Iranian Modernism*, Berkeley/Los Angeles/London, University of California Press, 1973.

ALGAR, Hamid. *Religion and State in Iran 1785–1906. The Role of the Ulama in the Qajar Period*, Berkeley/Los Angeles, University of California Press, 1969.

AMANAT, Abbas. *Resurrection and Renewal: The Making of the Babi Movement in Iran, 1844–1850*, Ithaca (NY), Cornell University Press, 1989.

AMANAT, Abbas. *Pivot of the Universe. Nasir al-Din Shah Qajar and the Iranian Monarchy 1831–1896*, Berkeley/Los Angeles, University of California Press, 1997.

AMANAT, Abbas. *Iran. A Modern History*, New Haven/London, Yale University Press, 2017.

AMIR-MOEZZI, Md Ali & Christian Jambet. *Qu'est-ce que le shî'isme ?*, Paris, Fayard, 2004.

ĀQELI, Bāqer. *Teymurtāsh dar sahne-ye Siāsat-e Irān*, Tehrān, Jāvidān, 1371/1992.

ARJOMAND, Said Amir (ed.). *Authority and Political Culture in Shi'ism*, Albany, State University of New York Press, 1988.

ARJOMAND, Said Amir. *The Turban for the Crown. The Islamic Revolution in Iran*, New York/Oxford, Oxford University Press, 1988.

ARMINJON HACHEM, Constance. *Chiisme et état. Les clercs à l'épreuve de la modernité*. Paris, CNRS-éditions, 2013.

ARSLANIAN, A. H. "Dunsterville's Adventure: A Reappraisal," *International Journal of Middle Eastern Studies*, 12 (1980), pp. 199–216.

ĀRYANPUR, Yahyā. *Az Sabā tā Nimā. Tārikh-e 150 sāl-e adab-e fārsi. I. Bāz-gasht, bidāri. II. Āzādi, tajaddod* [History of 150 years of Persian literature 1. 'return', awakening; 2. liberty, modernity], Tehrān, Jibi, 4th ed., 1354 (1st ed. 1350/1971).

ASADĀBĀDI, Mirzā Lotfollāh. *Sharh-e hāl va āsār-e Seyyed Jamāl ol-Din Asadābādi* [Life and works of Jamāl od-Din Asadābādi], Berlin, 1926.

ATABAKI, Touraj. *Azerbaijan. Ethnicity and Autonomy in Twentieth-Century Iran*, London/New York, British Academic Press, 1993.

ATABAKI, T. (ed.). *Iran in the 20th Century: Historiography and Political Culture*, London, Tauris, 2009.

AUBIN, Eugène. *La Perse d'aujourd'hui. Iran. Mésopotamie*, Paris, A. Colin, 1908.

AVERY, Peter. *Modern Iran*, London, Ernest Benn, 1965.

AVERY, Peter, Gavin HAMBLY and Charles MELVILLE (eds.). *The Cambridge History of Iran*, vol. 7, *From Nadir Shah to the Islamic Republic*, Cambridge/New York/Port Chester/Melbourne/Sydney, Cambridge University Press, 1991.

ĀZARI-SHAHREZĀ'I, Rezā (ed.). *Hey'at-e fowq ol-ādde-ye qafqāziye* [Documents about Sd Ziā's mission to Caucasus], Tehran, Markaz-e tārikh-e diplomāsi, 1379/2000.

ĀZARI, Ali. *Qiām-e Mohammad Khiābāni dar Tabriz* [Khiābāni's movement in Tabriz] Tehran, 1329/1950.

ĀZARI-SHAHREZĀ'I, Rezā (ed.). *Dowlat-e Irān va motakhassesān-e mohājer-e ālemāni (1310–1319s)* [Iran and the German experts, 1931–1940], Tehran, Sāzemān-e asnād-e melli, 1374/1995.

BAHĀR, Md-Taqi. *Tārikh-e mokhtasar-e ahzāb-e siāsi-e Irān* (History of political parties in Iran), I, Tehran, Jibi, 1357/1978.

Bahs-i dar bāre-ye marja'iat va ruhāniat [Discussion on the role of the guide in Shiism], Tehran, Sherkat-e sahāmi-e enteshār, 1341/1962 [On this collective book, see LAMBTON, "A Reconsideration of the Position … "]

BAKHTIAR, Chapour. *Ma fidélité*, Paris, Albin Michel, 1982.

BAMBERG, J. H. *The History of the British Petroleum Company*, vol. 2, *The Anglo-Iranian Years, 1928–1954*, Cambridge, Cambridge University Press, 1994. [vol. 1, see FERRIER]

BĀMDĀD, Mahdi. *Tārikh-e rejāl-e Irān. Qorun 12, 13, 14*, Tehrān, Zovvār, 1347–1351/1968–1972. [Biographical dictionary of Iranian elites, 18th to 20th centuries, 6 vols.]

BANANI, Amin. *The Modernization of Iran, 1921–1941*, Palo Alto (CA), Stanford University Press, 1961 [2nd ed. 1969].

BANISADR, Masoud. *Memoirs of an Iranian Rebel*. London, Saqi, 2004.

BARZIN, Nader. *L'Iran nucléaire*, foreword F. Khosrokhavar, Paris, L'Harmattan, 2005.

BAST, Oliver. *Les Allemands en Perse pendant la Première Guerre mondiale d'après les sources diplomatiques françaises*, Paris, Peeters (Travaux et mémoires de l'Institut d'études iraniennes), 1997.

BAST, Oliver (ed.). *La Perse et la Grande Guerre*, Téhéran, Institut français de recherche en Iran (Bibliothèque iranienne, 52), Louvain, Peeters, 2002.

BAST, Oliver. *Die persische Außenpolitik und der Erste Weltkrieg (1917–1921).* [La politique étrangère de la Perse et la Première Guerre mondiale (1917–1921)], Paris/Bamberg, Sorbonne Nouvelle/Universität Bamberg, 2003, unpublished dissertation.

BAYANDOR, Darioush. *Iran and the CIA: The Fall of Mosaddeq Revisited*, Basingstoke/New York, Palgrave Macmillan 2010.

BAYAT, Mangol. *Mysticism and Dissent: Socioreligious Thought in Qajar Iran*, New York, Syracuse University Press, 1982.

BAYAT, Mangol. *Iran's First Revolution. Shi'ism and the Constitutional Revolution of 1905–1909*, New York/Oxford, Oxford University Press, 1991.

BECK, Lois. *The Qashqa'i of Iran*, New Haven/London, Yale University Press, 1986.

BEHESHTI, Md-Hoseyn. *Mavāze'-e mā* [Our positions], Tehran, Hezb-e Jomhuri-e Eslami (1359/1981).

BEHNĀM, Jamshid. *Irāniān va andishe-ye tajaddod* [Iranians and the idea of modernity], Tehrān, Farzān, 1375/1996.

BEHNĀM, Jamshid. *Berlani-hā. Andishmandān-e irāni dar Berlan 1915–1930* [Iranian intellectuals in Berlin, 1915–1930], Tehran, Farzān, 1379/2000.

BERBERIAN, Houri. *Armenians and the Iranian Constitutional Revolution of 1905–1911: "The love for freedom has no fatherland,"* Boulder, Westview Press, 2001.

BHARIER, Julian. *Economic Development in Iran 1900–1970*, London/New York/Toronto, Oxford University Press, 1971.

BIALER, Uri. "The Iranian Connection in Israel's Foreign Policy – 1948–1951," *The Middle East Journal*, 2 (Spring 1985), pp. 292–315.

BLÜCHER, W. von-. *Zeitenwende im Iran: Erlebnisse und Beobachtungen*, Biberach a. d. Riss, 1949.

BOHAS, Georges & Florence HELLOT-BELLIER. *Les Assyriens du Hakkari au Khabour. Mémoire et histoire*, Paris, Geuthner, 2008.

BOROUJERDI, Mehrzad. *Iranian Intellectuals and the West. The Tormented Triumph of Nativism*, Syracuse, Syracuse University Press, 1996.

BROMBERGER, Ch. "Changements techniques et transformation des rapports sociaux ..., " in Y. Richard, Y., ed., *Entre l'Iran et l'Occident*, pp. 71–90.

BROWNE, Edward G. *The Persian Revolution of 1905–1909*, Cambridge, 1910.

BROWNE, E. G. trans. by H. JAVADI, *Letters from Tabriz: The Russian Suppression of the Iranian Constitutional Movement*, Washington (DC), 2008.

BUCHTA, Wilfried. *Die iranische Schia und die islamische Einheit 1979–1996*, Hamburg, Orient-Institut, 1997.

BULLARD, Sir Reader. *Letters from Tehran: A British Ambassador in World War II* "World War II" *Persia*, E. C. Hodgkin, ed., London, I.B. Tauris, 1991.

CALDER, Norman. "Accommodation and Revolution in Imami Shi'i Jurisprudence: Khumayni and the Classical Tradition," *Middle Eastern Studies*, 18, 1 (1982), pp. 3–20.

CALMARD, J. "Atābak-e A'zam, Amin-os-Soltān," *Encyclopædia Iranica, s.v.*

CALMARD, Jean. "L'Iran sous Nāser od-Din Chāh et les derniers Qadjar. Esquisse pour une histoire politique culturelle et socio-religieuse," *Le Monde iranien et l'islam. Sociétés et cultures*, 4, 1976–77, pp. 165–94.

CALMARD, Jean. "Les réformes militaires sous les Qājār (1794–1925)," in Richard, Y., ed., *Entre l'Iran et l'Occident*, pp. 17–42.

CALMARD, Jean. "Une dame française à la cour de Perse: Louise de la Marnierre (Paris, 1781-Shiraz, 1840)," *Studia Iranica*, 46 (2017), pp. 261–311.

CERTEAU, Michel. DE. *Histoire et psychanalyse, entre science et fiction*, Paris, Gallimard, 1982.

CHAQUÉRI, Cosroe. *The Soviet Socialist Republic of Iran 1920–1921. Birth of the Trauma*, preface by R. W. Cottam, Pittsburgh/London, The University of Pittsburgh Press, 1995.

CHAQUÉRI, Cosroe. *The Russo-Caucasian Origins of the Iranian Left*, [London], Curzon, Caucasus World, 2001.

CHAQUERI, C. "Communism, I," *Encyclopaedia Iranica*.

CHEHABI, H. E. *Iranian Politics and Religious Modernism. The Liberation Movement of Iran under the Shah and Khomeini*, Ithaca (NY)/London, Cornell University Press/I.B. Tauris, 1990.

CHEHABI, H. E. "Religion and Politics in Iran: How Theocratic Is the Islamic Republic?," *Daedalus*, 120, 3 (1991), pp. 66–92.

CHEHABI, H. E. "The Paranoid Style in Iranian Historiography," in T. Atabaki, ed., *Iran in the 20th Century: Historiography and Political Culture*, 2009, pp. 155–76.

CHEHABI, H. E. & V. MARTIN (eds.). *Iran's Constitutional Revolution: Popular Politics, Cultural Transformations and Transnational Connections.* London, Tauris, 2010.

CHELKOWSKI, Peter (ed.). *Ta'ziyeh: Ritual and Drama in Iran.* New York, New York University Press, 1979.

CLAWSON, Patrick see MATTHEE, Rudi.

CLAWSON, Patrick & Willem FLOOR, "Finance and Foreign Exchange for Industrialization in Iran, 1310–1319 (1931–1940/41)," *The Gulf in the Early 20th Century*, ed., R. I. Lawless, Durham, 1986.

COLE, Juan R. I. & Nikki R. KEDDIE (eds.). *Shi'ism and Social Protest*, New Haven/ London, Yale University Press, 1986.

CURZON, G. N. *Persia and the Persian Question*, London, 1892.

DAVĀNI, Ali. *Nahzat-e do-māhe-ye ruhāniun-e Irān be manzur-e defā' az osul-e moqaddas-e eslām* [Two months' struggle of Iranian clerics in 1962–63], Qom, 1341/1963.

DESTRÉE, Annette. *Les Fonctionnaires belges au service de la Perse, 1898–1915*, Leiden, Brill, 1976.

DIGARD, Jean-Pierre, Bernard HOURCADE & Yann RICHARD. *L'Iran au XXe siècle. Entre nationalisme, islam et mondialisation*, Paris, Fayard, 3rd ed., 2007.

DIGARD, Jean-Pierre. *Une épopée tribale en Iran: les Bakhtyāri*, Paris, CNRS éditions, 2015.

DOWLATĀBĀDI, Yahyā. *Tārikh-e moāser yā Hayāt-e Yahyā* [Memoirs], Tehran, 1328/1949.

DUDOIGNON, Stéphane A. *Voyage au pays des Baloutches (Iran oriental, an XXVIII–XXIe siècle – de la République islamique)*, Paris, Cartouche, 2009.

DUDOIGNON, Stéphane A. *The Baluch, Sunnism and the State in Iran: From Tribal to Global*, London, Hurst – New York, Oxford University Press, 2016.

DUNSTERVILLE, L. C. *The Adventures of Dunsterforce*, London, Edward Arnold, 1920.

EDMONDS, C. J. *East and West of Zagros: Travel, War and Politics in Persia and Iraq 1913–1921*, ed., Y. Richard, Leiden – Boston, Brill, 2009.

ELĀHI, Homāyun. *Ahammiat-e esterātezhik-e Irān dar jang-e jahāni-e dovvom* [Strategic importance of Iran in the 2nd WW], Tehrān, Markaz-e Nashr-e dāneshgāhi, 1361/1982.

ELWELL-SUTTON, L. P. *Persian Oil. A Study in Power Politics*, London, 1955.

ENTNER, M. L. *Russo-Persian Commercial Relations, 1828–1914*. Gainsville, Fl., 1965.

EPKENHANS, Tim. *Die iranische Moderne im Exil. Bibliographie der Zeitschrift Kāve*. Berlin, Kaus Schwarz, 2000.

ERFĀN-MANESH, Jalil (ed.). *Khāterāt-e 15-e khordād-e Shirāz* [Reports on 5 June 1963 in Chiraz], Tehrān, Howze-ye honari, 1375/1996.

ESHRAGHI, F. "Anglo-Soviet Occupation of Iran in August 1941," *Middle Eastern Studies*, 20, 1 (1984), pp. 27–53.

ESHRAGHI, F. "The Immediate Aftermath of the Anglo-Soviet Occupation of Iran," *Middle Eastern Studies*, 20, 3 (1984), pp. 325–51.

ETTEHĀDIYA (NEZĀM-MĀFI), Mansure. *Ahzāb-e siāsi dar Majles-e sevvom (1333–1334 h.q.)* [Political parties in the 3rd Majles, 1914–1915.], Tehrān, Nashr-e tārikh-e Irān, 1371/1992.

ETTEHĀDIYA (NEZĀM-MĀFI), Mansure. *Majles va entekhābāt: az Mashruta tā pāyān-e Qājār* [Parliament and elections from 1906 to 1925], Tehrān, Nashr-e tārikh-e Irān, 1375/1996.

FARDID, Ahmad, Md MADADPUR (ed.). *Didār-e farahi va fotuhāt-e ākhar oz-zamān* [Considerations on eschatology], Tehran 1381/2001.

FARDID, see HĀSHEMI, Md-M. – MIRSEPASSI, A.

FARDUST, Hoseyn. *Zohur va soqut-e saltanat-e Pahlavi*, vol. 1, *Khāterāt-e arteshbod-e sābeq Hoseyn Fardust* [Memoirs], Tehrān, Ettelā'āt, 1369/1990.

FAWCETT, Louise. *Iran and the Cold War: The Azerbaijan Crisis of 1946*, Cambridge/New York, Cambridge University Press, 1992.

FERRIER, R. W. *The History of the British Petroleum Company*, vol. 1, *The Developing Years, 1901–1932*, Cambridge, Cambridge University Press, 1982 [vol. 2, see BAMBERG].

FLEURY, Antoine. "Le pacte de Saadabad comme contribution à la sécurité collective dans les années trente," *Rev. Hist. des deux guerres mondiales*, 106 (1977).

FLOOR, books

FLOOR, Willem, see CLAWSON, Patrick; MATTHEE, Rudi.

FLOOR, Willem. *Labour Unions, Law and Conditions in Iran (1900–1941)*, Durham, 1965.

FLOOR, Willem. *The Persian Textile Industry in Historical* Perspective, *1500–1925*, Paris, L'Harmattan, 1998.

FLOOR, Willem. *A Fiscal History of Iran in the Safavid and Qajar Period*, New York: Bibliotheca Persica, 1999.

FLOOR, Willem. *Agriculture in Qajar Iran*, Washington (DC), Mage Publishers, 2003.

FLOOR, Willem. *Public Health in Qajar Iran*, Washington, Mage, 2004.

FLOOR, Willem. *History of Bread in Iran*, Washington, Mage, 2015.

FLOOR, articles

FLOOR, Willem. "The Customs in Qajar Iran," *Zeitschrift der Deutschen Morgenländischen Gesellschaft (ZDMG)*, 126 (1976), pp. 281–311.

FLOOR, Willem. "The Merchants (*tujjār*) in Qājār Iran," *ZDMG*, 126 (1976), pp. 101–35.

FLOOR, Willem. "The Bankers (*sarrāf*) in Qājār Iran," *ZDMG*, 129, 2 (1979), pp. 263–81.

FLOOR, Willem. "Changes and Developments in the Judicial System of Qajar Iran (1800–1925)," in Clifford E. Bosworth and Carole Hillenbrand, eds., *Qajar Iran: Political, Social and Cultural Change*, Edinburgh, 1983, pp. 113–47.

FLOOR, Willem. "The Revolutionary Character of the Ulama, Wishful Thinking or Reality," in N. R. KEDDIE, ed., *Religion and Politics in Iran*, 1983, pp. 73–97.

FLOOR, Willem. "The Secular Judicial System in Safavid Persia," *Studia Iranica*, 29 (2000), pp. 9–60.

FLOOR, Willem. "Tea Consumption and Importation in Qajar Iran," *Studia Iranica,* 33 (2004), pp. 47–111.

FLOOR, Willem. "The Rise and Fall of the Banu Ka'b. A Borderer State in Southern Khuzestan," *Iran,* 44 (2006), pp. 277–315.

FLOOR, Willem. "A Neglected Aspect of the Social History of the Iranian Oil Industry. The Case of Southern Khuzestan's Early Medical Infrastructure," *Studia Iranica,* 43 (2014), pp. 241–47.

FLOOR, Willem. "Custom duties," *Encyclopædia Iranica, s.v.*

FLOOR, Willem. "Judicial System from the Advent of Islam through the 19th Century," *Encyclopædia Iranica, s.v.*

FLYNN, Thomas S. R. O. *The Western Christian Presence in the Russias and Qajar Persia c. 1760–c. 1870.* Leiden: Brill, 2017.

FOUCAULT, M. "À quoi rêvent les Iraniens?" *Le Nouvel Observateur,* 727, 16–22 October 1978, reprinted in *Dits et écrits 1954–1988,* vol. 3, *1976–1979,* D. Defert, F. Ewald & J. Lagrange, eds., Paris, Gallimard, 1994.

FOUCAULT, M. "Lo scià ha cento anni di ritardo" [The Shah is hundred years late], *Corriere della Sera,* vol. 103, no 230, 1er octobre 1978, p. 1, reprinted in *Dits et écrits 1954–1988,* vol. 3, *1976–1979,* D. Defert, F. Ewald & J. Lagrange, eds., Paris, Gallimard, 1994.

FORUQI, Md-A., see VAREDI, A.

GARTHWAITE, Gene R. *Khans and Shahs. A Documentary Analysis of the Bakhtiyari in Iran,* Cambridge, Cambridge University Press, 1983.

GEHRKE, Ulrich. *Persien und die deutsche Orientpolitik während des ersten Weltkrieges,* Stuttgart, Kohlhammer, 1960.

GHANI, Cyrus. *Iran and the Rise of Reza Shah. From Qajar Collapse to Pahlavi Rule,* London/New York, I.B. Tauris, 1998.

GHEISSARI, Ali. *Iranian Intellectuals in the Twentieth Century,* Austin, University of Texas Press, 1998.

GILBAR, Gad G. "Demographic Developments in Late Qājār Persia, 1870–1906," *Asian and African Studies* (Jerusalem), 11 (1976), pp. 125–56.

GILBAR, Gad G. "The Big Merchants (*tujjar*) and the Persian Constitutional Revolution of 1906," *Asian and African Studies,* 11, 3 (1977), pp. 275–303.

GILBAR, Gad G. "Persian Agriculture in the Late Qājār period, 1860–1906: Some Economic and Social Aspects," *Asian and African Studies,* 12 (1978), pp. 312–65.

GILBAR, Gad G. "The Persian Economy in the Mid-19th Century," *Die Welt des Islams,* 19, 1–4 (1979), pp. 177–211.

GILBAR, Gad G. "Trends in the Development of Prices in Late Qajar Iran. 1870–1906," *Iranian Studies,* 16, 3–4 (1983), pp. 177–98.

GILBAR, Gad G. "The Opening up of Qājār Iran: Some Economic and Social Aspects," *BSOAS,* 49, *In Honour of Ann K. S. Lambton* (1986), pp. 76–89.

GOBINEAU, Arthur de-. *Les Religions et les philosophies dans l'Asie centrale*, *Œuvres*, II. J. Gaulmier, ed., Paris, Gallimard, 1983.

GOLNAZARIAN-NICHANIAN, Magdalena. *Revue d'histoire arménienne contemporaine*, vol. 7, *Les Arméniens d'Azerbaïdjan, histoire locale et enjeux régionaux, 1828–1918*, Paris, 2008.

HABIBI, Mariam. *L'interface France-Iran, 1907–1938. Une diplomatie voilée*, Paris, Groupe de recherche sur les économies locales, L'Harmattan, 2004.

HĀERI, Abdol-Hādi. *Nakhostin ruyāru'i-hā-ye andishegarān-e Irān bā do raviye-ye tamaddon-e buržuāzi-e qarb* [First encounter of Iranian thinkers with two faces of the western bourgeoisie], Tehrān, Amir Kabir, 1367/1988.

HAIRI, Abdul-Hadi. *Shī'īsm and Constitutionalism in Iran. A Study of the Role Played by the Persian Residents of Iraq in Iranian Politics*, Leiden, Brill, 1977.

HAERI, Shahla. *Law of Desire: Temporary Marriage in Iran*, London, Tauris, 1989.

HĀSHEMI, Md-Mansur. *Hoviat andishān va mirās-e fekri-e Ahmad Fardid* [Fardid and the issue of identity] Tehran, Kavir, 1383/2004.

HEDĀYAT, Sādeq. *Buf-e kur*, Bombay 1937.

HELLOT-BELLIER, Fl., see also BOHAS, Georges.

HELLOT-BELLIER, Florence. *France-Iran. Quatre cents ans de dialogue*. Paris, Association pour l'avancement des études iraniennes, 2007.

HELLOT-BELLIER, Florence. *Chroniques de massacres annoncés. Les Assyro-Chaldéens d'Iran et du Hakkari face aux ambitions des empires, 1896–1920*, Paris, Geuthner, 2014.

HINZ, Walther. *Iran, Politik und Kultur von Kyros bis Reza Schah*, Leipzig, Meyers kl. Handbücher, 1938.

HIRSCHFELD, Yair P. *Deutschland und Iran im Spielfeld der Mächte. Internazionale Beziehungen unter Reza Schah. 1921–1941*, Düsseldorf, Droste, 1980 (Schriftenreihe des Instituts für Deutsche Geschichte. Universität Tel Aviv, 4).

HOURCADE, Bernard, see also DIGARD, Jean-Pierre.

HOURCADE, Bernard. *Géopolitique de l'Iran. Les défis d'une renaissance*, nouvelle éd., Paris, Armand Colin, 2016.

HOURCADE, Bernard, Hubert MAZUREK, Mahmoud TALEGHANI & Mohammad-Hossein PAPOLI-YAZDI. *Atlas d'Iran*, Montpellier/Paris, Reclus/La Documentation française, 1998.

HUSHANG MAHDAVI, Abd ol-Rezā. *Siāsat-e khāreji-e Irān dar dowrān-e Pahlavi 1300–1357* [Politique étrangère de l'Iran sous les Pahlavi], Tehrān, Alborz, 1373/1994.

HUYSER, R. E. *Mission to Tehran*. Introduction by Gen. Alexander M. Haig, London, André Deutsch, 1986.

IRONSIDE, Edmund. *High Road to Command, the Diaries of Major-General Sir Edmnund Ironside 1920–22*, London, Leo Cooper, 1972.

ISSAWI, Charles (ed.). *The Economic History of Iran 1800–1914*, Chicago/London, Center for Middle Eastern Studies, 1971.

JAMĀLZĀDE, Md-Ali. "Seyyed Ziā va *Ketāb-e siyāh-e u*," [S. Zia and his "Black book"], *Āyande*, V & VI, 1359–1360/1981.

JONES, Geoffrey. *Banking and Empire in Iran. The History of the British Bank of the Middle East*, vol. 1, Cambridge – New York – Melbourne, Cambridge University Press, 1986.

KADIVAR, M., see VAHDAT, F.

KASRAVI, Ahmad. *Tārikh-e hejdah sāla-ye Āzarbāyjān yā sarnevesht-e gordān va dalirān. Bāz-mānda-ye tārikh-e Mashruta-ye Irān* [History of Azerbayjan after the Persian Constitution], Tehrān, Amir Kabir, 8th ed., 2536/1977.

KASRAVI, Ahmad. *Tārikh-e Mashruta-ye Irān* [History of the Persian Constitution], Tehrān, Amir Kabir, 13th ed., 2536/1977.

KATOUZIAN, Homa. *The Political Economy of Modern Iran. 1926–1979*, London/Basingstoke, Macmillan, 1981.

KATOUZIAN, Homa. *State and Society in Iran. The Eclipse of the Qajars and the Emergence of the Pahlavis*, London/New York, I.B. Tauris, 2000.

KAUZ, Ralph. *Politische Parteien und Bevölkerung in Iran: Die hezb-e Demükrāt-e Irān und ihr Führer Qavām-e s-Saltanä*, Berlin, Klaus Schwarz, 1995.

KĀZEMIYA, Eslām (ed.). "Yād-dāsht-hā-ye Seyyed Mohammad Tabātabā'i" [Autobiographical notes of Tabātabā'i], *Rahnamā-ye Ketāb*, 14, 7–8 (1350–1971).

KEDDIE Nikki R., see also COLE, J. R. I.

KEDDIE, Nikki R. *Religion and Rebellion in Iran. The Iranian Tobacco Protest of 1891–1892*, London, Frank Cass, 1966.

KEDDIE, Nikki R. *Sayyid Jamal ad-Din "al-Afghani": A Political Biography*, Berkeley/Los Angeles, University of California Press, 1972.

KEDDIE, Nikki R. *Iran: Religion, Politics and Society. Collected Essays*, London, Frank Cass, 1980.

KEDDIE, Nikki R. *Modern Iran. Roots and Results of Revolution*, with a section by Y. Richard [new expanded edition], New Haven/London, Yale University Press, 1981.

KEDDIE, Nikki R. *Religion and Politics in Iran. Shi'ism from Quietism to Revolution*, New Haven/London, Yale University Press, 1983.

KEDDIE, Nikki R. "The Roots of the Ulama's Power in Modern Iran," in *Scholars, Saints, and Sufis. Muslims Religious Institutions in the Middle East since 1500*, N. R. Keddie, ed., Berkeley/Los Angeles/London, University of California Press, 1972.

KERMĀNI, Mirzā Āqā Khān *Nāme-hā-ye tab'id* [Letters from exile], Bonn, Hafiz-Verlag, 1365/1986.

Kermāni, Nāzem ol-Eslām. *Tārikh-e bidāri-e Irāniān* [History of the Awakening of the Iranians], A.-A. Sa'idi Sirjāni ed., 2 vols., Tehrān, Bonyād-e Farhang-e Irān, 1357/1978.

Khalisi, Md-Mahdi al-. *La vie de l'ayatollah Mahdi al-Khalisi par son fils*, P.-J. Luizard ed. & trans., Paris, La Martinière, 2005.

Khāme'i, Anvar. *Khāterāt*, II, *Forsat-e bozorg-e az dast rafte* [Memoirs], Tehran, Hafte, 1362/1983.

Khoddami, Alireza. *Discours religieux des jeunes en Iran. Les nouveaux visages de la religion*, Paris, L'Harmattan, 2015.

Khomeyni, Ruhollāh. *Ketāb al-bey'* [On transactions], 5 vols., Najaf, 1390/1970–71.

Khomeyni, Ruhollāh. *Hokumat-e eslāmi* [Islamic government], Najaf, 1971.

Khomeini, Ruhollah. *Islam and revolution. Writings and declarations of Imam Khomeini*, trans. & intro. Hamid Algar, Berkeley, Mizan Press, 1981.

Khosravi, Md-Rezā. *Toqyān-e nāyebiān dar jariān-e Enqelāb-e Mashrutiat-e Irān* [The Revolt of Nāyeb's followers in the Constitutional Revolution], Tehrān, Beh-negār, 1368/1989.

Khosrokhavar, Farhad & Olivier Roy, *Iran: comment sortir d'une révolution religieuse*, Paris, Seuil, 1999.

Kiā, Tondar. Nahib-e jombesh-e adabi. Shāhin [Biography of Fazlollāh Nuri, Tehran, 1334/1956. Partially reprinted after 1979 as *Shahid hargez nemimirad* [The martyr never dies].

Kian-Thiébaut, Azadeh. *Les Femmes iraniennes entre islam, état et famille*, Paris, Maisonneuve et Larose, 2002.

Kian-Thiébaut, Azadeh. *Secularization of Iran: A Doomed failure? The New Middle Class and the Making of Modern Iran*, Paris, Peeters & Institut d'études iraniennes, 1998.

Kreiser, Kl. "Der japanische Sieg über Rußland (1905) und sein Echo unter den Muslimen," *Die Welt des Islams*, 21 (1981), pp. 209–39.

Ladier-Fouladi, Marie. *Population et politique en Iran. De la monarchie à la République islamique*, Paris, Ined, 2003.

Lambton, A. K. S. "A Reconsideration of the Position of the *Marja' at-taqlid* and the Religious Institution," *Studia Islamica*, 20 (1964), pp. 115–35.

Lambton, Ann K. S. *The Persian Land Reform 1962–1966*, Oxford, Oxford University Press, 1969.

Lambton, Ann K. S. *Qajar Persia. Eleven Studies*, London, Tauris, 1987.

Lashgari, Mahmud. "Dar nime-rāh-e konferāns-e solh-e Pāris," *Goftogu*, 65, 1393/2014.

Lerner, D. *The Passing of Traditional Society. Modernizing the Middle East*, New York, The Free Press, 1958.

Louis, Wm R. "Musaddiq and the Dilemmas of British Imperialism," in *Musaddiq, Iranian Nationalism and Oil*, J. A. Bill & Wm R. Louis, eds., Austin – London, University of Texas Press – Tauris, 1988.

Lytle, M. H. *The Origins of the Iranian-American Alliance, 1941–1953*, New York – London, Holmes & Meier, 1987.

Madani, Sd Jalāl od-Din. *Tārikh-e siāsi-e moāser-e Irān* [Political history of contemporary Iran], Qom, Daftar-e enteshārāt-e eslāmi, vā-baste be Jāme'e-ye modarresin-e howze-ye elmiye-ye Qom, 2nd ed., 1361/1982.

Marāqe'i, Zeyn ol-Ābedin. *Siyāhat-nāme-ye Ebrāhim Beyk* [Travelogue of Ebrahim Beyk], Tehrān, Nashr-e Asfār, 1364/1985.

Marashi, A. "The Nation's Poet: Ferdowsi and the Iranian National Imagination," in T. Atabaki, ed., *Iran in the 20th Century: Historiography and Political Culture*, 2009, pp. 93–111.

Martin, Vanessa, see also Chehabi, H. E.

Martin, Vanessa. *Islam and Modernism: The Iranian Revolution of 1906*, London, I.B. Tauris, 1989.

Martin, Vanessa. "Religion and State in Khumaini's *Kashf al-asrar'*," BSOAS, 56, 1 (1993), 34–35.

Matthee, Rudi, W. Floor & P. Clawson. *The Monetary History of Iran from the Safavids to the Qajars*, London/New York, I.B. Tauris, 2013.

Mauroy, Hubert de-. *Les Assyro-Chaldéens dans l'Iran d'aujourd'hui*, Paris, 1978.

McLean, David. *Britain and Her Buffer-State: The Collapse of the Persian Empire, 1890–1914*. London, Royal Historical Society, 1979.

Melzig, Herbert. *Reza Shah. Der Aufstieg Irans und die Großmächte*, Stuttgart, 1936.

Milani, Abbas. *Eminent Persians. The Men and Women Who Made Modern Iran, 1941–1979*, 2 vols., Syracuse (NY), Syracuse University Press, 2008.

Milani, Abbas. *The Shah*, New York, Palgrave Macmillan, 2011.

Mir Hosseini, Ziba. *Marriage on Trial: Study of Islamic Family Laws*, London, IB Tauris, 1993.

Mirsepassi, Ali. *Transnationalism in Iranian Political Thought. The Life and Times of Ahmad Fardid*, Cambridge, Cambridge University Press, 2017.

Moberly, F. J. *Operations in Persia 1914–1919*, intr. Dr. G. M. Bayliss, London, Imperial War Museum/Her Majesty's Stationery Office, 1987.

Moin, Baqer. *Khomeini: Life of the Ayatollah*, London/New York, I.B. Tauris, 1999.

Mojtahed-Shabestari, see also Richard, Y.– Vahdat, F.

Mojtahed-Shabestari, Md. *Imān va āzādi* [Faith and freedom], Tehran, Tarh-e now, 1379/2000.

Mokhber os-Saltana Hedāyat, Mahdi-Qoli. *Khāterāt va khatarāt. Toshe'i az tārikh-e shesh pādeshāh va gushe-i az dowre-ye zendagi-e man* [Memoirs], Tehrān, Zovvār, 2nd ed., 1344.

Momen, Moojan (ed.). *The Bábí and Bahá'í Religions, 1844–1944. Some Contemporary Western Accounts*, Oxford, George Ronald, 1981.

MOSADDEQ, Md. *Kāpitulāsyon va Irān* [Capitulations and Iran], Tehran (1914; recently reprinted).

MOSLEY, Leonard. *Curzon the End of an Epoch*, London, Longmans,1960.

MOTAMED OL-VEZĀRE, Rahmatollāh Khān & Kave BAYĀT (eds.). *Orumiye dar mohārebe-ye ālam-suz* [Urmia in the First World War], Tehran, Shirāze, 1379/2000.

MOTTAHEDEH, Roy. *The Mantle of the Prophet: Learning and Power in Modern Iran*, New York, Simon & Schuster, 1985/London, Chatto & Windus, 1986.

NAKASH, Yitzhak. *The Shi'is of Iraq*, Princeton, Princeton University Press, 1994.

NARAGHI, Ehsan. *From Palace to Prison: Inside the Iranian Revolution*. Chicago, Ivan R. Dee, 1994.

NARĀQI, Hasan. *Tārikh-e ejtemā'i-e Kāshān* [Social History of Kāshān], Tehran, Ent.-e Elmi va Farhangi, 2nd ed., 1365/1986.

Nāser od-Din Shāh, see Qāzihā, F.

NASIRI-MOGHADDAM, Nader. *La Révolution constitutionnelle à Tabriz à travers les Archives diplomatiques françaises (1906–1909)*, Saint-Denis, Connaissances et savoirs, 2016.

Nāteq, see Ādamiat – Pakdaman.

NĀTEQ, Homā. *Mosibat-e vabā va balā-ye hokumat* [Plague and cholera], Tehrān, Gostare, 1358/1979.

NĀTEQ, Homā. *Kārnāme va zamāne-ye Mirzā Rezā Kermāni* [Biography of Mirzā Rezā Kermāni], Santa Clara (CA), [Maple Press], 1363/1984.

NĀTEQ, Homā. *Irān dar rāhyābi-e farhangi. 1834–1848* [Iran and cultural change, 1834–1848], Landan, Payām, 1988.

NĀTEQ, Homā. *Bāzargānān dar dād-o setad bā bānk-e shāhi va Reži-e tonbāku (bar pāye-ye ārshiv-e Amin oz-Zarb)* [Retailers and the Tobacco Regie according to the documents of Amin oz-Zarb], Pāris, Khāvarān, 1371/1992.

NĀTEQ, Homā. *Kārnāme-ye farhangi-e farangi dar Irān / Les Français en Perse, Les écoles religieuses et séculières (1837–1921)*, Pāris, Khāvarān, 1375/1996.

NAVĀZENI, Bahrām. *Ahd-nāme-ye mavaddat-e Irān va Shuravi, 26 fevriye 1921* [A Study of the Treaty of Friendship between Iran and the Soviet Union – 1921], Tehran, Nashr-e Hamrāh, 1369/1990.

NEJĀTI, Qolam-Rezā. *Tārikh-e siāsi-e bist-o-panj sāle-ye Irān* [Political history of 25 years (1953–1978)], 2 vols., Tehrān, Resā, 1371/1992.

NURI, Fazlollāh, see TORKAMĀN, Md.

OLSON, William J. *Anglo-Iranian Relations during the First World War*, London, Frank Cass, 1984.

PAHLAVI, Md-Rezā. Shāh *Ma'muriat barā-ye vatan-am* [Mission for my country], Tehran, 1340/1961.

PAHLAVI, Md-Rezā. *Enqelāb-e sefid* [White Revolution], Tehran, Ketābkhāne-ye Pahlavi (1962).

PAHLAVI, Md-Rezā. Shāh *Be-suy-e tamaddon-e bozorg* [Toward the grand civilization], Tehrān, Ketābkhāne-ye Pahlavi, 2536/1977.

PAKDAMAN [-Nāteq], Homā. *Djamal-ed-Din Assad Abadi dit Afghani*, Paris, Maisonneuve et Larose, 1969.

PEARCE, Brian. *The Staroselsky Problem 1918–20. An Episode in British-Russian Relations in Persia*, London, SOAS, 1994.

PISTOR-HATAM, Anja. *Iran und die Reformbewegung im Osmanischen Reich: Persische Staatsmänner, Reisende und Oppositionelle unter dem Einfluß der Tanzimāt*, Berlin, Klaus Schwarz, 1992.

PISTOR-HATAM, Anja. "The Persian Newspaper *Akhtar* as a Transmitter of Ottoman Political Ideas," in Th. ZARCONE & F. Zarinebaf-Shahr, *Les Iraniens d'Istanbul*, Paris/Téhéran/Istanbul, IFRI/Institut Français d'Études Anatoliennes, 1993, pp. 141–47.

PISTOR-HATAM, Anja. "Progress and Civilization in Nineteenth-Century Japan: The Far Eastern State as a Model for Modernization," *Iranian Studies*, 29 (1996), pp. 111–26.

POTOCKI, Michel (trans.). *Constitution de la République islamique d'Iran, 1979–1989*, Paris, L'Harmattan, 2004.

PURJAVĀDI, N. "Irān-e mazlum," [Poor Iran], *Nashr-e dānesh* 7/5 mordād-shahrivar (1366/1987), pp. 2–10.

QĀZIHĀ, F. (ed.). *Ruznāme-ye khāterāt-e Nāser od-Din Shāh dar safar-e avval-e Farangestān* [Travelogue of the first journey of Naseroddin Shah to Europe], Tehran, Sāzemān-e asnād-e melli, Pazhuheshkade-ye asnād, 1377/1998.

RABINO, H. L. *Mashrute-ye Gilān az yād-dāsht-hā-ye Rābino, ... Vaqāye'-e Mashhad dar 1330 hq* [On the Constitutional movement in Gilan. Mashhad in 1911–12], Md Rowshan, ed., Rasht, 1352/1973.

RAHNEMA, Ali. *An Islamic Utopian. A Political Biography of Ali Shari'ati*, London, I.B. Tauris, 1998.

RAHNEMA, Ali. *Behind the 1953 Coup in Iran: Thugs, Turncoats, Soldiers, and Spooks*, New York, Cambridge University Press, 2015.

RAHNEMA, Ali. *Shi'i Reformation in Iran: The Life and Theology of Shari'at Sangalaji*, London/New York, Routledge, 2015.

RĀ'IN, E. *Qiām-e Jangal* [The Jangal upheaval], Tehran, Jāvidān 1357/1978.

RAMAZANI, Ruhollah K. *The United States and Iran*, New York, Praeger, 1982.

RASTEGĀR, N. "Majles-e mo'assesān-e 1303 va mokhālefān-e ān" [The 1925 Constituent assembly and its opponents], *Āyande*, 16, 9–12 (1369/1991), pp. 765–70.

REZUN, M. *The Soviet Union and Iran. Soviet Policy in Iran from the Beginnings of the Pahlavi Dynasty until the Soviet Invasion in 1941*, Alphen aan den Rijn, Sijthoff & Noordhof/Genève, Institut Universitaire de Hautes Études internationales, 1981.

RICHARD, Yann, see also DIGARD, Jean-Pierre.

RICHARD, Yann (ed.). *Entre l'Iran et l'Occident. Adaptation et assimilation des idées et techniques occidentales en Iran*, Paris, Maison des sciences de l'homme, 1989.

RICHARD, Yann. *Shi'ite Islam: Polity, Ideology and Creed*, trans. by A. Nevill, Oxford (UK)/Cambridge (USA), Basil Blackwell, 1995.

RICHARD, Yann (ed.). *Regards français sur le coup d'état de 1921 en Perse. Journaux personnels de Georges Ducrocq et Hélène Hoppenot*, Leiden/Boston, Brill/Tehran, IFRI, 2015.

RICHARD, Yann. "Ayatollah Kashani: Precursor of the Islamic Republic?" in N. R. KEDDIE, ed., *Religion and Politics in Iran*.

RICHARD, Yann. "Le coup d'état de 1921 et les sources historiques," *Studia Iranica*, 38, 1 (2009), pp. 69–103.

RICHARD, Yann. "Un théologien chiite de notre temps, Mojtahed Šabestari," in Md-A. Amir-Moezzi, M. M. Bar-Asher & S. Hopkins, eds., *Le Shiisme imāmite quarante ans après*, Turnhout, Brepols – Paris, EPHE, 2009.

RODINSON, M. *L'Islam: politique et croyance*, Paris, Fayard, 1993.

Roy, Olivier, see Khosrokhavar.

RUHĀNI, Sd Hamid. *Bar-rasi va tahlil-i az nahzat-e Emām Khomeyni dar Irān* [On the movement of Khomeyni in Iran], I, 1356/1978.

SABAHI, Houshang. *British Policy in Persia 1918–1925*, London, Frank Cass, 1990.

SABURI-DEYLAMI, Md-Hasan. *Negāh-i az darun be enqelāb-e mosallahāne-ye Jangal* [Glance from inside on the Jangal revolution], Tehran 1358/1979.

SĀDEQIPUR, Abdorrezā (ed.). *Yādegār-e gozashte: Majmu'e-ye sokhanrāni-hā-ye a'lā-hazrat-e faqid Rezā Shāh-e Kabir* [Discourses of Rezā Shāh], Tehrān, Jāvidān, 1346/1968.

SA'IDI-SIRJĀNI, A. "Baktiāri / Haj 'Ali-Qoli Kān Sardār As'ad," *Encyclopædia Iranica, s.v.*

SAFĀ'I, Ebrāhim (ed.). *Asnād-e Mashrute* [Documents on the Constitutional movement], Tehran, 2nd ed., 1352/1973.

SANASARIAN, Eliz. *Religious Minorities in Iran*, Cambridge/New York/Melbourne, Cambridge University Press, 2000.

SAYYĀH (Hājj-). *Khāterāt* [Memoirs], H. Sayyāh, ed., Tehran 1336/1977.

SCHAYEGH, Cyrus. *Who Is Knowledgeable Is Strong. Science, Class, and the Formation of Modern Iranian Society, 1900–1950*, Berkeley – Los Angeles – London, University of California Press, 2009.

SCHIRAZI, Asghar. *The Constitution of Iran: Politics and the State in the Islamic Republic*, London, I.B. Tauris, 1997.

SEPEHR MOVARREKH OD-DOWLE, Ahmad-Ali. *Irān dar Jang-e bozorg-e 1914–1918* [Iran in WWI], Tehran, 1336/1957.

Shaji'i, Zahrā. *Nokhbegān-e siāsi-e Irān az enqelāb-e mashrutiat tā enqelāb-e eslāmi* [Political elite in twentieth-century Iran], 4 vols., Tehran, Sokhan, 1372/1993.

Shamim, Ali-Asqar. *Irān dar dowre-ye saltanat-e Qājār* [Iran in the Qajar period], Tehran, Ebn-e Sinā, 1342/1964.

Shamshiri, Mahdi. *Asrār-e qatl-e Mirzā Ali-Asqar Khān Atābak* [Hidden truth in the assassination of Atābak], Houston (Tx), 1381/2003.

Shariati, Ali. *Bā makhātab-hā-ye āshnā* [Personal correspondance], *Majmu'e-ye āsār*, 1, Tehran, 1356/1977.

Shāyegān, Dāryush. *Bot-hā-ye zehni va khātere-ye azali* [Idols of the mind and perennial memory], Tehran, Amir Kabir, 2535/1976.

Shāyegān, Dāryush. *Āsyā dar barābar-e qarb* [Asia facing the West], Tehrān, Amir Kabir, 2536/1977.

Shayegan, Daryush (ed.). *L'Impact planétaire de la pensée occidentale rend-il possible un dialogue réel entre les civilisations?* Paris, Berg international, 1979.

Shayegan Daryush (with Ramin Jahanbegloo), *Sous les ciels du monde*, Paris, Éditions du Félin, 1992.

Shuster, Morgan *The Strangling of Persia. Story of the European diplomacy and Oriental Intrigue That Resulted in the Denationalization of Twelve Million Mohammedans. A Personal Narrative*, New York, The Century co., 1912.

Sykes, Brigadier-Gen. Sir Percy. *A History of Persia*, London, Macmillan, 2nd ed., 1921.

Taqizāda, Hasan. *Zendagi-e tufāni. Khāterāt-e siāsi-e H. T.* [A tumultuous life, political memoirs], I. Afshār, ed., Tehrān, Elmi, 2nd ed., 1372/1993.

Ettehādiye, Mansure. *Peydāyesh va tahavvol-e ahzāb-e siāsi-e Mashrutiyat (dowre-ye avval-o dovvom-e Majles-e Shurā-ye Melli)* [Creation and evolution of political parties of the constitutional period]. Tehrān, Nashr-e Gostare, 1361/1982.

Torkamān, Md (ed.). *Rasā'el, e'lāmiye-hā, maktubāt … va ruznāme-ye Sheykh-e Shahid Fazlollāh Nuri* [Writings of F. Nuri], Tehran, 1362/1983.

Torkamān Md. *Asrār-e qatl-e Razmārā* (The truth about Razmara's assassination), Tehran, Mo'assese-ye khadamāt-e farhangi-e Resā, 1370/1992.

Torkamān, Md. "Nezārat-e hey'at-e mojtahedin: seyr-e tatavvor-e ejrā-ye asl-e dovvom-e motammem-e Qānun-e asāsi dar dowre-ye dovvom-e taqniniye" [The application of art. 2 of the Supplement to the Constitution in the Second Majles], *Tārikh-e Mo'āser*, I, II & III, Tehrān, 1368, 1369, 1370 /1989–1992.

Vahdat, Farzin. "Post-Revolutionary Discourses of Mohammad Mojtahed Shabestari and Mohsen Kadivar," *Critique*, 16 (Spring 2000), pp. 31–54

Vāhed, Simā. *Qiyām-e Gowhar Shād* [The Revolt of Gowhar Shād Sanctuary], Tehran, Vez.-e Ershād-e eslāmi, 1361/1982.

VAREDI, Ahmad. *Muhammad ʿAli Furughi Zukā al-Mulk (1877–1942): A Study in the Role of Intellectuals in Modern Iranian Politics*, unpublished diss., University of Utah, 1992.

WILBER, Donald N. *Riza Shah Pahlavi: The Resurrection and Reconstruction of Iran*, New York, Exposition Press, 1975.

WRIGHT, Denis. *The Persians amongst the English. Episodes in Anglo-Persian History*, London, Tauris, 1985.

WYNN, Antony. *Persia in the Great Game. Sir Percy Sykes, Explorer, Consul, Soldier, Spy*, London, John Murray, 2003.

YARSHATER, Ehsan. "Communication," *Iranian Sudies*, 22, 1 (1989), pp. 62–65.

ZABIH, Sepehr. *The Communist Movement in Iran*, Berkeley – Los Angeles, University of California Press, 1966.

ZARCONE, Thierry & Fariba ZARINEBAF-SHAHR (eds.). *Les Iraniens d'Istanbul*, Paris/Téhéran/Istanbul, IFRI/Institut Français d'Études Anatoliennes, 1993.

ZARQĀM-BORUJENI, Jamshid. *Dowlat-hā-ye asr-e Mashrutiat* [Governments of the Constitutional period], Tehrān, 1350/1971.

ZIRINSKY, Michael. P. "Imperial Power and Dictatorship: Britain and the Rise of Reza Shah, 1921–1926," *IJMES*, 24, 4 (1992), pp. 639–63.

ZONIS, M. *Majestic Failure: The Fall of the Shah*, Chicago/London, The University of Chicago Press, 1991.

ZÜRRER, Werner. *Persien zwischen England und Rußland. 1918–1925. Großmachteinflüsse und nationaler Wiederaufstieg am beispiel des Iran*, Bern, Peter Lang, 1978.

INDEX